_Beyond
Civilization

**The world's four great streams
of civilization:**

their achievements,

their differences

and their future

KEITH CHANDLER

*To Muriel, whose art brought joy to
others and continual refreshment to me*

Library of Congress Catalog Number 92-09720
ISBN: 0-9636843-0-2 (paper trade)

Cover design by Dahl Kitchener. The medallions, clockwise
from the top are: Yin Yang symbol, Nataraj (Dancing
Shiva), Aztec Solar Disk, Da Vinci anatomical drawing.

Manufactured in the United States of America

CONTENTS

Walk tiptoe on the edge of the insatiable precipice and struggle to give order to your vision. Raise the multi-colored trapdoor of the mystery - the stars, the sea, men and ideas; give form and meaning to the formless, the mindless infinitude.

Gather together in your heart all terrors, recompose all details. Salvation is a circle; close it!

Nikos Kazantzakis
Saviors of God

ONE

What was Civilization?

Civilization had two faces. On the one hand, it was a specific way of organizing human society, a socioeconomic system. On the other, it was a way of thinking about reality, a cognitive structure. It was the dominant organizing force in human events for a very long time, five and a half millennia to be exact. The vast majority of human beings alive today were born into and shaped by some branch of civilization. Even those small remnants of the human race we call 'primitive' or 'aboriginal' have all been affected to some degree by contact with one civilized society or another.

The branch of civilization which is the American heritage is called Western Civilization. It began in the Fertile Crescent around 3500 B. C. and its offshoots eventually spread over Europe, much of what was the Soviet Union, the Middle East, Africa, Australia, New Zealand, and North and South America. Prophetic voices have been predicting the collapse of Western Civilization for many years. But predictions are no longer in order because at this moment Western Civilization *is* in the midst of collapsing. There are eddies of resistance, reaction and even revitalization in the torrent which is sweeping it away but nothing can save it because a revolution in the human mind is occurring which is even more radical than the mental revolution which first created civilization.

The current revolution is rooted in a radical freedom of the mind which neither primitive nor civilized human beings have ever before experienced. It can be terrifying, this new freedom which has emerged in only a few decades. It can and does lead to mental turmoil and social chaos. But it is also opening up a limitless expanse of possibilities for those who successfully pass through its terror and anguish. Their reward - and burden - will be a new mind, a *postcivilized mind*. The postcivilized mind will not be organized or motivated in the same way as the civilized mind was but it will be able to understand and draw upon the rich product of civilization in a way that will breathe new life into the past. If this is to be, then we need to understand with utmost clarity what the civilized mind was, what it enabled us to accomplish, and how it limited us. That is the purpose of this book.

The Problem of Defining 'Civilization'

> . . . states [i.e., civilized societies] first arise through the transformation and obliteration of typically primitive institutions. Thinkers of the most diverse backgrounds and intentions have, throughout history, grasped this cardinal fact of state formation. Lao-tzu, Rousseau, Marx and Engels, Maine, Morgan, Maitland, Tonnies, and many contemporary students of society have understood that there is a qualitative distinction between the structure of primitive life and civilization.
>
> Stanley Diamond (1a, 170)

It seems ironic that the phenomenon of civilization, central as it is to the human adventure, has never been adequately defined, let alone satisfactorily explained. *Encyclopedia Britannica* acknowledges:

> There has been relatively little empirical study of the quality, the consequences and the varieties of civilization. Particular aspects of certain civilizations have been well depicted by historians and others, but few scholars have used objective evidence to analyze the nature of civilization or have compared, one with another, the various civilizations which man has developed. (2, V, 831)

The scholars to whom we ought to be able to look for a comprehensive definition or a theory of civilization are historians. History is the chronicle of events which occurred during the period in which civilization grew and flourished. But historians have failed either to define civilization precisely or to propound a cogent theory of its origin and development. The results of this failure are twofold.

First, without a satisfactory definition or theory of civilization, it is impossible to develop analytical methods which are specifically applicable to history. Second, without definition, theory or appropriate methods, history is doomed to be anecdotal and conclusions drawn from it frivolous or sterile. An excellent example of the latter is the case of Will Durant, to whose six fat volumes on *The Story of History* he appended a slim volume called *The Lessons of History*. It contained the astonishing statement that 'the laws of biology are the fundamental lessons of history.' (3, 18) Durant went on to explain that these lessons are that *life is competition, life is selection and life must breed*. But if this is what a serious scholar wants us to learn from his thousands of pages of historiography, why not simply read a little Darwin and have done with it? The further pursuit of history would serve merely to entertain us or, as Durant more sanguinely puts it, to 'gather up our heritage, and offer it to our children.' (3, 4)

If *The Story of History* leaves our quest for the significance of civilization unsatisfied we might expect better luck if we turn to *A Study of History* by Arnold Toynbee. Here we have the result of a half century of dedicated, penetrating study of civilization by one of the greatest historians of all time. But with deference and respect to this great scholar's monumental work we have to observe that it is seriously flawed. I am not referring to the criticisms specialists have levelled at Toynbee for what they consider to be distortions of historical fact or the somewhat uncomfortable squeezing of societies into models of questionable fit. The fatal error in Toynbee is akin to that of Will Durant: *reductionism*. Reductionism is the interpretation of a phenomenon by breaking it down into simplistic elements which cannot account for the very special *elan* or integrity which gives the phenomenon its uniqueness. If Durant reduces history to biology, Toynbee reduces it to a species of behaviorist psychology. His primary analytical tool is what he calls *challenge and response*, a direct transplant from behaviorist *stimulus and response*. He compares civilized societies in terms of how they responded to similar challenges in the course of their development. Unfortunately, by imposing this kind of analysis on all civilized societies he manages to invest them with a uniformity which obscures their unique identities and often incompatible ways of thinking.

We will try then to avoid the error of reducing civilization (and history) to something less than it is and examine it on its own unique terms. We will ask what civilized human beings have been doing for the last five and a half thousand years that is more than simply competing, selecting, breeding, responding to challenges and building great societies only to have them degenerate or collapse.

General Definition of Civilization

While it is impossible to find a definition of civilization which is generally accepted, one would have to at least agree with Toynbee that it is '*a particular species of society.*' (4, 45, *emphasis mine.*). That having been conceded, the procedure usually followed in lieu of defining civilization is to list a series of attributes which are peculiar to civilized societies. For example: '...it may be said that civilization is that kind of culture which includes the use of writing, the presence of cities and of wide political organization and the development of occupational specialization.' (2, V, 831). Or, '...civilization is the state of cultural development at which writing and the keeping of written records is attained; *also* : the stage marked by urbanization, advanced techniques (as of agriculture and industry), expanded population, and complex social organization....' (5, 407) Such characterizations have two obvious deficiencies. In the first place, the attributes they ascribe to civilization are usually far too limited. We know a great deal more about it than they allow. In the second place, they lack coherence. They imply no systemic understanding of what gives civilization its uniqueness. Let us see if we can do a little better. To begin with, there are at least eight principal attributes which clearly characterize all civilized societies:

1. A hierarchical social organization dominated by a power elite which is not accountable to the powerless majority and for whose actions there is little or no redress.

2. Concentration of power and wealth in fortified urban centers.

3. Written language, the understanding and use of which is monopolized by the elite and its functionaries.

4. An economic system which vests title to the wealth produced by the society in the elite and controls that wealth by a strictly measured allocation of all industrial, agricultural, forestry and mining resources within the control of the central power.

5. Skills training and labor specialization designed to serve the goals of the power elite.

6. Extensive slavery or serfdom.

7. A grand mythology portraying society as originating from and continuing to be influenced by suprahuman powers with the elite as the conduit of that influence.

8. A military establishment which is utilized not only for external defense and aggression but for internal control and repression of the dispossessed majority.

If you question including slavery and serfdom among the essentials of civilization let me state categorically that no civilized society ever existed which did not depend on one or the other or both. Herbert J. Muller tells us,

> The poor have not always been with us. As a class, they came with civilization. There was also the new type of slave: victors in war had discovered that it was even more profitable to domesticate human captives than other types of animals. And outside its walls the city created still another type of man - the peasant. The villager had been preliterate, on a cultural par with his fellows; the peasant was illiterate, aware of the writing he did not know, aware of his dependence on the powers of the city, and liable to exploitation by them. (6, 34)

Lest we think that this situation was confined to ancient societies, let us remind ourselves that slavery was abolished by Great Britain no earlier than 1833 and by the United States nearly thirty years later. Although true slavery persists only in remote pockets of today's world, 'wage slavery', the degradation of women and children to the status of chattels, and the near-serfdom of the tenant farmer are by no means rare even now. However, allowing that slavery and serfdom have drastically diminished in modern times does not mean that those institutions are not essential to civilization. On the contrary, it means that during the last four centuries, and especially in the current one, civilization itself has been undergoing a tremendous upheaval which is transforming it into a new level of social organization. When we study civilization we are studying a system of the past in the process of being replaced. The universality of slavery in the period of civilization is an important piece of evidence about the nature of civilization which we will look at shortly.

There are two important observations to be made about the attributes I have ascribed to civilization. The first is that they are, as the opening quotation of this section implies, diametrically opposed to the attributes of precivilized societies. The second is that they are not isolable from each other, i.e., they are part of a system. You will not find a society with some of the attributes but lacking others. For this reason any society is clearly identifiable as either being or not being civilized.

The attributes of civilization describe a society characterized by the usurpation of power and the seizure of wealth by a relative few of its members. Primitive societies, on the other hand, are generally conceded to be based on social concensus and a concern for the general welfare, characteristics which generally express themselves in terms of extended kinship systems. The larger and more widespread a primitive society grows the more class divisions and variations in wealth and power it is likely to produce and the more hierarchical it becomes, but as long as it remains precivilized it also remains unified, that is, a product of broad social concensus. The ruler of the Natchez Indians, called 'the Great Sun,' was held in godlike awe and exercised nearly absolute power but, as Farb points out, he 'was not a complete despot. He could on whim order the execution of anyone who displeased him, yet in matters of general concern to the chiefdom he was very much limited by a council of elders.' (7, 156) Apart from the Great Sun and his brothers, who were also called 'Suns,' Natchez society was divided into three classes - Nobles, Honored People and *Stinkards* . Of these classes Farb observes,

> The Natchez class system has occasionally been regarded as a caste system, but such was not the case at all. A caste system rigidly isolates people, but the remarkable fact about the Natchez class system was that it did just the opposite. Every member of the three noble classes had to marry a Stinkard. Furthermore, marriage alliances were made only in certain combinations, and the offspring of these combinations almost always belonged to a different class from their father. (7, 159)

In other words, the inter-class marriage system was one way in which the Natchez kept their society unified even though it was hierarchical. That, in fact, was the *typical* structure of advanced precivilized societies. Whenever you find that rulers have dispossessed their people, appropriated their production, kept them illiterate and ignorant and, if that were not enough, suppressed them by military power, you are not confronting a primitive society. *You are face to face with civilization.*

What, then, accounts for the transition from the primitive to the civilized? Some writers are fond of contending that the decisive factor was technological innovations like those introduced in the Middle East between 5000 and 3500 B.C., the period immediately preceding the advent of Occidental Civilization. V. Gordon Childe lists 'fifteen' [sic]: 'artificial irrigation using canals and ditches; the plow; the harnessing of animal motive-power; the sailboat; wheeled vehicles;

orchard-husbandry; fermentation; the production and use of copper; bricks; the arch; glazing; the seal; and - in the earliest stages of the revolution [the urban revolution which initiated civilization] - a solar calendar, writing, numeral notation, and bronze.'(8, 180) Childe credits civilization itself with only two noteworthy innovations down to 700 B.C.: decimal notation and aqueducts for supplying water to cities.(ibid.)

Unfortunately, in all this concern for technology, Childe and many other historians overlook the single most important innovation which made civilization possible and gave it its distinctive structure: *the discovery by a few of the means to exercise absolute power over the many to accomplish ends of their own choice.* That was the *sine qua non* of civilization as a form of social organization. No primitive leader, as long as he remained primitive, had the capability to dispossess large numbers of his own people. It required an entirely new way of thinking about people and the world and, in essence, that is what civilization was - a new way of thinking which evolved a radically new set of institutions and symbols to produce human creations on a scale never before dreamed of.

The clear function of the precivilized societies, which were the product of the Neolithic agricultural revolution and which went on to create the technological inventions Childe lists, was to establish the human species as a viable, permanent population, no longer subject to the vagaries of hunting and gathering. This was a communal function based largely on concensus and undertaken for the common good of the people. But the function of civilization was entirely different and unless we understand that crucial difference we will get nowhere in understanding civilization. The founders of civilization built on the stable foundation and technological expertise of the preceding period but they did it not for the common good but *to achieve goals of their own choice.*

Childe clearly spotlights the evidence for this view although he draws the wrong conclusions from it:

Contrasting progress before and after it, the second revolution [the beginning of civilization] seems to mark, not the dawn of a new era of accelerated advance, but the culmination and arrest of an earlier period of growth....One partial explanation for such arrested growth may be detected in *internal contradictions evoked within the societies by the revolution itself.* The latter was made possible, it will be recalled, not only by an absolute accumulation of real wealth, but also by its concentration in the hands of gods or kings and a small class dependent on these. Such concentration was probably essential to ensure the production of the requisite surplus resources and to make these available for effective social use...None the less it meant in practice the economic degradation of the mass of the population. (8, 181, *emphasis mine*)

The error Childe makes is that 'the economic degradation of the mass of the population' was not the result of 'internal contradictions' in civilized society. This would be true only if one assumed that civilization was created for the benefit of the mass of the population and the evidence for that is nil. *That is why wherever you find civilization you find slavery and serfdom.*

The men who envisioned and built civilization were the proto-kings and -priests. They were men who understood that the means were at hand to undertake gigantic enterprises and they dedicated themselves to harnessing and directing all the human and natural resources they could command toward that end. But how could these early geniuses understand and accommodate to the awesome powers they were learning to exercise? Muller cites what he calls 'a paradox,' viz., '. . . man had come to depend more and more on supernatural means of power as he extended his own power over nature. Now, with the most triumphant demonstration of his creative powers, he became convinced of his utter dependence upon the gods, his utter powerlessness without them.' (6, 35)

But was this a paradox? What *concept of self* did these early creators have which could account for the dreams and visions which drove them to create and build? In precivilized society, allowing for gender differences and some craft specializations, wisdom and perceptions of the world and its possibilities were the common property of all the participants. No one dreamed far beyond his fellows, let alone thought of using them and their skills and labor to realize those dreams. But the strange, dynamic forces the proto-elite discovered at work in themselves were so prodigious that they could not be thought of as the product or property of puny human beings. They were perceived as akin to the great forces of nature, frightening and awe-inspiring. In order to accept them, the new elite, again building on arts derived from precivilized times, created larger-than-life scenarios, cosmic dramas, in which both their own powers and those of nature were personified on a scale that seemed appropriate to their awesomeness and in a manner that related them to the civilized enterprise. In this way the gods were created. As Henri Frankfort pointed out in *Before Philosophy*, myth was not proto-science. It was a way of dealing with the new forms of social organization man had created and differences in myths reflected differences between the societies in which they arose.

In addition, the grand mythologies, while not primarily created as 'the opiate of the masses,' were certainly a principal tool in maintaining authority over the masses who were given a place, however humble, in the cosmic drama. Farmers and laborers who would not give over a large share of their production to mere human beings could be persuaded that it was the due of the gods who made the whole society possible and to the rulers and priests who were the gods' holy vessels through whom their power was transmitted to the rest of the population.

Naturally, preserving and expanding the authority of the grand mythologies required great expenditures of energy, imagination and wealth. The rulers had not only to pursue a regular round of pious duties to the gods but put on periodic religious spectacles for the masses. Art and architecture were pressed into this service, creating vast monuments to the gods and their earthly representatives. It is in this sense and not merely that of size that we speak of civilized art and architecture as being 'monumental.' The central cities from which command was exercised grew around these monuments and the monuments expanded in size and extravagance as the cities became more populous and wealthy.

Writing was the single most important factor in the civilizing process. Its use betrays the advent of a new awareness in human life - the awareness of extensive future time. Writing was able to preserve information for posterity, the very desirability of which is foreign to the primitive mind. The primitive mind deals with the world as it was and is. It does not contemplate creating a world any different from that to which it is accustomed and it has no need to think about nor to project information any further than the immediate short-term future. John S. Mbiti has described this outlook very well in his book, *African Religions and Philosophy* . He uses two Swahili words to explain the African understanding of time. *Sasa* or Micro-Time, is current time, the past within living memory, the present and the practically foreseeable future, perhaps two years. Overlapping and inseparable from Sasa, is *Zamani* or Macro-Time, the infinite repository of past experience into which Sasa flows and disappears. Speaking of history and prehistory, Mbiti says,

> Each African people has its own history. This history moves 'backward' from the Sasa period to the Zamani, from the moment of intense experience to the period beyond which nothing can go. In traditional African thought, there is no concept of history moving 'forward' towards a future climax, or towards an end of the world. Since the future does not exist beyond a few months, the future cannot be expected to usher in a golden age, or a radically different state of affairs from what is in the Sasa and the Zamani . . . People constantly look towards the Zamani, for Zamani had foundations on which the Sasa rests and by which it is explainable or should be understood . . . It is by looking towards the Zamani that people give or find an explanation about the creation of the world, the coming of death, the evolution of their language and customs, the emergence of their wisdom, and so on. (10, 29-30)

Civilized man, however, did take the future seriously and writing was the vehicle by means of which he communicated with it. But writing also *objectified* information as myth objectified the forces of creation and destruction. Civilized man did not have to remember everything. He could 'look it up.' Preliterate societies depended on memory and oral transmission of information. Knowledge spread broadly throughout the culture as a way of ensuring its continuity. It would have disappeared had anyone tried to hoard or monopolize it because it would have died with the person who did so. Writing, however, made it possible to store information in archives and libraries which were centralized to make them easily accessible. Easily accessible, that is, to the rulers who were now in a position to monopolize information to whatever extent they wished. Monopolization of *written* information thus became an important instrument in the centralization of power. Not only were the libraries and archives restricted to the elite and their very important functionaries, the scribes, but access to them was in any case useless to the masses, who were illiterate. Mass literacy is a very recent phenomenon.

Finally, writing contributed directly to power centralization by making it possible for the rulers to remain in the seat of power while receiving lengthy reports from distant areas. One of the principle weaknesses of the 'Inca Empire' was its lack of writing. The Incas relied on a clever mnemonic device, a knotted cord called a *quipu*, which greatly facilitated oral transmission of information but one of the effects of its limitations was that the Inca king had to be constantly on the move from one end of his territory to the other to fill in the gaps in his information.

In addition to these means, the civilized elite employed armed force to hold and extend their sway. The huge surplusses amassed in the cities were partly used to finance standing armies and these in turn were utilized for the conquest of more human and natural resources. In the end, the gods and their earthly surrogates owned everything, not only natural resources and their products but even skills and control over skills-training. In a remarkable passage from the Sumerian civilization of 2000 B.C., the goddess, Inanna, Queen of Heaven and Earth, lists the gifts her father, Enki, gave her. Besides those which we might expect a god to give his daughter - the high priesthood, godship, the noble, enduring crown, the throne of kingship, etc. - we also find he has given her the crafts of the woodworker, the copper worker, the scribe, the smith, the leather maker, the fuller, the builder and the reed worker. (11, 16ff.) In other words, every important skill came from and remained the property of the gods and hence of the rulers.

We should not suppose that this 'divine connection' was peculiar to the civilizations of the West. It was universal. Even the Chinese, not given to elaborate mythologizing for reasons which will become clear later, recognized the divinity of the ruler and the creativity which flowed through him. Referring to the semi-historical Emperor Yao, who was thought to have reigned in the twenty-fourth century, B.C., the *Yao Tien* says,

> Examining into antiquity, (we find that) the Ti Yao [Grand Divine One] was styled Fang-hsun [The Highly Meritorious]. He was reverential, intelligent, accomplished and thoughtful, -- naturally and without effort. He was sincerely courteous, and capable of (all) complaisance. The bright (influence of these qualities) was felt through the four quarters (of the land), and reached to (heaven) above and (earth) beneath.
>
> He made the able and virtuous distinguished, and thence proceeded to the love of (all in) the nine classes of his kindred, who (thus) became harmonious. He (also) regulated and polished the people (of his domain), who all became brightly intelligent. (Finally), he united and harmonized the myriad states; and so the black-haired people were transformed. The result was (universal) concord. (8, 108)

Although the values credited to the Grand Divine One of China are somewhat different from those attributable to monarchs in other civilizations, the principal is the same. *Creativity comes through the ruler from a divine source.*

There is thus a very clear dividing line between primitive societies, however they may vary in size and complexity, and civilized

societies. A society is either civilized or it is not. If it is, it will have
all the attributes I have listed. If not, it will have none of them.
With this in mind, we can now offer a General Definition of
Civilization which describes a system rather than simply lists
attributes.

> *Civilization is a type of social organization in which a*
> *relatively small power elite, in pursuit of its own goals, exercises*
> *authority over and preempts the production of a large,*
> *powerless majority through the monopolization of information,*
> *the sanctification of myth, the centralization of key*
> *institutions, and the utilization of regimented armed force.*

'Civilizations' that Weren't

Since historians have never had a comprehensive definition of
civilization, some advanced precivilized societies have been regarded,
even by the great Toynbee, as civilized when, in fact, they were not.
Two of the most prominent examples are the Minoan society of Crete,
which Toynbee included in his 'Aegean Civilization,' and the Incan
society of Peru, which he called the 'Andean Civilization.' An
examination of the Minoan and the Incan societies in the light of the
General Definition of Civilization will not only demonstrate the value
of the definition but throw a new light on how we should think about
those two remarkable cultures.

Crete is an island about 250 kilometers long and fifty kilometers
at the widest. It lies southeast of the Greek Peloponnesus and
divides the Mediterranean from the Aegean Sea. Its ancient culture,
called 'Minoan' after its legendary king, Minos, is related to another
culture called 'Mycenean' or 'Mycenean Greek' which spread
throughout the Aegean, its cities including Homeric Troy. Minoan
culture had a written script which linguists call 'Linear A' while the
Mycenean script is called 'Linear B.' Considerable progress has been

made in deciphering Linear B but little on Linear A. Historians and archaeologists generally consider Minoan Crete 'civilized.'

Minoan culture was abruptly destroyed around 1450 B.C., probably by a Krakatoa-type explosion of the nearby volcanic island, Thera. In the absence of written records and of cultural continuity after the cataclysm, the burden of establishing what Minoan society was like falls on the shoulders of archaeologists. Since 1900 four complexes called 'palaces' have been excavated: Knossos (the largest), Phaistos and Mallia in east central Crete, and Zakros in its southeast corner. All are near the seacoast.

Writing in *Scientific American*, Peter M. Warren characterizes the palaces as follows:

> Each palace was the main building at its site, which was generally a major Minoan town. Each palace included a central court; generally there were other courts as well. Around the central court were grouped storage facilities, production areas, archives of inscribed tablets, rooms for ritual activity and rooms for state functions. Great power was concentrated in these elaborate structures: both the secular and the religious authorities of Minoan societies lived in them. Recent scholarly work has concentrated on the economic functions of the palace. It has been shown that the palace rulers probably had considerable control over agriculture in the region around the palace and also over Crete's rich foreign trade. (13, 74)

The thing Warren finds most striking about the Minoan palaces was that *they were not fortified* . There are two reasons for centers of civilization to be fortified. The first is to protect against foreign invaders. Aristotle long ago noted that the interior of Crete was so difficult of access that it discouraged invasion and Warren adds that Crete did not need defenses against foreigners because 'the island was far enough from mainland powers such as the Egyptians, the Hittites and the Mycenean Greeks to discourage frequent attacks.' He backs up his opinion convincingly with the fact that from the beginning of the Age of Palaces in 1930 B.C. to its cataclysmic end in 1450 B.C. 'no trace exists of foreign invaders.' (13, 77)

The other reason for fortifying civilized centers is to protect the rulers and their accumulated wealth from uprisings by the dispossessed masses, the people whom Toynbee called the 'internal proletariat.' The absence of fortifications suggests to Warren that 'they were built with the collective acceptance of the community. None of the palaces is in a physically commanding position and all four of them are readily accessible from the surrounding towns.' (ibid.) This leads him to the conclusion that 'Bronze Age society on Crete was hierarchical but not divisive. Under the authority of the palace the various social groups appear to have lived in relative harmony.' (13, 74)

But Warren is not comfortable with this conclusion. He finds the fact that 'the various social groups appear to have lived in relative harmony' puzzling in the extreme and asks,

> What was the source of the relative harmony of Minoan society? . . . At the heart of what we call civilization is the sublimation of aggressive impulses: their redirection toward higher and more abstract purposes than killing other human beings. Why that capacity appeared in a highly developed form among the seafaring inhabitants of a small, sun-baked island in about 2000 B.C. remains a profound and intriguing mystery. (13, 81)

There is nothing I enjoy more than a profound and intriguing mystery. But what Professor Warren has given us is not a mystery but a misconception which arises from his premise that 'at the heart of what we call civilization is the sublimation of aggressive impulses: their redirection toward higher and more abstract purposes than killing other human beings.' Cultural anthropology clearly contradicts the notion that it is precivilized peoples who go about killing and brutalizing their own members and that civilization exchanges such savagery for 'higher and more abstract purposes.' Wasn't it the *civilized* Romans who crucified rebellious slaves by the thousands and fed members of their internal and external proletariats to wild beasts in the arenas from Palestine to Gaul?

Wasn't it the *civilized* Europeans who transported millions of Africans to the new world to live and die as slaves? Wasn't it the *civilized* Indians who created the degrading caste system? Wasn't it the *civilized* Amerindians who sacrificed thousands of victims annually on their blooddrenched altars? Of course, the Chinese, as they were so fond of telling us, were eminently civilized. The story is told of Kao-hsin, favorite concubine of a prince, who became jealous of another concubine, Wang ch'ing. When it was discovered that Wang ch'ing had committed the grave offence of having her portrait painted in the nude, the prince allowed Kao-hsin to punish her, with the following result:

> . . . Wang ch'ing was first whipped and tortured with red-hot needles, then had her hair ripped out. At this point she managed to tear herself free and rushed towards a well with the intention of jumping into it. The attempt failed, she was seized and brought back to Kao-hsin who ordered that 'she be staked to the ground and red-hot irons inserted into the Jade Pavilion [vagina].' When Wang ch'ing lost consciousness, 'she was then cut to pieces, beginning with the facial flesh, and the remains at last thrown down the well she had been so determined to reach. (14, 58)

Incidentally, Hao-hsin was credited with having had fourteen women similarly tortured to death in her career. You can see for yourself from these few examples how well civilization managed to sublimate aggressive impulses.

The notion that civilized societies are hierarchical but not divisive and that precivilized or early civilized societies ought to show evidence of divisiveness has no basis either in history or anthropology. The exact opposite is the case. Once we dispose of the misconception that civilization overcomes divisiveness, the solution to the Minoan 'mystery' is obvious: *Minoan society was not yet civilized*. It was certainly a highly advanced precivilized society which might have taken the leap to civilization in another century or two but had not yet done so at the time it was destroyed. If we examine what Warren's excellent work tells us about Minoan Crete it will be

evident that nothing in the General Definition of Civilization applies
to its society. There is no evidence of the usurpation of authority or
the preemption of production. On the contrary, the 'palaces' appear
to be organizational, storage, recreation and religious centers for the
community. The fact that there was no need for armed force to
protect usurpers accounts for the lack of fortifications. Even the
centralization of key institutions is absent. The dispersion of the
'palaces' across the small island clearly contradicts centralization.
Although Knossos was the largest, there is nothing to indicate that it
exercised hegemony over the others. Finally, in contrast to the Egypt
and Assyria of the time, there was no monumental art or
architecture in Minoan Crete.

> In Aegean art, notably in that of Crete, we find nothing of the
> quiet, somber dignity found in Egyptian art or of the dim
> mysteriousness of the Egyptian temple, but a style directly
> expressive of a democratic people intimate with nature. It is
> a refreshing, sprightly art, imaginative and naturalistic
> rather than abstract. Its restlessness and movement reflect
> an exuberance of body and mind. The adventures of the
> Cretans on the sea were equaled by the love of pleasure at
> home to which their palaces bear witness. These palaces
> with their equipment and articles of personal adornment
> constitute practically the entire Cretan art expression, except
> for similar articles made for trading. They were equipped
> comfortably, even luxuriously, and their walls were gay with
> frescoes which picture life on land and on sea, and decorate
> as well. (65, 116)

In precivilized Crete, there was no power elite which needed
monumental art to support its grand social scheme, so art was free
to simply be enjoyed by everyone.

As I pointed out earlier, knowledge cannot be monopolized in a
preliterate society because it has to be remembered and passed
along to living people. But once you can write it down you can put it
away and mark it 'secret,' 'classified,' or 'for our eyes only.' Of course,
if you don't teach the masses how to read you don't have to mark it
at all. If the General Definition of Civilization is correct, a society

which does not have the other hallmarks of civilization will also not have a written language. *From this we can infer that Minoan Crete did not have a written language* . Then what about Linear A? It will probably turn out to be something like a reckoning system rather than a written language. A reckoning system, of course, has the potential of becoming a written language. Some written languages certainly originated in reckoning systems as the brilliant work of Denise Schmandt-Besserat has demonstrated (Cf. Scientific American, June 1978). But a reckoning system is not a written language, not something capable of objectifying speech and thoughts. Peter Warren himself seems to bear out my opinion of Linear A when he says, 'it is probable that the Minoan writings consist mainly of economic accounts.' (13, 74)

Minoan Crete is a fortunate example which supports my theory of civilization, fortunate because had the Minoans found it necessary to build fortifications against external enemies we might have assumed that they were used to control internal rebellion as well. In the case of Crete, that source of ambiguity is removed and we have a chance to see what an advanced precivilized society looked like. The second outstanding example of an advanced precivilized society which has been mistaken for civilized is the Incan society of Peru. The Incans' lack of writing has often been noted by other writers who generally treat them as an exception to the rule. They are, however, like the Minoans, an exception that proves (probes, tests) the rule. What Toynbee calls the 'Andean Civilization' actually meets none of the criteria for a civilization. It was another hierarchical but not divisive society. Although it was ruled by an absolute ruler, *the* Inca, the society was clearly founded on social concensus as has often been noted. It was guided by a concern for the general welfare rather than the exclusive interests of the elite. Incan towns, like Minoan, were generally not fortified but, unlike the Minoans, Incans were sometimes subjected to external attacks, so they built forts near their towns to which people could repair when they needed to defend themselves. Military power was used for the defense of the population rather than its repression. On the basis of the General Definition of Civilization, the Incans no more qualified as a civilization than did the Minoans. In fact there are remarkable similarities between the organization and function of Incan and Minoan towns which are well worth comparative archaeological study.

Nearly three thousand years after the disaster which destroyed Minoan society, Incan society was destroyed by another kind of disaster named Francisco Pizarro. Would the Incans have produced the Andean Civilization with which Toynbee wrongly credited them had not the murderous Spaniard arrived when he did? Inca culture was barely five hundred years old and, in my view, was *regressive* in terms of the trend toward civilization. If we rank societies on a scale of one to ten from the simplest, most primitive bands to full-blown civilizations, I would rank the Incans at about eight. *But some of their predecessors had been nines.* The Incans steadfastly denied they had any antecedents, professing to be the originators of high culture in their domain, but their claim was false. They were preceded by the Chavins, the 'Mochicas,' the Tiahuanacans and the Chimus. Some of their predecessors, particularly the Tiahanacans and the Chimus, had reached the brink of civilization but as it turned out, close as they were, none of the pre-Incan cultures did make the leap. Incan society, with its powerful social cohesion, nipped South American civilization in the bud and moved society backward from a nine to an eight (perhaps not unhappily for the Incan people.)

What the Incans might have done without Pizarros's help is anyone's guess, but we do have one clue as to the direction in which they might have been headed. After the death of the Inca, Huayna Capac, in 1527, the succession was expected to pass to one of his many sons, Huáscar. But another less pestigiously born son named Atahualpa contested the succession. After five years of civil war Huáscar was defeated and Atahualpa became Inca. Clearly the usurpative mentality which precurses civilization had emerged in Incan society. Had the Incans had the chance we might today have direct and recent information about how a society makes the transition from pre-civilization to civilization. But they did not get the chance. On November 16, 1532, while Atahualpa was at evening prayers, his unarmed bodyguard was ambushed and slaughtered by Pizarro's Christian soldiers. On August 29, 1533, after a kangaroo trial, the last Inca was unceremoniously garrotted. Which proves the superiority of tens over eights.

The Mental Revolution

The question we now have to ask ourselves is, Why? Why was the prodigious social system we call 'civilization' created? It originated independently in several widely separated parts of the earth and yet, as we have seen, it was not for the good of the mass of the people but of a small elite. What motivated its creators to accept the burden of responsibility for such an enormous and unprecedented enterprise? For indeed it was a great responsibility. Failure to carry it off spelled the untimely deaths of many a ruler in the course of history. If we can gain some insight into the motivation of those extraordinary innovators we will be in a better position to address the question we left unanswered in the first section of this chapter: What have civilized human beings been doing for the last five and a half thousand years?

Perhaps it was simply greed that motivated the proto-rulers. Perhaps they only wanted to amass great fortunes and live in styles to which no one had ever before been accustomed. Considering the risk and burden of their venture, I find that explanation difficult to support. In his classic treatise on *The Theory of the Leisure Class*, Thorstein Veblen observes correctly that 'so far as regards those members and classes of the community who are chiefly concerned in the accumulation of wealth [which the proto-rulers certainly were], the incentive of subsistence or of physical comfort never plays a considerable part.'(15, 26) In other words, *it isn't the wealth that's*

important, it's something derived from the wealth. According to
Veblen that something is the 'evidence of the prepotence of the
possessor of [the wealth] over other individuals within the
community.'(15, 28). 'The dominant incentive,' he claims, 'was from
the outset the invidious distinction attaching to wealth, and, save
temporarily and by exception, no other motive has usurped the
primacy at any later stage of development.'(15, 26) Wealth earned
esteem in the 'community', the more wealth, the more esteem and,
by reflection, the more self-esteem for the possessor. Of course, one
always has to cope with competition from other wealth-accumulators,
so in order to maintain the esteem of the community and,
consequently, self-esteem, one has to keep accumulating more
wealth. As Veblen put it, '...as fast as a person makes new
acquisitions, and becomes accustomed to the resulting new standard
of wealth, the new standard forthwith ceases to afford appreciably
greater satisfaction than the earlier standard did. The tendency in
any case is constantly to make the present pecuniary standard the
point of departure for a fresh increase of wealth; and this in turn
gives rise to a new standard of sufficiency and a new pecuniary
classification of oness self as compared with one's neighbors.'(15, 31)

   Veblen's prehistoric-historic sequence is somewhat confusing.
Once he gets beyond the stage of 'peaceable savagery' it is never
quite clear whether he is talking about ancient Egypt, Periclean
Athens, 'the higher stages of the barbarian culture; as, for instance
in feudal Europe or feudal Japan,' or *fin de siecle* New England
(where he studied and taught). His analysis, as mentioned in the
preceding paragraph, sounds most like what one might have found in
the last, i.e., 'keeping up with the Joneses'. If we go back to the time
when his analysis ought first to apply, to that of the enormous
accumulation of wealth in proto-civilization, then his theory is clearly
inadequate. The proto-rulers monopolized all the wealth within
their domains. Who were the 'Joneses' they had to outdo by
'invidious pecuniary comparison?' It seems absurd to suppose (and I

know of no evidence to support) that the Akkadian kings worried about whether the Egyptian kings had more wealth than they or *vice versa*. What *all* the kings were concerned about was *whether they had enough wealth to do what they wanted to do*. If they didn't, they set about to get it. That's what started wars very early in history.

At one point Veblen cautions that 'What has just been said must not be taken to mean that there are no other incentives to acquisition and accumulation than this desire to excel in pecuniary standing and so gain the esteem and envy of one's fellow-men.'(15, 32) He admits, for example, that '*the power conferred by wealth also affords a motive to accumulation*' (ibid., *emphasis mine*). But no sooner has he said that than he lapses back into his anachronistic psychosocial notions and thus misses the crucial point.

Bluntly put, what other conceivable motive could anyone have had to accumulate such enormous wealth and therewith create the 'enterprise of great pith and moment' we call civilization, with all its drain on human energy and imagination, its hazards, costs and sacrifices, except *power?* It wasn't the 'self esteem' derived from 'evidence of prepotence' that led to the monopolization of wealth. It was the prepotence *per se*, the *actual power* it conferred on the proto-rulers and their successors. The only real question is why they wanted that awesome power and the answer to that lies in how they used it.

If, as Childe claims, the centuries following 3500 B.C. did not produce much in the way of seminal inventions they certainly saw the expansion of human creativity in other ways at an explosive pace. The half-millenium before 3000 saw the flowering of Sumerian civilization with its great temples at Eridu, Uruk and Al Ubaid and the introduction of the first cuneiform writing. By the end of that period Upper and Lower Egypt had been united under Menes. The next thousand years produced the series of massive Egyptian pyramid tombs starting with the two hundred-foot high 'step pyramid' of Zoser in the 28th century and culminating, if not ending, scarcely a hundred years later in the Great Pyramid of Khufu at

Gizeh, the largest stone structure ever constructed. This period also encompassed the beginnings of civilization in India, the growth of seagoing trade on a wide scale, the introduction of international warfare, the forging of iron, the first fixed 365-day calendar, careful and systematic astronomical observations, epic religious poetry, the idea of the god-king - and beer. The succeeding centuries and millennia were all filled with achievements. In one place and time they would flow from one segment on the spectrum of human imagination, at other places and times from different segments but something extraordinary was always going on somewhere.

The Neolithic Revolution and the technological innovations of the millennia which followed had created the infrastructure for civilization but what finally made it possible was a revolution in the human mind. Throughout his many thousands of years on earth, man had been learning to cope in more and more effective ways with the world in which he found himself. Then, in the fourth millennium before Christ, a new kind of man with a different way of thinking came on the scene. That new man, the proto-ruler-priest, was no longer interested in merely coping with the world. His dream was *to make a world of his own design,* a design generated by his own vision. The worlds such men brought into being were integrated complexes of symbol and value. Each of them was *the world* to its participants, the all-embracing scheme in terms of which life was defined. They were not mere 'superstructures' of the material base as the topsy-turvy view of Marx and his followers would have it. Power and wealth were needed to build and expand the infrastructure for those worlds and the accumulation of power and wealth became, in turn, evidence that the divine connection of those worlds remained intact.

The Civilized Mind

The preliminary answer to the earlier question we asked - What have civilized human beings been doing for the last five and a half thousand years? - is that they have been engaged in a series of attempts to build, expand, preserve and defend their visionary worlds. They have been the successors of the Mental Revolution, the heirs and followers, for good or ill, of the world-makers. Toynbee implied this understanding of civilization when he wrote,

> Following Whitehead's lead, I should define civilization in spiritual terms. Perhaps it might be defined as an endeavour to create a state of society in which the whole of Mankind will be able to live together in harmony, as members of a single all-inclusive family. This is, I believe, the goal at which all civilizations so far known have been aiming unconsciously, if not consciously. (4, 44)

This 'state of society' is, of course, the ultimate 'challenge' to which Toynbee believes all civilized societies are called to 'respond'. In essence it is neither an environmental nor socio-political challenge but, as Toynbee says, 'spiritual.' In his view it leads to the attempted establishment of the 'Universal Church' and the 'Universal State.' While I think this conception of the 'whole of Mankind' as 'members of a single all-inclusive family' is overly influenced by Toynbee's own Western-Christian bias, he is right in identifying the prime motivating force in civilization as 'spiritual' in the sense that the whole enterprise was essentially a matter of creating self-contained, symbolic value-worlds.

If this view is correct, then history ought first to concern itself about the world view of each civilized society and the ways in which the society sought to build, maintain and expand its unique world according to that view. In such an approach, politics and economics would lose the dominant place they have gained in historiography and would be treated in the context of the vision which motivated each society as a whole. It would be seen that each civilized society came into being on the tide of a new world view or of a reformulated, reinvigorated version of an ancient world view. It would also be seen that the most severe crisis a civilized society could face was the threat of collapse of its world view, or, to put it another way, the threat that its fundamental symbols and values had become severed from the 'divine connection.'

However, it is not my purpose to rewrite history. The subject at hand is the nature of the mind which began and sustained history, the civilized mind. From what has already been said we can conclude that that mind was creative and bold, visionary and arrogant, more free from the constraints of tradition and social pressure than any mind had ever been but understanding itself as the conduit of superhuman powers of which it stood in awe.

These characteristics apply to the civilized mind in all places and at all times from the beginnings of civilization to the modern era. The civilizers' methods of acquiring wealth and power and the exploitative social structures they engendered were very similar from one civilization to the next. But knowing that is only an introduction to understanding civilization. It is like thinking we understand a human being when we have only described the bone structure he has in common with all other human beings. What is far more pertinent to truly understanding him is his *modus vivendi*, how he behaves and, even more deeply, how he thinks. If its world view was the primal creation of the civilized mind then we cannot understand that mind without examining the world views it created. That in turn compels us to ask whether the civilized mind was limited in its creativity only by its own imagination. Was it free to devise whatever kind of world it could envision? Or did it have a deeper structure, a structure which guided and molded its world views? To answer that question we have to look at a different kind of evidence. So far we have looked at what made all civilizations alike. But the essential clue to the nature of the world's great civilizations is to be found in what made them different - their *mindsets*.

TWO
Civilized Mindsets

The Four Civilizations

> . . . every manifestation by any human being who belongs to any civilization is stamped from the outset - *a priori* , in the strictest Kantian sense - with an idiosyncrasy that goes far deeper than any conscious judgment or endeavor and which is recognizable, by its style, as belonging to a particular civilization.'
>
> Oswald Spengler (16, 382)

Civilization arose independently in four parts of the earth. *Occidental Civilization* was the earliest, producing civilized societies in the Fertile Crescent by 3500 B.C. The other three civilizations followed at remarkably close to thousand year intervals: *Indic Civilization* in the Indus valley by 2500 B.C., *Sinic Civilization* in China by 1500 B.C. and *Amerindic Civilization* in the New World by 500 B.C. Many civilized societies sprang from these origins over the millennia (Toynbee counts about thirty) but the civilizing process never again occurred *de novo* .

Spengler is only one of many philosophers of history who have recognized the profound differences in styles of life and thought between the world's civilizations. When, however, it comes to describing and explaining these differences, scholars again desert us. In his *Study of History*, Toynbee is concerned about how civilizations exemplify certain general principles, not how and why each is unique. Although he acknowledges Spengler's assertion as having some merit, he does not credit it with any particular significance for the understanding of history. Again, when one of the most seminal minds of our time, Teilhard de Chardin, confronts the phenomenon of civilization, we are disappointed to find him able to make only a simplistic distinction between *passive* civilizations (i.e., Eastern) and *active* ones (the West). Being a devoted Westerner himself, Teilhard has no doubt that the future of man arises from the active West. The comprehensive minds failing us, more parochial ones fare no better. Proponents of 'the East' contrast its spiritual and intuitive qualities with the materialistic and analytic qualities of 'the West.' Apologists of the latter prefer to make the distinction between a rational and scientific approach to life and one that is mystical and superstitious. Finally, some thinkers, Aldous Huxley, for example, prefer to ignore differences altogether and extract from all civilizations a refined essence which they cite as a 'perennial philosophy.' None of these viewpoints is satisfactory. Nowhere do we find the conviction expressed by Spengler that civilizations do markedly differ matched by a theory which tries to explain the reasons why they differ - with one notable exception.

One of the most original thinkers of this century, Gerald Heard, addressed himself to this problem in a lecture delivered at Washington University in 1951. Reviewing the three prime civilizations which originated in the Old World - the Occidental, the Indic and the Sinic - Heard, unlike Toynbee, was not content to fit them into models which revealed only their similarities. As an anthropologist specializing in cultural evolution, he asked what adaptive specializations were evident in the three civilizations. What were they attempting to accomplish? In what did they excel? He formulated his answer in terms of three basic questions put by life, hypothesizing that each civilization specialized in answering a different one. The West sought an answer to the question, *Where am I?* This was the physical question, that of man's relation to nature, particularly nature conceived as space and mass. Out of this concern came the West's interest in engineering and science and its eventual strides toward the conquest of nature.

Indic Civilization, on the other hand, had turned inward, seeking an answer to the question: *Who am I?* From its obsession with the psychological question came the probing of the sages and yogis into the innermost layers of human consciousness.

Finally came China and the social question: *What am I?* How best can I manage my relations with my fellow man? While almost continually beset by strife from inside and out, Chinese civilization remained viable and continuous for well over three thousand years. This, as Heard saw it, was due to the Chinese expertise at maintaining social integrity while absorbing alien intrusions, with the result that, one after another, invader groups were converted to the Chinese way rather than destroying it.

One merit in Heard's approach was rightly perceiving that East is *not* simply East as the words of Kipling's ironic poem would have it. He made a clear distinction between the Sinic and Indic civilizations of Asia. Sometimes a single word can do more to obscure truth than volumes of erroneous theory. Such a word is 'East.' It was once used to denote the whole of the Eurasian land mass beyond the Aegean Sea. More recently it has been used to refer to the further reaches of that vast area which include India, China and Southeast Asia. The latter are meant when someone speaks of the 'Eastern mind' or 'Eastern culture.' But it is one thing to refer to a certain area by its direction from oneself and quite another thing to allow that designation to label it with a cultural or spiritual unity which does not exist. Yet that is precisely what happens when we try to make generalizations about 'the East' which embrace both Indic and Sinic civilization. The error becomes a serious intellectual distortion when it is perpetrated by scholars of the stature of Teilhard, Coomaraswamy and Northrop. Fortunately, other scholars have taken the opportunity to correct it. As the author of a major work on Far Eastern art says, '...the idea that the cultures of Asia are one, that there exists such a thing, for example, as the 'Oriental mind,' or that all the peoples of these regions are united by a highly developed metaphysical approach to life, is false...' (17, 18)

Heard's second achievement was to correctly identify and

document the unique achievements of the three civilizations he examined. Finally, he was right to locate the source of their differences in a fundamental divergence in point of view rather than in something external, such as differences in the environments in which the civilizations arose.

But his analysis did not go far enough. It failed both in scope and in depth. First, he considered only the three civilizations of the Old World, ignoring that of the New World entirely. Although we know much more about the Old World civilizations, no understanding of civilization can be complete which fails to take into account the peculiarities of Amerindic Civilization. Second, the conceit of the 'three questions', while useful, is nevertheless essentially a literary device. It begs the question of why the three civilizations chose to answer the questions they did. Even more importantly, it fails to tell us why they were so successful in their answers. Merely choosing the question is no guarantee of giving a satisfactory answer.

To understand the fundamental differences between the four prime civilizations (those which originated *de novo*) we have to go deeper than Heard did, deeper indeed than anyone has gone before, to expose the fundamental structure of the minds which created and sustained them. The civilizing process required a mind structured in quite a different way from that of either animals or primitive (precivilized) peoples. Animal experience is largely structured by heredity. Although animals are certainly capable of learning, for the most part their experience of the world is filtered through inherited mechanisms and their responses to stimuli come from a predetermined repertoire adequate to cope with their normal environment. If an animal meets a circumstance for which it has no available response in its repertoire, it simply cannot survive. A duck has no appropriate response to being soaked with oil and so, without outside help, it dies.

The primitive mind operates in similar fashion except that its repertoire is almost entirely learned, largely symbolic and much more flexible than that of any animal. According to A. Irving Hollowell,

> . . . self-identification and culturally constituted notions of the nature of the self are essential to the operation of all human societies and . . . a functional corollary is the cognitive orientation of the self to a world of objects other than self. Since the nature of these objects is likewise culturally constituted, a unified phenomenal field of thought, values, and action which is integral with the kind of world view that characterizes a society is provided for its members. The behavioral environment of the self thus becomes structured in terms of a diversified world of objects other than self, discriminated, classified, and conceptualized with respect to attributes which are culturally constituted and symbolically mediated through language. Object orientation likewise provides the ground for an intelligible interpretation of events in the behavioral environment on the basis of traditional assumptions regarding the nature and attributes of the objects involved and implicit or explicit dogmas regarding the 'causes' of events. *Human beings in whatever culture are provided with cognitive orientation in a cosmos; there is 'order' and 'reason' rather than chaos.* (1b, 50, *emphasis mine*)

It is to this 'cognitive orientation' that we must look in order to understand not only what makes the civilized mind different from the precivilized but what differentiates the mental structures of the four prime civilizations. The cognitive orientation which the young primitive learns is essentially a complete *map* of his limited world. By this I mean not merely a territorial map, although knowing his territory is an essential part of it, but a map that shows how every phenomenon and every kind of behavior he is ever likely to encounter is to be identified and related to himself - which are useful, which to avoid, which are sanctioned, which tabooed. This is the meaning of Hollowell's statement that the 'behavioral environment of the self thus becomes structured in terms of a diversified world of *objects other than self*, 'discriminated, classified, and conceptualized with respect to attributes which are culturally constituted and symbolically mediated through language.' The *objects* are the contents of the primitive's cognitive map. Obviously the cognitive map is not objective and impartial but thoroughly pragmatic, determined by the role the individual is expected to play. For this reason, in any primitive culture there are at least two 'submaps,' one for males and one for females, which, while they may overlap, nevertheless exclude each other to some extent.

The maplike character of this primitive orientation and the fact that it must be learned piece by piece in great detail cannot be overemphasized. It is what enables primitives to engage predominantly in what Kurt Goldstein (1c) calls 'concrete behavior,' which entails an immediate grasp of any situation on the basis of predetermined, learned signs and which does not require abstraction or generalization. It is also what guarantees the persistence of unchanged traditions through many generations, discourages innovation, and makes primitives loath to move from their original locale to another where a large part of their orientation maps might be inapplicable, a fact that the American government tragically missed in its dealings with Native Americans.

The Emergence of Mindsets

The essential limitations of the cognitive 'map' are what made the primitive mind unsuitable for the civilizers. Civilization was an enterprise of creativity, innovation, and expansiveness both in time and space, all qualities alien to the primitive mind. The limited primitive behavioral system, conservative by its very nature, had no capacity to handle the novelty, the creative imagining and the complicated relationships that civilization required. The cognitive map is perfectly suited to passing on a limited, unchanging tradition. It is of no use in exploring uncharted territory, which is exactly what the civilizers were doing. While primitive modes of thought were never entirely dispensed with in civilization, they were relegated principally to the internal relationships of subgroups. In fact, the elite were always happy to have the masses thinking at a primitive level and engaging only in 'concrete behavior,' provided the cognitive maps in their minds were consonant with the world the elite had designed for them. But that kind of thinking was not for the elite themselves. It could not be. Relating to the whole of the civilizing process, for those who created it and envisioned its enormous possibilities, required an entirely different way of experiencing and responding to that experience. Yet they needed some kind of guide, an orientation system that would keep them from squandering their energies in aimless wandering.

What they needed was not a map but a cognitive *lodestone*. A lodestone is a piece of magnetite which always points in the same direction - north. Which brings us to the primary thesis of this book: the lodestone which replaced the primitive cognitive map and provided orientation for the civilized mind was a *mindset*. A mindset is an *a priori* psychological matrix which guides experience and behavior in a predetermined 'direction.' The primitive mind had structured the *contents* of experience as they were received and understood through tradition. But the civilized mind utilized a structure, the mindset, which imposed itself on *all possible experience* rather than to a particular range or particular contents of experience. The way such a structure works can be seen in a limited context in the analysis of psychological *positions* originated by Eric Berne (18, 270) and Thomas E. Harris. The positions are mindsets operating in interpersonal relationships. They originate by dichotomizing social experience into two poles: *I* and *you*. Next, a value, *OK* or *not-OK*, is assigned to each term. The four possibilities resulting from this early childhood process can be tabulated as follows:

	I	YOU
1.	OK	OK
2.	OK	NOT-OK
3.	NOT-OK	OK
4.	NOT-OK	NOT-OK

About the four positions, Berne comments, 'It is evident that only position 1 is intrinsically constructive, and therefore, existentially possible. Position 2 is essentially paranoid, 3 depressive, and 4 futile and schizoid.' We will have occasion later to reflect back on this observation, but let us note here that the positions do not depend on the specific content of interpersonal experience. They do not involve evaluating each 'you' that comes along as to relative 'OK-ness.' If I adopt position 2, then in *every* 'I and you' experience I am automatically OK and you are automatically not-OK. A mindset is inherently prejudicial. It operates as a subconscious structuring of experience.

My contention is that the civilized mindsets were built on *positions* exactly like those identified by transactional analysis. The civilizers used the same method that, according to Berne, a child does in formulating its life world view (equally subconsciously, I am sure), that of dichotomizing experience and assigning a value or coefficient to each of the poles. But the simple interpersonal *I* and *You* would hardly have suited their needs. After all, they were world-builders. They needed something comprehensive and fundamental upon which to base their world views, a dichotomy which encompassed the totality of experience rather than a limited area such as interpersonal relationships. The problem was, what possible division of all experience can one make which is comparable to 'I and you' in interpersonal relationships?

The solution was, in retrospect, incredibly simple, yet it marks a quantum leap in the development of the human mind. Man, on the threshold of becoming civilized, divided experience into the two poles of *order* and *non-order*. *The different ways in which he conceived the relationship between those two poles became the cognitive lodestones or mindsets which oriented the course of the four prime civilizations and their successors.*

Before we investigate what the civilizers did with that dichotomy, let us examine and clarify the meaning of the two poles. In everyday experience, *order* is experienced as the known, the rational, the familiar. *Non-order* is the mysterious, the nonrational, the strange. The closest synonym we might find for the rather cumbersome word 'non-order' is 'mystery.' Hereafter I will use the two words almost interchangeably. Obviously we hardly ever experience pure order or pure non-order. The experience of a catatonic schizophrenic may come close to pure order and that of a mystical experience (cosmic consciousness) to pure non-order, i.e., ineffable, undifferentiated, etc., but apart from those extremes every experience has both ordered and non-ordered aspects. Let us take a simple example. We find ourselves in a room full of people. We recognize them to be people. That is *order*. We distinguish men and women, tall and short, dark and blonde. That also is *order*. But *who* are the people? Perhaps their faces are not familiar; perhaps they are all strangers to us. At that point we confront *non-order* or *mystery*. Or, to take another example from the world of poetry, everyone would recognize that 'A rose is a rose' is a tautology. It is a perfect example of order, a thing known for certain. But let Gertrude Stein say 'A rose is a rose is a rose' and the certainty disappears. We are puzzled by what this apparent redundancy means. The third rose has introduced an element of non-order and opened up the mind to mystery.

To make the idea of ordered and non-ordered experience still more concrete, following are a list of concepts, the first column representing order, the second, non-order:

Order	Non-order
Familiar	Strange
Trite	Novel
Earthly	Alien
Mundane	Sacred
Stable	Unstable
Rigid	Flexible
Law and Order	Lawlessness
Tyranny	Freedom

The righthand term in each horizontal pair clearly denotes a lower degree of order (or higher degree of mystery) than its opposite on the left. If we can borrow a principle from Indian philosophy, that the first step in the creation of order is the ascription of name *(nama)* and form *(rupa)*, then it is obvious that the non-order concepts above refer to realities which cannot be named (strange, novel, alien, sacred) or which have dubious or unpredictable form (unstable, flexible, lawlessness, freedom.) In the case of 'sacred' we can recall that the true names of gods were often taboo. This was precisely because the experience of the supramundane or divine is at one level a non-order experience *(mysterium tremendum et fascinosum)*. Giving it a name would impose an order upon it and, therefore, dilute its mystery. Of course, you can easily construct your own list of order/non-order antonyms to satisfy yourself that language is rife with this fundamental polarity in experience but let us have a second look at the preceding list.

In the list the concepts are not only paired horizontally but vertically as well. The vertical pairs are words which denote roughly the same idea but which have quite different conventional connotations. The first in each pair has a positive connotation (in current American culture), the second, a negative. Their antonyms have opposite connotations. The purpose of this vertical pairing is to illustrate that order and non-order do not carry intrinsic valuations. We assign them values as 'I' and 'you' were assigned the values 'OK' and 'not-OK' in the transactional analysis table. Take the last pair as an example. Both the terms 'law and order' and 'tyranny' denote a high degree of social control. Political conservatives positively value such control as 'law and order' and praise its resulting social stability while deprecating its opposite as 'lawlessness.' On the other hand, radicals take a very negative attitude toward the same degree of control and call it 'tyranny.' Its opposite then has the positive connotation of 'freedom' rather than 'lawlessness.'

It is not even necessary that one term of an order/non-order polarity be negative and the other positive. Either term can have either valuation. A good illustration of this is the following table involving the order concept of marriage and the non-order concept of divorce as evaluated by persons in different situations:

Marriage	Divorce	As viewed by:
OK	OK	An impartial marriage counselor
OK	not-OK	The Roman Catholic Church
not-OK	OK	A miserable spouse
not-OK	not-OK	An unadjusted divorcee

This illustrates the crucial point for understanding mindsets, that both order and non-order can either be affirmed or negated, that is, a positive or negative value can be ascribed to either. It should also be clear from the preceding illustrations that the four positions or mindsets are mutually exclusive. For example, you cannot assert that 'marriage is good and divorce is bad' and, at the same time, 'marriage is bad and divorce is good' without contradicting yourself. In fact, you cannot assert *any two* of the positions at the same time without contradiction. With these points in mind, let us apply what we have discovered to the civilized mind.

The Four Civilized Minds

In setting out the relationship between order and non-order adopted by each of the civilized mindsets I will continue to follow Berne and Harris in using the terms, 'OK' and 'not-OK'. But we need to bear in mind that, simple as these words are, they reveal decisions about life made thousands of years ago which formed the matrix of the civilized societies in which the vast majority of mankind lived thereafter. The character of those societies was shaped by those primordial decisions and the minds of all civilized men who followed were molded by them. For that reason it must be understood that, in that primordial context, an 'OK' to either order or non-order meant that it was affirmed, desired, searched out and embraced. It was believed, to borrow a phrase from Paul Tillich, that it was 'rooted in the Ground of Being,' essential to the meaning of life. On the other hand, a '*not-OK* ' to either order or mystery meant that it was negated, rejected, avoided and feared. It was not rooted in the Ground of Being and held no final meaning for life. With that in mind, we can now present the four mindsets which are theoretically possible.

<u>Mindset</u>

<u>Order</u>	<u>Non-order</u>
OK	OK
OK	not-OK
not-OK	OK
not-OK	not-OK

If you wonder whether the first, double affirmative, mindset wouldn't allow a civilization to ride off in all directions, which is what mindsets are supposed to prevent, the answer is 'No.' The second and third mindsets have a special intensity, a wholeheartedness, a thrust toward one pole and a kick against the other, but the first mindset lacks the kick. Since it cannot 'cathect' order and non-order with equal intensity, it aims at a balance between them. If you wonder how any mind could adopt the fourth, double negative, mindset, then bear in mind that what it means is that neither order nor non-order is 'rooted in the Ground of Being,' neither is independent or self-sustaining. Since, however, any world involves both poles, something extra must be injected, as we shall see, into a world structured by the fourth mindset in order to make it viable.

The next question, of course, is how to assign these theoretical mindsets to the four prime civilizations. The table on the following page answers that question. The first column in the table is the list of civilized mindsets. The second column indicates the civilization which adopted each mindset. The third gives what I consider to be the best one-word description of the overall view of life produced by each mindset, the *dominant theme*. The last column shows four major categories of experience to which each civilization traditionally gave special attention. These categories are called the *dominant concerns*. The dominant concerns of the first three civilizations agree with the 'specializations' propounded by Gerald Heard. My scheme, however, adds a fourth specialization, *time*, as the dominant concern of Amerindic Civilization.

| Mindset | | Prime | Dominant | Dominant |
Order	Non-Order	Civilization	Theme	Concern
OK	OK	Sinic	Balance	Society
OK	not-OK	Occidental	Transformation	Nature
not-OK	OK	Indic	Transcendence	Self
not-OK	not-OK	Amerindic	Precariousness	Time

These mindsets are the cognitive structures or orientations of the minds which created and carried forward civilization. They were the 'fixed coordinates' of the four civilizations, the guarantors of their uniqueness and durability. As long as the mindsets did not change and the civilizations therefore retained their fundamental identities, endless cultural variations could be generated as creativity or the exigencies of time required. Without the mindsets as primal guides civilization would have been impossible. Given the enormous creativity, energy and arrogance of the civilizers the whole enterprise would have drowned in anarchy at its inception.

But what is the significance of the fact that there were *four* mindsets, only four, and that they were mutually exclusive? The significance is simply that there was, in fact, no such thing as *a* civilized mind. There were *four* civilized minds. *In each civilization, what it meant to be civilized was not only different from but incompatible with what it meant to be civilized in the other three civilizations.*

In the remainder of this chapter we will briefly review the four mindsets in turn and examine how each dealt with those four categories of experience which I have referred to as dominant concerns. In doing so we will see not only that the mindsets were incompatible with each other but also why each was prone to a different dominant concern. For the sake of clarity I have decided to begin with the second (Occidental) mindset rather than the first because it is my own and probably that of the earliest readers of this book. If we first understand the mindset which is our heritage we will more easily grasp the nature of mindsets in general.

The Occidental Mind:
Transforming Chaos into Cosmos

The structure of the Occidental mind is reflected in its earliest creation myths. It is a mind which is obsessed with the ordered, the rational, the ideal, the male, and deeply suspicious of the non-ordered, the intuitive, the material, and the female. Mythically, non-order is expressed as Chaos, that which is 'without form and void,' terms with essentially negative connotations. In the act of creation, Chaos is transformed, sometimes through epic struggle, sometimes by fiat, sometimes spontaneously, into Cosmos. This implies that the very essence of life, to the Occidental mind, is the *transformation* of non-order into order. Further, the triumph of that process is in some way assured despite the persistent threat that life may be engulfed by mystery, accident, evil, or entropy. The Deluge comes but the primeval waters of Chaos do not succeed in destroying man. Non-order cannot prevail because only order is 'rooted in the Ground of Being.'

The Occidental mind saw the *self* as, at best, an arena of conflict between non-order and order. It discerned non-order in the vagaries of fortune, the force of passion and the certainty of death. The Greek perception of the first two is reflected in an interchange between

Medea and Creon in Euripides' play (19, III, 70):

> Medea. Oh what an evil to men is passionate love!
> Creon. That would depend on the luck that goes along with it.

That good luck was hardly something to be counted on in life was a recurrent theme in Greek tragedy:

> . . . grief and joy come circling
> to all, like the turning paths
> of the Bear among the stars.
> Sophocles, *The Women of Trachis* (19, II, 283)

The Occidental mind developed two strategies for transforming the non-order of the self, including the inevitability of death, into order. The first is as old as Western civilization itself. It consisted essentially in transforming death into a new - and everlasting - life. The tomb became the gateway to heaven. The process was not automatic, of course. Conditions had to be met during earthly life, conditions which in themselves imposed a certain order on the contingencies of life. Sometimes it was sacrifice to supernatural powers, sometimes a code of morality, sometimes an act of faith. ('Whosoever believeth in me shall not perish, but have everlasting life.') However the conditions might differ, the first century Christian would have been entirely comfortable with the joyful paean of the Egyptian scribe from three thousand years earlier: 'Boundless eternity hath been granted to me, and, behold, I am the heir of eternity; to me hath been given everlastingness.' (20, 310)

The everlasting life strategy sometimes brought the whole self, including the body, into the transformation process. This was the purpose of mummification for the Egyptians, to whom an afterlife without a body was difficult to imagine. In Pauline theology the body was to be resurrected in a transformed condition, the exact nature of which Paul left his successors to ponder.

The other prominent view of everlasting life was that it involved only a special component of the self called the soul or spirit. It was this component that the Greeks turned to in creating the second strategy for bringing the chaotic and hapless self into the realm of order. The world is rational, reasoned the Greeks. That rationality is beyond the vicissitudes of chance and decay. Therefore, to the extent that the spirit or mind understands and is guided by the rational, the self escapes the misfortunes of the flesh. One can even, like Socrates, accept death calmly, knowing that one is participating in the highest order of which life is capable. Both strategies persisted throughout Occidental civilization.

Self was clearly a problem for the Occidental mind. It was something to be dealt with, not explored. Dionysian and mystical propensities, which led beyond the rational and regulated, were always suspect in the West. Not until the twentieth century would the West, in the person of Sigmund Freud, feel comfortable with investigating the self's hidden layers. But even after four centuries devoted to breaking the hold of civilization on the West, the influence of the Occidental mindset was still strong enough to make Freud's view of the unconscious essentially Dionysian.

Time, on the other hand was not a problem for the West. The Occidental mind thought of posterity, of the persistence of dynasties. It also conceived of 'everlastingness' or 'eternity' as a religious concept. But, in a cosmic sense, until quite recently the West has behaved as though time did not exist. A modern scientist says,

> The real time scale of the universe that has been developed
> by science can be regarded as having liberated the perception
> of time from the limitations of the human mind. (21, 194)

If we substitute 'the Occidental mind' for 'the human mind,' the statement is accurate. It would not be accurate for any of the other three civilizations. The West's peculiar attitude toward time is not difficult to understand. Time was judged by the Occidental mindset to be a fundamental non-order concept contrasting with the perfect order of eternity. It was associated with change, decay and death. As it passed, all things passed with it, individuals in years, dynasties in decades, nations in centuries. Time simply swallowed up life and one did not need to be reminded of that. It was not until the nineteenth century in the West that time, under the guise of evolution, was seriously entertained as a universal organizing principle.

Society implies order and one might expect that a mind which prizes order and eschews disorder might be especially good in the social sphere. That is not necessarily true. It is one thing to apperceive order as being rooted in the Ground of Being, but quite another thing to accord a particular social order the same status. The temptation to do so was always a danger in the West. The society of the divine Pharaohs persisted for millennia in Egypt. It also alternately stagnated and suffered violent upheavals. When change finally came, it often erupted as anarchy. Of the Egyptian revolution in the twenty-third century B.C. Neubert says,

> The revolution was not directed against a particular social class, but against property owners everywhere. Its object was not merely the abolition of 'privileges' but the abolition of law itself...Brother fought with brother, father with son. Foreigners infested the land, all was chaos. Murder was no crime and the Nile ran red with blood. (22, 98)

The history of Western civilization is replete with examples of societies which imposed their sanctified order so rigidly that the only avenue of change was revolution; so much so that Marx could write the history of the West in terms of its revolutions. The redeeming alternative the West found to identifying order with the *status quo* was law, law conceived not as a specific code but as a system of principles on the basis of which particular laws could be formulated, repealed or altered. In this sense law was a perception of order higher than but related to society. It was an active force which produced civilization out of barbarism and sometimes rescued civilization from reverting to barbarism. But only sometimes. The rule of law in society can be heavyhanded and slow to change. Law can easily be used by both reactionaries and revolutionaries and is often not a sufficiently sensitive fine tuning mechanism for either social change or stability.

It is in the realm of *nature* that the second mindset produced its finest results and Gerald Heard was quite right in identifying nature as the dominant concern of the West. It is important to note that 'nature' does not mean here the nature of naturalists and ecologists. It means the physical world of space and mass. The West's success with the physical world was not the result of any geographical or environmental peculiarity of the areas in which Western civilization originated. Rather it was due to the West's primal obsession with order. Astronomical systems and geometric principles had been devised long before the Greeks, but it is to to the latters' credit that they indulged their interest in such matters for its own sake, quite apart from priestly or practical considerations. The Greeks invented philosophy and science simply because their minds were driven to find out what kind of order lay behind the phenomena. Although pure science was neglected and even suppressed in Europe for nearly two thousand years after the Greeks, it was never extinguished. It was kept alive under Islam and revived in Europe in the Renaissance. In the last four hundred years it has accelerated enormously with the development of an experimental method of inquiry which has the capacity to further and further define the order of nature with extreme mathematical precision.

These, then are the fruits of the Occidental civilized mind: an atomized, troublesome sense of self; an impoverished concept of time; a workable, if somewhat cumbersome, method of managing society through law; and a superb grasp of the laws of nature. Let us bear this in mind as we turn to the Indic mind, the inverse of ours.

The Indic Mind:
Ascent from Order to Mystery

Indic Civilization was a huge system of many layers built up throughout the course of a long history. There can be little doubt, however, that the Indic mindset derived from the deepest layer, the Indus Valley civilization which was already flourishing a thousand years before the Aryans, distant cousins of the Greeks, commenced their invasions around 1500 B.C. Ritual bathing tanks consonant with later Indian usage were already present at Mohenjo-Daro and Harappa and one beautifully carved seal clearly shows a masked figure, perhaps a god, seated in a yoga posture (*siddhasana*). The spiritual 'revolution' of the sixth century B.C. which produced the Upanishads was undoubtedly less a revolution than a renaissance of the long-established Indic mindset in the context of an imported Aryan mythology. Belief in a primal, ineffable, non-ordered Ground of Being overshadowed every institution and system of behavior in Indic civilization. Nothing ordered could be rooted in the Ground of Being, not gods nor souls nor law. That which was final and ultimate in experience was the mystery of it. To the Indic as to the Occidental mind, order and non-order were always in opposition. But the Indic myths of creation related a primeval separation from oneness, a descent of the world from formless ultimate reality. Order, beginning in its most primitive guise as name and form, was a vast and treacherous illusion (*maya*). There was only one reality and about that one could only say, 'It is not this - it is not that'. To say anything else would be to ascribe order to what is unorderable. The closest one might come, in order to convey the ultimate positive valuation of non-order, was to say that it was Pure Being, Pure Consciousness and Pure Bliss (*satcitananda*). The ultimate meaning of life when viewed from this mindset was the *transcendence* of all experience of form and a return to that which is formless.

This view subjected the *self* to a peculiar duality. On the one hand the self was that primal non-ordered reality (Self with capital 'S').   It had to be since that was all that really was. On the other hand, the self (small 's') existed in some way as an individual soul (*jiva*) trapped in *maya* or *samsara* (time, ceaseless change). That self was subject to all the laws and conditions of the temporal world, particularly the rigorous order of *karma* (law of cause and effect) and reincarnation. Every deed one did became a future determinant that either positively or negatively affected one's ability to transcend the round of rebirths and achieve final liberation (*moksha* or *nirvana*). The Egyptian scribe rejoiced that he had been given individual 'everlastingness.' To the Indic mind such a notion was unthinkable because it would mean an eternal separation from that pure mystery which is what the self really was (*tat tvam asi* : That thou art). Contrast with the passage from the Egyptian Book of the Dead quoted in the preceding section the following passage from the Bardo Tödol, the Tibetan Book of the Dead :

> Those who are voraciously inclined toward this [i.e., temporal existence], or those who do not at heart fear it, -- O dreadful! O dreadful! Alas! -- and those who have not received a guru's teachings, will fall down into the precipitous depths of the Sangsara in this manner and suffer interminably and unbearably. (23, 180)

Note that this passage is not threatening hell-fire.   It is merely speaking about being reborn in further earthly lives.   Evans-Wentz says, 'Normally, existence in the Bardo ever tends to lead the deceased back to birth; and this is due to karmic propensities, which are the opposition, the forces opposing the Enlightenment of Buddhahood. Hence the deceased must oppose this innate tendency with every help available.' (23, 176, Footnote 2) Thus, whereas self was a non-order concept to the Occidental mind, to the Indic mind self (small 's') is an order concept. Since, however, the Western mind negated non-order and the Indic mind negated order, the self was problematic in both worlds.

Time likewise had a negative 'coefficient' in both civilizations, also for opposite reasons. Whereas time in the West was a non-order concept, the destroyer of order, in India it was the matrix of karma and reincarnation, that is, the epitome of order. The attainment of liberation from the world of *samsara* was a prodigious task. In effect, it amounted to reversing the process of creation. In the Indic world view it was not the work of one lifetime but of many. In fact, it was a neverending process involving innumerable souls over inconceivable eons. While, in the West, time was the insidious 'conqueror worm,' symbol of death and decay, to the Indic mind it was a vast and virtually interminable oppression.

How did a mindset which led to abhorrence of the primal order of birth itself manage to create and preserve *society*? If the whole realm of order is an illusion, not rooted in the Ground of Being, it is yet the nature of an illusion that it appears to be reality. One must deal with it as long as one is fooled by it but in such a way that one has progressive opportunities to be less fooled. Indic society was therefore organized on transcendent principles, that is, in ladderlike stages. Each person's relative position on the ladder leading to ultimate release was his caste which depended on his accumulated karma. Indic society simply assumed that each person was born into the caste where he belonged. With few exceptions, there he stayed. At the top of the ladder were the Brahmins, the priestly caste, highest on the scale of transcendence. Transcendence also dictated the stages of life. One was expected to have religious training as a child, then go on to raise a family and be a responsible householder. But in the later years it was accepted that a man might leave his home and become a wandering ascetic, meditating to open his consciousness and project it toward death with added *karmic* merit.

The most ironic aspect of the Indic mind's influence on society is
that, while disaffirming order, it created a society which was one of
the most rigidly ordered and reactionary the world has known. The
reason is not far to seek. Recall that in the West it was the idea of a
law above society that often rescued Occidental Civilization from
becoming mummified. Order being rooted in the Ground of Being,
the relative order of society at any time could be called into question.
Society was always, at least in principle, subject to transformation.
But in India the social order could not be called into question by a
higher order because there was no such thing as higher order. The
Bhagavad Gita contains an excellent illustration of this. When
Prince Arjuna, on the battlefield, shrinks from killing foes, some of
whom are his kinsmen, Krishna, the divine avatar, tells him,

> I am come as Time the waster of the peoples,
> Ready for that hour that ripens to their ruin.
> All these hosts must die; strike, stay your hand - no matter.
> Therefore, strike. Win kingdom, wealth and glory.
> Arjuna, arise, O ambidextrous bowman.
> Seem to slay. By me these men are slain already.   (24)

Krishna was reminding Arjuna that, as a member of the warrior
caste, it was his caste obligation to 'win kingdom, wealth and glory.'
No principle or law, let alone personal feeling, had any power of
judgment over that obligation. The implication is that history is
merely the arena in which certain predestined roles are acted out.
The acting has significance only for the karmic merit of the
individual, none for history itself. History is, therefore, meaningless.
This is underscored by Krishna's blunt announcement, 'By me these
men are slain already.'

Heinrich Zimmer contrasts the differences wrought by the
Occidental and Indic mindsets on concepts of politics and rulership
as follows,

> Apparently the Western man of action has to regard himself
> as the noble instrument of a mysterious plan for the history of

> mankind, the arm of the universal spirit, working changes
> and driving toward evolution. . . No such mandate from
> Providence, history, or mankind descends to form a wreath
> around the head of the Hindu despot. (25, 103-4)

The Indic ruler was strictly on his own, without justification of higher principles. The social result was that apart from those institutions which lent themselves to transcendent orientation - the caste system itself, religious obligations within the castes, the stages of life - social, political and, as we shall see in Chapter 8, even sexual activities - became a law unto themselves.

Nature, whether the world of space and mass or the naturalist's world, held little interest for the Indic mind. Like all civilizations, the Indic developed astronomy to the extent that it served astrology, so it clearly grasped the idea of order in nature. Apart from its significance for rituals and prognostications, however, that order was not important to a mindset which ultimately valued only that which was beyond order. What was important to the Indic mind was how we *experience* nature. If the mind is caught in the web of illusion, it is of vital concern to know how that illusion operates. Long before the beginning of the Christian era, Hindu and Buddhist philosophers were already developing analyses of experience far more complex and subtle than those of the English philosophers of two thousand years later.

What, then, were the fruits of the Indic mindset? An architectonic sense of *time* as the matrix of endless rounds of birth and death; a concept of *society* as oriented toward a transcendent goal and neither susceptible to nor warranting amelioration in time; virtually no understanding of *nature* as a sphere independent of spirit but a profound analytical treatment of the *experience* of nature; and, finally, a view of the *self* which extends beyond the confines of individuality to embrace infinity. It was this view which produced the most extraordinary outgrowth of Indic society, the *sadhus* and *gurus* - holy men and spiritual teachers - who followed the mystery of experience to its limits and plumbed those depths of consciousness where knowledge gives way to ecstasy and order to that which was before it.

The Sinic Mind:
Harmonizing the Opposites

If some clichés produce gross distortions of truth, others contain more than a grain of it. So it is when we speak of 'the inscrutable Oriental (i.e., Sinic) mind.' No Western writer has so well depicted that inscrutability as James Clavell in his novels, *Shogun* and *Tai Pan*. Even after reading the novels and knowing the denouement, one has the impression that one has missed something in the thinking processes of the Japanese and Chinese. A second reading fails to dispel that impression.   In this century the Indic mindset has made some significant penetrations into the West, beginning with the arrival of Ramakrishna's disciple, Vivekananda, to attend the world Parliament of Religions in Chicago in 1893. Since that time, the West, particularly the United States (and, more particularly, California) has been inundated with gurus, swamis and maharishis, none of them lacking for disciples. But, innumerable Chinese restaurants and Arthur Waley notwithstanding, we have not become well acquainted with the Sinic mind. In fact, its influence only began to be felt after World War II and then through the back door, so to speak, in the gradual popularization of Chinese and Japanese martial arts. I believe the reason for this is that it is much easier for a Westerner to understand the Indic mind than the Sinic. All that is required for the former is that you turn your outlook upside down and think of everything in the opposite way from that to which you are accustomed. Pavlov was able to get even dogs and monkeys to do that. But the Sinic mind is not diametrically opposed to the Occidental. It affirms order as we do but it also affirms mystery in a way we cannot. While we come to the fork in the road and insist that only one road can be followed, the Sinic mind, says,

'No, you can take both at the same time.' We find that understandably confusing. In this section we will try to clear up some of that confusion. However, we should be forewarned that that is far easier to do intellectually than it is existentially. I suspect that when we have finished, the Sinic mind will still remain, at 'gut level,' somewhat inscrutable.

To the Sinic mind, order and mystery were equally rooted in the Ground of Being. They were complementary and their interplay was the essence of life. Because both were affirmed, neither could be allowed to assume exclusivity or final dominance over the other. This is expressed as follows in the *Tao Te Ching* of the sage, Lao-Tse:

> Being and non-being interdepend in growth;
> Difficult and easy interdepend in completion;
> Long and short interdepend in contrast;
> High and low interdepend in position;
> Tones and voice interdepend in harmony;
> Front and behind interdepend in company.   (26, 47)

Order and non-order had always to be kept in *balance*, not a static balance but a dynamic one in which the two tussled creatively with each other but neither ever permanently gained supremacy. It was a conflict leading to harmony. In China this dynamic balance was traditionally symbolized by the Yin Yang:

Yang represented the ordering, active principle which was identified with the male, and Yin was the non-ordering, passive, female principle. They interpenetrated and interfecundated each other.

The double affirmative mindset conduced to a holistic concept of *self* which was quite unlike that found either in the West or India. To the Chinese, the self was the focus of a complex web of relationships involving the universe, society and the opposite sex. All of those relationships involved conflicting demands and the challenge was not to get rid of them by transforming or transcending them but to accept and harmonize them. This challenge was nowhere more clearly recognized than in the Chinese attitude toward sex. While the Western mind moralized about it and the Indic mind treated it either with mechanical eroticism or mystical symbolism, the Chinese, from the earliest times, discussed sex in all its aspects with absorbing and candid seriousness, not, however, without a generous admixture of humor. An extensive discourse on sex was attributed to the legendary founder of Chinese civilization, the Yellow Emperor Huang Ti, to whom tradition assigns a ninety-nine year lifespan beginning in 2697 B.C. From this earliest treatise to ones dating as late as 1500 A.D., according to Humana and Wang,

> . . . there is a remarkable consistency in the approach to sexual relations. This can be seen in their acceptance of the ancient beliefs of the Yin and Yang theory, of Harmony and the cosmic properties of the Vital Essence, and of the need to indulge in such relations with a certain moderation. (14, 15)

To the Chinese, sexual intercourse was literally a battle of the sexes and the metaphors used in speaking about it were often martial in tone - e.g., they spoke of the man's 'assault on the Jade Pavilion,' the latter, of course referring to the female sex organ. It was not, however, a rancorous battle. It was a pleasurable and exciting one for both parties, leading to a mutually beneficial exchange of life forces. In other words, sex reflected the basic conflict leading to harmony, the dynamic balance which the Sinic mind saw as the essence of life. Through sex the self was connected to the Ground of Being.

When it came to the question of life and death, the Chinese always sought the best of both worlds. While the quest for immortality (in a kind of 'astral' body) was central to early Taoism, considerable effort was also expended on the attainment of earthly longevity. When Buddhism entered China, around the first century A.D., it brought with it the Indic concern for transcendence. Nothing illustrates the force of the Chinese mindset more clearly than the way in which it altered the Buddhist doctrines of life and death. Although rebirth remained a tenet of Chinese Buddhism as did karmic merit, the rigid determinism of karma was sidestepped by a doctrine of grace and the horrific connotations of rebirth typical of Tibetan Buddhism were ameliorated by the idea of a kind of interim immortality of a pure and pleasant nature in *ch'ing't'u*, the Pure Land, where the soul awaited final Nirvana. Final transcendence, yes, but not too soon and not too much grimness during the interval. Typically, the Chinese managed to keep the most disparate concepts of the self and its destiny in a viable balance.

As Gerald Heard rightly noted, the Sinic mind was at its best in matters of *society*. This was not so much because it 'specialized' in social matters, but because its mindset singularly equipped it for the delicate adjustments required for longterm social stability. '. . . the Chinese,' says Joseph Needham, 'wise before their time, worked out an organic theory of the universe which included nature and man, church and state, and all things, past, present and to come.' (27, 308) Sinic civilization, like all the others, had to recognize and contend with the polarity of social continuity (order) and innovation (non-order). Unlike the West, which constantly struggled with the polarity, or India, which suppressed it, the Chinese emphasized it. Rather than trying to codify their governing principles into laws for all time, they spawned numerous schools of social philosophy which were in constant contention. Nobles, governors and bureaucrats received ongoing input from the social philosophers. Sometimes one school prevailed, sometimes another. Radical innovations were often introduced by an attack on the currently dominant social philosophy and often its adherents were persecuted. This practice persisted to some extent even in modern communist China. But none of the schools was permanently outlawed and another season would see the persecuted regaining their influence. Although the Chinese had a powerful respect for elders and an entrenched class system, they saw to it that young commoners of exceptional ability were regularly brought into the bureaucracy. This assured fresh ideas and innovation.

The key to Chinese social expertise was, of course, the emphasis on balance which derived directly from the Sinic mindset. 'In every dynasty,' says E. A. Kracke, 'realization of good government and dynastic survival itself called for a careful balancing of power among the persons and organs through whom the emperor acted.' (28, 317) Again,

> The principle of balance was reflected also in collegial organization of the various ministries and other central agencies, commonly headed by two officials similar in rank and authority. In provincial and local government and in military command it was obviously necessary to confide responsibility for a given function in a given area to a single official, but even here structural checks were provided. (28, 318)

To complete the system of checks and balances, China added the institution of the Censorate. The function of censorship was not, as in Western society, to assure conformity with rules laid down from above. It worked in the reverse manner. The censors at times functioned like ombudsmen, directing their criticism toward high policy and high office. In general they were a thorn in the side of officials prone to injustice and corruption.

The Chinese treated both *time* and *nature* in a very practical way. Neither assumed architectonic importance for the Sinic mind, that eminence being reserved for society. The Sinic mind was not one to leap into the future, either materially or spiritually, but rather moved cautiously with a veneration for the past. While Chinese mathematicians toyed with Buddhist concepts of vast time and calculated dates millions of years in the past, their main concern was the computation of ordinary diurnal and lunar time. It was the Chinese who invented the first mechanical clocks.

As long as nature was harmonious and man in harmony with it, a condition they portrayed so well in their architecture, art and poetry, the Chinese were not driven to probe its secrets. Their astronomy was well-developed and they invented an armillary sphere for determining the exact positions of the heavenly bodies. The list of technological innovations which they made and put to practical use is formidable. Yet they were never obsessed, as was the West, with conquering space and mass nor with looking for the hidden order behind phenomena. Their mindset did not demand that everything be ordered. In fact, it did not expect that everything would be.

To summarize, we find that the Chinese mind lacked the frenzy and drivenness which resulted from the imbalances in both the Western and Indic mindsets. It produced a sense of self that was earthy and secure, a longlived society that was carefully adjusted to both maintain tradition and permit change, and conceptions of time and nature which were basically practical. We miss, in Sinic civilization, both in China and its affiliated civilizations of Asia, great heights of speculation, mysticism or even material achievement. What we do find is an extraordinary degree of social cohesion and responsiveness which is without parallel in any other civilization.

The Amerindic Mind:
Fusing the Opposites

Before we review the Amerindic mindset, let us clarify what we mean when we speak of the Amerindians or Mesoamericans. Some people still think history in the Americas began with Columbus and that the peoples of what is now Mexico and Central America were merely savages. Even if we recognize that there were people inhabiting these continents before 1492, it is quite another thing for us to realize that there were civilized societies here whose achievements were every bit on a par with those of Europe, Asia and Africa. On the other hand, some writers who do recognize the high level of Meso-american Civilization have been reluctant to grant that it was the product of the indigenous population. As one example, early efforts were made to give credit for it to such peoples as Egyptians or Lost Tribes of Israel. Victor von Hagen writes,

> Such attitudes were still popular when, in 1840, William H. Prescott began to write the *History of the Conquest of Mexico*. Few then believed that the Aztecs had reared the buildings ascribed to them; few accepted the fact that the American Indian had ever been capable of producing the civilization described by the early Spaniards. So Prescott went to the original unpublished records that lay in Spanish archives. With the appearance of his *Conquest of Mexico* in 1843, the evidence he had amassed was so formidable and the style of his writing so impressive that Prescott in that one book succeeded in giving America back to the Indians.(29, 14)

Notwithstanding the fact that Prescott proved his point more than a century and a half ago, occasional writers still try to convince us that Mesoamerican Civilization was the work of someone other than Amerindians, such as 'Visitors from Outer Space,' 'Atlanteans' or even globetrotting Egyptians. But the overwhelming weight of scholarship bears out the conclusion that Mesoamerican Civilization was the sole creation of indigenous peoples whose ancestors had populated North and South America many thousands of years ago.

The generally accepted theory is that these immigrants came from Siberia, crossing the Bering Sea when it was frozen over during the last Ice Age, perhaps 25,000 years ago. In time they spread over the entire length of the two American continents, from Alaska and Labrador to Tierra del Fuego, becoming the Eskimoes, the many Indians of our own history, the great Andean social organizers, the jungle dwellers of the Amazon, and, finally, the first inhabitants of what is now modern Guatemala, Honduras, El Salvador, Belize and Mexico - 'Mesoamerica.' This last group were the builders of Amerindic Civilization.

There were several groups of Mesoamericans, all of them culturally related - Olmecs, Totonacs, Zapotecs, Mixtecs, Mayans, Toltecs, and Aztecs. Of these, the Zapotecs of the Oaxaca Valley in southwestern Mexico were the earliest builders of the great ceremonial cities which were typical of Amerindic Civilization.. They were responsible for the center of Monte Alban which is dated at no later than 500 B.C., the date which I have taken as the beginning of Amerindic Civilization. Proto-Mayan villages in Central America have been dated to the third millennium B.C. but the great system of Mayan ceremonial centers was begun after 100 A.D., eventually spreading across southern Mexico into the Yucatán peninsula. The Aztecs - or Tenocha - were latecomers in a series of precivilized *Chichimeca* peoples who invaded central Mexico from the south in the 10th century A.D. Their own civilization lasted barely two hundred years, from the founding of Tenochtitlán - Place of the Tenocha - on the site of present-day Mexico City about 1325 to its final destruction by Cortés in 1521. The Aztecs contributed little new to Mesoamerican Civilization except an obsession with human sacrifice which seemed extraordinary even to peoples ideologically committed to human sacrifice and a talent for self-defeat which made them relatively easy prey for the conquistadors.

The Aztecs, however, adopted and were faithful in recording and perpetuating the substance of the civilization which they and their

Chichimec predecessors had conquered - the Toltec. Unlike the Mayans, the Toltecs do not present us with a long prehistory. They appear as an identifiable culture in the Valley of Anáhuac (present Valley of Mexico) two centuries before Christ and by 100 A.D. their great city, Teotihuacán - Place of the Gods - was already well underway. The city eventually reached eight square miles in area and the size of its massive Sun Temple takes second place in the annals of stone building only to the Egyptian pyramids. Toltec cultural dominance was felt all over Mexico and Central America. Around 900 A.D. they abandoned Teotihuacán and built a new capital, Tula, to the west. In 987, Tula's ninth ruler, Topiltzin, was driven from the city by civil war. With a large army he moved southeast into Yucatán, conquering some of the Maya lords who ruled there and allying with others. Taking the sacred name of *Quetzalcoatl* - or its Mayan equivalent, *Kukulcan* - Topiltzin refounded the Yucatán city of Chichen Itzá as his capital and from that time on Toltec and Mayan cultures were inextricably joined.

I originally developed the theory of mindsets to account for the differences between the prime civilizations which originated in the Old World. But the theory resulted in a quadratic model as we have seen. The model clearly predicted a fourth mindset. The obvious solution was to look to the fourth independent source of civilization, namely the New World, to see if it bore any correspondence to the fourth mindset. That solution, however, presented two difficulties. In the first place, it seemed to me that the implications of the fourth mindset were so horrendous that I could not conceive how any civilization based on it could get started, let alone survive. I recalled that Berne called his fourth psychological position (I'm not OK - you're not OK) 'futile and schizoid.' For a mindset to negate both order and non-order means that order is apperceived as uncertain and undependable and mystery as malignant and horrific. Neither are rooted in the Ground of Being. This mindset is in all respects opposite to the Sinic. Like the latter it involves a kind of balance but the balance, far from being firm and secure, is intrinsically precarious. Like the latter again it involves a constant conflict between the two poles, but the conflict never leads to harmony. It leads instead to further conflict and insecurity. Where the Sinic self is secure, having the best of this world and the next, its opposite is insecure and hapless in both. Where Sinic society was stable and life-oriented, a society based on the fourth mindset would be unstable and harried by death. I found it hard to believe that such a grotesque society could be a viable one.

The second difficulty lay in the extent of our information about Amerindic Civilization. If one had only to consider the Aztecs, a good *prima facie* case could be made that the Amerindic mind did reflect the fourth mindset. But the Aztecs were latecomers in the history of Amerindic civilization and many scholars considered their bloody ways a freak in that history. The key was the Mayas, the other durable branch of Amerindic civilization. Barely twenty-five years ago the Mayas were thought to be cut from an entirely different cloth than the Aztecs. As late as 1969, Britannica stated flatly that 'the classic Maya society was not oriented toward war; conquest, tribute-taking and a warrior class were foreign to their way of life.' (30, 55) I was flummoxed by that opinion because I was convinced that mindsets are involved in the very origin of civilization and that they shape *all* the civilized societies in the area of genesis. The dilemma was resolved by one simple fact - earlier opinions of Mayan society *were dead wrong*. Subsequent intensive Mayan research has given us an entirely different picture of that extraordinary civilization. In an article in National Geographic, La Fay concluded, 'Recurring strife characterized the Classic age [of Mayan civilization], and artists memorialized it in striking murals at Bonampak . . . One series of paintings depicts a raid against another Maya community, from the battle to the final ritual sacrifice of prisoners.' (31, 739) The Mayas and the Aztecs, it turned out, were brothers under the skin and the evidence is now overwhelming that they shared the double negative mindset.

What did such a mindset entail for Amerindic life? The evidence shows that *precariousness* was indeed its very essence. Precariousness in life has been recognized by all societies - the Book of Job deals with precisely that quality - but nowhere except in Meso-America was it accepted as life's final condition. Farb says, in *Man's Rise to Civilization,* 'The cosmogony the [Aztec] priests taught depicted man as living on the verge of doomsday, and the world as barely escaping from cataclysm after cataclysm.' (7, 182) The mindset which this world view expressed created a quality of life in which one literally lived from 'moment to moment.' The sun did not simply rise and journey across the sky. It had to wage war against the forces of darkness just to be able to appear each day. According to Valliant, '. . . an eternal war was fought symbolically between light and darkness, heat and cold, north and south, rising and setting sun. Even the stars were grouped into armies of the east and the west . . . This sacred war permeated the ritual and philosophy of the Aztec religion.' (32, 175) This was *nature* as the Amerindic mind grasped it, an awesome battleground of cosmic forces.

Naturally the *self* was overshadowed by this titanic conflict. The greatest honor was to die in war. An Aztec song declares,

> There is nothing like death in war,
> Nothing like the flowery death
> so precious to Him who gives life;
> far off I see it: my heart yearns for it. (7, 179)

All war was holy. If the Aztecs did not have a good opportunity to wage a real war on a neighbor, they waged one among themselves, a 'War of Flowers.' As in Islam, the Aztec warrior who died on the battlefield went immediately to 'heaven,' or at least into the presence of the Sun God. But unlike the Moslem warrior the Aztec did not get to stay in heaven. After a time he was sent off to become a cloud or bird spirit. *Even heaven was precarious.* The

Amerindic mind conceived of no paradise in the Western sense and no release in the Indic sense. The fate that awaited most people after death was an everlasting darkness in which to suffer for their sins.

The ultimate denigration of the self in Amerindic society was, of course, human sacrifice. 'Human sacrifices have been practised by many nations, not excepting the most powerful nations of antiquity;' says Prescott, 'But never any on a scale to be compared with those of the Anahuac [Aztecs]. The amount of victims immolated on its accursed altars would stagger the faith of the least scrupulous believer. Scarcely any author pretends to estimate the yearly sacrifices throughout the empire at less than twenty thousand, and some carry the number as high as fifty.' (33, 59) Many of the victims were captured in war, but not all. In China the most concrete symbol of the self's relation to the universe was sex. In Meso-America it was human sacrifice.

However, we would make a serious mistake if we concluded that the Amerindians practiced human sacrifice out of sheer cruelty or bloodthirstiness. They did it because of their mythology which was in turn based on their mindset. As I remarked earlier, the double negative mindset cannot sustain a world without something else being injected. For the Chinese, both order and non-order were rooted in the Ground of Being and they produced the world through complementary action. For the Amerindians, order and non-order were in conflict and *could not* act in harmony. They had to be *fused* by some extraordinary energy and that energy came from sacrifice. The Amerindian world was an immense struggle between opposites which could only be unified by the day to day fusing effect of sacrificial and penitential acts.

It was in the context of this cosmic struggle that *time* became the dominant concern of Amerindic civilization. Every hour was important because it might be the last, unless the proper rituals and sacrifices were performed. 'Above all,' says La Fay, 'Time obsessed

the Maya. They envisioned it in terms we can never understand.'
(ibid.) There were special ceremonies for every month and every day
and each of the thirteen hours of day and nine hours of night had its
own god. Certain times were especially precarious, such as the five-
day hiatus between the end of one 360-day year and the beginning of
the next. Even more so was the end of each fifty-two year cycle,
when the gods were most likely to let the world end. For this reason
the Mesoamericans constructed their incredibly accurate calendars.
It was crucial to know when each potentially catastrophic period
would occur.

A mindset which produces such a precarious outlook on life
seriously obstructs the capacity to sustain *society*. Amerindic
civilization was, in fact, the most shortlived of the prime
civilizations. Latest to start, its total span of life was barely two
thousand years. Granted it was brought to an abrupt end by the
Spanish conquest, it nevertheless already contained the seeds of its
own destruction. The incidence of human sacrifice had accelerated
and under the Aztecs took a staggering toll. But there were other
factors. Had Moctezuma not believed and acquiesced in the portents
of doom for Mexico derived from the Quetzalcoatl legends of the
Toltecs, history might have taken a different turn for the vastly
outnumbered Spaniards. A Western or a Sinic mind would, in all
likelihood, have sought more encouraging portents. Yet Moctezuma's
failure of nerve was not the only reason for the Spanish success.
Cortes could not have succeeded had he not been aided by tributary
cities of the 'Aztec empire.' There was, in fact, no Aztec empire.
Toynbee's notion that the Aztec empire was the universal state of
Mesoamerican Civilization is fanciful. Farb more accurately
concludes, 'To understand the rise of the Aztec and their precipitous
decline, one has to realize they displayed every characteristic of an
orderly and well-administered state - yet it was an illusion.' (7, 173)
Empires are high forms of social order which need a sense of purpose
and permanence. They cannot be long sustained by minds which are

occupied solely with survival - not the survival of people in the world, but of the world itself.

A poignant sadness pervades Aztec poetry. Reading it, we cannot but feel compassion for the first civilizers of our own continent, whose mindset burdened them with a *self* overshadowed by death, a bizarre cosmic drama in which *nature's* very survival hung on the whims of demonic gods, a *society* obsessed with war and sacrifice and a sense of *time* as a living oppressor which had to be meticulously served. A mindset which negates both order and non-order does not conduce to longterm social stability, let alone create empires, nor yet is it able to conceive of a destiny which transcends all order. It has the worst of all worlds.

Origin of the Mindsets

The foregoing sections have served merely to establish a *prima facie* case for the existence of civilized mindsets. The next six chapters will argue that case in much greater detail from an examination of the mythology, philosophy, law, art, physical discipline and sexual practices in the four civilizations. Mindset Theory argues that civilization, while basically one type of socioeconomic organization, was, in fact, fragmented into four streams which had incompatible *a priori* cognitive structures and therefore produced incompatible outlooks in every sphere of life. I do not believe that any other explanation can account for the remarkable consistency and coherence of outlook which we find in the product of the four prime civilizations and their offspring. We certainly cannot explain it by such vague notions as *ur* -images or even mythology. As we shall see in Chapter 9, the modern West demonstrates how mindsets continue to structure thought even after the civilized socioeconomic system has been substantially dismantled. The mindsets certainly antedate any product of civilization, even its earliest myths, and have a powerful influence on all its products from the very beginning.

Answering the question of how the mindsets originated and how they came to be selected by their respective civilizations is really beyond the scope of the task I have set myself in this book, namely, establishing their existence and operation in history. Nevertheless, a few tentative observations about their origin are appropriate here.

If you were a proto-king selecting with complete freedom one of the four mindsets to bolster the vast new enterprise you were undertaking, which mindset would you be likely to select? The second, of course - the Occidental mindset. The second mindset was, in fact, chronologically the first. Its emphasis on the supremacy of order seems most nearly to reflect what all the civilizers were actually doing, bringing a new kind of order out of chaos, creating a new world by fiat like the God of Genesis. Why then should we not expect that each civilization in turn would not simply adopt the same sort of mindset? We should, but that is where history trips us up and what seems eminently reasonable turns out to be contradicted by the facts. A thousand years after the founding of Western Civilization (3500 B.C.) a second civilization was born far to the east in the Indus Valley. Indic Civilization not only failed to copy or recreate the Western mindset, it adopted one which was the exact opposite. Of course, a mindset in which non-order reigns supreme and all forms of order are relative does not at all reflect or parallel the process of civilizing as the Occidental mindset does. So the mindsets were not selected merely to mirror what the civilizers were doing. Obviously some other consideration was operating in the selection process. About 1500 B.C., after *another thousand years*, Sinic Civilization ignored the first two mindsets and introduced a third in which supremacy was accorded to the balance between order and non-order. So three of the four possibilities had been selected and the one that was left was the most bizarre and paradoxical, the one which focussed on the precarious interaction of order and non-order. Having seen the regular eruptions of civilization from west to east we would almost be compelled to expect that another civilization would erupt after a thousand years somewhere east of China and that it would be based on the fourth mindset. That, of course, is exactly what happened in Meso-America!

I have no idea why those thousand year intervals (give or take a hundred years) between civilizations are so regular but with regard to the mindsets it seems that once one had been selected, it was no longer available for the next civilization. In my opinion the selection process was not contemporary with the beginning of civilization. On the contrary, it must have taken place many thousands of years before civilization. It could not have been the result of interaction between each group of civilizers and those that went before them because each civilization arose in relative isolation from the others. Significant contact between them did not begin until all three of the Eurasian civilizations were well established, and the only proven contact with Amerindic Civilization was virtually simultaneous with its destruction by the West. I can only conclude that the mindsets or predispositions to them originated well back in the Stone Age, certainly prior to the migration of the Asiatic nomads who crossed the Bering ice bridge 25,000 years ago.

Homo Civilis

During the past hundred years, Evolution, i.e., the idea of an evolving universe, has gradually established itself as the architectonic framework for all the sciences. The theory of evolution started with subhuman animals, expanded to cover man's physical emergence until he reached a fully modern form some fifty thousand years ago, then worked its way backwards all the way to the Big Bang in which the whole process began. One scientist, Steven Weinberg, wrote a book about what happened in the first three minutes of the universe, telling the story in great detail and even being somewhat apologetic that the first twentieth of a second was still a bit hazy. (35) And since Weinberg wrote, I understand cosmologists have worked their way back to the first trillionth of a second - more or less.

In the late nineteenth century it was assumed by progressive thinkers, led by Herbert Spencer, that history ought to fall within the scope of evolution. Yet, after a hundred years, historians have still made no significant link between the two. Many historians and philosophers of history, Toynbee and R. G. Collingwood, for example, flatly reject the attempt. Collingwood's specific grounds are that evolution is a natural - i.e., mindless - process, while history is the product of mind. This view, shared by many historians, overlooks the fact that evolution, as the theory has been developed in the twentieth century, is not a qualitatively homogeneous process. At each major stage it exhibits properties and mechanisms quite different from those of preceding stages. Biological evolution based on selection is different from (though continuous with) geological and astrophysical evolution. Sexualized evolution is again different from pre-sexual biological evolution. There is no obvious reason why, at some point, the main thrust of evolution should not become psychic and no reason why history should not be viewed as a stage in psychic evolution, provided we understand that history, like every preceding stage, introduces new factors into the process. The idea of psychic evolution was a keystone in the thought of both Teilhard de Chardin and Gerald Heard.

The beginnings of civilization have all the hallmarks of a species subdividing or ramifying, a species we might call *Homo Civilis* . The ancestors of the prime civilizations had dispersed across the face of the earth and settled in four relatively isolated areas, a typical prelude to ramification. They did not, of course, grow apart genetically. All human beings today are capable of interbreeding. Instead, the four groups diverged psychically. While all four groups had a similar 'agenda' leading to the development of arts and institutions which were remarkably alike in function - class structures, monumental art, grand mythologies, written language, educational systems, elaborate technologies - their orientations and styles were dissimilar to the point of incompatibility. The similarities of the four groups stemmed from the requirements of the civilizing process itself. The dissimilarities came from the distinctive mindsets they brought into that process.

Evolution is not amorphous. At every stage it occurs within dynamic structures which channel its energies. Man emerged from a mammalian structure which emerged from a reptilian structure which was a variety of tetrapodal structure and so on back. As I conceive them, the mindsets are a late evolutionary structure, psychic rather than physiological. They both empowered and limited each civilization's ability to cope with life. History, therefore, can be defined as the expansion of human life structured by mindsets or, to put it somewhat differently, as the evolutionary adaptation of psychic subspecies to new environments. But the environments were ones to which no animal and no primitive human being had ever had to adapt. Civilized human beings confronted life on a new level because they were in the radical process of designing and creating their own environments. The worlds to which they had to adapt were worlds of their own making.

If, as I have proposed, the creative enterprise of civilization would have been dissipated without the mindsets, it is interesting to speculate what mankind would have been like if every civilization had been structured by the same mindset, namely, the first, Occidental mindset. There would have been no rich cultural heritage comparable to that of India and China. All civilized societies would have been cast in the same mold and when, because of its inherent limitations, the Universal-Occidental mindset inevitably broke down, as we shall see in Chapter Nine is now happening, we would have no alternative heritages to draw on as resources to engage the future without mindsets. *The existence of multiple mindsets and the diversity of cultural product they made possible was, by design or chance, a safety net for the time when mankind reached the stage when it had to abandon mindsets altogether.*

As the four subspecies of Homo Civilis developed in isolation, their mindsets were continually reinforced through religion, art, philosophy and every other civilized activity. The first significant and irreversible contact between the prime civilizations occurred with the Occidental (Moslem) expansion into India. After that, contact accelerated. The impact of the Occidental (European) expansion into Mesoamerica brought on the complete disintegration of Amerindic Civilization. The Amerindic subspecies was selected out of history as a civilization, although remnants of its mindset are still to be found in Mesoamerica. The Indic psychic subspecies has been challenged both externally (by the West) and internally (by the pressure for social change). Its tenacious hold on existence has been purchased at enormous cost to India's population. While China underwent a 'Marxist' revolution, it remains very much a product of the Sinic mindset, a formidably successful one as we have seen. But none of the mindsets will long survive except as relics of the past. All forms of civilization have failed or are failing. At the moment of the Western mindset's greatest triumphs in this century, scientific and technological triumphs, a revolt has occurred which in scarcely three decades has made all mindsets obsolete. Homo Civilis is an endangered species. As Neanderthal man was once displaced by Cro-magnon, Homo Civilis is now being displaced by a new species with a different kind of mind, an *unset* mind or, to put it in another way, a radically *free* mind.

In the last two chapters of this book we will become acquainted with this new species, but in those intervening we will get to know the minds of the four subspecies of Homo Civilis as they revealed themselves in six different areas of human experience. We will try to do so with empathy and compassion because even though man is going beyond civilization he will need to draw on its legacies in creating the models of postcivilization.

THREE

Mythology: Life, Death and Beyond

The Nature of Myth

A comprehensive book on 'Man's Religions' tells us the following about myths:

1. 'the making of myths is universal among mankind;'
2. 'Occasionally. . . myths are developed in order to explain and to give the weight of a supernatural origin and authority to the customs, ceremonials, and rituals of the tribe;'
3. 'Myths also have their genesis in dreams . . . because somehow they suggest the beginnings and meanings of things;'
4. 'the myth sometimes arises because an imaginative person was asked some question like 'How did the sky get up there?', etc.;
5. 'More profoundly, myths are expressions in fantasy-form of subconscious criticism of the injustices and maladjustments of familial and social organizations;'
6. 'The quasi-historical myth is . . . the elaboration of an original happening, involving usually a hero or martial figure, into a tale of wonder.' (36, 23-24)

To avoid the bewilderment which may arise from this kind of list, let us define three terms as they will be used in what follows:

Myth: an archetypal story which gives meaning and significance to some aspect of human existence and defines the limits and possibilities within that aspect.

Mythology: an integrated system of myths peculiar to a particular society.

Mythopeia: the intellectual process which produces myths.

Mythopeia is not unique to civilization. As the author previously quoted rightly says, 'the making of myths is universal among mankind.' It is a fundamental activity of every human society, primitive or civilized. Story-telling must be nearly as old as human speech, but not all stories are myths. A primary purpose of stories has always been to entertain and for adults novelty in such stories is important. We are entertained by new stories, not by 'the same old story' (unless of course it is told in the form of a play or an opera, for example, the appeal of which lies in the manner in which it is written and performed, not in what may be a quite simple story line). Myth, on the contrary, is meant to be repeated. 'It is the reiterated presentation of some event replete with power, ' in Van Der Leeuw's words. (37, 413)

Mythopoeia goes on around us all the time but we probably fail to recognize it for what it is. When I was a child my parents used to visit frequently with a favorite aunt and uncle. Whenever my father and my uncle were together, they enjoyed telling stories but I noticed that many of them were the same stories, stories of the bright days of their youth in the Ozarks. The repetition of the stories bored me at eight years of age but they never bored my father and my uncle. I realized many years later that they did not repeat those tales merely to entertain themselves, but to confirm and celebrate who they were, the significance of their lives . The stories had become myths and, to them, gained power, never staleness, in the retelling. The myths we are interested in here, of course, deal with levels of human experience far more profound than those which my father and uncle recalled in their personal myths. But the principle is the same. The myth is told over and over through countless generations to confirm and celebrate basic understandings of life. These understandings are so basic that no one dare change the myth in which they are encapsulated. Stuart Piggott observes that 'Although certain Hindu religious texts were written down in the Indian Middle Ages and later, the whole tradition of the Brahmins vehemently opposed this desecration of the holy word by committing it to written form.' (38, 254) This illustrates that in some traditions even the writing down of a myth constitutes unacceptable tampering with it. That is why a myth, although originating as an oral story and not being written down for a thousand years, may reach the written page in substantially its original form.

To say that mythopeia is universal, that it is found alike in primitive and civilized societies, is not to say that there is no difference between primitive and civilized myth. On the contrary, the difference between the two is profound, as profound as the difference we have seen in the preceding chapter between primitive and civilized society. Let us consider, for example, creation myths. These myths purport to be stories about the beginning of the world, something that happened a long time ago. Some modern theologians and philosophers of religion, however, contend that what they are really talking about is something quite different. The respected theologian, Paul Tillich, tells us in his Systematic Theology, 'The doctrine of creation is not the story of an event which took place 'once upon a time.' It is the basic description of the relation between God and the world.' (39, 252) And, to quote Van Der Leeuw again, 'Myth takes the event and sets it up on its own basis, in its own realm. Thus the event becomes 'eternal': it happens now and always, and operates as a type. . . The mythical occurrence, then, is typical and eternal; it subsists apart from all that is temporal. If nevertheless we attempt to fix it in time, we must place it at either the beginning or the end of all happening, either in the primeval era or at the conclusion time, that is before or after 'time'.' (37, 414, *emphasis mine*) In other words, myth embodies, as we have seen in the first chapter, man's most profound understanding of the relationship between himself, his world and the power he perceives as surrounding and affecting both.

But just as there is a radical difference between primitive and civilized societies in every other respect, they also differ as to their use of myth. Primitive myth is essentially adaptive. It deals with the world as it is and was. The primitive mind wants to be assured that its world continues and replicates the past. It does not contemplate a world with any major surprises or creative endeavors in it. John Mbiti contends that all African myths concern events of the Zamani, the infinite past. A primitive creation myth, therefore, is not about a 'typical' and 'eternal' event because the primitive mind does not deal with that kind of events. To the primitive mind the very fact that the world came into being once and for all in the ancient past is an assurance that it is going to stay the way it is and that nothing can undo it. In Mbiti's words,

> African peoples expect human history to continue forever, in the rhythm of moving from the Sasa to the Zamani and there is nothing to suggest that this rhythm shall ever come to an end: the days, months, seasons and years have no end, just as there is no end to the rhythm of birth, marriage, procreation and death. (10, 30f.)

When we come to civilized myths, the 'eternal', 'timeless', 'typical' character which Tillich and Van Der Leeuw ascribe to them is an *added dimension*. I see no reason to deny that at one level the civilized mythmakers were talking about an event which took place 'once upon a time.' Even if the world began with a 'Big Bang' as modern scientific cosmogony theorizes, that would have been the time that the basic 'relation between God and the world,' to repeat Tillich's phrase, would have been established. All creation myths are the opening scenes in mythological sagas and, as such, refer to time past. But, unlike the primitive mind, the civilized mind was also aware of future time as a significant dimension and it made myths about the end of the world or the end of life or the end of time which it foresaw as real future events. I recall reading a passage about the second coming of Christ written by St. Basil in the fourth century A.D. Basil had no doubt that Christ would really reappear sometime in the future. His only question was what form the reappearance would take.

But even though civilized myths have a 'real time' referent, they also have that timeless dimension to which Tillich and Van Der Leeuw point. Rather, however, than characterize the content of that dimension in theological terms, I believe we can understand it perfectly well if we understand it as portraying the *mindset* of the civilizers who created it. It tells in story form the primal stance toward order and non-order on which the civilization is founded and which will be the template of all that it creates.

We will now examine myths of the four civilizations but as we do let us bear three points in mind. First, we will limit our discussion to the mythological treatment of three themes: creation, the source of evil, and human destiny. The restriction is necessary because of the sheer volume of myth the human mind has produced and this particular selection has been made because these themes most directly reveal the underlying mindsets.

Second, the myth not only exemplifies the mindset, i.e., exposes its position with regard to order and non-order, but clarifies what phenomena are to be classed under each category. As we saw previously, 'self' in Indic civilization is an order phenomenon while in Occidental civilization it belongs to non-order.

Third, the need for the supportive power of myth (and religion) is directly proportional to the inherent instability of the mindset. If we consider the four mindsets in the order they were first listed - Sinic, Occidental, Indic, Amerindic - it will become apparent that they display increasing instability vis-á-vis living in this world of time and space. The relationship between life and the power which makes it possible becomes progressively more tenuous with each mindset. Consequently, we should expect to find that resort to myth, which embodies that power, and religion, which acknowledges and implores it, becomes progressively more urgent and demands more and more of each civilization's resources.

Occidental Myths - Tragedy and Redemption

A precedent was set in the second chapter of examining
Occidental Civilization first. For the same reasons given there we
will follow that precedent in this chapter and in the rest of the book.
The Occidental   creation myth with which we are most familiar
begins as follows,

> In the beginning God created the heaven and the earth.
> And the earth was without form, and void, and darkness
> was upon the face of the deep. And the Spirit of God moved
> upon the face of the waters.
> And God said, Let there be light, and there was light.
> And God saw the light, that it was good. And God divided
> the light from the darkness.
> And God called the light Day, and the darkness he called
> Night. And the evening and the morning were the first day.
> And God said, Let there be a firmament in the midst of the
> waters, and let it divide the waters from the waters.
>
> And God made the firmament, and divided the waters which
> were under the firmament from the waters which were above
> the firmament, and it was so.
> And God called the firmament Heaven. And the evening and
> the morning were the second day.
>
> (40, Genesis, I, 1-8)

While Genesis is a late product of Western mythopeia, it opens a
clear window on the earliest Mesopotamian creation stories. The
Hebrew phrase translated as 'the Spirit of God' translates equally
well as 'the wind of God' and hearkens back to Enlil, the 'Lord
Wind' of Sumeria whose character was later incorporated into
Marduk, the great creator God of Babylonia. 'The deep' or 'the
waters' are the waters of primeval chaos which, in Mesopotamian
mythology, were represented by Tiamat, whom Marduk had to
defeat in order to create the world. Tiamat is also recalled in 'the
darkness' which was 'upon the face of the deep.' Finally, the division
of the primeval waters into those above and those below is basic to
Mesopotamian cosmogony. This is not to say that the Genesis myth

is 'the same as' or 'copied from' earlier myths. It is, rather, a variation on a fundamental Western theme, a kind of revision which is typical of a new society originating within an ancient civilized tradition. Therefore we can look behind the idiosyncrasies which make it unique to the basic mindset which relates it to its parent civilization.

The words 'without form,' 'void,' 'darkness,' 'the deep,' 'the [primeval] waters' all clearly bespeak non-order and all clearly have a negative connotation in Genesis. Whatever God does, on the other hand, has a positive connotation. If there is any doubt about this, we are told no less than six times in the first chapter that what God has created is good and once that it is *very good!* And what God has done is create *order*. He takes the undifferentiated primal deep and divides it into two parts. One part is the firmament which He puts up above and calls Heaven. To the rest He gives form by gathering it together, calling it Seas, and raising dry land out of it. In Verse 14 He sets lights - sun, moon, stars - in heaven. These heavenly lights give order to time: '. . . and let them be for signs, and for seasons, and for days, and years. . .' He then produces by fiat the whole biological world including man and, having finished, rests on the seventh day which he blesses and sanctifies in commemoration of all the order He has created.

Thus we see that the first chapter of Genesis amounts to a resounding affirmation of order. Furthermore, the myth states that self, nature, time and, by inference, society were, as created, ordered, perfect and, therefore, affirmed. As I noted earlier, Genesis is a variation on the basic Western theme. All Western societies affirmed order although they told the story of its origin differently. In Mesopotamia it was the result of an epic battle, in Egypt a rather peaceful arising of order out of chaos (the goddess, Nun), and in Israel and Zoroastrian Persia the work of one, all-powerful and all-wise god, an idea the Greeks, too, finally came to accept, although they did not get around to it until the third century B.C.

But it was clear to Western man that the perfectly ordered world he affirmed was not the world he lived in. The righteousness of the self and the lawfulness of society which were man's birthright no longer prevailed. Even time, the benign measure of the seasons, had been corrupted into the inescapable harbinger of death and nature had become the venue of human toil rather than a bountiful storehouse. The stars above kept their perfect orderliness but that was because they were not of nature but of the heavens. ('The heavens declare the glory of God and the universe showeth his handiwork.') Evil had entered the world God had created and, with it, the tragic view of life.

Morse Peckham, interpreting Genesis, describes the tragic dilemma poignantly,

> Man, therefore, knows of a world radiant with order and value, and is ignorant of its deceptiveness; he lives in a world of hunger, toil, and sin. It is the contrast between the two worlds that gives him his awareness of the character of the world he lives in. It is his consciousness of his fate, his ability to remember, to experience in his imagination, an infinitely better world that makes this one so bitter and cruel. Man is the victim of a cosmic joke the point of which he can never see -- and consequently he can respond only to its cruelty but never to its humor. (41, 48)

Tragedy, therefore, springs from an affirmation of order coupled with a perception of its unattainability. Let us return to the Genesis myth to see how it accounted for the origin of the tragic condition. In the third chapter a serpent rears its ugly head. Who is this serpent? We are told that it was 'more subtil than any beast of the field,' which means ingenious, crafty and cunning, qualities suited to an Iago, certainly not belonging to a world of perfect order. But if we look further into its pedigree we will find that this is no ordinary snake in the grass. Its ancestor was Tiamat, the monster serpent of Mesopotamian origin who represented primeval chaos. Different Western societies would give this monster different names. To the Persians it was Ahriman, 'the Destructive One,' to the Egyptians

Sekhet, symbolized by the water-monsters, the crocodile and the hippopotamus. Genesis is telling us that non-order has reasserted itself in that 'place of perfect beauty and order,' to use Peckham's words. But it can only do so because there is a lacuna in the order God has created.

The lacuna is the will of man and that, of course, is no accident. What all civilized myths are about is the creative powers of man and the suprahuman forces which both enable and constrain those powers. Man knows himself to have a choice and in Genesis that choice is symbolized in the one rule God lays down for him, that he must not eat of the fruit of the tree of the knowledge of good and evil (the Bible never said it was an apple). The knowledge that Adam and Eve would gain by eating the fruit is not a catalogue of good and bad things nor a list of rules and regulations. The serpent tells Eve, 'For God doth know that in the day ye eat thereof, then your eyes shall be opened, and ye shall be as gods, knowing good and evil.' 'Knowing good and evil' is the power of evaluating and, more than that, of creating, the power of calling into question what has been given as perfect order and conceiving of how it might be changed. When the fruit has been eaten, God confirms what the serpent said, 'Behold, the man is become as one of us [sic], to know good and evil.' But the mythmaker knew very well that, unlike a god, man's evaluative and creative powers are not unlimited and that perfect order is beyond his grasp. The story makes that clear with a vengeance.

The idyll of Eden is abruptly terminated. Adam and Eve are driven from its perfect order. Self, nature, society and even time have been corrupted by non-order. The self has 'sinned and come short of the glory of God,' as a later writer would put it. The very ground is cursed. 'Thorns also and thistles shall it bring forth to thee and thou shalt eat the herb of the field.' Time becomes the bearer of death. 'In the sweat of thy face shalt thou eat bread, till thou return unto the ground; for out of it wast thou taken: for dust thou art, and unto dust shalt thou return.' And, in chapter four of Genesis, the paradigm of social conflict arises when Cain murders Abel.

Thus is expressed in one form the Western mind's passionate yearning for order and its grievous alienation from it. While the Occidental mindset sets the highest value on order it perceives the whole of life as corrupted by non-order. The images of order and the specific source of non-order in life vary from one Occidental tradition to another, but this basic sense of alienation from order pervades them all and is reflected in all their myths.

The tragic view of life is one which inexorably leads to pessimism and despair. The best one can derive from it is an admiration for those who endure its contradictions nobly, a quality of character the Greek tragedians portrayed so magnificently. But the Occidental mind was not prepared to accept tragedy as life's final condition. It mounted a two-pronged assault on the problem. The first was philosophical, leading to schools such as stoicism, epicureanism and neoplatonism. The second approach, which is the one relevant to this chapter, was by way of religious revelations.

Revelations are authoritative addenda to myths delivered by divinely-inspired prophets. In the West three principal addenda to the basic creation-and-fall mythology survived: the Judaic, the Christian and the Islamic. The revelations of Judaism and Islam were of the same basic type. They said, in effect, that while the perfect order of creation has been corrupted it can be restored for those people who are willing to accept and abide by certain very specific laws and observances. In this respect, Huston Smith's comments about Islam are worth quoting at length.

> The distinctive thing about Islam is not its ideal but the detailed proposals it sets forth for achieving it. . . The Koran in addition to being a manual of spiritual exercise is an immense body of moral and legal ordinance. When its innumerable laws are supplemented with only slightly less authoritative Hadith or tradition based on what Muhammed did or said informally. We are not surprised to find Islam the

most socially vocal of man's enduring religions.
Westernerswho define religion in terms of personal experience
would never be understood by Muslims whose religion calls
them to establish a very explicit kind of social order. Faith
and politics, religion and society are inseparable in Islam.
(42, 215)

Islam reasserted the Western passion for order with an
uncompromising zeal. Its monotheism was absolute as was its
belief in the individuality and indestructibility of the human soul. It
staked everything on the individual's adherence to the divine order in
this one life. Every soul's performance was entered in the divine
record and that alone would determine his everlasting fate on
Judgment Day:

In the name of the merciful and compassionate God.
When the heaven is cleft asunder,
And when the stars are scattered,
And when the seas gush together,
And when the tombs are turned upside down,
The soul shall know what it has sent on or kept back!
O man! what has seduced thee concerning thy generous Lord,
  who created thee, and fashioned thee, and gave thee
  symmetry, and in what form He pleased composed thee?
Nay, but ye call the judgment a lie! but over you are
  guardians set, --noble, writing down! they know what ye do.
Verily, the righteous are in pleasure, and, verily, the wicked
  are in hell; they shall broil therein upon the judgment day;
  nor shall they be absent therefrom!
And what shall make thee know what is the judgment day?
Again, what shall make thee know what is the judgment
  day? a day when no soul shall control aught for another; and
  the bidding on that day belongs to God!
                                    (43, 518 , Surah LXXXII)

Here we see that order has been restored to time. It began at one
specific point - creation day - and will end at another - judgment day.
The Christian revelation treated time in the same way. In fact, the
early Christians were so convinced that the end of time was near
that, in contrast to Judaism and Islam, they did not promulgate a
body of laws and observances. 'The kingdom of Heaven is at hand!'
meant that God would soon be restoring the perfect order He had

created. The Christian began with the premise that there was no way he could perfect his own life. What he could do - and all he had to do - was to accept the new revelation in an act of faith and let the power of God order his life. Radically different as the Christian revelation was from that of Judaism and Islam, the goal, for the purposes of our analysis, was the same -- the restoration of God's perfect order to a world which had fallen from it.

It is worth noting here that, strange as Islam may sometimes seem to Christians, its underlying world view is common to that of both Christians and Jews. The Prophet himself recognized that in accepting the historical foundation of the Old Testament as well as Jesus as an antecedent prophet. Far from being alien to the Western mindset, Islam is one its three principal heirs This will become even more apparent as we turn now to the mythology generated by the mindset exactly opposite to ours -- the Indic.

Indic Myths - Bondage and Release

Indic creation myths also portray a world born out of primeval non-order. A beautiful and enigmatic creation hymn from the Rig Veda, dating from at least a thousand years before the Book of Genesis, uses some of the same terms found in Genesis but the entire tone is different from that of any Western creation myth.

> Then was not non-existent nor existent: there was no realm
>   of air, no sky beyond it.
> What covered in, and where? and what gave shelter?
>   Was water there, unfathomed depth of water?
> Death was not then, nor was there aught immortal: no
>   sign was there, the day's and night's divider.
> That One Thing, breathless, breathed by its own nature:
>   apart from it was nothing whatsoever.
>
> Darkness there was: at first concealed in darkness this
>   All was undiscriminated chaos.
> All that existed then was void and formless: by the
>   great power of warmth was born that unit.

> Who verily knows and who can here declare it, whence
>   it was born and whence comes this creation?
> The gods are later than this world's production. Who
>   knows then whence it first came into being?
> He, the first origin of this creation, whether he formed
>   it all or did not form it,
> Whose eye controls this world in highest heaven, he
>   verily knows it, or perhaps he knows not. (44, 32)

Here we find none of the negative attitude toward non-order which typifies Western myth. Instead we find an attitude of awe before the 'darkness', the 'void and formless,' the 'All' that was 'undiscriminated chaos.' (I suspect, in fact, that 'chaos,' with its negative Western connotation, is probably a less than perfect choice to translate the original.)

We are told that perhaps not even the creator, the one who actually brought the world into being, knows how it happened or where it ultimately came from. One thing is certain: the Indic mind never thought of the world as wrested from chaos by force or fiat. The power of generation came from the 'All' itself, by the great power of warmth . This fundamental notion that order was generated by a creative power within non-order itself was repeatedly developed in Indic mythology. The Satapatha Brahmana tells the story of the primordial man, Prajapati, and the creation of the gods,

> Verily, in the beginning this universe was water, nothing but a sea of water. The waters desired, 'How can we be reproduced?' They toiled and performed fervid devotions; when they were becoming heated a golden egg was produced. . . this golden egg floated about for as long as the space of a year.
> In a year's time a man, this Prajapati, was produced therefrom. . . Desirous of offspring, he went on singing praises and toiling. He laid the power of reproduction into his own self. By the breath of his mouth he created the gods. . .by the downward breathing (flatulence) he created the Asuras [demons]. (44, 37-8)

The gods, whom the Indic mind counted in thousands, and the world, to which it ascribed incredible vastness both in space and time, are created by a process of proliferation out of the one, undifferentiated, primordial All. Order is generated by non-order and there is nothing in the early creation texts to indicate that the ordered world as created is any more perfect than the world as we currently find it. Although later theologians would introduce doctrines of cycles in which the world gradually deteriorated from age to age (over a period of 4 billion years) until its final destruction, the creation myths accept the world of order as it is without moral judgment.

Doesn't this directly contradict what we have claimed about the Indic mindset? Isn't this acceptance of creation tantamount to saying that the Indic mind does affirm order? It would be, except for one crucial proviso: although the Indic mind does not make a moral judgment about the world, as the Western mind does, it makes an *ontological* judgment. It says, in effect, 'The world is okay for what it is but what it is isn't real. It's an illusion.' In one passage in the Upanishads the sage Yajnavalkya is asked how many gods there are. He first answers, 'As many as are mentioned in the formula of the hymn of praise addressed to the Visvedevas, viz. three and three hundred, three and three thousand.' But upon being pressed about how many there really are, he admits to thirty-three, then six, three, two, one and a half, and, finally, one. 'Who,' he is then asked, 'are these three and three hundred, three and three thousand?' His reply: 'They are only the various powers.' (44, 50)

In another part of the Upanishads we are told,

> And when they say, 'Sacrifice to this or sacrifice to that god,' each god is but his manifestation, for he is all gods.
> He (Brahman or the Self) cannot be seen, for, in part only, when breathing, he is breath by name; when speaking, speech by name; when seeing, eye by name; when hearing, ear by name; when thinking, mind by name. All these are but the names of his acts. And he who worships (regards) him as the one or the other, does not know him, for he is apart from this when qualified by the one or the other. Let men worship him as Self, for in the Self all these are one. (44, 39-40)

'Self,' as it is used here does not refer to an individual, personal self. The Sanskrit word is Atman and it is used interchangeably with another word, Brahman. They both refer to the same thing, that undifferentiated All, the plenum void out of which all things were generated. Brahman is the All conceived of as undergirding the external world. Atman is the same All conceived of internally as a Universal Self. When the Indic mind says the world order - including nature, self, society and time - is an illusion it means that it has no independent reality. It is a manifestation or appearance of the pure non-order which underlies it.

As we have seen, the Occidental mind affirms order (symbolized in Genesis by Eden) and therefore disavows this world because it is corrupted by non-order. The Indic mind also disavows this world but for the opposite reason. It affirms non-order (symbolized by the Atman-Brahman) and disavows this world because its order obscures the ultimate truth that all is One, that plurality is an illusion. The claim that has often been made by Occidentals that the West is life- and world-affirming whereas India is life- and world-denying is a red herring. Neither the Occidental nor the Indic mind affirms the world as it is. The difference is in what they try to do about it, the former living in hope of its redemption, the latter trying to escape its snare.

For, to the Indic mind, this world is a snare and a bondage. Evil is not a corruption of order by non-order as it is in the West. It is the obscuring of the divine non-order by treating the fantastic, alluring multiplicity of this world as real. 'The mind in its ignorance . . ,' says Zimmer, 'superimposes a world of duality and plurality on the nondual, unique identity of jiva [the individual self] and Brahman -- thus bringing into view, like a wonderful mirage, a multitude of beings, interests, and conflicting opposites.' (25, 421). Through ignorance of its own divine identity, therefore, the self is trapped in its individuality and subjected to the rigorous order of karma, the universal law of cause and effect, and to reincarnation, the cycle of death and rebirth. 'The experiences of pleasure and of pain within

Maya [universal illusion],' Swami Prabhavananda tells us, 'are in fact due to the good and evil deeds of an individual's past: they are the direct result of karma operating in an individual's life.' (45, 111)

While bondage to the illusion of individuality and plurality might be said to be the ultimate, absolute evil in human life, Indic religion also recognized relative good and evil within the world of illusion. To quote Prabhavananda again,

> Good and evil, that is to say, as they exist in Maya, are relative -- in the sense that the one without the other is meaningless. Shankara [India's great Vedanta philosopher], therefore, distinguishes Maya as being of two kinds -- avidya (evil) and vidya (good). Avidya is that which causes us to move away from the real Self, or Brahman, drawing a veil before our sight of Truth; vidya is that which enables us to move towards Brahman by removing the veil of ignorance. As we receive illumination and come to know the Self, we transcend both vidya and avidya and cease to submit to the dominion of Maya. (ibid.)

Indic religion became a way -- in fact, an enormous variety of ways -- of building good karma and cultivating vidya, both with the aim of increased enlightenment. The end result of that eonic process involving innumerable rebirths was the final stripping away of all illusion and realization of the self's oneness with that original, uncreated, universal Self. Then there would be no more karma, no more rebirth, no more Maya. The bondage of the world would have been transcended and release achieved.

As I remarked in the second chapter, Indic society was organized on lines which reflected its transcendent orientation. While release was theoretically possible at any moment, in the meantime one had to stick to one's own caste, observe all the relevant rites and customs, and climb the spiritual ladder through the long reincarnation process. It was a realistic compromise between a vision of distant spiritual triumph and the demands and delights of worldly life. But in the sixth century B.C., about the same time the

Upanishads were being created, a man was born who rejected that compromise. He was a young prince named Siddhartha Gautama. Despite every effort of his father to keep him ignorant of suffering in the world, Siddhartha became aware of it. After long pondering the meaning of old age, sickness and death, he decided that he could no longer be satisfied with the pleasures and riches life had afforded him, left them behind, and became a wandering ascetic. In 'The Light of Asia' Edwin Arnold has Siddhartha say,

> For now the hour is come when I should quit
> This golden prison where my heart lives caged
> To find the truth; which henceforth I will seek,
> For all men's sake; until the truth be found. (46, 103)

And so he did. For six years he practiced stringent austerities and meditated. Finally, at the age of thirty-five, convinced that austerities were not getting him anywhere, he took a little food, sat down under a tree and determined not to get up until he had achieved the ultimate enlightenment (bodhi). That night, under the full moon of May, in deep meditation, he stripped away layer after layer of illusion until his craving for individuality was extinguished(nirvana) and he was ever after honored as the Buddha, the Enlightened One.

> . . . in me emancipated arose the knowledge of my emancipation. I realized that destroyed is rebirth, the religious life has been led, done is what was to be done, there is nought [for me] beyond this world. . . Ignorance was dispelled, knowledge arose. Darkness was dispelled, light arose. So is it with him who abides vigilant, strenuous, and resolute. (46, 22)

What Buddha taught for the remaining forty-five years of his life was the essence of simplicity, the Four Noble Truths:

1.All life is suffering.
2.The cause of suffering is craving for individuality.

3. Suffering ceases when craving is extinguished.

4. The way to extinction (nirvana) of craving is through a regimen
   of morality and meditation called the Noble Eightfold Path.

What Buddha had achieved was nothing more than Indian
religion had always claimed to be possible, namely, to transcend the
bondage of self, discover the true universal identity and no longer be
subject to karma and reincarnation.   But he had done it without
waiting for another life and another caste position and without
depending on rites and religious observances.   Not only that, he gave
a prescription for doing the same thing to others which had nothing
to do with their caste or circumstances.   In so doing, he bypassed the
entrenched structure of Indian society and made the basic social unit
involved in spiritual growth the monastic Order.   The result was that
while Buddhism grew in India for fifteen hundred years and
produced one of the world's richest religious systems, by 1000 A.D.
Indian society had effectively rejected it in all its forms and, except
for a relatively few adherents, it abandoned India for other lands.
As one author puts it,

> This decline was inevitable.   Buddhism was too deeply
> confounded with Hinduism and Tantrism.   Its central
> emphasis on the Order deprived it of the popular support
> of the mass. (47, 96)

The critical thing to note is that Indic society finally rejected
Buddhism not because it was non-Indic but because it was so
uncompromisingly Indic that it threatened to make traditional
society impossible.   And that also is the reason -- because Buddhism
was so purely Indic -- that although it vigorously proselytized China
the Chinese were never really comfortable with it.   They changed it
drastically to suit their own mindset but at the deepest level they
always recognized it was antithetical to their basic world view.

Sinic Myths - Strife and Harmony

'Chinese literature, unlike the literatures of other world cultures, such as the Greek and the Indian, does not begin with great epics embodying primordial mythological lore. If there were priests in China to systematize and instutionalize the myths, and bards to adorn these myths and present them for education and edification, their works have not been preserved.' (48, 642)

There are many historical and social reasons given for the absence from China of significant, widely-accepted myths involving the gods and their relation to the world. While each of these reasons undoubtedly has some validity, I suggest that the Sinic mindset militated against giving such cosmic stories a dominant place in life. A mindset committed to a balance between order and mystery and prizing the freedom to affirm both would, it seems to me, be burdened and unsettled by the great spiritual pressures we found to characterize both the Occidental and Indic minds. In fact, some of the Chinese myths which do survive from early times seem to make just this point. For example:

Originally, the gods, dwellers in heaven, and the human dwellers on earth do not seem to have mixed. A relaxation of this segregation eventually occurred . . . so that human beings could ascend to heaven; then the gods also took to descending to earth. This situation came to an end when one of the gods, Ch'ih-yu . . , aspired to the position of Shang-ti, the Lord on High, and corrupted the human beings to support his rebellion. . . Those among men who were incorruptible and were slaughtered in consequence complained to the Lord on High, who sent heavenly soldiers to punish Ch'ih-yu and exterminate the bad people. Thereupon, the Lord on High [established] a barrier so that mankind could no longer ascend to heaven nor the gods descend to earth. (ibid.)

Note that the strife described in this myth was not initiated by men, but by a god. The myth seems to be saying that too much concern with the superhuman (mankind ascending to heaven) and too much interference by the gods in human affairs, both of which were inescapable in the Western and Indic traditions, led to nothing but trouble and therefore ought to be eliminated. Chinese history followed that prescription. The Sinic mind was never obsessed by divine mythology as were those of the other civilizations.

This is not to say that China was poor in mythology. There was always an ultimate deity to be reckoned with, whether called Shang-ti, T'ai I (the Lord of Heaven), or T'ai Chi (the Great Ultimate or Terminus). For practical purposes one could define that deity as what lay beyond the final boundary at which Chinese mythopoeia stopped, the point beyond which the Sinic mind declined to speculate. There were also rank upon rank of celestial figures associated with imperial rites and observances, their importance usually depending on the favor of the Emperor. And, of course, over the centuries the Chinese entertained innumerable aboriginal, parochial and imported foreign myths and deities in addition to those supplied by Buddhism and popular Taoism. But, bearing in mind that myths are not necessarily about deities, that they are, in essence, archetypal stories with special meanings for human life, perhaps China's most typical mythopeia is the vast literature revolving around its great sages, who were more venerated and heeded than its gods. The honor paid in China to sages such as Confucius and Lao-Tse was on a par with that paid to Moses, Jesus, Mohammed and Buddha in other parts of the world. The lives and teachings of the great sages represent the real mythology of China.

Although Confucius (K'ung Fu-tzu - Grand Master Kung) is undoubtedly the most famous and honored Chinese sage, largely because of Confucianism's central place in the Chinese educational system, Lao-Tse (the Grand Old Master) has a very special place in Sinic tradition. In *The Religions of Man*, Huston Smith recounts the following anecdote about the two sages:

Confucius, intrigued by what he had heard of Lao Tzu, once visited him. His description suggests that he was baffled by the strange man yet came away respecting him. 'Of birds,' he told his disciples, 'I know that they have wings to fly with, of fish that they have fins to swim with, of wild beasts that they have feet to run with. For feet there are traps, for fins nets, for wings arrows. But who knows how dragons surmount wind and cloud into heaven. This day I have seen Lao Tzu. Today I have seen a dragon.' (42, 176)

The story is doubtless apocryphal. Lao Tzu himself may even be entirely legendary. Neither point would be terribly important to the Chinese who regularly made men out of legends, gods out of men and history out of fiction. In this sense they were congenital mythmakers, the importance of the story for the conduct of life being what counted. They attributed to the shadowy Lao Tzu one of the most profound of all their writings, the Tao Té Ching, 'The Way and Its Power.' The following is its first 'chapter.'

> The Tao that can be told of
>   Is not the Absolute Tao;
> The Names that can be given
>   Are not the Absolute Names.
> The Nameless is the origin of Heaven and Earth;
> The Named is the Mother of All Things.
> Therefore:
> Oftentimes, one strips oneself of passion
>   In order to see the Secret of Life;
> Oftentimes, one regards life with passion,
>   In order to see its manifest forms.
> These two (the Secret and its manifestations)
>   Are (in their nature) the same;
> They are given different names
>   When they become manifest.
> They may both be called the Cosmic Mystery:
> Reaching from the Mystery into the Deeper Mystery
> Is the Gate to the Secret of All Life.   (26, 41f.)

I have no intention of trying to explain this passage. As Huston Smith points out, both Tao (the Way) and Té (Power) have three quite distinct meanings making an exegesis of the Tao Té Ching a very complicated matter. For the reader who wants to explore this remarkable book further I recommend that he read the chapter on 'Taoism' in *The Religions of Man*. All I wish to point out is the stance the foregoing passage takes toward order and non-order. Lin Yutang remarks in a footnote to his translation that 'Miao [which he translates as 'Secret'] may also be translated as 'Essence'; it means 'the wonderful,' the 'ultimate,' the 'logically unknowable,' the 'quintessence,' or 'esoteric truth.'" (ibid.) Clearly, the 'Nameless,' the 'Absolute Tao,' the 'Secret' are all terms denoting pure non-order. On the other hand, this pure non-order manifests itself as order and, as such, is 'the Mother of All Things.' There is nothing in the passage to indicate that either manifestation is more real or more desirable than the other. Both are affirmed. They are two sides of the same coin and which side you see at any time depends on how you look at it, with passion or without.

The Taoist Chuang Tzu gives a little more detail about the origin of things:

> In the beginning of things, there was a time when even nothing did not exist, and then something came into existence which had no name. From this, One arose but this one did not yet have form. The source from which things come into being is called teh [Té] (character, or Tao embodied). Things have not yet received their form, but the division of the yang (positive) and yin (negative) principles which are intimately related to each other already appear. This is called natural constitution. When (the yin and the yang) begin to move, things come into being. When things are formed in accordance with the principles of life -- this is called form. When the bodily form shelters the spirit where each part behaves according to its own pattern -- this is called the thing's nature. (26, 113)

I have already introduced yin and yang in Chapter 2. The yin-yang figure is one of the most perfect symbols of a world view ever devised by the human mind. Wing-Tsit Chan characterizes yang and yin as,

Passive and active principles, respectively, of the universe, or the female, negative force and the male, positive force, always contrasting but complementary. Yang and yin are expressed in heaven and earth, man and woman, father and son, shine and rain, hardness and softness, good and evil, white and black, upper and lower, great and small, odd number and even number, joy and sorrow, reward and punishment, agreement and opposition, life and death, advance and retreat, love and hate, and all conceivable objects, qualities, situations, and relationships. (47, 157)

This perception of complementarity and balance in the very structure of the world pervaded the Chinese spirit. To the Sinic mind the world was not created perfect and then corrupted. It came into being through the creative interplay of opposites. So it has remained and so it will remain. 'Heaven's [nature's] ways are constant. It does not prevail because of a sage like Yao; it does not cease to prevail because of a tyrant like Chieh.' (12, 174)

Nature, then, is neither good nor evil. It has its good side and its bad side - bounty and famine, rainfall and drought, tranquility and disaster. But, on the whole, nature makes human life and peaceful, productive society possible. The Sinic mind affirmed the world we live in with its good and bad sides and never expected it to be perfected by divine intervention or saw it is a prison to be escaped. It was a levelheaded view. After all, knowing what we know about the billions of years life has existed on this planet and the millions of years the human species has existed, the idea that the world is a viable place seems pretty realistic!

What, then, did the Sinic mind regard as evil in life? *Strife and disorder.* 'Are order and disorder due to the heavens?' Hsün Tzu asked and then replied:

. . . the sun and moon, the stars and constellations revolved in the same way in the time of Yü as in the time of Chieh. Yü achieved order. Chieh brought disorder. Hence, order and disorder are not due to the heavens. (49, 176)

Are order and disorder due to the seasons, to the land, to strange occurrences and portents (such as falling stars and eclipses), Hsün Tzu goes on to ask, to all of which the answer is 'No.' 'Stars that fall, trees that give out strange sounds,' he says, '-- such things occur once in a while with the changes of Heaven and earth and the mutations of the yin and yang. You may wonder at them, but do not fear them.' He then concludes,

> Among all such strange occurrences, the ones really to be feared are human portents. When the plowing is poorly done and the crops suffer, when the weeding is badly done and the harvest fails; when the government is evil and loses the support of the people; when the fields are neglected and the crops badly tended; when grain must be imported from abroad and sold at a high price, and the people are starving and die by the roadside--these are what I mean by human portents. . . [When] fathers and sons begin to doubt each other, superior and inferior become estranged, and bands of invaders enter the state -- these too are human portents. Portents such as these are born from disorder, and if all three types occur at once, there will be no safety for the state. The reasons for their occurrence may be found very close at hand; the suffering they cause is great indeed. You should not only wonder at them, but fear them as well. (45, 177)

In other words, if man suffers in this world it is because he brings it upon himself. Nature acts according to Tao (the Way) and if man also acts according to Tao, he will find nature adequate for life and peace.

> Let the State of Equilibrium and Harmony exist in perfection, and heaven and earth would have their (right) places, (and do their proper work), and all things would be nourished (and flourish).
>
> From The Book of Rites (48, 49)

As one might expect, each sage had his own interpretation of what living according to Tao meant. None of them claimed to be original (although they often clearly were). All gave credit for the Tao they expounded to the ancients. The Confucians emphasized being 'true to the principles of one's own nature' *(chung)* and 'the application of those principles in relation to others.' *(shu)* (47, 148). Confucius was asked, 'Is there any single saying that one can act upon all day and every day.' His reply: 'Never do to others what you would not like them to do to you.' (48, 10) The Moists and Taoists emphasized different traits of character but they all shared the concern for the restoration of harmony and goodness to society and the individual. The supreme goal of human life was to be a good, loyal, respectful person in a peaceful, well-ordered state.

Buddhism flourished for many centuries in China but it underwent profound changes to adapt to the Chinese mind.

> . . .the esoteric Mystical (Chên-yen) and the intuitional Meditation (Ch'an) Schools, which were formed and developed in China, did not last. They were either too extreme or too mystical for the Chinese. From the earliest days of Buddhism in China to the present, the Chinese have clung to the more practical and more moderate aspects of the system.. (47, 97)

By the time the Chinese finished adapting Buddhism to their own propensities it was so different from the heroic spirituality of the Buddha that he would undoubtedly have been mystified by it. This is well illustrated by the widespread cult of Kuan-yin with whom most Westerners are familiar through her representation in delicately graceful figurines (Cf. Plate 10). Of her cult, E. Zürcher comments,

> Even more popular [than the cult of Maitreya, a Buddha yet to appear] was the cult of the Bodhisattva Avalokitesvara, who in China, probably again under the influence of indigenous folk-lore, came to be represented as a female figure, named Kuan-yin. He (or she) was believed to rescue from danger and distress, to preserve from sin, and to bestow all kinds of happiness and prosperity. Kuan-yin was closely associated with Amitabha, the Buddha of the Western Paradise, and was believed to lead the 'souls' of the believers to that region of light at the moment of their death. There, in . . .'the Pure Land' (ch'ing-t'u) they remain until the

moment of their Nirvana, dwelling in perfect purity and unsullied happiness. The popular cult of Amitabha represents the culminating point of devotionalism and doctrinal simplification: the devotee simply surrenders to the grace of the Buddha, and salvation is not the result of mental and bodily discipline or metaphysical insight, but of faith in Amitabha's miraculous power, expressed by a simple invocation of his holy name. (50, 67)

Nevertheless, for all its attempts to adapt to Chinese ways and for all its popularity among some segments of the Chinese population, Buddhism tended to remain a thorn in the side of the elite and, after all, it is the interests of the elite which are crucial in any civilization. An 845 A.D. decree of the emperor T'ang Wu-tsung proclaimed,

I have heard that there was no Buddhism before the Three Dynasties and it began to spread only after the Han and Wei dynasties. Slowly and gradually it spread; its adherents multiplied with the passage of time. It corrupted and undermined our way of life; the process was so slow that we hardly noticed it ourselves. It seduced people with its beguiling, and the masses fell increasingly into its deceiving traps. . . Buddhist monks flourished, and their temples rose higher and higher each day. Manpower was wasted in temple building, and gold and other valuables which should have been people's private wealth were taken away to decorate Buddhist temples. Disregarding their duty towards their king and their parents, the monks and nuns pledged loyalty and obedience only to their Buddhist superiors. They violated the vow of matrimony by deserting their spouses so that they could abide by the so-called rules of discipline. Nothing in the world was so harmful to man and his good customs as this alien belief called Buddhism.

*   *   *

When this measure takes effect, more than 4,600 temples will be demolished, and more than 260,500 monks and nuns will be returned to civilian life and registered as taxpayers. No less than 40,000 monasteries are also scheduled to be demolished. (51, 74-5)

Although as a popular religion Buddhism managed to survive even such persecutions as this passage suggests, it remained beyond the pale as far as the Chinese elite were concerned. Its emphases remained too Indic and it was perceived as interfering with that harmony and balance in life which were in accord with Tao.

Amerindic Myths - Entropy and Sacrifice

One of the most intriguing aspects of the Mindset Theory is the ability of its quadratic model to make predictions about how each Civilization can be expected to deal with specific areas of experience. For example, having seen what myth is about and gotten used to its terminology in three of the Civilizations we can make some fairly clear generalizations about the myths of the fourth. This does not mean we can predict the specific details of Amerindic mythology. After all, the details are the product of human creativity operating in living situations. But the general structure of myth, as of all civilized endeavors, reflects the mindset and is to that extent predictable.

The Amerindic mindset, as we saw in the preceding chapter, is the opposite of the Sinic. Instead of affirming both order and non-order, it negates both. It grants ascendancy to neither and views neither as rooted in the Ground of Being. The creation myths which it shapes, therefore, will, like those of China, involve a kind of balanced interaction of opposites. But there will be a fundamental difference in the kind of interaction. Whereas Yin and Yang are interdependent and mutually fulfilling forces, both rooted in the Tao, the Mesoamerican opposites will be independent of each other and mutually antagonistic. While they may be forced to interact as they must to produce a world, if left to their own natures they could not do so but would exhaust each other and culminate in destruction. This result is mandated by the internal logic of the Amerindic mindset.

The best-known Amerindic myths are those of the Toltecs which were adopted and transmitted by the Aztecs. Toltec myths not only typify Mesoamerican Civilization, they profoundly influenced all its branches. That these myths are still available to us owes nothing to the Spanish church hierarchy which ordered the voluminous ideographic writings of the Aztecs destroyed. Only a tiny fraction of those invaluable records survived. Our knowledge of Toltec myths, hymns, songs and legends is due largely to the work of one man, sixteenth-century Franciscan friar Bernardino de Sahagún, who compiled his monumental *History of the Things of New Spain* from surviving Aztecs' accounts of what they had been taught in their youth.

The Aztecs, having adopted Toltec culture as their own, traced their history back to the legendary founder and first king of Teotihuacán, Quetzalcoatl, whose name meant 'Feathered Serpent' or 'Bird Serpent.' Whether Quetzalcoatl was a historical individual will likely never be known. If he was, he may have lived sometime during the first century A.D. and have been given the title Quetzalcoatl out of reverence for his message as Jesus was called 'the Messiah' or Gautama 'the Buddha.' The Toltecs certainly regarded him as the originator of civilization. They would have said of him as Aeschylus did of Prometheus,

> One brief word will tell the whole story: all arts that mortals
> have come from Prometheus. (19, I, 329)

In 770 A.D. a great temple was erected for Quetzalcoatl at Teotihuacán. By that time, probably much earlier, he had become a god incarnate, the creator not only of civilization but of man.

> His essential role as founder of [Toltec] culture was never questioned by any of the historians of the sixteenth and seventeenth centuries, who always state that, just as our era began with Christ, so that of the Aztecs and their predecessors began - approximately at the same time - with Quetzalcoatl. His image, the plumed serpent, had for Pre-columbian peoples the same evocative force as has the Crucifix for Christianity. . . Besides being invoked as the creator of man and his work, he was patron of two institutions which were the foundation of all Aztec social and religious life: the priesthood and the college of princes. (52, 25)

It was thus the most sacred title of Mesoamerica which Topiltzin adopted when he left Tula to conquer the Yucatán, for that one word, Quetzalcoatl, encapsulates the Amerindic understanding of man and the world. What it symbolizes is a fusion of opposites but not attracting opposites like Yin and Yang. Serpents do not fly and birds do not crawl in the dirt. Serpents are earthbound while birds soar to heaven. They have no intercourse with each other except as enemies. They symbolize repulsing, not attracting, opposites which could only be united by some act of extraordinary power.

Let us turn now to the Toltec creation myth recorded by Fr. Sahagún as he heard it from Aztecs who had survived the Spanish holocaust. It is the story of how the Fifth Sun came to be.

'. . . They used to say that before there was day in the world the gods met together . . . and said one to another: 'Who shall have the task of lighting the world?' Then to these words a god called Tecuzistecatl answered and said: 'I shall take charge of lighting the world.' Then again the gods spoke and said: 'Who else?' At that moment they looked at one another and conferred who should be the other, and none of them dared offer themselves for the task; they were all afraid and excused themselves. One of the gods to whom they were paying no attention, and who was afflicted with scabs, did not speak but listened to what the other gods said. The others spoke to him and said: 'Be thou he that shall light the world, scabby one,' and he with a good will obeyed what they ordered and answered: 'Mercifully I receive what ye order; so be it.' And then the two began to make penance for four days. Afterwards they lighted a fire in the hearth that was built in a rock. . . . Everything the god named Tecuzistecatl offered was precious, for instead of branches he offered rich feathers . . . instead of pellets of hay he offered pellets of gold, instead of maguey thorns he offered thorns fashioned of precious stones: instead of bloody thorns he offered thorns of red coral, and the copal he offered was good. The scabby one, who was called Nanautzin, instead of branches offered green canes tied three by three, amounting to nine in all; he offered pellets of hay and maguey thorns and he annointed them with his own blood, and instead of copal he offered the scabs of his sores . . . to each of these gods they built a tower like a mountain; in these mountains they did penance for four nights . . . then they threw them the jars and all the other things with which they had done penance. This was done at the end . . . of their penance when the next night, at midnight, they had to begin their tasks; when the fire had burned for four days . . . the gods arranged themselves in two ranks, some on side of the fire, some on the other, and then the two above-mentioned placed themselves before the fire, facing it, in the midst of the two ranks of gods, all standing, and then they spoke and said to Tecuzistecatl: 'Ea, Tecuzistecatl, enter thou into the fire!' And then he prepared to throw himself into it; and as the fire was large and burning greatly, he felt great heat, was afraid, and dared not throw himself in, but turned away. Again he turned to throw himself into the flames, gathering strength, but reaching it he stopped; four times he tried, but never dared throw himself in. There was a law that none should try more than four times. So when he had tried four times the gods then spoke to Nanautzin, and said to him: 'Ea, then, Nanautzin, try thou.' And when the gods had spoken to him he made an effort and closed his eyes, and rushed forward, and cast himself into the fire like one roasting. When Tecuzistecatl saw he had cast himself into the fire and was burning, he rushed forward and threw himself into the flames. . . (52, 74)

Through their self-immolation these two gods became the sun (Nanautzin) and the moon (Tecuzistecatl) - *but,*

'. . . When the sun began to rise it seemed very red and it lurched from side to side and none could look at it, for it took sight from the eyes, it shone, and threw out rays splendidly, and its rays spilt everywhere; and afterwards the moon rose in the same part of the east, on a par with the sun; first the sun, and behind it the moon. And those who tell tales say that they had the same light shining, and the gods saw that they shone equally, and they spoke again and said: 'Oh gods, how can this be? Is it well that they go side by side? Is it well they shine equally?' And the gods pronounced sentence and said: 'Be it so.' And then one of them went running, and flung a rabbit in Tecuzistecatl's face, and his face darkened, his splendour was put out, and his face remained as it is now. After both had risen upon earth, they were still, not moving from one place, the sun and the moon; and again the gods spoke and said: 'How can we live? Does the sun not wag? Must we live among the lowly? Let us all surround him that he revive through our death.' And then the air set to killing all the gods, and killed them . . . and they say that though the gods were dead the sun did not therefore move; and then the wind began to blow with a strong blast, and made the sun move on its course. . . ' (52, 76)

Recall that this is the story of the creation of the *Fifth* Sun.. According to Toltec mythology there were four creations before this one. Each creation was presided over by a different sun but the first four suns were destroyed. The first, the Sun of Night (or Earth) perished without any living thing being preserved. The second, the Sun of Air left behind a world populated only by monkeys. The heritage of the Sun of Rain of Fire was the birds and that of the last sun, The Sun of Water, was the fishes. Only under the Fifth Sun was man created. Its symbol was a human face, the same face which appears at the center of the famous Aztec Calendar Stone.

Before we venture to interpret this seemingly bizarre story, we should note that many writers still tend to treat Mesoamerican myths as we used to treat Occidental myths, as either magical superstition or primitive science. Von Hagen tells us, for example,

> Huitzilpochtli, the Hummingbird Wizard, was the Aztecs' own. He was the sun, the ever-youthful warrior who fought battles with the other gods for man's survival. Each day he rose, fought the night, the stars, the moon, and, armed with sunbolts, brought on the new day. Since he fought these battles for them, the Aztecs could only repay him by nourishing him for his eternal wars. The proferred food could be neither the watered-down intoxicant pulque, nor corncakes such as mortal man ate - the god must be nourished on the stuff of life: blood. It was the sacred duty of every Aztec - for all were part of an agrarian militia - to take prisoners for sacrifice in order to obtain for Huitizilopochtli the nectar of the gods - human hearts and blood. (29, 100).

The foregoing passage was published in 1962, after Karl Jung, after Henri Frankfort, after Suzanne Langer, after Joseph Campbell, after nearly everyone had learned that myth was multidimensional, that it had something to do with the structure of human consciousness and man's vision of the world in which he was both creator and creature. Yet von Hagen, an otherwise very competent scholar, portrays Amerindic myth as an equation as simple as 'X gives Y sunshine and, in return, Y gives X blood.' And too many other writers have made the same mistake.

Fortunately for us, one notable scholar, Laurette Séjourné, has probed Toltec mythology for its underlying spiritual significance rather than treat it from an external point of view as a collection of prescientific nature myths or grotesque culture stories. Séjourné's book, *Burning Water: Thought and Religion in Ancient Mexico*, is a masterpiece of insightful and compassionate analysis and I have found it invaluable in the preparation of this section.

To return to the myth of the Fifth Sun, note that it begins with a decision of the gods that there shall be a new sun. These gods make laws, judgments and decisions about the world. All those powers are described in the myth. The gods represent order. But the order they represent is seriously flawed. In the first place, the world has already gone through four creations presided over by four different suns but each sun in turn has perished and none have been the warm, lifegiving sun necessary to sustain man, a very poor success record for the gods. Second, the gods clearly do not have the power to form a new creation by fiat as does the god of Genesis. And finally, we learn that one of the gods, Nanautzin, is afflicted with sores and scabs, indicating that the gods themselves are subject to decay and disintegration.

If there is one thing Occidental Civilization, with its resounding affirmation of order, was certain about, it was that God (or the gods) and the heavens which declared His glory did not decay. Order, in other words, was 'rooted in the Ground of Being.' Not so for the Amerindians. The first principle which flowed from their mindset was:

Order inexorably decays into non-order.

As you will recognize, this principle is today called *entropy*. It is one of the foundations of modern physics, stated in the Second Law of Thermodynamics. I am not suggesting, of course, that the Toltecs had any prescience about modern physics, simply that their conviction about the inevitable decay of order enshrined the concept of entropy in their world view. But entropy, to the Mesoamericans, involved not only physical or natural decay but moral decay as well, a kind of corruption which afflicted even the gods as evidenced by the four days of penance required of Nanautzin and Tecuzistecatl before their self-sacrifice.

Let us recall how creation was accomplished in the other three Civilizations. In the Occidental it was by the power of order to conquer and transform non-order. In the Indic it was by generation from within non-order itself, by proliferation. In the Sinic it was by the harmonious interaction of order and non-order. By contrast with all of these, creation in Amerindic myth arose out of the sacrificial destruction of decaying order. It is not a cyclical concept in the usual sense because the cycle of decay does not end before re-creation occurs. The gods are in process of decay but the process is arrested by their self-immolation and while they are destroyed a new order results. Thus the second cosmological principle which derived from the Amerindic mindset was:

Entropy is overcome only by sacrifice.

It is important to recognize that this is not a natural process. It involves intentional sacrifice of life. Furthermore, we see in the myth that once the Sun and Moon have come into being they are afflicted by counterparts of entropy - inertia in the first instance and irregular motion in the second. Getting them to move regularly calls for the sacrifice of all the gods, indicating that self-sacrifice is a universal requirement. What is still more important is that even the martyrdom of all the gods is insufficient to overcome inertia and entropy. The sun moves only when 'the wind began to blow with a strong blast.' The wind referred to here is Quetzalcoatl, giver of all culture, he who fused within himself order and non-order. Why is this footnote about the wind - the breath of Quetzalcoatl - necessary? Why, we have to ask, after this long story about the gods sacrificing themselves to bring about a new creation, are we told that it all comes to naught without the intervention of Quetzalcoatl? Recall that Quetzalcoatl is the Feathered Serpent god in whom repulsing opposites are brought together. The extraordinary power which brings them together is nothing other than sacrifice. Another Toltec myth tells how Quetzalcoatl created man and then immolated himself. His intervention in the creation myth tells us that the destructive-creative interaction between order and non-order through sacrifice as told in the myth is not a one-time occurrence, that, on the contrary, sacrifice is of the very essence of life.

In my opinion this view of the life is one of the most extraordinary ever put forth by the human mind. The Sinic mind conceived of order and non-order as interacting in a compatible, fruitful way. It was a sexual interaction. But the Amerindic mind could only imagine the opposites interacting through sacrifice. Thus, because it portrayed the fundamental structure of experience, the myth of the gods' sacrifice became the paradigm for a continuing burden of sacrifice placed on man.

The sacrifices entailed not only the tearing out of hearts on blooddrenched altars but self-inflicted pain, drawing of ones own blood and adherence to a strict moral code. The civilized Mesoamerican believed that his failure to uphold the moral and sacrificial demands placed upon him would jeopardize the very existence of the world. Even more tragically, he accepted that all his efforts would finally be futile His myths told him that his era would end and a new world follow in which human beings would have no place. It was a world view which produced profound feeling and much poignantly memorable poetry like the following two examples.

> The fact is that here we are but slaves.
> Men are simply standing
> before him through whom everything lives.
> Birth comes, life comes upon earth.
> For a short while it is lent us,
> the glory of that by which everything lives.
> Birth comes, life comes upon earth. (16)

> We come only to sleep,
> We come only to dream:
> It is not true, not true we come to live on the earth:
>
> Spring grass are we become:
> It comes, gloriously trailing, it puts out buds, our heart,
> the flower of our bodies opens a few petals,
> then withers. (17)   (52, 63)

Laurette Séjourné maintains that Toltec religion was essentially spiritual or mystical and that its Aztec heirs 'later betrayed [it] in its most sacred essence so that the interests of a temporal structure ruled by an implacable will to power might be upheld.' (52, 16) She believes that Toltec myths and symbols having to do with sacrifice were symbolic of an 'interior,' spiritual life concerned with the fusion of matter and spirit and the emergence of individuality from precivilized collective darkness.

> All that can be said is that the laws of interior preparation
> revealed by Quetzalcoatl were used by the Aztecs to prop up
> their bloody State. The mystic union with the divinity, which
> the individual could achieve only by successive steps and
> after a life of contemplation and penitence, was thenceforth
> considered to be the result merely of the manner of a man's
> death. We are here dealing with low witchcraft: the material
> transmission of human energy to the sun. The exalted
> revelation of eternal unity of the spirit was converted into a
> principle of cosmic anthropophagy. The liberation of the
> individual, the separate 'I,' came to be understood with
> crude literalness only, and achieved through ritual killings,
> which in their turn fomented wars. (52, 28)

Regrettably, I find this position untenable. There is now little, if any, evidence to dispute and much to support that all Mesoamerican civilizations practiced extensive human sacrifice from the earliest times, Toltecs and Mayas included. It was at Tula, the second Toltec capital that the grim figure of the Chac-Mool first appeared, the reclining expressionless statue holding a stone dish into which the hearts of human sacrificial victims were thrown. It was the Toltecs, not the Aztecs, who transplanted that same symbol of

human sacrifice to Mayan Chichén Itzá. Although the Aztecs may
have expanded human sacrifice beyond all their predecessors, they
did not invent the practice. It clearly traces directly back to the
Toltecs and the Mayas. In fact, one passage in the Toltec creation
myth which I omitted earlier for brevity relates how one of the gods,
far from immolating himself or allowing himself to be sacrificed for
the creation of the Fifth Sun, did not want to die. He ran but was
hunted down and killed by 'the air' (Quetzalcoatl). Thus the
groundwork was laid in the creation myth itself for sacrificing those
who were not willing victims. What I believe Séjourné overlooks is
that the Amerindic preoccupation with the fusion of order and non-
order involved vastly more than the 'interior' life. It involved the
whole cosmos and the peculiarity of the Amerindic view was that,
unlike any other civilization, it saw the world's only connection to the
Ground of Being in the acts of human beings, particularly their acts
of sacrifice .

The thing we need to remember about the scale of Aztec
sacrifices is that by the time of the Spanish conquest the Aztec
leadership had become obsessed with evil omens which foretold their
society's downfall and were desperately using every means at their
disposal, religious and temporal, to maintain their precarious
position in Mexico. That is why the number of human sacrifices
became more and more outrageous. But the fact that the Aztecs took
that course to help solve their problems stemmed from the theology
they had inherited and the unstable mindset on which that theology
was founded. If you believe your world came into being through
sacrifice and can survive only through sacrifice, what do you do when
you are convinced that that world is approaching catastrophe? The
logical, if tragic, solution to such a dilemma, it seems to me, is that
you accelerate the pace of sacrifice. *And that is exactly what the
Aztecs did!*

FOUR

Philosophy: Appearance and Reality

The Thought that Followed Myth

Ph. D. stands for the 'Doctor of Philosophy' degree, the highest you can receive from educational institutions. Having the Ph. D. after your name is a sign that you have successfully run the academic gauntlet to its conclusion and been awarded the laurel wreath. More accurately, I should say 'gauntlets,' because only a tiny portion of Ph. D.'s are awarded in the field of philosophy *per se*. The vast majority are awarded for achievement in the many other fields of knowledge. Why, then, don't we use names like Doctor of Chinese Literature, Doctor of Sociology, Doctor of Nuclear Physics, and so forth? Why call everyone Doctor of Philosophy? Simply because philosophy is the mother of all fields of knowledge. Long before there were astronomers and physicists and biologists and psychologists there were philosophers, and philosophers were interested in learning about everything.

The word, 'philosophy,' comes from two Greek words, *'philos,'* meaning 'loving,' and *'sophos, '* meaning 'wise.' Etymologically, therefore, it denotes the love of wisdom or knowledge. In the Greece of the fifth century B. C., however, its connotation was something close to 'curiosity.' (53, 25) The Greek philosophers were the ones who unleashed their curiosity, asked questions about the world, and proposed answers. Despite the crudeness of the experimental and observational tools available to them, they were, in the truest sense of the word, scientists, examining evidence, constructing hypotheses, and testing them. In the course of three centuries they laid the groundwork for most of the fields of knowledge in our modern repertoire, from mathematics and mechanics to biology and psychology to history and political science. Well into the modern era the physical sciences were still called 'natural philosophy.' Consequently, to call a person who has reached a high level of academic achievement a Doctor of Philosophy is a high honor which places him or her in a long and distinguished tradition.

The Greeks were heirs of the other great Western civilized societies, in which the highest form of thought had always been mythopeia. But something peculiar happened to Greek mythology which was unparalleled in any other Western society. That something was a poet named Homer. In his great epics about the Greeks' war with Mycenean Troy and its aftermath, Homer had given the gods roles which often made them seem all too human. His stories stripped them of the awe-inspiring, *numinous* quality gods are supposed to have. The progressive religious poet, Xenophanes, complained,

> Homer and Hesiod [later poet, author of the *Theogony*] have ascribed to the gods all deeds that are a shame and a disgrace among men: thieving, adultery, fraud. (54, 49)

After Homer, stories about the gods assumed the aspect of fables rather than myths. Myths, as we saw in Chapter 3, are stories which you believe and which connect you in a vital way to the ultimate meaning of life. Fables, on the other hand, are stories which you don't believe but from which you can derive a moral, like the fables of Aesop. The effect on Greek culture of transforming the gods from mythic to fabulous beings was twofold. The first effect was on the common folk, who always tended thereafter to look backward for a religious foundation in either local chthonic cults or in the cults of the old Mycenean gods which had been strongly influenced by the religions of Egypt and western Asia Minor. The second effect was on a small group of uncommon folk who, from the sixth century B. C., were enabled to seize an unprecedented opportunity to think *without the structure of mythology*. Those who did so were the first philosophers. Although the kind of thought in which they engaged was unprecedented in any human society, it can be characterized fairly simply:

Philosophy is the effort to provide an abstract, reasoned explanation for the contents of human experience.

If this seems like a very broad definition, it is intentionally so because the subject matter of philosophy is unbounded. In today's specialized world the philosophical quest has become fragmented into a multitude of sciences but they all follow the same impulse toward reasoned explanation which motivated the Greek philosophers 2500 years ago. It will be important to remember, particularly when we look at the philosophy of non-Western civilizations, that what is included in 'the contents of human experience' and what portion of those contents are considered important may vary considerably from one civilization to another. Abstract reasoning, however, is a development common to all civilizations (except the Amerindic which was destroyed before it reached the level of abstract thought.) When I use the terms 'abstract' and 'reasoned,' I mean the following:

Abstract. Mythical explanations are always personal and concrete, i.e. personified gods perform concrete actions which account for how some natural phenomenon or social institution came to be. An *abstract* explanation, on the other hand, is one which employs generalizations, principles, and concepts, any of which may be thought of as *real* in some sense but not as personal.

Reasoned. Myths are not the product of reasoning. They are revealed and are not required to be consistent or non-contradictory nor to form a coherent whole. In any group of myths the same event may be narrated in many different versions. Even the remarkably lucid Genesis myth has, in fact, two different and not entirely consistent versions of creation, that of Chapter 1, verse 1 and that of

Chapter 2, verse 4. The second version was obviously added to explain the origin of sin and to establish the subordinate position of women but no attempt was made to reconcile or amalgamate the two stories. Philosophy, however, allows itself no such latitude. It starts by examining certain phenomena, theorizes about what causes them to appear the way they do and checks its theories to find out if anything was overlooked. It strives to be faithful to experience, to be consistent with itself, and to bring its theories into a single, coherent system, leaving nothing unaccounted for. Very few philosophers have actually produced a universal system but from the beginning that has always been their ultimate goal.

Philosophy has much in common with *theology*. It has, in fact, been called 'the handmaiden of theology.' In the first place, scarcely any philosopher is silent about God, even if he simply concludes that God does not exist. Secondly, there is a branch of philosophy called *natural theology*, which aims to show that the existence of God is either a logical necessity or an empirical probability. The latter means, in effect, that the existence of the universe and life as we know it as the result of chance alone, without design, is so highly improbable as to be absurd. The writings of St. Thomas Aquinas (using arguments originated by Aristotle) take the logical necessity approach while Lecomte du Noüy (55) and Gerald Heard (56) founded their arguments on empirical probability. Finally, although there is such a thing as fundamentalist theology which is mainly a matter of cataloguing and clarifying the revealed word, more sophisticated theologians, such as Aquinas, always sought to build their work on a solid philosophical base, which is to say, a view of the world which was acceptable to intelligent, knowledgeable persons of their particular time.

Nevertheless, the primary concerns of philosophy and theology are quite different. Although it may be selective in what it emphasizes, the focus of philosophy is on the totality of human experience. Contrariwise, the focus of theology is on mythology and

the revelations which supplement it. Aquinas, who was one of the
most brilliant thinkers the West produced, could undoubtedly have
been remembered as a great philosopher. But, although he
incorporated philosophy skillfully in his system, he was a theologian,
not a philosopher. His work was abstract and reasoned but its
purpose was not to explain the contents of human experience but to
explicate and justify the Christian revelation. As Abû Hamid
Muhammad al-Ghazâli, the great Muslim scholar and mystic, wrote
about theology two centuries before Aquinas,

> I commenced, then, with the science of Theology. . . , and
> obtained a thorough grasp of it. I read the books of sound
> theologians and myself wrote some books on the subject.
> But it was a science, I found, which, though attaining its
> own aim, did not attain mine. *Its aim was merely to preserve
> the creed of orthodoxy and to defend it against the deviations
> of heretics.* (57, 214, *emphasis mine.*)

Because philosophy is the mother of all the sciences and, in
principle, nothing is beyond its purview, we can hardly consider
everything that philosophers talked about in this brief chapter. In
the following four chapters we will refer from time to time to various
philosophical views which influenced attitudes toward art, law,
physical discipline and sex. But in this chapter I propose to confine
our investigation to the one key question with which philosophers of
all civilizations have been concerned: *What is reality and how does it
come to appear the way it does to us?* This is called the *ontological
question.* It implies that what appears to sense and common sense
can be and needs to be explained by reference to something more
fundamental, that there is a depth to the world we live in which
needs to be plumbed before that world can become meaningful. No
matter what other inquiries they have conducted, the ontological
question has occupied philosophers of all ages and places. In the
West it has been the central concern of thinkers from the sixth
century B. C. down to this century, reflected in the titles of such
books as F. H. Bradley's *Appearance and Reality* (1893) and Alfred

North Whitehead's *Process and Reality* (1929).

I hope we can avoid some common misconceptions about philosophy, namely, that it is obscure, difficult and irrelevant. It is not philosophy but experience which is obscure. Behind our simplest perceptions and notions lie enigmas and paradoxes of which we are scarcely aware until we begin to question what we previously took for granted and try to find answers to our questions. Philosophy is the attempt to think with the *utmost clarity* about our experience. It is true that that kind of thought is often difficult and philosophy is not now and never was an occupation for lazyminded persons. But the difficulty is not of the same kind as a person encounters trying to keep from drowning in floodwaters, the opinions of many first-year philosophy students notwithstanding. It is rather the difficulty of the Channel swimmer striving toward a goal. And is the goal of philosophy relevant or irrelevant to your life? If it is preferable to be the victim of the world you live in without making any effort to understand the forces which shape your life, then it is indeed irrelevant. If it is preferable to live in a thought-world pieced together, like Frankenstein's monster, from a patchwork of inputs provided by specialists without a clue as to how to make it a living whole, then again philosophy's goal is irrelevant. But if it is preferable to gain a comprehensive view of experience, to be able to 'see life clearly and see it whole,' to make rational rather than irrational judgments and decisions, then it is clearly not irrelevant. Because that *is* the goal of philosophy.

The West: Matter and Form

One day my wife and I were explaining to some of our poorly educated Jamaican staff how astronauts went to the moon and landed there. From the questions they asked we understood that they were not at all clear about what the moon was and how far away or, for that matter, even that the earth was round. So we got out a globe and a ball and attempted to demonstrate that the moon is a satellite circling the earth at a great distance and that a rocket is simply a vehicle which you shoot from the earth to the moon. They still seemed skeptical and when we inquired what the problem was, one of them said it wouldn't be possible to shoot a rocket to the moon because it would not be able to get through the clouds. They apparently thought clouds were great solid masses in the sky.

The incident brought home to me how much we take for granted as common sense which is actually the result of many centuries of investigation and theorizing. The fact that the simple people to whom we were talking did not know the nature of clouds or the moon or gravity was a matter of education. No one had taught them. But consider the Greeks of the sixth century B. C. They had little more knowledge than our Jamaicans but it was not because of lack of education. They could not learn from someone else because no one else had the knowledge to teach. The only way they could learn was to teach themselves by observation and by reasoning about their observations.

The starting point of the Greeks were those very things we were discussing with our Jamaicans, the phenomena of the heavens. They made no distinction originally between astronomical and meteorological phenomena. Events in the distant heavens, those in the nearby skies, and those of earth and sea were not only part of the same world but seemed to interact in a much more intimate way than we understand them to. When they began to sort out their observations about the world the early philosophers were impressed by the fact that everything changed, nothing endured. 'You cannot step in the same stream twice,' said Heraclitus of Ephesus (late 6th century). Change was seen in the transitory character of life itself and in the movements of nature. The sun not only moved across the sky in day only to disappear in darkness at nightfall, but changed the position of its course with the seasons. The moon followed a similar course but also changed its shape, waxing and waning over the course of a month. Warmth and cold, light and darkness, dryness and moisture not only alternated but seemed to strive with each other in unending conflict.

The Greeks, of course, were not alone in noting the endless change and alternation in the world. It was a fundamental observation of all civilizations. But it was such an affront to the Occidental mindset that it stamped the plinth of Western philosophy with a mark of gloom and pessimism which was never quite erased. John Burnet, one of the outstanding modern interpreters of Greek philosophy, tells us,

> The Ionians [Greeks from cities on the west coast of Asia Minor, the home of the first philosophers], as we can see from their literature, were deeply impressed by the transitoriness of things. There is, in fact, a fundamental pessimism in their outlook on life, such as is natural to an over-civilized age with no very definite religious convictions. We find Mimnermos of Kolophon preoccupied with the sadness of the coming of old age, while at a later date the lament of Simonides, that the generations of men fall like the leaves of the forest, touches a chord that Homer had already struck. Now this sentiment always finds its best illustrations in the changes of the seasons, and the cycle of growth and decay is a far more striking phenomenon in Aegean lands than in the North, and takes still more clearly the form of a war of opposites, hot and cold, wet and dry. It is, accordingly, from that point of view the early cosmologists regard the world. The opposition of day and night, summer and winter, with their suggestive parallelism in sleep and waking, birth and death, are the outstanding features of the world as they saw it. (53, 8)

I don't think we need to take very seriously the statement that pessimism is 'natural to an over-civilized age with no very definite religious convictions.' The Chinese in many ages amply contradict that notion. But that pessimism due to a perception of 'the transitoriness of things' did characterize the early Greeks is indisputable. Transitoriness to the Western mind means *non-order*, and the Western mind abhors non-order. Pessimism is simply the outcome of a belief that life is swallowed up by non-order or chaos and it recurred throughout Greek, Hellenistic and Roman philosophy right down to the last great Stoic philosopher, the emperor Marcus Aurelius.

But the apperception of chaos and the pessimism which accompanied it were not by any means the dominant themes of Greek or later Western philosophy. No sooner did you say 'NON-ORDER!' to the Occidental mind than it homed like a heat-seeking missile on ORDER. No sooner did you say 'CHAOS!' than it targeted COSMOS. (The Greek word, *cosmos* , 'meant originally the discipline of an army, and next the *ordered* constitution of a state.') (53, 9, *emphasis mine*) Burnet states the same thought from a slightly different perspective:

> No sooner did an Ionian philosopher learn half-a-dozen geometrical propositions, and hear that the phenomena of the heavens recur in cycles, than he set to work to look for law everywhere in nature, and, with an audacity almost amounting to [*hubris* or overweening pride], to construct a system of the universe. (53, 25)

The early Greek philosophers adopted two strategies for uncovering the hidden order which they were certain must underly the empirical world: *simplification* and *organization*. Simplification involved finding a primordial substance *(Arché)* or stuff *(Physis)* from which everything else could be derived. The first philosopher, Thales, who was born around 624 B.C., suggested that everything might arise from *water* or, perhaps more accurately, *fluid*. It is important to remember that whenever the Greek philosophers used concrete terms they rarely meant them in the common way but rather as abstractions. When Anaximenes proposed that the primary stuff was *air* he meant something more like vapor. Air as we know it was discovered by Empedocles in the fifth century and he called it 'ether.' Thales' contemporary, Anaximander, hypothesized a completely abstract Arché, the *Apeiron* or Boundless. The Boundless had no beginning or end and no spatial limit but did have an inherent natural motion. Nothing new originated in the Boundless, even motion. Everything sensible was merely the result of combination, separation and recombination of what was already there. *Nothing comes from nothing* was a fundamental presupposition of early Greek philosophy.

The simplification strategy was adopted by other philosophers. Heraclitus accepted the ever-changing character of reality. The Arché for him was an abstract *fire:* 'this ever-active, mobile, self-transforming 'something' is a divine Fire which has always existed and always will be operative according to 'fixed measures' or a definite order.' (54, 41) But Heraclitus introduced an emphasis on the second way of ordering the foundations of reality: *organization.* The 'fixed measures' or 'definite order' which regulated the permutations of the universe resulted from an intrinsic property of the 'divine Fire' which Heraclitus called the *logos* or word, a term which was to become one of the permanent fixtures of Western philosophy. Another was promulgated by Anaxagoras of Clazomenæ: *nous* or mind. Anaxagoras taught that matter and mind *(nous)* were coexistent and coeternal and that mind was the cause of order. Interpreting this concept, Warbecke says, 'Mind is an eternal cause of order, an *intelligent* energy more and more widely determining the motions of the world.' (54, 75)

But while the Ionian philosophers were busy weaving their ontologies and cosmologies and teaching their doctrines from Asia Minor to Sicily, trouble was brewing for them in a place called Elea on the west coast of Italy. In 515 B.C. Elea produced Parmenides who deserves the title of the first Western *logician*. Logicians are a cantankerous lot. Their main purpose in life is to show that other people don't know what they are talking about. They do this by demonstrating that the profound statements of constructive thinkers have implications which are contradictory, inconceivable or impossible. Parmenides saw that all the Greek philosophers had been trying to simplify the empirical world into one or at best a few common substances and then trying to organize the activities of those substances so that they could account for the appearances. In all of their speculations, the philosophers accepted one assumption without question: *whatever is real is corporeal*. They did not conceive of anything real, even soul, mind or logos which did not have body, that is, dimension and substance. A void, to them, was nothingness and not only could nothingness not be but it could not give rise to something. What Parmenides did was merely to show that all their schemes implied the existence of nothingness or that *what is not, is* , which is contradictory and, therefore, impossible. His arguments went something like this: *What is*, is. *What is not*, is not. *Therefore,*

1. If you say that *what is* changes into something else, then it would no longer be *what is* but would have to be *what is not*. IMPOSSIBLE!
2. If you say that *what is* is something else, e.g., water, air, fire, or elements (Thales, Anaximines, Heraclitus, Empedocles), then *what is* would no longer be *what is* but something else. But the only thing other than *what is* is *what is not*. IMPOSSIBLE!
3. If you say that *what is* can expand or contract (Anaximenes), then there must be something for it to draw on to expand and something to dispose of to contract. But *what is* could only draw on *what is not* to make more of itself and it could only lessen itself by turning *what is* into *what is not*. IMPOSSIBLE!
4. If you say that *what is* can be divided (Anaxagoras) then *what is* would have to contain some of *what is not* 'to hinder it from holding together.' (53, 175) IMPOSSIBLE!
5. If you say that *what is* is infinite (Anaximander) then *what is* is not complete within itself ('it is in need of nothing' (ibid.)) IMPOSSIBLE!

And so on. Having cut the ground out from under all prior ontologies and some which were yet to come, Parmenides stood fast by the implications of his own logic:

And there is not, and never shall be, anything besides what is, since fate has chained it so as to be whole and immovable. Wherefore all these things are but names which mortals have given, believing them to be true - coming into

being and passing away, being and not being, change of place
and alteration of bright color. . . [*What is*] is complete on
every side, like the mass of a rounded sphere, equally poised
from the centre in every direction; for it cannot be greater or
smaller in one place than in another. For there is no nothing
which could keep it from reaching out equally, nor can ought
that is be more and less there than what is, since it is all
inviolable. (53, 176)

Or, as Burnet summarizes Parmenides' conclusions,

What *is*, is a finite, spherical, motionless corporeal *plenum,*
and there is nothing beyond it. The appearances of
multiplicity and motion, empty space and time, are illusions.
(53, 182)

'If you want a primal substance which is the quintessence of
order,' Parmenides said, in effect, 'I'll give you one in spades.' What
could be more orderly than a 'finite, spherical, motionless corporeal
plenum'? The problem with Parmenides' scheme is that he answered
the first half of the ontological question, *What is reality?*, in a way
that made an answer to the second half, *How does it come to appear
the way it does to us?*, impossible. If reality does not change, there is
no way to account for appearances. Therefore, appearances must be
an illusion. What seemed like a triumph for order as the foundation
of the world turned out to be sterile because it could not account for
the world we experience. While Parmenides' logic may have
appealed to the Greek passion for order, to write the world off as an
illusion seemed like intellectual anarchy to the constructive
philosophers.

Thus Greek philosophy was dichotomized into conflicting trends.
On the one side were the Ionians who emphasized flux, change,
divisibility and infinity. Their motto was the Heraclitean 'You cannot
step in the same stream twice.' On the other side were the Eleatics
to whom reality was motionless, unchanging, indivisible and finite.
Their epigram was the Parmenidean 'What is, is; what is not, is
not.' As might be expected, subsequent philosophers worked

tirelessly to find a way out of the impasse. Two groups produced solutions which were to make lasting contributions to Western thought.

The first group were the *atomists*. Originated by Leucippus and Democritus, atomism rejected the assumption that empty space is not real. Space, the atomists said, is a three-dimensional continuum in which things move, and the things that move in space are *atoms*, invisible, indivisible particles, each a miniature, self-contained Parmenidean sphere. While for Parmenides there was only one such finite sphere, for the atomists there were an infinite number in infinite space, and all the phenomena we observe were caused by combinations and arrangements of atoms. Atomism is sometimes referred to as a *mechanistic* view of the world but if by 'mechanistic' we understand a world functioning like a machine, the atomists cannot be given that much credit. The machine is the epitome of order but the lack of a developed principle of order was a major flaw in the atomists' cosmology. They had no satisfactory explanation of what organized the randomly moving atoms to bring them into larger structures or of what accounted for repeating and reduplicating structures, invoking such vague notions as vortex motions and affinities of like for like. In short, they did little to satisfy the philosophical search for order. When the Western world eventually found the ordering principle it needed for an atomic world-view it was in the concept of *natural law* formulated by another school of corporealist philosophers, the Stoics. The combination of a primal substance consisting of atoms and a natural law which those atoms obeyed was what made possible a truly mechanistic view of the world, but that combination did not become viable until the modern era when new experimental methods made the investigation of atomic configurations feasible. So atomism was put on the shelf until it was revived nearly two thousand years later to form the basis of modern physical science. Incidentally, the idea of natural law was also sidelined until the modern era as far as understanding physical phenomena was concerned, but as a *moral* concept it played a major role in the development of Western legal theory as we shall see in the next chapter.

The second group of philosophers to attack the Ionian-Eleatic impasse I call the *rationalists* because of their insistence on the primacy of the mind and reason in scientific investigation.   The rationalists, chief among whom are the three most famous names in Western philosophy - Socrates, Plato and Aristotle - were quite self-consciously dealing with the dilemma bequeathed by their predecessors. Socrates says, in the Theætetus,

> I am about to speak of a high argument in which all things are said to be relative; you cannot rightly call anything by any name, such as great or small, heavy or light, for the great will be small and the heavy light - there is no single thing or quality, but out of motion and change and admixture all things are becoming relatively to one another, which 'becoming' is by us incorrectly called being, but is really becoming, for nothing ever *is*, but all things are *becoming*. Summon all the philosophers - Protagoras [a leading *Sophist*], Heracleitus, Empedocles, and the rest of them, one after another, and with the exception of Parmenides they will agree with you in this. (58, V. II, 154)

Unlike atomism, rationalism was not to be shelved until the modern era, but was, in fact, to provide the thought structure for all subsequent Occidental Civilization. Socrates, Plato and Aristotle saw that it was necessary to bring philosophy back to earth or, to put it another way, if the purpose of philosophy was to explain experience, then they needed to examine experience itself more closely and carefully. When they did so they quickly realized that the dichotomy between philosophies of change and the philosophy of strict logic was a false one.

It is not experience, the rationalists saw, which leads to the Eleatic paradoxes but false assumptions, such as the unreality of space, the restriction of reality to the corporeal, and the rigid disjunction between what is and is not. Nor does experience confirm that reality is nothing but an Ionian flux. Experience tells us we *can* step in the same stream twice although it may not be the same water. When as a boy I used to swim in the Missouri River the current was swift and strong and I never thought I swam in the same *water* on two occasions. But in some sense it was the same *stream* each time. Although its contents were always different, its shape, size and location remained relatively constant. The lesson of experience is that there is change but that something abides through change. For Plato (with whom I include his mentor, Socrates) an infinite, divisible *matter* is what changes and receives the impress of unchanging *forms* or *ideas* which give it definition and make it intelligible. Matter and form cannot be separated as the Ionians and the Eleatics tried to do. Together they form the *substance* of the world. That means that the ultimate reality is *inherently and inescapably unified and ordered* by the ideas and the ideas can be examined in a refined and coherent way by the use of dialectic reasoning.

> The world is presented [by Plato] as an individual, the Supreme Unity, whose *matter* (in the technical sense) is the complex of all substances, together with the motions appertaining to them, and whose *form* is the order and harmony of the whole. The structural concepts are three: time, space and cause. Time is the 'enduring essence' of the world; it cannot be confined to days, months and years, its natural divisions, but is 'the moving image everlasting.' It is a continuum; it has no beginning and it will have no end. It is the central index of the harmony of motion. Scarcely less significant is space which establishes the internal relations of the cosmos, and denotes continuity, expansion, and the unified whole. Plato lets Timæius call it the 'receptacle of all becoming,' which appears to mean that the 'planes' of individual bodies would have no 'home,' were they not connected by the unseen but coercive factor of space. Hence space guarantees the *order* of nature and forbids us to accept the theory of a void which would destroy the symmetry of the system. (59, 102)

The third, equally important structural concept, cause, can best be left until we get to Aristotle. Plato went on to say that there is one archetypal idea or form, the Idea of the Good. There is, of course, a 'good' for each kind of individual, which is what is best for it, its *raison d'être*, what it ought to be at its full potential. In Chapter 8 (on Sex) we will examine what the Idea of the Good meant for man. Here, however, we are concerned about the universe, the reality underlying the totality of experience. For Plato, the world, although uncreated, was nevertheless purposeful and that purpose was the harmonious, orderly functioning which was made possible because all substance was unified by the Good.

Scholars sometimes tend to set Socrates and Plato off against Aristotle but in actuality they differ more in emphasis than basic orientation. When we come to Aristotle, Socrates' great personal passion for the principles which rule life has been left behind (as it had indeed by Plato in his later years). Aristotle is the consummate, dispassionate investigator, the prototype of our modern scientists. He agreed with Plato that reality has both a material and a formal aspect and that the formal aspect is not a particular but a universal which renders a thing intelligible. But for him matter is more than something which receives the impress of a form. It has the *potential* of changing to other forms and not just any other forms, but quite specific ones. The acorn can become an oak tree but not a peach tree. Thus matter is an active rather than a passive principle in that it is selective about what forms it can take. Aristotle considers both matter and form causes of change and to complete his view that the world as it appears is an orderly, intelligible process he adds two more causes, the *efficient* cause which is the activity or energy which actually brings about the change and the *final* cause which orders and guides that activity to consummation.

> . . . Aristotle speaks of matter as *Potentiality* and of its combination with form as *Substance*. What is realized when the intangible (Form) completely develops the potentiality of matter is *Entelechy*, or completeness. At the two poles of

Being, then, are the limits of formless Matter and matterless Form - but we never experience these limits except as necessary distinctions in Logic, or as mathematical infinities never actually reached. *Pure* potentiality would be formless matter or absolute chaos; its opposite pole, matterless form or pure actuality. (54, 301f.)

It seems to me that one of the important differences between Plato and Aristotle is that the former would argue that 'matterless form' *is* within the realm of experience precisely to the extent that it can be an object of abstract contemplation as Socrates describes in *The Republic* :

For he . . . whose mind is fixed upon true being, has surely no time to look down upon the affairs of earth, or to be filled with malice and envy, contending against men; *his eye is ever directed towards things fixed and immutable, which he sees neither injuring nor injured by one another, but all in order moving according to reason;* these he imitates, and to these he will, as far as he can, conform himself. (58, V. I, 761, *emphasis mine*)

Passages like this, where Socrates speaks of the mind being 'fixed on true being' and the inner eye being 'ever directed toward things fixed and immutable' have led some scholars, including A. E. Taylor, to call Socrates a mystic and to regard his contemplation of the Idea of the Good as a mystic vision. I do not think there is the slightest justification in Plato for that view. There is a profound difference between the mystic and the rationalist. As an example, the nineteenth century Hindu saint, Ramakrishna, reportedly had love for everyone because he had a *direct experience of the divine* shining through everyone, even the most wretched human being. That is mysticism. Albert Schweitzer also manifested a universal love but he was motivated not by a mystical vision but by an impelling principle which he called 'reverence for life.' That is rationalism. Socrates was far more of a Schweitzer than a Ramakrishna. He was the supreme rationalist, abstracting rigorously and determinedly from experience to find what was intelligible about it. The abstract principle, uncloyed by a specific embodiment or skewed by emotion, was an enormously powerful reality to him, so powerful, in fact, that it led to his death when he refused to compromise his principles. Socrates' obsession with abstraction of that level and force was totally new in the history of Western thought. Compared to Socrates the earlier philosophers had been engaged in child's play.

Plato and Aristotle. with some help from Stoicism, created the *thought-structure* which dominated the Western world until the modern era. Their answer to the ontological question was that what is *real* is matter and form and that what *appears*, the world as we know it, is a universal, dynamic *substance* which is the result of the creative interaction of the *potential of matter* and the *actuality of form*. As we would expect from Mindset Theory, Western philosophy, whatever the differences among its many schools, is generally united in the view that although change occurs, it occurs only within a matrix of order and there is no escape from that order. Because reality is *inherently ordered* it is accessible to reason. And just as there is no reality above or outside the dynamic substance which is our world, there is likewise no human faculty above or transcending reason.

India: Illusion and Knowledge

India never had a Homer, so the Indians never had the opportunity to consider the world in quite the secular way the Greeks did. No people have ever been such inveterate mythologizers as the Indians, welcoming countless gods into their pantheon and weaving great epics, such as the Ramayana and the Mahabharata, around them. Probably the best example of the Indic passion for mythology is the fact that in less than three hundred years after Buddha introduced what was essentially an anti-mythological, anti-speculative, spiritual way of life his followers had invented a vast mythological universe containing innumerable worlds, each with its hierarchies of Buddhas and bodhisattvas (Buddhas-to-be). In view of the sharp distinction I made earlier between theology and philosophy you might well wonder if the Indic mind ever could produce an 'abstract, reasoned explanation of the contents of human experience' without resort to mythology.

The fact, however, is that it did because, contrary to conventional opinions, the Indic mind did go through a 'demythologizing' process comparable to that in Greece. As I pointed out earlier in this chapter, different civilizations may emphasize different aspects of human experience. For that reason the demythologizing process which led to philosophy in India took an entirely different turn than it did in the West. Whereas the Greeks used as their starting point experience of the external world, the world of nature, the Indians started from experience of the internal world, the world of spirit. The demythologizing vehicle in India was a series of works called the *Upanishads*. The Upanishads were accepted as the last part of the Vedas, the Indic scriptures, and were therefore also called the Vedanta, 'the end of the Vedas.' They were composed over a several hundred year period from perhaps as early as 1000 B.C. down to around 300 B.C. The ten (of 108) most important were probably composed before Buddha (6th century) and may have been known to him.

In my opinion the Upanishads represent a revival of the ancient Indic tradition which preceded the Aryan takeover of India in the middle of the second millennium B. C. I suspect that the idea of life's four stages, the last of which involved putting behind one's family and dwelling away from settled communities in the forest as a seeker of enlightenment, was at least in part a strategy of the Indic mindset to counter the essentially Occidental character of Aryan religion. The forest dwellers were not rationalists, but rather intuitionists, seeking in their meditations a direct, immediate experience of ultimate reality in the depths of consciousness. The

Upanishads they composed, which are also called the Aranyakas or forest books, were not so much philosophy as testimony to that experience and how it affected mythology. The experience was of the universal, timeless All or Atman as the ground of the self and of the identity of the Atman with Brahman as the ground of the universe. We have already seen in Chapter 3 how that experience affected mythology. From its ultimate point of view the world and its creatures, heaven and its gods lost their independent reality and became manifestations, expressions, or appearances of the one reality.

When you stop regarding the contents of myth as real and think of them only as ways of expression or appearances necessary for the unenlightened you have gone just as far along the road to demythologizing as if you regarded them merely as fables. Thus the groundwork had been laid for Indic philosophy to seek an explanation of human experience just as Homer had done for the Greeks. The critical difference between the two was that the Indic mind had to consider one content of human experience which the Greek mind, looking outward, never did: *the direct experience of the World Self on a spiritual level.*

There are two great streams of Indic philosophy, both of which are the equal in scope and analytic power to anything in the West. The earliest was Mahayana Buddhist philosophy which culminated in the Vijñanavadin (ultimate reality is consciousness, *vijñana*) school of the brothers Asanga and Vasubandhu in the 4th century A.D. Following closely on and stimulated by dialogue with Buddhist philosophy were the six Hindu systems, the foremost of which and still most honored today was the Advaita (non-dualist) Vedanta of Shankara, a brilliant young philosopher who died at the age of thirty-two in 820 A.D. The differences between Vasubandhu and Shankara are, I believe, just about as consequential or inconsequential as those between Plato and Aristotle. Their systems are both squarely within the matrix of the Indic mindset, so

I will confine myself in this section to the salient features of Shankara's system.

Superficially, Shankara's thought is similar to that of Parmenides. What is real to them both is singular, timeless, changeless, complete within itself. Whatever changes or becomes cannot be real. Therefore the world of appearance, which does change, must be an *illusion*. But there the resemblance between the two philosophers ends. Parmenides' philosophy is an exercise in logic based on the assumption that the real is corporeal and winds up with the sterile notion that the real is a corporeal, finite, sphere. But Shankara's view of reality is based on *evidence* of the underlying infinite spiritual reality derived from *mystical experience*. We can never understand the force of Shankara's arguments unless we understand that he accepts as fully confirmed *by experience* the unity of Atman and Brahman. It is not merely that ancient compositions such as the Upanishads say so but that the truth has been repeatedly confirmed by holy men down through centuries from time immemorial to Shankara's time and even, as many would say, to our time. In Radhakrishnan's words,

> [Shankara] does not start, as theological philosophers do, with a discussion of God's attributes. He is indifferent to, and even critical of, the arguments which are adduced in favour of a great First Cause and Creator of the world. For him integral experience, or anubhava ['mystical' experience], is the basal fact. It is the highest religious insight. It supplies the proof - if proof be the name for it - of man's awareness of a spiritual reality. Brahman is present to every man and is the universal fact of life. (60, V. II, 534)

As I pointed out in Chapter III the Atman/Brahman is pure non-order. We can call it pure consciousness but in so doing we are not speaking of consciousness as we know it because there is no distinction in it of subject and object or any of the other categories in terms of which we can define order. It is beyond all dualities and categories but that does not mean it is nothingness or unreality:

Brahman has nothing similar to it, nothing different from it,
no internal differentiation, since all these are empirical
distinctions. As it is opposed to all empirical existence, it is
given to us as the negative of everything that is positively
known. [Shankara] declines to characterise it even as one
except in the sense of secondless, but calls it non-dual,
advaitam. It is the 'wholly other' but not non-being. (60, V.
II, 535)

It should never be supposed that because Vedanta recognized
Brahman, the pure non-order, as the only reality, that it therefore
denied that the empirical world or the individual self *exist*. Of course
they exist. If they didn't exist why would we have to explain them
and why would release from bondage be necessary? As far as the
external world is concerned, the Indic philosophers analyzed it quite
thoroughly, using many of the same concepts, such as space, time
and causality, as did the Greeks. As for the self, they analyzed it in
far greater detail than the West, which is understandable because if
you have to make your way through the complexities of the inner
world to experience the ultimate World Self, then you need to
understand those complexities. We will examine some of the
practical consequences of Indic psychology in a later chapter but here
we are concerned with psychological processes only as they, like
external events, are objects in the empirical world.

However much of a structured cosmos the empirical world,
including our 'internal' world, may be, Shankara tells us, it does not
have the same status as Brahman. You cannot say that it is real
because only Brahman is real. On the other hand, you cannot say it
is unreal, because it exists as an object of experience. We call
something which is neither real nor unreal an *illusion*. When a
magician saws a box with a woman inside it in half, and apparently
the woman as well, we cannot say that what he does is real because
he doesn't actually saw through the woman. But neither can we say
that it is unreal because we see that it appears to happen. So we
call the magician an illusionist. Shankara uses the example of our
mistaking a piece of rope on the path for a snake. The snake is not

real because it is actually a rope. But it is also not unreal because we see it. However, when we realize that the snake is really a rope, the illusion is gone and that is the nature of enlightenment or release. The world exists in all its complexity until we realize it is truly only Brahman, then we know it for the illusion it is and its spell no longer has any power over us.

> The ultimate truth, as realised by a *jivanmukta* [enlightened soul], denies the world while affirming the underlying reality of Brahman which is given in all presentations as positive being *(sat)* and with which we may therefore be said to be constantly, though not consciously, in touch. (61, 157)

It should be noted that the *jiva* or individual self does not stand in quite the same illusory relation to Brahman as the world does. When I look at a white flower through rose-colored glasses I see the flower as it is but attribute a mistaken color to it. When I take off the glasses the flower does not disappear, it simply displays its true color. That is a different kind of illusion than that of the snake which entirely disappears. Hiriyanna explains,

> This difference . . . has a vital bearing on the Advaita doctrine, and [Shankara] consequently lays particular emphasis on it. It brings out clearly what is meant by the identity of the *jiva* and Brahman which is of fundamental importance to the doctrine. The *jiva* is not false or illusory as the world is; for, if it were, there would be none to be saved and the whole teaching of the Upanishads would then be nullified. Salvation implies survival. The liberated *jiva* is not thus lost in Brahman. But, at the same time, it should be remembered that it would not be quite correct to say that it is preserved, for it is only as Brahman that it continues to be, losing its limitations which are all false. (Op. cit., 157f.)

The 'limitations,' of course, are part of the 'false and illusory' empirical world. Although there are many ways *(yogas* or *margas)* to enlightenment in the Indic scheme, the most intellectually severe and demanding is *jñana yoga*, the yoga of knowledge, in which the mind attempts to strip away the layers of order which structure our empirical world and mask the World Self within, constantly reminding itself, 'It is not this, It is not that.' The order of the empirical world, which the West tried so strenuously to comprehend through reason, was the realm of *illusion* to the Indic mind, ultimately to dissolve in the experiential *knowledge* of That to which no name, no form, no order of any kind could be ascribed.

China: Yin and Yang

The reason Occidental philosophy began and ended with the empirical world and Indic philosophy began and ended with the spirit world was not a matter of arbitrary choice. *The area of experience which held the greatest attraction for a civilization was determined by its mindset.* The West was intrigued by the physical world because it was obsessed with order and order is most obvious in the mensurable regularities of nature. The inner world, on the other hand, the world of feelings, desires and dreams, tended to baffle and try the Western mind. The Indic mind, obsessed with mystery, followed the inward path to an ultimate truth beyond order and, therefore, gave the empirical world short shrift. What area of experience, then, would we expect to engage a mind which cathected a balance between order and mystery? That area in which peace and strife, balance and imbalance, harmony and discord are most directly detectable and critical, *the sociopolitical area.*

Sociopolitical problems were, in fact, the chief preoccupation of Sinic thinkers from the time of Confucius who lived in the sixth century B.C. Confucius is generally regarded as the first Chinese 'philosopher,' yet Westerners have seriously questioned whether that title is appropriate either to him or to the many thinkers who came after him, just as they have questioned whether it ought to be given to Indic philosophers. The question does not imply that sociopolitical phenomena are not as legitimate a subject for philosophy as physical or spiritual phenomena but indicates a doubt that the Chinese dealt

with them in an 'abstract, reasoned' manner. A. C. Graham states
the problem cogently.

> . . . Chinese thought continues to puzzle Western readers,
> even to leave many of them doubtful as to whether it truly
> deserves the name of 'Philosophy'. The great Chinese
> thinkers are moralists, mystics, and political theorists,
> concerned with the conduct of the individual and the
> organization of society, but seldom interested in constructing
> metaphysical systems. By itself this fact may not deter
> readers today as much as a generation ago, metaphysics
> being at present rather out of fashion; but it is far from
> obvious to many people that Chinese thinkers can be credited
> with thinking rationally at all. Admittedly they are not
> religious prophets and do not appeal to divine revelation,
> but the two most influential documents, the *Analects* of
> Confucius and the *Tao te ching* ascribed to Lao-tzu, do
> not appeal to reason either. To what extent was the
> Greek discovery of rational discourse paralleled in China?
> (62, 28f.)

Graham goes on to show quite clearly that whatever their
distinctive styles of expression the Chinese did approach
sociopolitical problems in a reasoned way and did search for abstract
principles which could explain and therefore make possible the
alleviation of those problems. The following is an example of early
Chinese philosophizing by Mo Tzu who lived after Confucius, from
480 to 390 B. C.

> Now at the present time, what brings the greatest harm to
> the world? Great states attacking small ones, great families
> overthrowing small ones, the strong oppressing the weak, the
> many harrying the few, the cunning deceiving the stupid, the
> eminent lording it over the humble - these are harmful to the
> world. So too are rulers who are not generous, ministers who
> are not loyal, fathers who are without kindness, and sons
> who are unfilial, as well as those mean men who, with
> weapons, knives, poison, fire, and water, seek to injure and
> undo each other.

> When we inquire into the cause of these various harms, what
> do we find has produced them? Do they come about from
> loving others and trying to benefit them? Surely not! They

come rather from hating others and trying to injure them. And when we set out to classify and describe those men who hate and injure others, shall we say that their actions are motivated by universality or partiality? Surely we must answer, by partiality, and it is this partiality in their dealings with one another that gives rise to all the great harms in the world. Therefore we know that partiality is wrong.

. . . Whoever criticizes others must have some alternative to offer them. To criticize and yet offer no alternative is like trying to stop flood with flood or put out fire with fire. It will surely have no effect. Therefore. . : Partiality should be replaced by universality.

But how can partiality be replaced by universality? If men were to regard the states of others as they regard their own, then who would raise up his state to attack the state of another? It would be like attacking his own. If men were to regard the cities of others as they regard their own, then who would raise up his city to attack the city of another? If men were to regard the families of others as they regard their own, then who would raise up his family to overthrow that of another? It would be like overthrowing his own. Now when states and cities do not attack and make war on each other and families and individuals do not overthrow or injure one another, is this a harm or a benefit to the world? Surely it is a benefit. (63, 39f.)

In this passage Mo Tzu begins with a question - 'What brings the greatest harm to the world?' - which he follows with a series of examples which are virtually a self-evident answer. Next he inquires what is the common factor in all these examples - universality or partiality? - to which again the answer is obvious: partiality. Then he follows the basic Confucian principle that having knowledge is no good unless you use it and offers an antidote for the harm being inflicted on the world: Partiality should be replaced by universality. Finally he proposes how that general prescription can be made into a specific ethical principle: Do unto others as if they were yourself.

This is clearly philosophy. Had it been written in dialogue form, the method would be Socratic. It is abstract and reasoned and although it is not highly sophisticated it is no less sophisticated in its own sphere of interest than sixth century Greek philosophy was with regard to the empirical world. As we might expect, over the centuries Chinese philosophy became more sophisticated, more systematic and more polemic as it had to cope with outside competitors, particularly Buddhism, but it remained at heart sociopolitical. It was not until the 11th century A.D., at about the same time that Taoism and Buddhism became extinct as philosophies (though not as religions) that cosmology came to the fore in the form of Neo-Confucianism.

While concentrating on sociopolitical philosophy, Chinese philosophers had always had at their disposal a kind of primitive cosmology which viewed the world as the product of five alternating elements: metal, wood, water, fire and earth. There was nothing unique to China in this notion. Similar groups of elements were recognized both in the West and in India. However, a second conception implicitly accepted by nearly all Chinese philosophers was unique - the Yin Yang doctrine. The idea of Yin and Yang, which we discussed in the preceding chapter, was not so much a philosophy as *a direct, intuitive expression of the Sinic mindset.* It is a very old idea, probably as old as Chinese civilization, and it underlies one of the most important Chinese compositions, the system of divination known as the *I Ching*, The Book of Changes, the first two 'trigrams' of which are:

▬▬▬▬▬▬▬▬▬	▬▬▬▬ ▬▬▬▬
▬▬▬▬▬▬▬▬▬	▬▬▬▬ ▬▬▬▬
▬▬▬▬▬▬▬▬▬	▬▬▬▬ ▬▬▬▬
Ch'ien standing for	*K'un* standing for
the Yang principle	the Yin principle

The I Ching antedates all Chinese philosophy. It was well known to and greatly honored by Confucius and its use as a guide to living has always been an integral part of Far Eastern life. The design of the modern South Korean flag is made up of the Yin Yang symbol and four I Ching trigrams, including the two shown above. Not surprisingly, then, Neo-Confucianism built its cosmology on principles underlying the Yin Yang symbol and the I Ching along with the notion of the five elements, although the latter were always subordinated to the former and sometimes dispensed with altogether.

Not a few writers have suggested that Chinese philosophy is strongly influenced by the nature of their pictographic writing. My own opinion is that the converse is true, that the Chinese retained their preference for pictographic writing because their mindset resisted the tendency to dichotomization implicit in Aryan (both Greco-Roman and Sanskrit) languages. Be that as it may, related to their long adherence to pictographic writing was a Chinese penchant for abstract symbols and diagrams. Diagrams, like aphorisms, are an excellent way of making a statement while leaving a great deal unsaid and therefore open to further, if not endless, interpretation. The Taoist and Neo-Confucian philosophers were particularly fond of diagramming their cosmologies. The diagram on the following page is attributed to Chou Tun-i, the founder of Neo-Confucianism (1017-73 A.D.). Dai Liu interprets it as follows,

> The empty circle at the top represents the Supreme Ultimate (*t'ai chi*), which generates yang through movement and the yin through quiescence. The circle below it, with inner crescents of alternating black and white, represents the opposition and interaction between yin and yang. Notice that the yang side contains yin within it, just as in the T'ai Chi T'u [referring to the Yin Yang symbol - see Chapter II - with its small white and black circles within the larger black and white 'fish' areas]. Below this circle there is a pattern that contains five smaller circles symbolizing the five elements, which come into being through the interaction between yin and yang.
>
> The large circle below the five small ones represents the male and the female joined. Thus the five elements are formed

from the yin and yang once again. The lowest circle represents the results of the union of female and male *(yin* and *yang):* reproduction of the next generation of man and in the universe, the production and evolution of all things. (64, 27)

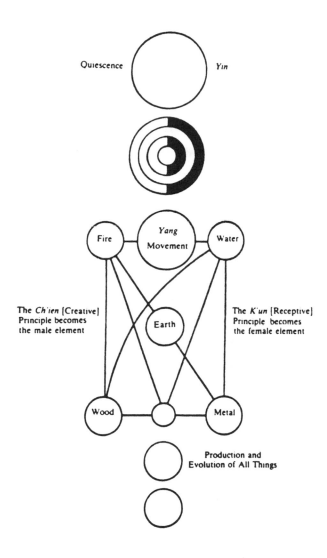

T'ai Chi T'u of Ch'en Tuan

Diagram of the Supreme Ultimate that Antedates Heaven

(From Fung Yu-lan, *A History of Chinese Philosophy,* V. 2, p. 439)

Note that in Chou Tun-i's diagram the top circle represents two concepts, both of which refer to the final, universal reality. It is called, in the first place, 'the Ultimateless!' (or Non-Ultimate) which essentially means limitless, unbounded, undifferentiated, inactive, that which the Tao Te Ching called 'the Nameless Tao.' As an abstraction it is very similar to the Indic Brahman but Chinese philosophy does not think of it as a World Self or Atman which can be directly experienced. It is completely transcendent. On the other hand, the Ultimateless is also the Supreme or Great Ultimate (the Tao which can be named), in which character it produces the changing empirical world through the complementary powers of yin and yang.

The Neo-Confucianists differed in many respects but, like Western and Indic philosophers, they tended to agree on certain basic points. Some, like Chang Tsai, identified the Great Ultimate with a material force and played down *yin* and *yang* and the elements as merely aspects of that force. Others slighted the corporeal side of the world and emphasized creative, productive *li* or principle as the essence of the Great Ultimate, making the universe more of a living, reproducing organism. But they all agreed that the cosmological process was *good*, coming around in the end to saying that its essence was *jen*, humaneness or universal love, the fundamental Confucian virtue. The greatest of the later Neo-Confucianists, Chu Hsi (1130-1200 A.D.) finally produced a synthesis in which the Great Ultimate appeared as the formless (in the corporeal sense) reservoir of the principles or forms of all things. The forms were actualized in matter which was a kind of ubiquitous gas similar to the Stoic's *pneuma* but lacking inherent reason. Since all things material were produced from the perfect forms in the Great Ultimate, all things ought to be perfect and would be if there were not inescapable defects in matter. But Chu Hsi and those who followed him were all quite certain that the defects, particularly in man, could be remedied through one form of discipline or another.

Chu Hsi's cosmology is not exactly a great triumph of philosophy. His cosmic gas was something of a *res ex machina* and his system was not worked out with the precision either of an Aristotle or a Shankara. But the Chinese were happy with it because it achieved what they wanted from philosophy. Chu Hsi had demonstrated that order and non-order were equitably and harmoniously balanced in the universe as they were intended to be in society and that was all the Chinese needed to be assured of. So after Hu Hsi nothing notably innovative occurred in Chinese cosmology. The transcendent unordered, i.e., the Ultimateless or 'Great Vacuity' as Chang Tsai had called it, was lurking unapproachably behind the phenomena, and the Great Ultimate or Great Harmony was functioning to keep the world a viable place for human life. Thus the Sinic mindset had been satisfied and subsequent Chinese philosophy was content to leave well enough alone.

Mesoamerica: The Perilous Moment

Thanks to Hernan Cortés and Company there were no Amerindic philosophers, so we could simply skip this section with regrets. Alternatively we could play the role of an Amerindic philosopher, trying to think as he might one day have thought, but that would be fruitless speculation. Even though you understand a people's mindset, you cannot predict how they will work out its implications in a particular area of experience. A mindset merely provides a matrix or probability structure for experience, not its specific content. Nevertheless, I think we know enough about how the Amerindians thought to make some reasonable guesses about the kind of philosophy they would have developed.

In the first place, the double negative mindset with its emphasis on the precariousness of the cosmic process, led to an obsession with *time* from the very beginning of Amerindic civilization, an obsession which resulted in the development of an extraordinary *calendar*.

Calendars were, of course, established early in all civilizations and throughout history were subject to revision and improvement. Certain problems occupied chronologists the world over, such as the precise length of the solar year, coordinating the solar year with lunar cycles, and trying to make sure that both solar and lunar cycles bore the same relation to seasonal changes in each succeeding year (so that the beginning of summer, for example, didn't start out in June one year and some years later wind up in January). The Western Gregorian calendar, which is virtually a universal civil calendar today, has 365 days and 12 months in its year, each month being almost the same in length with just enough variations to make up the extra five days. Since the actual solar year is about 365 1/4 days, an extra day is added to February every fourth year. All civilized societies, with minor variations, arrived at similar calendars. This not only made possible accurate historical and current civil dating but was essential to one of civilization's most ingrained activities - astrology.

Although the Toltecs and Aztecs attributed their calendar to Quetzalcoatl, it was actually the Mayans who invented it. The Mayan calendar, which was adopted by all succeeding Mesoamerican societies, was one of the most remarkable creations of the ancient human mind. It was, in fact, two calendars which, when combined, produced amazing results. The first calendar can be called the Ritual Calendar. It consisted of 13 cycles of 20 days each or 260 days. Each of the Ritual Calendar days bore a number and a name, both of which were required to identify it. But while there were twenty names there were only thirteen numbers. Since thirteen and twenty have no common denominator, when you cycle the names over the numbers any one combination does not come up a second time until you have completed thirteen cycles and that begins another 260 day period. Therefore every day in each 260-day period has a unique number-name designation.

To make things more complicated there was also a Seasonal

Calendar which comprised 18 months of 20 days each or 360 days called a *tun*, to which were added five days at the end to bring the total to a 365 days. That added five day period was called by various fearful names indicating that it was a time of dire and uncertain omen in which the whole cosmos was in special peril. In the Seasonal Calendar each of the 18 months had a name and each day had a number from 1 to 20. (Strictly speaking, there was no 20. The last day of the month had a sign indicating that it was the last of the month or the day preceding the next month, as if we were to call March 31st 'the last of March' or 'the day before April.') Therefore each day of the *tun* had its own number and month designation just as our days do.

But now imagine what happens if you cycle the 365 days of the Seasonal Calendar around the 260 days of the Ritual Calendar? You would then have for every day a Ritual number and name plus a Seasonal number and name. To use Mayan names a day might be designated,

1 Cimi (day name) 7 Yaxkin (month name)

Now the mathematics of cycling 365 days over 260 days are such that this same four-element combination cannot recur for 18,980 days or 52 years, a period called by scholars a Calendar Round. Every day in the Calendar Round has a unique four-element name which is not repeated for 52 years! For longer periods of time the Mayans used the Long Count, a system based on a 360-day *tun* and its multiples: *katun (20 tuns), baktun (20 katuns), pictun (20 baktuns), calabtun (20 pictuns), and kinchiltun (20 calabtuns)* . A kinchiltun adds up to 1,152,000,000 days or 3,200,000 years. The Mayans seldom used the kinchiltun but began their Long Count dates by recording how many baktuns, katuns, tuns, uinals (months) and kins (days) had elapsed since a certain date which they regarded as the beginning of their era. They also had a way of incorporating

Calendar Round dates in Long Count chronology. One final calendric intricacy stemmed from the fact that every date was 'ruled' by one of nine 'lords of the night' in uninterrupted succession. Since the 18,980 dates of the 52-year Calendar Round leave a remainder of eight when divided by nine, the first day of each of nine successive Calendar Rounds was ruled by a different lord of the night. Consequently, if you add the symbol or glyph of the ruling lord of the night to a four-element date you have a unique five-element designation for each day which cannot occur for 9 x 52 or 468 years.

I have mentioned these details of the Amerindic calendar to give you an idea of the extremes to which they carried it. The importance of their calendar and the cosmic order it represented was far greater to the Amerindians than to any other civilization. To them the calendric order was not something merely devised by man for practical purposes. It was the very fabric of the universe and of life. In any Amerindic philosophy, therefore, time would have undoubtedly been the major structural concept and it may have been employed somewhat as follows.

A basic feature of time is that it is divisible into units. In each of those units, to borrow terms from the Greeks, substance is created by joining matter and form. As long as that is a congenial process, as the Greeks viewed it, a process in which matter is receptive to form, time is merely the duration of change or an index of 'the moving image everlasting.' But the Amerindians would not have regarded the creative process as congenial. They would have denied that matter is receptive to form, pointing out that, quite the contrary, it is hostile and resistant. If they were to use a favorite example which the Greeks used to illustrate the four causes, that of a sculptor making a statue, they would have drawn quite different conclusions from it. The marble, said the Greeks, is the *material* cause having the potential to be shaped into a thing of beauty, the *formal* cause. The sculptor's activity is the *efficient* cause and his plan of completion the *final* cause. It makes sculpting sound like a very smooth procedure. But no, the Amerindic philosopher would have said, what the sculptor is actually doing is forcing recalcitrant material to take form. Form and matter are not merely joined, they have to be *fused*. And the fusion may not succeed because matter is essentially entropic, tending to disorder, resisting form. Because of that resistance, substance may or may not be created. *Each moment of time, therefore, is the perilous arena in which the issue is decided.* The question is always moot: will fusion succeed or will it not?

What determines success or failure? An extraordinary input of energy into the fusion process to overcome entropy. Where does that energy come from? From human life. It is *human energy* that makes the difference. This is not a concept that should be strange to us. We well recognize that we often have to sacrifice a part of ourselves, a part of our energy to achieve some worthwhile purpose. But whereas we think in terms of quite limited achievements being dependent on our sacrifices, the Amerindians believed the entire universe was dependent on theirs. Sacrifice to them meant not the destruction of life but giving meticulous attention to the demands of the cosmic process, i.e., making certain that every unit of time received its necessary input of energy through ritual, observance of duty, and, from time to time, the sacrifice of human lives. By the time the Amerindians had got around to philosophy I imagine they would have found a way to turn the concept of sacrifice into something less deadly, perhaps more symbolic than it was when Cortés arrived. But I doubt that Amerindic philosophers could have entirely dispensed with the idea of sacrifice in some form because any cosmology consistent with the Amerindic mindset would have required it.

FIVE

Art: Window on the Mindset

What is Art?

> What is art? We do not know. The essential nature of that
> mysterious, intangible, indefinable something that we call
> art baffles us. On the other hand, we do know definitely that
> from the earliest times until today human beings the world
> over have given expression to human experience in concrete
> tangible forms which we call works of art. And we know that
> art is essential to man's well-being. Take away the finest of
> our buildings, our pottery, pictures, music, poetry, drama,
> and the dance. What kind of life would result?
>
> Helen Gardner, *Art through the Ages* (65, 1)

I have always found this opening paragraph in the fourth edition
of Helen Gardner's classic text remarkable. On the one hand she
tells us that art, the subject matter of her excellent survey, is
mysterious, intangible, indefinable and baffling. On the other, she
avows that we cannot live, in any worthwhile sense, without that
enigmatic thing. Most remarkable of all, she goes on to write no less
than 851 pages about it. If you wonder how a scholar of Gardner's
stature can write so prolifically about a subject whose nature baffles
her, the answer is really quite simple. She proceeds in the same way
as historians who write volumes about civilization without defining
it, except that, instead of telling us about nations, dynasties, wars,
classes and governments, art historians write about schools,
movements, influences, styles and techniques. In that way one can
produce an endless stream of erudite and fascinating observations
about art without ever focussing on the pivot around which it all
revolves -- the meaning of art in human experience.

But that method is not possible in this chapter because the matter in hand is not the history of art but art in history or *art in civilization*, which is the same thing. The Theory of Mindsets implies that art, along with all civilized endeavors, is structured by the mindsets of the four Civilizations and, therefore, that the essential nature of art in each Civilization will be not only different from but incompatible with what it is in the other three. To prove that proposition requires two steps:

1.A general definition of art similar to the general definition of civilization in Chapter I. This is necessary in order to make certain that we are comparing the same phenomena, that is, that we are not comparing art with something else -- sports, for example.

2.A demonstration that the general definition contains at least one term which is susceptible to the four radically different interpretations required by the Theory of Mindsets, thus giving rise to four incompatible specific definitions of art.

General Definition

Not everyone believes art is indefinable and baffling. Attempting to define it is the province of *aesthetics*. Experiences evoked by art are commonly called *aesthetic experiences*. In its original Greek meaning 'aesthetic' is a good word to use when talking about art. *Aisthetikos* meant 'perceptive,' especially through feeling. Unfortunately, around 1750 a German philosopher named Baumgarten used the cognate German noun, *Aesthetik*, to designate the science of sensuous knowledge, the goal of which he said was *beauty* in contrast with logic whose goal was supposed to be truth. Although this usage was rejected by Immanuel Kant, it was revived in the philosophy of fine arts elaborated by the idealist philosopher, Hegel, in the eighteen-twenties. So influential was Hegel that his identification of art with beauty became a virtual presupposition of aesthetic theory for over a century.

If, as someone said, yesterday's philosophy (or science) is today's common sense, we probably have Georg Wilhelm Friedrich Hegel to thank for the fact that many people still think that all art is, or is supposed to be, beautiful. Undoubtedly much of civilized art has been intended to produce the experience of beauty, that is, an exciting and delightful experience for the senses and the mind. The so-called 'decorative arts' have that as their sole function. They raise ordinary objects to a level above the trivial and commonplace, making them not only useful but a pleasure to behold. There are also particular eras, such as that of Louis XIV, the Sun King, in which art in all its forms is called upon to produce little else than sheer beauty.

But it is absolutely erroneous to equate art with beauty or the aesthetic experience with the experience of beauty! If we set aside our preconceptions and make even a cursory survey of what are considered great works of art in Western Civilization, from Egypt to the Renaissance, we will readily see that most of them were not created to be beautiful. Take the enormous temple complex of Karnak with its forest of gigantic columns or the colossi of Abu Simbel. Majestic, awe-inspiring, yes. But beautiful? No! In fact, most Egyptian sculpture is rather dull and heavy and much Egyptian painting is stilted and stylized. That is not because Egyptian artists did not know how to create beauty. They left a legacy of sheer loveliness in many of their wall paintings, especially those depicting simple scenes from nature. The reason that that loveliness is the exception rather than the rule is that, for the most part, Egyptian art was not intended to be exciting and delightful. It was intended to produce *an experience of awe before great majesty*.

At the other end of Western Civilization, take Michelangelo's Sistine ceiling. To call that ceiling beautiful is to depreciate it. It was not painted, like baroque ceilings, for the sake of beauty but as a magnificent confirmation of faith and the full aesthetic experience it can produce is one which incorporates that sense of confirmation. If the corporeality of the Sistine figures distracts us from experiencing its sublimity, as it undoubtedly did some of the Vatican clergy in Michelangelo's time, then we need only lower our eyes to the chapel wall on which the same artist painted The Last Judgment. The Last Judgment is not a *beautiful* fresco. Any human beauty depicted there is contrapuntal to the overriding doom of the scene. To stand before that enormous work and think in terms of beauty is preposterous. The aesthetic experience, by which we mean the experience evoked by that great work of art, is one of *mortality and horror*.

I could, of course, produce a whole catalogue of Western art to prove the point that art is not exclusively nor even predominantly devoted to beauty and that the aesthetic experience is only sometimes one of beauty. Nor would the catalogue need to be confined to the visual arts. All the arts, including the literary, the dramatic and the musical, may at times create beauty and at other times something quite different. Pity and terror, the emotions Aristotle said were appropriate to Greek tragedy, are hardly emotions we feel toward the beautiful. We could also extend our catalogue to the art of other civilizations in which case the point would be so obvious as to be self-evident. Who could stand before the statue of the Aztec goddess, Coatlicue (Plate 13), with her serpent head and girdle of skulls or look on the sarcophagus lid of the ruler of Palenque (Plate 12), showing that mighty lord descending into the gaping jaws of the earth monster, and think that art has to be beautiful. But we do not have to compile our own catalogue because any comprehensive book on the history of art, such as Gardner's, will do as well. You only have to look through the pictures and ask yourself of each work, 'Is this beautiful or is it more than, different from, or contrary to the beautiful?' The point will prove itself.

The history of thought is replete with examples of intelligent men spending lifetimes trying to solve problems created by their predecessors' mistakes when the real solution lay in taking a fresh look at the evidence. So it was with the mistake Hegel handed down to his successors. Stuck with the notion that art and beauty were inseparable, the post-Hegelians had to account for the fact that there is so much ugliness and evil in art. This was called the aesthetic 'Problem of Evil.' It was a problem which never should have arisen but it led intelligent men to devise ruses such as what we may call the 'Sugar-coated Pill Theory of Art.' One of its first exponents was George Santayana who wrote in *The Sense of Beauty*, published in 1896,

> Art does not seek out the pathetic, the tragic, and the absurd; it is life that has imposed them upon our attention, and enlisted art in their service, to make contemplation of them, since it is inevitable, at least as tolerable as possible.
>
> The agreeableness of the presentation is thus mixed with the horror of the thing; and the result is that while we are saddened by the truth we are delighted by the vehicle that conveys it to us. (66, 136)

It is, of course, nonsense to say that art does not seek out the pathetic, the tragic and the absurd. Life did not impose Macbeth on Shakespeare or Medea on Euripides. The artist chooses his subjects and they often are pathetic, tragic or absurd because pathos, tragedy or absurdity is the experience the artist wants to communicate. Do *Macbeth* or *Medea* really delight us by the 'agreeableness of the presentation' or do they overwhelm us with revulsion at the murder of innocents, with sympathy with the murderers who seem driven by a malign destiny, and with horror at their inevitable destruction? So disagreeable, in fact, is Medea's murder of her own children, that the event is made to take place off stage. The point is not for the presentation to be agreeable but to be effective and appropriate to the subject. The function of the artist is not to sugar-coat unpalatable facts of life but to convey with integrity what his mind envisions. If the subject is evil the form will not delight but focus and intensify the experience of evil in every nuance. If the subject is sublime the form will stimulate the senses and the mind to heights of ecstasy. With this in mind let us now try to unravel the tangled skein of phenomena we call art.

One way to proceed with a complex definition is to build up to it by discussing its elements first, then combining them into a whole. That is how we presented the definition of civilization in Chapter I. In this chapter let us adopt the opposite approach, giving the full definition first, then explaining its parts.

Art is a mature human activity which creates and produces objects or events intended to evoke specific and significant experiences in those expected to observe them.

Now for the constituent elements of the definition. First, art is a *mature human activity*. Although in many traditions the artist is thought to be divinely inspired, art is an activity of mature human beings. Gods do not produce art unless they use human hands and brains to do it. Nor do animals or small children (apart from those rare prodigies who are really premature adults) produce art. It may be fun to turn a chimpanzee or a tot loose with paints and paper and compare what it does with what Jackson Pollack did. But the chimp and the tot are not Jackson Pollack. They are *playing* with artist's materials. What they produce may be entertaining or interesting to psychologists but it is not art for reasons we shall see.

Second, art *creates and produces*. The activity of art involves both creating and producing works of art. It is necessary to emphasize the distinction between these two phases of the process because the definition is intended to cover all the arts. In painting, sculpture and literature, creating and producing are generally, though not always, accomplished by a single person in one continuous act. But in architecture, music, and drama, creating and producing are separate functions. The architect creates a plan, the composer a score, the playwright a script. Production falls to the master builder, the conductor, and the director respectively. However, in the history of these arts it has been common for the creators to perform the productive functions as well. Architects have frequently built their own buildings and composers and playwrights frequently acted as or with conductors and directors, especially in the first performances of their works, because out of those performances may arise the need for vital changes.

Third, art produces *objects or events*. Again, this distinction is required to make the definition comprehensive. An object can be defined as a product in which change or activity in time is negligible. An event is one in which time and activity dominate. All the arts produce one or the other. It is not difficult to sort them out on this basis. Some arts, such as plays or operas, combine events and objects (stage sets). Although the twentieth century is not, strictly speaking, within the scope of this book, it is worth noting that modern artists have been very innovative in producing both objects, such as fences which meander miles across the countryside, and events, such as unrepeatable, self-destructing ensembles. When we have finished this definition it will be clear that such works clearly fall within the scope of art, untraditional as they may be.

Fourth, art is intended to evoke *a specific . . . experience* Although there may be playlike elements involved in the spontaneity of artistic creation, art is essentially work, not play. It is *goal-directed*. Unlike 'children's art' or 'therapeutic art,' genuine art is not done merely for expression ('getting something out') or 'for its own sake.' The goal of art is not vague or random but a *specific* experience which can only be evoked by the completed work of art. It does not pre-exist in the artist's mind. What does pre-exist and motivates the execution of the art work is what we call *artistic vision*. When the artist has produced a work which, in his judgment, does evoke the experience he envisioned, the work is complete. It is well-known that artists work in different ways and their visions occur in different ways. Mozart's musical vision was highly integrated. A whole symphony seemed to present itself in his imagination to be merely written out. Beethoven's vision, on the other hand, was sequential, unfolding slowly as he labored through endless trials and revisions. But no matter how the vision comes or the work is executed, the artist is the sole judge as to when the work is finished. The story is told of Whistler that, having painted a woman's portrait which others thought was a masterpiece, he went to his studio one night and discovered that he was not satisfied with the way he had painted the lady's wrist. So he began to repaint it. He painted and painted and the more he painted the more dissatisfied he became and the more changes he made. By morning the entire painting was a shambles and it was never exhibited. What others had been ready to accept as finished had not completely fulfilled the artist's vision.

Fifth, someone is *expected to observe* works of art. In what kind of observer is a work of art supposed to evoke an experience? First and foremost, in the artist. He is its first judge and critic. But most artists expect their work to be observed by others and hopefully to evoke in others an experience similar to their own. It is in this sense that art communicates. Such communication, the evocation of a common experience, implies a similarity of tradition, taste and values between the artist and his public. The communicative power of art is reduced to the extent that that similarity is absent. Bernard Berenson, the great American art expert, although he possessed a fine collection of Chinese art, saw no aesthetic value in it. Rather than be shocked by such parochialism in a great mind we should remind ourselves that Chinese artists would doubtless not be shocked at all. They would not expect Berenson to appreciate their work because it was created for Chinese, not Americans. The artist expects to communicate with a specific kind of audience, not simply with anyone who happens to come across his work.

Sixth, art evokes a *significant experience* . Here we come to the hub not only around which our general definition of art revolves but through which we will find our connection to the civilized mindsets. Significance in art means several things, two of which I wish to emphasize. Firstly, all art is significant in the sense that the experience it is intended to evoke is *important*. Although a great deal of art, especially at the decorative level, is not *very* important, the one thing art absolutely cannot be is routine, trivial or commonplace. These characteristics form the minimal level below which it is meaningless to speak of art. The very least art must do is to produce an object or event which is beyond the ordinary. Someone who makes a serviceable pot or bowl is a craftsman. He becomes an artist when the bowl is finely turned so as to be something good simply to look at, or when a scene is painted on its surface as in a Greek *kylix,* or when it is masterfully designed and cast as were Chinese bronzes. Above that first level of decoration and design the significance of a work of art depends on how powerful and impressive an experience it evokes. Art *can* affect us at every level of our being - sensory, emotional, intellectual, spiritual. The more it succeeds in reaching all those levels in an integrated manner - all on the same wavelength, so to speak - the more significance we accord it.

In the second place, art becomes more significant when the experience it evokes is *meaningful*. Meaning is, in fact, the crux of aesthetic significance. But it is also one of the most debated concepts of the twentieth century. A very influential group of semanticists have contended that only statements which can, in principle, be verified in shared experience, as scientists do, are meaningful. Some aestheticians try to fit art within this narrow definition by claiming it does provide semantically meaningful information of a sort which cannot be derived by other means. One author who makes this claim is Nathan Knobler in a generally well thought-out and readable book, *The Visual Dialogue* (67). For example, he produces a number of drawings and black-and-white photographs and one floor plan of Rouen Cathedral which he says provide a certain amount (though far from complete) information about the Cathedral. If we consider photographs and floor plans as the visual equivalents of statements, then there is a good case for accepting them as meaningful information. It is in this sense that we say, 'A single picture is worth a thousand words.' But on this relatively safe foundation Knobler builds the following contention:

> The French Impressionist Claude Monet saw the cathedral of Rouen in still another way. For him, and for the other Impressionists painting late in the nineteenth century, light reflected from the surfaces of buildings and landscape was a major factor in the perception of the real world. The physical objects might remain constant, but their appearance changed radically under different conditions of light and atmosphere. Monet took the facade of Rouen Cathedral as his subject in a series of paintings . . . In each of them, using technical devices that helped to create a painted equivalent for the effects of light, the artist communicated information about the cathedral that could not have been comparably expressed in any of the other visual forms mentioned above. (67, 54)

Here I think Knobler has gone too far. He includes reproductions of two of the Monet paintings, one of the cathedral in full sunlight and one at sunset. The one in full sunlight is somewhat monochramatic but with deep, sharp shadows in doors, windows and niches. In the other, the architectural details are etched in light and the openings are filled with the deep russet of the setting sun. In its own way each of the two paintings evokes a strong reaction. Knobler is saying - I believe - that the Monet paintings inform us that Rouen Cathedral looks or can look such and such a way at a particular time of day. But frankly I doubt that Rouen Cathedral ever looks the same to anyone as it did to Monet and I doubt that it even looked to Monet the way it does in his paintings. Monet's experience of the cathedral combined with his fascination for luminous color and reflected light to stimulate his artistic vision. The result was a series of paintings. We, the observers, experience those paintings but that aesthetic experience tells us little about Rouen

Cathedral. Knobler himself says almost the same thing when he refers, in a later paragraph, to Monet's 'choice of light reflection, rather than the specifics of modeling, as *the salient feature of his personal response to the building.* ' (ibid., *emphasis mine*) The paintings give us not information about a cathedral but *a personal response* to a cathedral.

On the other hand, while I think Knobler's example is a poor one, a good case can be made that some visual and literary art conveys information which is meaningful in a strict semantic sense. Take Holbein's famous portrait of Henry VIII. At an informational level the portrait tells us what Henry VIII looked like and that is, in principle, verifiable. The same can be said of Audubon's paintings of birds and the Western paintings of Remington and Price. As information, they are *pictorial equivalents of statements about reality* and, therefore, semantically meaningful. We also get a great deal of information from historical novels and plays.

But the informational content of works of art is secondary and often suspect for the simple reason that, for the artist, *aesthetic meaning always takes precedence over semantic meaning.* If the artist has to distort or even contradict historical or scientific fact in order to produce the experience he envisions, he is compelled to do so. Controversy still rages in England over whether Shakespeare's portrayal of Richard III as a humpbacked villain is historically accurate but most of us would doubt that the question affects the aesthetic value of the play. One of the most notorious examples of the direct contradiction of historical fact in art is Friedrich Schiller's play about Joan of Arc, *Jungfrau von Orleans*, in which Schiller not only alters many details of the milieu in which Joan lived but actually has her escape from the English and die on the battlefield, even though history records that she died at the stake.

To summarize, some art contains information which is meaningful in the semantic sense of verifiable statements or their graphic equivalents but that sort of information is usually incidental to the art work and often quite unreliable, if not downright false. Art involves another kind of meaning to which semantic meaning is subordinated. What is that other kind of meaning? The same semanticists I referred to previously contend that unverifiable statements, that is, statements which cannot be tested for truth or falsity, are mere expressions of emotion, like 'Wow!' or 'Aha!' Works of art, they contend, belong in the same category. Since they cannot be tested for truth or falsity, so the argument goes, they cannot be meaningful or rational and, therefore, can only be emotional expressions because anything which isn't rational must be emotional. A number of theories have been advanced to get art off the horns of this dilemma. One of the most original is found in Suzanne K. Langer's *Philosophy in a New Key*. But rather than pursue those theories, let us see what kind of meaning we ourselves can find in a well-known poem.

OZYMANDIAS

I met a traveller from an antique land
Who said: Two vast and trunkless legs of stone
Stand in the desert . . . Near them, on the sand,
Half sunk, a shattered visage lies, whose frown,
And wrinkled lip, and sneer of cold command,
Tell that its sculptor well those passions read
Which yet survive, stamped on these lifeless things,
The hand that mocked them, and the heart that fed:
And on the pedestal these words appear:
'My name is Ozymandias, king of kings:
Look on my works, ye Mighty, and despair!'
Nothing beside remains. Round the decay
Of that colossal wreck, boundless and bare
The lone and level sands stretch far away. (68, 589)

'Ozymandias' is a gem of a word picture. One can well imagine the scene described being painted. But obviously Shelley's words are not meant to be verified. No one supposes the poet really met a 'traveller from an antique land' who described the scene to him. Taken as a statement of fact the poem would be false - a fiction as is most literary art - but no one takes it as a statement of fact. Yet, if the words are not statements of fact or information, are they then merely expressions of emotion? The problem with saying that art is merely emotional expression is that emotion is never 'mere.' It comes from involvement in life and that involvement includes the physical, the intellectual, and the spiritual. There is a strong emotional component in the experience evoked by 'Ozymandias' but the emotion proceeds from something else in the poem, the *statement* it makes about the fate of men who pretend to great power and the fragility of their 'mighty works.' Such a statement reflects a *viewpoint* and while a viewpoint cannot be verified in the same way as a statement of fact, it can be understood and accepted or rejected. Meaning in art, therefore, lies in its viewpoint and the effectiveness of any work of art depends on how compellingly it expresses that viewpoint. Art is meaningful to any human being to the extent that it evokes an experience which involves his being, his values, and his outlook on life. This is what we mean when we say colloquially that art 'speaks to us' or that it 'reaches us where we live.'

You will recall that when we undertook a general definition of art it was partly to make sure that we did not confuse art with something else - sports, for example. So let us test our definition and see if it effectively excludes sports such as football, baseball, cricket, tennis or golf. The choice of sports for comparison is not random because sports have much in common with art. Unlike art, however, sports are not engaged in merely for the experiences observers get from them. They are contests primarily intended to test the participants. Nevertheless, it cannot be denied that public sporting events often evoke very significant experiences in observers. The reaction of sports enthusiasts has traditionally been so extreme that it has earned them the designation, 'fans,' - short for 'fanatics.' The strong emotion produced by two teams or players battling with each other for supremacy is the reason that sports have been the theme of so many movies. But there is a crucial difference between sporting events, which are not works of art, and movies about sporting events, which are. That difference lies in the fact that sporting events are not the result of an integrated creative process proceeding from an artistic vision but of competing processes and a significant chance component. No one can (legally) envision and produce a specific outcome for a game between two major league teams, but a writer and director can produce a specific outcome for a movie about such a game. The experiences sporting events evoke are simply not specific to a single creative vision as our definition requires.

Civilized Art

Art is always capable of surprising us by revealing new dimensions we hadn't noticed before. An interesting example is recorded in National Geographic:

> Based on Yale University archaeologist Michael D. Coe's observation that the artistic style of many Maya funerary vessels resembled that of the codex artists, Dr. [Francis] Robiscek examined 186 vases and showed that such vessels put in proper sequence, can themselves be read like codices. The artists had used pottery - a material far more durable than bark - to portray the complex Maya mythology. . . (69, 464)

In this case Dr. Robiscek has shown that art which might have been regarded as 'merely decorative' or as being meaningful in a superficial way actually has a much deeper meaning when put into a proper context.

You will have noticed that our general definition of art included none of the traditional distinctions between the 'fine' arts and the decorative arts, art 'for its own sake' and the practical arts, or the pure and the industrial arts. That was because I do not believe any difference in kind can be made between the various arts, only differences in degree of significance and depth of meaning. These kinds of artificial distinctions have only led to more historical arguments which never should have arisen, such as whether architecture was to be considered a 'fine' art in view of the fact that buildings have a practical function. *All arts have a practical function.* Given a blank wall you can either paint the whole thing blue or have an artist paint a fresco on it. The result in either case is that a blank wall gets covered with something. That is practical. The fresco is art because of the significant way in which the artist covers the wall as opposed to the trivial way in which the house painter covers it (even though a plain blue wall, I hasten to add, can be elevated to art when it is part of an integrated interior design). Leroy Nieman once commented that New York City is the modern world's greatest art market because it has more walls to cover than any other place. (70)

It may not be obvious that music and literature have an equally important practical function but they do. They *occupy and structure time*, which is an extremely important function but one which can be also be performed by trivial pursuits. What makes music and literature art, again, is the significant way in which they perform that practical function. What about that moldy controversy over architecture? Architecture is the artistic development of the building craft, which is the craft of structuring space and, if we consider that buildings are not merely to be looked at or stood in but also walked through, it is also a way of structuring time. Architecture performs that complex set of functions significantly rather than routinely and the experience of being in and moving through the world's great edifices is one of the most meaningful of aesthetic experiences. Architecture was, in fact, *the master art of Western Civilization*, to the enrichment of which painting, sculpture, mosaic, landscaping and other arts were often devoted.

We now have before us the task of demonstrating that the practice and appreciation of art was approached in radically different ways in the four Civilizations and that the art of those civilizations was a transparent window on their mindsets. The arts are so many that I intend to restrict this demonstration principally to painting and sculpture but you will undoubtedly see as we go along that evidence can be mustered from all the arts with equal facility. The first thing to observe about civilized art is that the mindsets influenced it in two ways, *externally* and *internally*. The external influence was reflected in the *content* of art. Some of that content had to do with the elite themselves and the symbols of their power. This kind of self-aggrandizement had less to do with the mindset than with the nature of civilized men in general, although when the elite had their own grandeur portrayed, it was often with some deference to their place in the mythological scheme of things. A much more important subject matter of civilized art was the mythology itself. Art was foremost among the means of reinforcing and transmitting mythology. We have already seen that the mythologies were shaped by the civilized mindsets. That means that the content of art would likewise be shaped by the mindsets. It is fairly easy to demonstrate this external influence simply by reviewing *what* the artist chose to portray and what statement he made about it.

But the mindset exerts a more profound influence on art, the *internal* influence, which is not quite as easy to demonstrate. This influence results from the fact that the artist, if not actually a member of the elite in terms of power, was always a close associate of the elite and participated fully in its world view. His artistic vision, therefore, and the creative process by which he produced meaningful statements were also shaped at the deepest level by the mindset of his civilization. We can get fairly direct evidence of this from artists themselves and from aestheticians in the three civilizations of the Old World. But the evidence from Amerindic Civilization will be mostly indirect, as it will in other areas we will consider, because Amerindic Civilization never reached the point of consciously examining and evaluating its own works or institutions in the same way the other civilizations did.

Plate 1: Ceiling painting from the tomb of Ramses VI. On either side
the vault a panoply of Egyptian gods, each with his or h
distinctive form and hieroglyphic designation, is portraye

...neath overarching renditions of the skygoddess, Nut. The priesthood had
...parently convinced the pharoah not to slight any deity, however minor,
...his determination to insure his immortality.

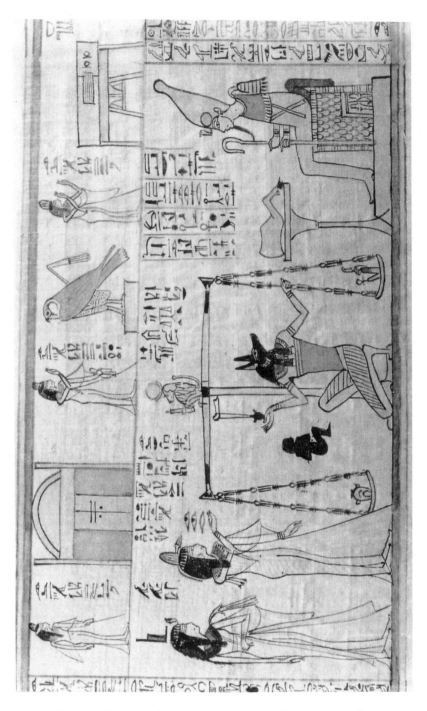

Plate 2: Anubis weighing the heart of the Princess Entiu-ny
before Osiris, Judge of the Dead. From the tomb of
Queen Meryet-Amun, at Bahri, Thebes.

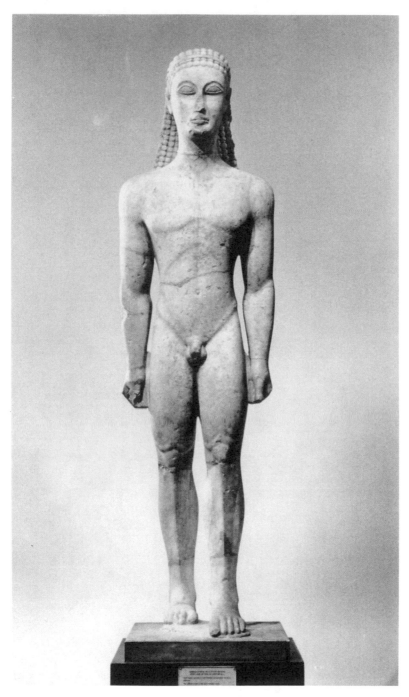

Plate 3. Kouros (honorary or memorial statue), ca. 600 B.C.

Plate 4. Hermes with the infant Dionysius.

Plate 5. Kailasanatha Temple at Elura (Ellora). A *sculpture* out of
the living rock! The elephant is life-sized.

Plate 6. Buddhist Chaitya Hall (meeting place) at Carle. Note the
freestanding *stupa* surmounted by parasol at far end.

Plate 7. The great *stupa* of Borobodur, central Java, ca. 800 A. D.
Aerial view from the southeast.

Plate 8: Chinese bronze tripod cauldron *(ding)*, Shang dynasty, 11th century B.C.,

Plate 9: Chinese bronze bird-shaped wine container *(Niao Zun)*,Shang dynasty, 12th-11th century B.C.

Plate 10. Kwan Yin (Guanyin), Tang Dynasty, late 8th cent.

Plate 11a. 19th century Chinese porcelain screen.
"Old Man Crossing Bridge with Stick in Hand."

Plate 11b. Center panel of 11a.

Plate 12. Sarcophagus Cover of Pacal at Palenque. Pacal, in the center, is entering the gaping jaws of the Earth Monster.

Plate 13. Coatlicue, the Aztec Mother Goddess and Goddess of Death.
Imagine yourself as an Aztec before this eight and a half
foot statue symbolizing the meaning of *your* life!

1. Solar Disk   2.Earth Monster

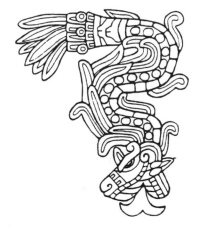

3.Feathered Serpent

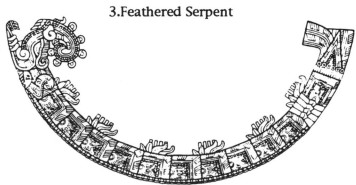

4.Fire Serpent

Plate 14: Aztec Emblems (after Pasztory)

Plate 15. Facade of the great temple of Quetzalcoatl at Teotihuacan. Note the alternating symbols of Quetzalcoatl, the Fire Serpent, and Tlaloc, the Water Deity.

Western Art: Vision of the Eternal

The period of time we are considering in discussing Occidental civilized art (or any other civilized activity) is the five thousand years from 3500 B.C. to 1500 A.D. When we think of the outstanding art of those fifty centuries, five venues come immediately to mind - Egypt, Greece, Byzantium, Renaissance Italy and 'Gothic' France. What common basis unites the art of such diverse societies? *A preoccupation with the eternal!*

'Eternal' has two meanings. It can mean 'everlasting' or 'beyond time.' To the Egyptians and the early Christians it meant the former. In an ancient [Egyptian] religious text, a deceased king asks of the creator-god, 'O Atum, what is my duration of life?' And the deity replies, 'Thou art destined for millions of millions of years, a lifetime of millions.' (71, 17) Over two thousand years later another writer would declare, 'For God so loved the world that He gave his only begotten Son, that whosoever believeth in Him shall not perish but have everlasting life.' (John 3: 16) As we have seen previously, 'everlasting life' was a solution to the tragic dilemma which stemmed from Western man's conception of himself and his world as mired in non-order while his mind was enamored of order. As we have also seen, everlasting life was not a free gift. It was linked to the idea of judgment from the earliest times. The judgment of the deceased's life by the Egyptian god, Osiris (Plate 2), was the direct antecedent of the Judgment Day passage from the Koran quoted in Chapter 3 and of Michelangelo's 'Last Judgment.' From first to last, Western Civilization was obsessed with overcoming human mortality. Mythology, theology and philosophy strove mightily to defy the inevitability of death, but it was art that gave Western man his most vivid experience of eternity.

Western artists dealt with the eternal in three ways:

1.By producing art works that were themselves intended to be imperishable;

2.By portraying the divine order of the world which guaranteed human triumph over death; and,

3.By depicting human subjects as embodiments of archetypes or ideals while diminishing their individuality.

Egyptian artists employed all three methods but the first method produced their earliest and most conspicuous achievements. Not only the pyramids but later temples to the gods and divine rulers where literally intended to last forever. An inscription on a temple to Amon erected by Amenhotep III at Thebes reads,

> Behold, the heart of his majesty was satisfied with making a very great monument; never has happened the like since the beginning. He made it as his monument for his father, Amon, lord of Thebes, making for him an august temple on the west of Thebes, *an eternal, everlasting fortress* of white sandstone, wrought with gold throughout; its floor is adorned with silver, all its portals with electrum...; it is made very wide and large, and *established forever.* (71, 120, *emphasis mine*)

The monumental art of Egypt impresses us even today. How much more significant an experience it must have produced in the people who shared the world view it represented. But much of the art of Egypt was not made to impress the Egyptian people, not even the nobles. Its most important 'observers' were intended to be the gods themselves, who alone could guarantee immortality. The tomb paintings, which often showed the deceased making offerings to the gods or recounted his good deeds during life, were sealed from public view and intended to be viewed only by the gods throughout eternity.

The practice of building pyramids gradually died out in the Middle Kingdom period (2134-1785 B.C.) but the desire for imperishable architecture was rekindled in the New Kingdom which began with the XVIIIth dynasty in 1557 B.C. This time art satisfied the desire in the form of temple complexes of astounding magnitude, such as those at Karnak and Luxor. In the New Kingdom, however, artists were increasingly influenced by theologians and attempted to convey the eternity experience through wall paintings portraying the divine order. A magnificent ceiling painting (Plate 1) from the tomb of Ramses VI depicts the confusing panoply of gods, each hieroglyphically identified, arrayed in ranks beneath the overarching body of Nut, the sky goddess. Portraits of pharaohs and nobles receiving the (favorable) judgment of Osiris (Plate 2) are common. From being eternal itself, Egyptian art turned increasingly to *portraying the eternal.*

Coming to the third way in which the Egyptian artist dealt with the eternal, you will recall we observed earlier in this chapter that most Egyptian art, particularly architecture and sculpture, lacks grace and beauty. It tends to be static and heavy. But it was effective. Generally oversized, frequently colossal, its purpose was to portray the essence of majesty or divinity. The Egyptian artist followed strict canons of what constituted aesthetic validity as did artists of other civilizations. As one writer puts it,

> In the Egyptian language, characteristically enough, there is no word for 'art' or 'artist'; a sculptor is denoted by a hieroglyph showing a bow-drill. Prime importance attaches to workmanship rather than to artistic imagination. The function which the sculptor had to perform left him no opportunity to develop an individual style; for he was not expected to express his subjective experience but *to reproduce an object of eternal value* in accordance with a definite schematic pattern. (72, 82, *emphasis mine*)

The point is well taken that the Egyptian artist was producing an object of 'eternal value', that is, an object which reflected an enduring type. In three thousand years of Egyptian art, while there were stylistic innovations from time to time, they were never radical by modern standards. For the most part the canons and customs were scrupulously observed. But the Egyptian's passion for order did not extend merely to reproducing the order demanded by theology. Gardner remarks about the great pyramid of Khufu at Gizeh,

> . . . without modern surveying instruments and machinery, and with only a knotted rope for laying out the huge base and only human labor to drag stones of two-and-one-half tons into place - so accurate is the work that the most delicate modern instrument can detect only about one-half inch of error in the measurement of one side. (65, 49)

This kind of meticulous attention to measurement stems from what I called the internal influence of the mindset. No external pressure dictated such precision.

These, then, were the three methods by which Egyptian art strove to impose order on the ultimate mystery of death and decay. The Egyptian was the only civilization in history which employed the first method, the creation of architectural monuments truly intended to be everlasting Of course, we know that intent was in vain, for all those great monuments have long since become ruins. It was, in fact, a fallen statue of Ramses II which inspired Shelley's poem, 'Ozymandias.' Subsequent Occidental civilizations built enduring buildings but no one ever seriously thought they were imperishable. We shall soon see how Christian art developed the other two methods but, first, let us turn to a civilization in which 'eternal' meant not 'everlasting' but 'timeless' - Greece.

The Greeks were a people of extraordinary intellectual energy and curiosity. Around 750 B.C. they were producing art of the so-called Geometric style which was clearly influenced by Minoan-Mycenean styles but which went a step further. The .art of the Geometric period was essentially an effort to portray the 'essence' of a thing (virtually an abstraction). By the seventh century B.C. the Greeks were experimenting with the Egyptian type of sculpture in the round but it did not take them long to transform the Egyptian style into something more typically Greek. The sixth century Kouros in Plate 3 is clearly influenced by Egyptian praxis on the one hand.

Note how the left leg with its thick ankles is pushed forward, the shoulders are squarely set, and the arms are held rigidly at the side. But the Kouros already departs from Egyptian stylization in its softer, more human rendering of the face and in the girdle of muscle around the waist which would typically be seen in the bodies of young Greeks who wrestled in the *palaestra* or competed on the athletic field.   Within another hundred and fifty years, the transformation of Greek sculpture was complete.   Sculptors were producing sensitively sublime statues of their gods and goddesses like the Hermes with the infant Dionysius (Plate 4), a work by the great Praxiteles.

It is sometimes said that the style of the Classic Period was 'naturalistic,' but that is a misnomer.   Greek art was *idealistic* rather than naturalistic.   It flowed from a mind which had learned to seek out the essential in the Geometric period and had developed an incomparable skill at sculpture in the Archaic period.   The Greek sculptor followed nature only to a point, then elevated it to express something timeless and true.   He did not make a god or goddess to look like a human being.   He made them look as they would look *if they took on human form*.   Even today they stir us with an admiration for the perfection they represent.

The Good, the True, the Beautiful - to the Greek mind they were somehow all one.   You could not truly seek or find one without seeking and finding the others.   The Greeks were aware that art was a powerful force which could produce experiences other than beauty. Socrates was especially suspicious of the power of music and poetry to debase the character but he was also very positive about the power of art, particularly sculpture and architecture, to ennoble the mind.   'We shall not appreciate his position,' says A. E. Taylor,

> . . . unless we understand quite clearly that he is in
> downright earnest with the consideration that the connexion
> between aesthetic taste and morality is so close that
> whatever tends to ennoble our aesthetic taste directly tends
> to elevate our character, and whatever tends to foster a

'taste' for the debased in art tends equally to deprave a man's whole moral being. . . [The] young 'guardian' [of Socrates' hypothetical Republic] is to be subjected from the first to the positive influences of lofty art of every description. . . The growing boy or girl is to live in an environment of beauty, and the appreciation of the beauty of the environment is expected to lead insensibly to appreciation of whatever is morally lovely and of good report in conduct and character. (73, 280)

But. for the Greek, the love of art - the ideal, the sublime - was more than merely ennobling. It was a unique path to immortality. The Greeks flirted with earlier ideas of judgment and immortality. Socrates discusses them in several Platonic dialogues, such as *Gorgias, Phaedo* and *The Laws* but such notions seem to have had little impact on Greek civilization and played no part in Greek art. In discussing Plato's *Symposium,* Taylor says,

The true 'life for a man' is to live in the contemplation of the 'sole and absolute Beauty', by comparison with which all the 'beauties' which kindle desire in mankind are so much dross. Only in intercourse with It will the soul give birth to a spiritual offspring which is no 'shadow' but veritable 'substance,' because it is now at last 'espoused' to very and substantial reality. This and only this is *the true achieving of 'immortality.'* (73, 230)

The 'glory that was Greece' lasted very briefly. Its greatest achievements occurred between 600 B.C. and 300 B.C. But it bequeathed to Occidental Civilization one of its most important treasures - *the vision of the Ideal.* That vision, expressed in art and philosophy, gave Western man an alternate conception of eternity, the conception of a timeless realm of perfection by contemplation of which the soul could reach for immortality.

The spirit of Greece was abruptly killed in the sixth century A.D. when the emperor Justinian forbade the pursuit of philosophy in Athens. Earlier in that same century Justinian had decreed the building, in Constantinople (formerly Byzantium), of what was, up to its time, the greatest of all Christian churches - Hagia Sophia, the

Church of Holy Wisdom. Built between 532 and 537 A.D., Hagia
Sophia represents a kind of religious architecture quite different from
any of its Occidental predecessors. Both Egyptian and Greek
temples were essentially built to be seen from the *outside*. The
religious celebrants who attended them gathered in the forecourts or,
as in the case of the Parthenon, on the Acropolis in front of the
temple. In the case of Hagia Sophia, on the contrary, the interior
was what counted.

What the Byzantine architect and artist aimed at was to create a
building for the faithful, the interior of which would be a self
-contained Christian universe. The sheer vastness of Hagia Sophia
declares the glory of God. Its great dome is 180 feet high and 150
feet across. Nor was its statement left to its vastness:

> The decoration of *Santa Sophia* [Hagia Sophia latinized] . .
> is filled with meaning. The characters or episodes move in
> hieratic succession from the more human scenes on earth,
> scenes relating to the life of the Virgin and of Christ, through
> the figures of angels, saints and prophets on the walls, to the
> four cherubim in the pedentives, and finally to the
> Pantocrator [Christ as Sovereign Ruler of the Universe], in
> the crown of the dome: 'Know and behold that I am.' Thus
> the movement of lines and volumes is paralleled by a literary
> movement of ever-increasing sanctity and awe culminating in
> the symbol of the heart and mystery of the Christian faith.
> (65, 260)

The idea of the self-contained Christian universe is further
explained by Pierre Francastel,

> For Byzantium the problem of place and time was a well-
> defined one. All representation was linked to the
> Christological dogma upon which the social hierarchy of the
> universe was based. The function of painting was therefore to
> materialize the dimensions of a space whose attributes were
> entirely determined by divine law. There was, so to speak, no
> figurative space: the space represented was actual, whether
> in the case of the walls and vaults of a church or on the
> surface of a picture. . . When a Byzantine painter decorated a
> church, he laid out his symbols in an order that reproduced
> the supernatural arrangement of the world. (74, 190)

Byzantine art, like Egyptian, devoted itself to portraying the eternal order that governed the world. It is also well-known that the sacred art of Byzantium employed a rigid set of conventions which made its painted saints, Virgins and Christs instantly recognizable, a repetition of the third artistic method used in Egypt.

Since this is not a history of art we do not need to consider every period of Occidental art but a few remarks about the Renaissance and Gothic periods are in order. The Renaissance is unique because it drew together in its art the two meanings of eternity, the everlasting and the timeless ideal. This is especially well illustrated in the work of Michelangelo. The Sistine ceiling is a work portraying the divine order as set forth in Genesis. In that sense its function is linked to that of Egypt, Byzantium and the Middle Ages. But Michelangelo departed radically from the conventional representation of sacred figures. Nor are the figures he painted 'naturalistic.' What he did was to adopt the Greek method of portraying the ideal. God the Creator as we see Him on the Sistine ceiling is not a humanization of God. It is God *as He would be if he appeared in human form*. Adam is, of course, human but he is the first, the ideal human, Adam as Michelangelo conceives God would have created him. Vasari says of Michelangelo,

> He would construct an ideal shape out of nine, ten and even twelve different heads, for no other purpose than to obtain a certain grace of harmony and composition which is not to be found in the natural form, and would say that the artist must have his measuring tools, not in the hand, but in the eye, because the hands do but operate, it is the eye that judges. (75, 184)

In this preoccupation with the ideal Michelangelo wedded Greek and Christian art as Thomas Aquinas had long before done with philosophy.

The Italian Renaissance masters deplored the great French and German cathedrals which made their appearance in the twelfth and thirteenth centuries. The cathedrals lacked the classical restraint so much admired by architects like Bramante, prompting the Italians to refer to them by the pejorative term, 'Gothic.' Nevertheless the Gothic cathedrals rank among the most remarkable achievements of world architecture. Although most of their elements had precursors in the Romanesque period, those stupendous buildings with their soaring vaults, towering spires, and flying buttresses are a monument to the zeal of master artisans inspired by religion. A mighty focus of Christian life and faith in transalpine Europe, their great height dwarfed the surrounding towns and their towers could be seen for miles, an everpresent reminder to the faithful. They served as the venue not only for daily mass and all the high celebrations of the Christian calendar but also for the miracle and morality plays which played such an important role in the life of the medieval community.

We noted above how artists had used the interior walls and ceilings of Christian churches to illustrate a self-contained world of religious images utilizing mosaic or paint. Those iconographic interiors were lit either by artificial light or by windows made of a material which would keep out the elements. The use of glass for windows gradually succeeded the use of translucent materials such as alabaster in early Christian churches. Not only clear but colored glass was available and the latter was installed in many of the great churches such as Hagia Sophia in Constantinople.

But in Northern Europe, in the ninth and tenth centuries, artisans devised a new technique which was to revolutionize the presentation of Christian iconography - *figured stained glass.* When the Gothic cathedrals were being built in the 12th and 13th century, vast areas of wall space were no longer needed for murals. Huge openings were made in their massive walls and the openings were filled with glowing murals made of glass. Instead of admitting merely white light or colored light the cathedral windows blazoned forth the images of Christ and the saints, of prophets and scriptures. Those windows must have seemed a miracle to the faithful upon whose gaze they fell. The mighty 'rose' windows of that most awesome of all Gothic cathedrals, Chartres, are more than forty feet in diameter and with the lancet windows beneath them they form a composition nearly eighty feet high. According to Enrico Castelnuova,

> . . . the glass windows of [Gothic] churches, which allowed the light to pass through and offered protection from storms, were likened to, or actually identified with, the prophets, the Apostles, the doctors of the church, or the Holy Scriptures, in short, with all that enlightens the faithful and shields them from evil. In his *Rationale Divinorum Officiorum* Gulielmus Durandus of Mende wrote: 'The glass windows in a church are Holy Scriptures which expel the wind and the rain, that is all things hurtful, but transmit the light of the true Sun, that is God, into the hearts of the faithful . . . (76, 354)

The Gothic glaziers did not intend merely to produce an emotional or aesthetic experience as twentieth century stained glass artists often do. Their intent was to present the divine Christian order in all its glory. The windows were didactic and instructive, living images to largely illiterate congregations. One cannot but be impressed in Rome by the bright shaft of white light which streams through the open dome of the Pantheon. But that light is the pagan light of the Sun God. The True Sun of whom Gulielmus speaks is not the Sun God. His symbol is therefore not natural white light but light ordered by the scriptures and the hagiography through which He revealed his plan for the world. What the Gothic masters had achieved in their stained glass was a double transformation. On the one hand they changed a nearly universal symbol of paganism, the Sun, into a source of illumination for the Christian message. And on the other, they transformed clear light, another nearly universal symbol of mysticism (the 'clear light of the Void') into a vehicle of divine order. Whether or not their achievement pleased the Italian Renaissance masters, it was a triumph for the Western mind.

It has no doubt occurred to you by now that artistic creativity in the Western world is analogous to God's creativity as we encountered it in Chapter 3, that is, the transformation of non-order into order.

In his book, *Genius and Creativity,* Milton C. Nahm calls this analogy between the artist and God the 'great analogy.' Although there have been innumerable analogies and metaphors applied to artists, Nahm says, 'the analogy of the artist to God is unique.' (77, 64) He goes on to make a very cogent exposition of the difference it makes whether one conceives the artist's powers as analogous to that of the Hebraic-Christian Creator or the Maker of Plato's *Timaeus.* But that distinction, while interesting, is not relevant here. What is important, as we turn to Indic art, is remembering that the Occidental artist's function, like that of the Occidental God, is to create something ordered and superior out of something less ordered and inferior. The task of the Indic artist, as we shall see, is quite different.

Indic Art: From the Many to the One

If you want to immerse yourself in the look of Indic art there is no better survey of it than Sherman E. Lee's *A History of Far Eastern Art* (which has the additional advantage of also providing an excellent review of Chinese art). Westerners are more familiar with Chinese art than with Indic because Chinese art and art motifs have long been used in the West for decoration. Indic art, on the other hand, is inextricably bound to mythology. A simplistic way to demonstrate that Indic art is shaped by the Indic mindset would be to say that since the art portrays the mythology and we have already shown that the mythology reflects the mindset, then we can deduce that the art reflects the mindset. True as that may be it is not a very satisfying demonstration since it involves only what I called the *external* influence of the mindset on art through its subject matter. To make a really effective demonstration of our point we need to describe how the Indic mindset also impresses itself on the artist *internally* and affects his choice of media and methods.

Suppose we begin by applying the 'great analogy' (between the Creator and the artist) to Indic art. To do this we must first recall that, to the Indic mind, creation was not a matter of forming order out of chaos but of the proliferation or generation of order out of the primal All. Modified to fit that understanding, the 'great analogy' would then imply that the Indic artist's task was to bring forth forms from a material substrate which not only symbolized but was a real connection to the All. The forms so created would not be embodiments of eternal types or ideals as in Western art but manifestations of the All, luring the soul back to it. The Indic artist would bring forth the Many from the One but, as with all things Indic, with the purpose of leading from the Many back to the One.

We will find evidence for this hypothesis from two sources. First, we will look to the art historian for his opinion as to what special characteristics display themselves in the great art works of India. In this respect, Sherman Lee's comments are invaluable. Second, we will listen to the voice of Indic aesthetic theory, especially as expounded by Ananda K. Coomaraswamy.

Perhaps the greatest art work in Indic history is that shown in Plate 5, the great temple complex of Kailasanatha at Elura (Ellora) in central India. The complex is a forest of columns and shrines reaching a height of nearly a hundred feet. Bearing in mind that the statues of Abu Simbel are sixty-seven feet high and the massive columns of the Amon temple at Karnak sixty-nine may prepare us somewhat to appreciate the colossal magnitude of Kailasanatha. The elephants are lifesized and the people in the picture are dwarfed by their surroundings. Yet you will be correct if you say that there are larger buildings in the world than this Indian temple.

But Kailasanatha is not a building! It is a sculpture!

Although the exact dates are not certain, it was certainly the work of at least a hundred years (between the eighth and ninth centuries A.D.) to hollow out a great bay in the surrounding escarpment and carve Kailasanatha's monuments from the living rock in the process. As Lee says,

> The Indian genius is primarily sculptural.   There is no question that if one were to name the great sculptural styles of the world, one would have to include the Indian. If it is true that the Indian genius is primarily sculptural, it would seem to be confirmed as well by their architecture, as Medieval Hindu architecture demonstrates. The Indian does not conceive of architecture as primarily enclosing space. He conceives of it as a mass to be modeled, to be formed, and to be looked at and sensed as a sculpture. Perhaps, then the practice of carving in living rock is understandable. It is possible that primal ideas of fertility are involved, of penetrating the womb of the mountain, or the desire for security in the womb. (17, 90)

I have one problem with this passage.   At Elura we are witnessing a highly developed, civilized art.   To suggest that the practice of carving in living rock is attributable to 'primal ideas of fertility' or 'the desire for security in the womb' at that advanced level seems discordant to me. There are, of course, often many levels of symbolism in civilized art but the art of Elura reaches far beyond the primitive chthonic level. We have to remember that the ultimate source of fertility, the primal womb, to the Indic mind, was *that first All out of which all things were generated.*   At the civilized level, it was the Universal Soul, the first origin of things, which the living rock represented to the Indic artist and when he carved and modeled that rock he was repeating the process of creation.   In another context, Lee adds,

> A further and significant characteristic of Hinduism is the concept of macrocosm and microcosm, of the desire to have the artist represent on a small scale the huge scale of the universe. For example, the Kailasanatha Temple at Elura . . is not simply a massive stone cutting, but an attempt on the part of the architect and the sculptor to visualize the universe in a monument ninety-six feet high, and to orient and build it in such a way that it becomes a magical structure, one which contains the world within its compass. Thus the orientation of the plan is to the Four Directions, and in the cell of the

temple - the basic unit for individual worship in the Hindu faith - there was planted a copper box containing 'wealth of the earth, stones, gems, herbs, metals, roots, and soils.' At this time the Earth Goddess was invoked: 'O thou who maintainest all the beings, O beloved, decked with hills for breasts, O ocean girt, O Goddess, O Earth, shelter this Germ.' This, in the words of some Hindu texts, inseminates the temple and gives it life.(17, 175)

But again, let us look beyond the image of the Earth Goddess just as we did the image of the womb. As Lee himself tells us, 'In theory, and to the most initiated and adept of the Hindu faith, the image is not a magical fetish, worshiped in itself, but stands for something higher - *a manifestation of the Supreme Being.* ' (17, 174) If this is so, and an endless list of authorities will tell us it is, then the Earth Goddess which gives the sculptured monument life is a manifestation of the Supreme Being. It is the ultimate '*thou who maintainest all the beings,*' not merely a chthonic deity, to which the artist is connected as he brings forth forms from the stone.

Recall that I said at the beginning of this section that 'the 'great analogy' would then imply that the Indic artist's task was to bring forth forms from a material substrate which not only symbolized but was a real connection to the All.' Lee says of Kailasanatha, '*The whole complex must be imagined as a sculpture - or rather as architecture in reverse, with the forms created by removing stone to 'release' them.*' (17, 193, *emphasis mine*) We have here an entirely different approach to art and the material base of art than we found in the West. The Occidental artist, so to speak, removed his material from its natural context and created a new form in isolation from its origin, a form answerable only to the ideal or type which informed it. The Indic artist, on the other hand, released his forms reverently from their matrix, aware that it was only through the matrix and the All to which it was connected that those forms had any meaning or existence.

It should not be supposed that the rock-cut character of Kailasanatha was unusual. On the contrary, it was the most typical

mode of Indic monumental art. Plate 6 shows the interior of a
Buddhist assembly hall or *chaitya* at Karle (Carli) which dates from
the second century A.D. The columns and vaulting of Karle do not
support a roof. They are carved from the walls of a manmade cave a
hundred and fifty feet deep and forty-five feet high. At the far end of
the nave is a hemispherical mound called a *stupa* set on a cylindrical
base. The *stupa* played an important part in Indic monumental art
and underwent substantial development over the centuries. When
Buddha was dying, he is said to have instructed that his body be
cremated and the ashes be distributed across the land and buried in
earth mounds to commemorate his *paranirvana* or final release from
the cycle of birth and death. Those reliquary mounds were the
legendary origin of the *stupa* although archaeologically they recall pre-
Buddhist burial structures. In the chaitya hall the *stupa* was
freestanding so that the devotee could walk around it. Other *stupas*
were built in the open, often in high places overlooking broad
stretches of land. These *stupas*, like the ones in *chaitya* halls, were
solid mounds with no accessible interior.

> Around the mound proper, a path was laid out so that the
> pilgrim to the holy spot could make a ritual, counterclockwise
> circumambulation of the *stupa*, walking the Path of Life
> around the World Mountain. This path around the *stupa*
> was enclosed by a railing pierced by gates at each of the Four
> Directions. The railing and the four gates provided the
> occasions for rich sculptural decoration. The *stupa*, like so
> much Indian architecture, is not so much a constructed space-
> enclosing edifice as it is a sculpture - a large, solid mass
> designed to be looked at and to be used as an image or
> diagram of the Cosmos. (17, 184)

It seems clear that the mound of the *stupa* had an intensely
symbolic character. It was the All from which all things came and,
since for the Buddhist it represented Buddha's *paranirvana*, it was
also a symbol of the All as that to which all things eventually return.
In time, not only the railing and gates around *stupas* standing in the
open were richly carved but the mound itself became the substrate

for epic devotional imagery based on the *Jatakas* (stories of previous incarnations of the Buddha), scenes from the life of Buddha and the typically Indic proliferation of Buddhas and bodhisattvas which inhabited the heavens of Mahayana Buddhism. Nowhere was this tendency carried to such an incredible extreme as in the *stupa* of Borobodur (Plate 7) in Indonesia, of which Lee says,

> The greatest example of Buddhist art in Southeast Asia and Indonesia is certainly the Great Stupa of Borobodur, situated on the central Dieng Plateau of Java . . . The monument, carefully preserved and restored by Dutch archaeologists, is a fantastic microcosm, reproducing the universe as it was known and imagined in Mahayana Buddhist theology. The monument dates from about A.D. 800, and apparently was built in a relatively short period of time -- a colossal achievement. It is approximately 136 yards long on each side and some 105 feet high. There are in all more than ten miles of relief sculpture. . . Borobodur is, then, a magic monument, an attempt to reconstruct the universe on a small scale. The interior is rubble faced with the carved volcanic lava stones. The pilgrim enters the magical structure and performs the rite of circumambulation, which figuratively recreates his previous lives and foreshadows his future lives. While pursuing his pilgrimage, he sees the reliefs of the previous lives of the Buddha, the Life of the Buddha, and those depicting the various Heavens. (17, 128)

Although this is an excellent description of Borobodur, I am again uncomfortable with Lee's repeated use of the word 'magical' in reference to monuments like it and Kailasanatha. They were products of high civilized religion and were essentially devotional and ritualistic, not magical in any strict sense of the word. I can testify that even to a non-Buddhist, to walk the miles of relief-covered open corridors of Borobodur as my wife and I did, then to emerge at the top amid the concentric rings of hollow *stupas* and the tranquil figures of meditating Buddhas and to look out over the sweeping vista of central Java is an awe-inspiring experience. It is truly a spiritual journey from the sea of plurality and change to the realm of peace and timelessness.

To the Western mind there is one striking or even shocking
feature of both Hindu and Buddhist art That is the inclusion of
sensual figures, male and female, and sexual symbols in essentially
religious works.   Both Hindu and Buddhist places of worship
frequently portray voluptuous female and virile male figures.   The
two are sometimes combined in a *mithuna,* a couple in sexual
embrace. As if that were not enough, completely realistic sculptures
of the *lingam* (penis) is an accepted symbol of the god Shiva. (For
more on this, see Chapter 8) No other civilization countenanced the
sensuality in its *monumental* art that the Indic did. It is virtually
nonexistent in both Occidental and Sinic monuments. Some writers
suggest that it was the Indic way of relating high spiritual content to
earlier, more primitive mythology in much the same way that local
cults in many countries have been incorporated into and transformed
by Roman Catholicism.   Lee says, 'As images on a religious
monument the Yakshi and Yaksha [female and male deities]
certainly served as supports for Buddhism, for the lesser folk, the
illiterate, the great mass of people who but dimly understood the
significance of the teachings of the Buddha, could be comforted when
they saw the local tutelary deities, male and female, welcoming them
to the austere and abstract *stupa*.' (17, 89) I would find this
assessment easier to accept if we found the sensual-spiritual
coexistence mostly in early Indian art as a transitional stage but, in
fact, we find it in every period and it must have had the full
acceptance of the Indic mind. It is easier to explain if we understand
that to the Indic mind all life was linked together in the great cycle of
existence, from the deepest hells to the highest heavens. Sensuality
was no less a part of that cycle than sainthood. The Indic mind was
deeply aware of the enormous energy of life but it did not, like Freud,
attribute that energy to libido or sexual drive. It viewed libido as
only one manifestation of the vast outflowing energy of the All. The
Indic artist's sensual figures burst with that cosmic energy but they
are also part of a great series of figures which, taken as a whole, are

meant to help the isolated self find its way back to the Universal Self.

To summarize, Indic art does indeed seem to proceed in opposite directions from Western art. While the Western artist adumbrated the eternal order through the portrayal of ideal or eternal types, the Indic artist portrayed images which come from and lead back to the ultimate non-order which is the source of all things. While the Western architect erected soaring churches which imitated the vault of Heaven and the heavenly cohorts ruled by an ultimate God who created order from chaos, the Indic sculptor-architect carved his microcosm from the living rock which symbolized the ultimate One who generated order from and called it back to Itself. However, all these conclusions about Indic art are based on an interpretation of certain unique characteristics which art historians ascribe to Indic art. What evidence is there that Indic artists think this way or that Indic aesthetics views art this way?

The best source we can turn to for such evidence is the work of the late Ananda K. Coomaraswamy, former Curator of Indian Art at the Boston Museum of Fine Arts. Coomaraswamy was a powerful advocate of the notion that Indian and Chinese (and, for that matter, Medieval Christian) art had a basic unity and common philosophy. Since that approach is antithetical to the one taken in this chapter, I obviously disagree with it. But since others much more adequate to the task than I have thoroughly criticized that aspect of Coomaraswamy's thought, I will simply draw on his unparalleled grasp of Indian aesthetics.

First, as to the artistic process itself, Coomaraswamy writes,

> The whole process, up to the point of manufacture, belongs to the established order of personal devotions, in which worship is paid to an image mentally conceived. . .; in any case, the principle involved is that true knowledge of an object is not obtained by merely empirical observation or reflex registration . . . , but only when the knower and known, seer and seen, meet in an act transcending distinction . . . To worship any Angel in truth one must become the Angel:

'whoever worships a divinity as other than the self, thinking
'He is one, and I another,' knows not' . . . (78, 35)

We are being told here that artistic creation begins (and
continues right through the execution of the art work) as an act of
worship or Yoga during which the artist has to concentrate on the
subject so completely that he becomes absorbed in or united with it.

> To generalize, whatever object may be the artist's chosen or
> appointed theme becomes for the time being the single object
> of his attention and devotion; and only when the theme has
> become for him an immediate experience can it be stated
> authoritatively from knowledge. (ibid.)

This union of the artist's consciousness and his subject matter is
necessary in order to achieve two principles which are considered
paramount in Indic art. First is *sadrsya,* 'visual correspondence,'
which does not mean correspondence between the art work and the
model but between the 'mental and sensational factors in the work'
itself. In other words, the artist has to get himself so absorbed in
the essential meaning of his subject that when he sculpts or paints it
the meaning and the appearance of the work will exactly correspond.
The second principle of Indic art is *pramana*. *Pramana* is also a
kind of correspondence but not, like *sadrsya,* a correspondence self-
contained in the art work but rather a correspondence between the
aesthetic design and a norm or 'inwardly known model.' 'Thus,' says
our authority,

> . . .the idea of *pramana* implies the existence of types or
> archetypes, which might at first thought be compared with
> those of Plato and the derived European tradition. But
> whereas Platonic types are types of being, external to the
> conditioned universe and thought of as absolutes reflected in
> phenomena, Indian types are those of sentient activity or
> functional utility conceivable only in a contingent world.
> (78, 41)

This is a quite clear statement of the fact that Indic art does not follow the Occidental method of portraying the ideal or the eternal type. The author states elsewhere that 'we should err equally in supposing that Asiatic art represents an 'ideal' world, a world 'idealized' in the popular (sentimental, religious) sense of the words, that is, perfected or remodeled nearer to the heart's desire; which were it so might be described as a blasphemy against the witness of Perfect Experience, and a cynical depreciation of life itself.' (78, 37) It is not clear to me why Coomaraswamy qualifies 'ideal' with the adjectives, 'popular,' 'sentimental' and 'religious.' He has already ruled the Platonic ideal out of Indic art so it seems certain that the representation of an ideal world in *any* sense is foreign to 'Asiatic' (i.e., Indic) art.

Getting back to *pramana* , Coomaraswamy describes it as a kind of aesthetic conscience:

> Just as conscience is externalized in rules of conduct or the principles of thought in logic, so aesthetic *pramana* finds expressions in rules. . ., or canons of proportion. ., proper to different types, and in the *laksanas* of iconography and cultivated taste, prescribed by authority and tradition; and only that art 'which, accords with canonical standards. . . is truly lovely, none other, forsooth!'. . . As to the necessity for such rules, contingent as they are by nature, and yet binding in a given environment, this follows from the imperfection of human nature as it is in itself. (78, 41)

Now let us recall that, according to Coomaraswamy, Indic art is a form of yoga, a spiritual act which involves a union between self and subject matter. The more that spiritual unification is developed the less rules, principles and canons are required and, ultimately,

> . . .a condition of spontaneity. . . outside of and above ascertained rules, though not against them, can be imagined. . . But if the liberated being (*jivanmukta*) or saint in a state of grace is thus free to act without deliberation as to duty, it is because for him there no longer exists a separation of self and not-self . . . All art thus tends toward a perfection in which pictorial and formal elements are not merely

reconciled, but completely identified. At this distant but ever
virtually present point all necessity for art disappears. . .
(78, 43)

This is a remarkable statement. It depicts the Indic artist as
involved in a spiritual endeavor in which he tries to match the
meaning and the representation of his subject (formal and pictorial
elements), trying to *see* the meaning and following traditional rules
and canons until he reaches a point at which he *does see* the meaning
and knows that it is the Oneness between himself and all subjects.
At that point he no longer needs art because the perception of duality
on which art is based no longer exists.

But what the artist has done for himself, he does in the same
way for those who observe his work with *proper preparation and
devotion*. The latter is quite important in Indic aesthetics.

Aesthetic experience is thus only accessible to those
competent. . . Competence depends on purity or singleness . .
. of heart and on an inner character or habit of obedience. . .
tending to aversion of attention from external phenomena;
this character and habit, not to be acquired by mere
learning, but either innate or cultivated, depends on an ideal
sensibility . . . and the faculty of self-identification . . . with
the forms . . . depicted . . . *Just as the original intuition arose
from a self-identification of the artist with the appointed
theme, so aesthetic experience, reproduction, arises from a self-
identification of the spectator with the presented matter;
criticism repeats the process of creation.* (78, 60, *emphasis
mine*)

With that I believe we can consider my thesis about Indic art
sufficiently well established. The Indic artist produces a multiplicity
of images but the thrust of his creativity is that each of those images
shall lead back to the divine One out of which all images came.
What Mindset Theory predicted, Coomarawamy confirms:

It is of the essence of [Indic] art to bring back into order
[oneness] the multiplicity of Nature, and it is in this sense
that [the artist] 'prepares all creatures to return to God.
(78, 45)

Chinese Art: The Way of Nature

I remarked earlier in this chapter that there are some eras in which art is called upon to do little else than create beauty, that is, to produce art works which are sheer delights to the senses and the mind. Throughout Chinese history a great deal of artistic energy was always put into production of the beautiful. In some periods, of course - the T'ang, Sung and Ming Dynasties, for example - that production was more notably lavish than in others. The Sinic preoccupation with beauty seems to have burgeoned in the last phase of the Chou Dynasty, between 600 and 222 B.C.

The Late Chou period was a time of great civil strife in China. The Chinese themselves called the years between 481 and 221 B.C. the period of Warring States. But intellectually and spiritually the Late Chou was probably the most creative period in their history. It was the era of the great sages - Confucius, Mo-tzu, Lao-tzu, Mencius - whose thoughts embodied the Sinic mindset for all succeeding generations. The wisdom of the sages not only laid the groundwork for the Chinese mastery of statesmanship, it created the guidelines for Chinese art as well.

There was a substantial tradition of art in China before the age of the sages. The earliest dynasty, the Shang, which commenced around 1500 B.C. produced impressive stone work, pottery and, most notable and most valued by Chinese collectors, the famous bronzes (Plates 8 and 9). The bronzes were small ceremonial vessels of many different shapes and functions cast in pottery molds. They were highly prized by their owners and held in great reverence. As for their appearance, Helen Gardner says, 'The decorative motifs are similar on all the bronzes: highly conventionalized representations of dragons, cicadas, snakes, birds, or animals connected with an agricultural people and undoubtedly symbolic in their formative period.' (65, 211) One has to wonder just how far back that formative period went. Sherman Lee sees a possible connection

between Shang decor and 'Northern' or Siberian geometric
decoration.' Lee also makes another interesting observation. He
describes the 'unique quality of Shang art' as 'a combination of
elegant and refined detail with tremendously powerful silhouettes
and shapes that contribute to an effect that is, on the whole,
frightening. We are inspired with awe and terror when looking at
these beasts with gaping mouths, and at these birds of prey.' (17,
32) What strikes me when I look at a vessel like the tripod cauldron
(ding) in Plate 8, its side covered with an 'ogre mask,' is how
reminiscent it is of Mesoamerican stone reliefs. Unless something is
grossly wrong with current scholarship, Shang Chinese had no
contact with pre-Columbian Americans but the ancestors of both did
have a common connection many thousands of years earlier - in
Siberia.

Before we consider the meaning of endemic Chinese art in the
tradition of the great sages, it should be mentioned that Mahayana
Buddhism had an important influence on art in China. It was the
principle stimulus for the development of sculpture in the round.
Beginning in the fourth century A.D., Chinese sculptors faithfully
copied Indian styles. But, as we have seen earlier, the Chinese mind
profoundly transformed Buddhism to suit its own standards,
standards which were formulated in the age of the sages. The same
kind of transformation was responsible for the change in Buddhist
art from Indic to Sinic. For example, the Chinese replaced the
austere *stupa* of early Buddhism, which we saw developed into the
colossal world mountain of Borobodur, with the *pagoda*. The exact
function of *pagodas* is uncertain. Perhaps, like *stupas*, they were
commemorative monuments or shrines for wayfarers, perhaps also a
highly visible way of earning merit for their builders. In origin, the
pagoda is really an extension of the symbolic tiered parasol which
you can see atop the *stupa* at Karle in Plate 6. However, in China it
became a tall, graceful tower with many tiers - as many as thirteen
- which were set in the landscape like beacons which could be seen

for miles. When it came to Buddhist sculpture, within a few hundred years the Chinese had discarded virtually everything Indic and created the delicate and beautiful, altogether Chinese, style of the T'ang Dynasty (618-907 A.D.). It is the latter style, exemplified by the elegant Kuan-yin (Guanyin) in Plate 10, which has so often been copied and so well received in the West.

Michael Sullivan puts the case for the Sinicization of Buddhist art very clearly,

> China, it is clear, was forced to adopt the language of Indian Buddhist sculpture, not only because her own sculptural tradition was unable to meet the challenge, but also because it was essential that 'authentic' imported images be copied as closely as possible if they were to be considered efficacious. Here there was no choice. Nevertheless, without any significant sacrifice of iconographic requirements, China did succeed in imposing her own aesthetic upon the Indian model: first in the startlingly flat and linear sculpture of the late fifth and early sixth centuries, and again from the mid-T'ang onwards. While in the first instance the linear flatness proclaims a total victory for the Chinese brush line, in the second the Chinese line is used to convey an Indian feeling of plasticity. In both cases the crucial factor is the influence on sculpture of the ideals and techniques of Chinese painting. (79, 226)

Although from time to time the Indic mindset exerted an influence on Chinese art through Buddhism, it never gained the upper hand in the greatest of Chinese art forms, the one that also most clearly exemplifies the Sinic mindset - painting.

> In China, painting, and more especially landscape-painting, is mistress of the arts. That this should be so seems not unnatural when we consider that one of the aims of Chinese philosophy and religion has always been to discover the workings of the universe and to attune man's actions to them. A Chinese painting, therefore, not only embodies the visible forms and forces of nature, but also displays the painter's understanding of their operation. His purpose is to present the subtle and complex forces of nature as harmoniously interacting, to show man in his true relationship to her, and to convey the life that is in all things by means of the springing vitality of his brushwork. In a sense, therefore, every picture, however slight, is a general-

ized philosophical, or rather metaphysical statement, even though it may be inspired by a particular place or memory. For the painter is not concerned with individual events, or with the accidents of time and place. (79, 193)

Lee calls landscape painting 'one of the most significant contributions of China to the art of the world' and states that 'few can deny the unique characteristics of Chinese landscape painting.' (17, 268) These 'unique characteristics' are apparent in the painted porcelain screen shown in Plates 11a and 11b. Its title, 'Old man crossing bridge with stick in hand,' derives from the larger central panel. Note the delightfully detailed little woodland vignettes in the foreground of the panels. Bent as he is, the old man obviously has only a short way to go for food and rest in the neat little house. There is something about this idyllic scene which pulls you into it. You don't have to be Chinese to want to walk through the woods, cross the little bridge and perhaps, after a time, take tea in that fragile house. The screen is not hoary with age but it is over a hundred years old. My wife and I acquired it in China some years ago. Whenever the cares of the world or the stress of my work get me down I simply stand or, preferably, sit in front of the screen and look at it. My mind is drawn into those woods and I can feel what it is like to walk over that simple bridge or sit quietly in the little fishing boat. (Chinese painters were very fond of little fishing boats.)

What the screen first accomplishes is to refresh my cluttered, disordered mind with a vision of pure, simple order. But looking now above the foreground I see mountains (actually the same mountain, Pearl Mountain, seen from several perspectives). But the mountains are not painted in the same detail as the foreground. It is not that they are simply suggested or incomplete. They are intentionally painted to be mysterious, to leave everything to the imagination. Nature, to the Sinic mind, could not be encompassed in a simple woodland scene. That was a part of Nature, to be sure, but the painter never lets us forget that mystery (non-order) is just as much a part of Nature. This is the significance of the mist that partially obscures the mountains. We are invited to enter the mist just as we were invited to the woodland. Frequently, Chinese painters would put paths on their mountains, paths which, as likely as not, would turn a corner and vanish into the mist. This small screen is a statement about life, that order (the familiar) is always balanced with non-order (the mysterious).

Chinese landscape painting thus invites us to be refreshed by its simple order but then erases boredom by its inherent mystery. Says Sullivan,

> The Chinese painter's aim is always to present a view of the world that is satisfying and spiritually refreshing; consequently only themes which carry this message would he consider worthy of his brush. He would regard with horror the rapes, executions, and massacres which, whether of religious inspiration or not, we are trained to contemplate as works of art; for to him art is indivisible, and our Western ability to admire colour, form, and composition in a picture without being in any way affected by distasteful subject-matter implies, if not a corrupt view of the world, then at least a dangerously fragmented one. (79, 196)

I think this latter 'Western ability' is an outcome of what I have called the 'Sugar-coated Pill' conception of art, the notion that you can separate the 'form' of an artwork from its content and call the former 'beautiful' even though the latter may be evil or grim. It *is* a dangerously fragmented view.

The Chinese never developed extensive aesthetic theories any more than they did metaphysical ones. They were outspoken critics and their criticism implied a highly developed aesthetic sense but they did little to codify that sense. The most famous general pronouncement on aesthetics were the 'six principles' of Hsieh Ho, a painter and critic who lived around 500 A.D. Sullivan translates the principles as follows:

1. Spirit-consonance and life-movement;
2. The 'bone method' in the use of the brush;
3. Conformity to the shapes of objects in nature;

4. Conformity to their colours;
5. Care in placing and arranging the elements in the composition;
6. Transmission of the tradition by copying past models. (79, 197)

There are just about as many explanations of these principles as there are experts writing about them. There is no need to repeat an explanation of all of them here but I would like to highlight two, the first and sixth. The translation of the first offered by Lee is *'animation through spirit consonance,'* qualified in Soper's translation by the phrase, *'sympathetic responsiveness of the vital spirit. '* (17, 253) He goes on to explain,

> Animation through spirit consonance is interpreted as a kind of resonance or rhythm in the painting, an expression of the heavenly inspiration of the artist himself. The painting must have what the Chinese call *ch'i yun*, the spirit or breath of life. . . *Ch'i yun*, the life spirit, is the quality that separates the sheep from the goats, the great masters from the lesser ones. Acker relates the meaning of this particular canon to a very complex combination of Confucian and Taoist ideals involving concepts of the rhythm implicit in the *Tao Te Ching* of Lao-Tze and of the Confucian principle, *li*, by which man regulates his actions. (17, 254)

This brings us back to the point made in the opening paragraph of this section, that the 'wisdom of the sages . . . created the guidelines for Chinese art.' But one does not really have to search quite as deep as 'a complex combination of Confucian and Taoist ideals' to arrive at this understanding. If we apply the 'great analogy' to Chinese painting it is transparently clear that the Sinic artistic process is a matter of bringing order and non-order, familiarity and mystery together in a kind of vital balance. The artist was following Tao, the creative Way of Nature. Chinese art pointed neither to an eternal order as in the West, nor to the timeless source of all things as in India but rather to the ongoing creative wellspring of life.

A Chinese painting, therefore, is a lasting contact with that which, to the civilized Chinese, is the very   essence of life:

> When [the eye of a Chinese gentleman] falls on the miniature porcelain tripod standing on his desk, not only does he savour the perfection of its form and glaze, but a whole train of associations are set moving in his mind. For him his tripod is treasured not simply for its antiquity or rarity, but because it is a receptacle of ideas, and a visible emblem of the ideals by which he lives. (79, 206)

Therefore, what is most important about a Chinese work of art is that it properly *preserves the tradition and the understanding of life embodied in that tradition*. That is why I wanted to highlight Hsieh Ho's sixth canon, 'Transmission of the tradition by copying past models.' Aware that this canon might be disconcerting to modern Occidentals with a mania for originality and authenticity, Sherman Lee says, 'The making of copies was the discipline by which the painter, through the study of the brush of his predecessors, learned control of his own. Such copying was not done to deceive, but as a way of study. . .' (17, 255) But copying was not canonized merely because it was a study method, but rather for the reason the canon gives. *The tradition needed to be transmitted, passed on, kept alive.* To insure that the tradition so transmitted remained authentic, Chinese collectors often validated a painting by imprinting on it their stamp or *chop*, a practice completely outrageous to the Western collector. Sometimes a painting which had passed through many hands would have a large section covered with *chops*, each of which testified that a previous owner agreed that it produced the aesthetic experience for which it was prized - a sense of tranquility, harmony and being in tune with the living Way of Nature.

Amerindic Art: Vitality through Sacrifice

In the realm of Amerindic art there is no Plato or Aristotle, no Coomaraswamy, not even a laconic Hsieh Ho to whom we can look for guidance in understanding what must be the strangest aesthetic conceived by the civilized mind. There is no work comparable to

Lee's *A History of Far Eastern Art* and no body of aesthetic theory to which we can appeal as we approach Amerindic art. Most 'surveys' of this great corpus of artistic achievement are little more than catalogues. That leaves us in the position of having to do rather more of our own interpretation than was necessary in the three preceding sections.

Fortunately we are not left totally adrift. There are a few books which venture to explain some aspects of Amerindic art rather than simply list specimens of it. Two of these are Paul Westheim's *Prehispanic Mexican Art* and Esther Pasztory's excellent *Aztec Art*. Also of great help as always is Laurette Séjourné's *Burning Waters* which, while not specifically about art, nevertheless deals extensively with Toltec-Aztec symbolism.

Taking as a starting point 'the Great Analogy' between artistic and cosmic creation, we should expect that Amerindic art would be characterized by certain traits analogous to those we came across in reviewing Toltec-Aztec mythology. Recall that, like the Chinese, the Mesoamericans viewed the world as arising from the interaction of opposites, but, unlike the Chinese, they conceived the opposites as inherently hostile and never of themselves capable of creativity. The essential fusion of order and non-order required for creation could only be brought about *through sacrifice*. Just as the Indic artistic process depended on the proper yogic discipline and devotion, Amerindic art, from conception to completion and installation, involved the kind of religious discipline typical of the Amerindians - fasting, penitential acts, sacrifice in some degree. That this was the case is confirmed by Esther Pasztory in relation to Aztec art.

> Artistic activity was not without the pervasive ritualism of Aztec life. Certain calendric days, such as 7 Flower, were propitious for an artist's birth. Nor were ethical and aesthetic considerations kept separate - a morally bad person could not be a good artist, as this passage from Sahagún indicates:

And the symbol Seven Flower
was said to be both good and bad.
When good, they celebrated it
with great devotion;
the painters honored it,
they painted its image,
they made offerings to it.
The embroiderers were also joyful
under this symbol.
First they fasted in its honor,
some for eighty days, or forty,
or they fasted for twenty days.

And this is why they made these supplications
and performed these rites:
to be able to work well,
to be skillful,
to be artists like the Toltecs,
to order their work well,
whether embroidery or painting.

And when this symbol was bad,
when an embroiderer broke her fast,
they said that she deserved to become a woman of the streets,
this was her reputation and her way of life,
to work as a prostitute.

But for the one whose actions were good,
who worked well, who guided herself,
all was good; she was esteemed. . .

(From Sahagún's Codices Matritenses
Trans. León-Portilla, 1963, PP. 170-71) (80, 92)

So serious was the transgression of a mere embroiderer who broke her fast that she *deserved to be treated like a prostitute!* Sacrificial acts, of which fasting is one type, were, therefore, an integral part of the artistic process. We are not told in this passage what kind of sacrifices were required from those who sculpted the great statues and reliefs or built the vast pyramidal temple platforms nor what degradation would follow failure to perform those sacrificial duties but we can be certain they were far more stringent than those for the embroiderer!

We can also be certain that it was not alone the sacrificial acts necessary for the artistic process which made the work of art successful. To the Amerindians any work of art had to be a living reality and the only way it could achieve that condition was to be *vitalized through sacrifice*, the same way the world of the Fifth Sun was vitalized. The greater the art work the greater the sacrifice was required. According to Prescott,

> At the dedication of the great temple of Huitzilopotchli, in 1486, the prisoners, who for some years had been reserved for the purpose, were drawn from all quarters of the capital. They were ranged in files, forming a procession nearly two miles long. The ceremony consumed several days, and seventy thousand captives are said to have perished at the shrine of this terrible deity! (33, 59)

To be sure, Huitzilopotchli was indeed a 'terrible deity', the traditional clan-god of the Aztecs, and the sacrifices to him were doubtless more horrendous than those of other gods. Still, we are talking about the inauguration of a great work of architecture and the sacrificial process which was the way *and the only way* it could be instilled with the living power it was intended to embody. Although the artistic process itself was interlaced with sacrificial ritual, the art work had no vitality until it received the invigoration of the god to whom sacrifice had to be made, just as the we saw the Fifth Sun did not move until it was sent on its way by Quetzalcoatl.

By comparison let us recall that the Indian temple of Kailasanatha was dedicated by planting a copper box containing 'wealth of the earth, stones, gems, herbs, metals, roots, and soils' in a worship cell and invoking the 'Earth Goddess.' Contrast this simple ceremony to 'inseminate' a temple with the sacrifice of thousands of people to accomplish the same purpose. The difference lies in the fact that the Indic artist, through the artistic process, an act of devotion, created an icon which was rooted in the Ground of Being. The temple was already alive because it was carved from the living rock, the embodiment of the ultimate One. The simple ceremony of planting the box containing 'wealth of the earth' merely acknowledged that fact. But the Amerindic temple was a dead thing, sundered from the Ground of Being, until it was *forcefully fused* to the divine order by the power of sacrifice!

Between the extremes of the embroiderers' work and the great temple of Huitzilopotchli extends the great range of Amerindic sculpture and painting. We simply do not have enough information to say for certain what degree of sacrifice and ritual was demanded for the execution and final acceptance of those works. We do know, however, that many statues were anointed with blood at their installation and, with what we now understand about the Amerindic mind, I consider it unlikely that any significant art work could have been produced without reference to sacrifice from beginning to end.

What, then, was the nature of the art produced by this sacrificial-artistic process? 'The primary function of Aztec art,' says Pasztory, 'was the communication of ideas about man's place in the cosmos and in human society. Works of art presented and handed down information about the appearance and relationships of gods and men. They could take the form of propaganda, expressing current values or justifying political realities. The works often served to identify one or more individuals as belonging to a certain group or class, or performing certain tasks.' (80, 71) This description in itself does very little to distinguish Amerindic art from that of other civilizations. Most Western and Indic and much of Sinic art served the same function. What presented special problems and evoked special solutions for the Amerindic artist was the *unique nature of Amerindic ideas about the cosmos,* or, put another way, *the peculiarities of the Amerindic mindset.* To demonstrate this, let us consider the options available to the artists of the other civilizations as we have outlined them earlier in this chapter.

1.*Producing monuments intended to be imperishable (Egypt).* Obviously this option would be meaningless to a society which did not even expect their world, let alone monuments, to last forever. On the contrary, the Amerindians expected the world of the Fifth Sun to be destroyed, for all human life to vanish and a world inhabited only by the planets to follow.

2.*Portraying the divine order of the world which guaranteed human triumph over death (Egypt, Christendom).* That this option was unavailable to Mesoamericans was touchingly expressed by Moctezuma on seeing his own carved portrait at Chapultepec:

> If our bodies were as durable in this life as this carved effigy is upon this rock, who would be afraid of death? But I know that I must perish, and this is the only memorial that will remain of me   (Durán, 1964, p. 254). (80, 94)

3.*Depicting subjects as embodiments of archetypes or ideals (Egypt, Greece, Christendom).* As the foregoing quotation illustrates, the Amerindic elite were quite well aware that they, along with the entire world, were caught in the cosmic crunch and, although they might have the artist show them in the paraphernalia of power, routing their enemies and slaying their captives, we never find them portrayed as more than human.   In Plate 12 we see Pacal, ruler of the Mayan city of Palenque, depicted on his magnificent five-ton sarcophagus lid. He is reclining serenely in death, his hands appearing to be set in what Hindus would call a *mudra,* as his body is about to be engorged by the Earth Monster, symbol of ultimate destruction. Although the ruler remains altogether human, he is portrayed with such nobility that his certain defeat by death becomes all the more poignant.

4.*Depicting multiplicity as manifestations of the ultimate non-ordered All (India).* Alas, the ultimate non-order was no refuge for the Amerindian nor something the artist cared to point to in his work because non-order was, in Mesoamerica, an object of even more horrendous dread than it was in the Occident. Non-order is, in Pasztory's words, '. . . the chaos of darkness, unmeasured time, and unformed matter.' (80, 82) And its symbol is, of course, that very *Earth Monster* we encountered on the Palenque sarcophagus

'No emblem can alternate with the earth monster,' says Pasztory, 'which is *chaos par excellence*.' (ibid., *emphasis mine*) (Plate 14, Emblem 2)

5.*Depicting the harmonious Way of Nature (China)*. To the Amerindian, the idea of nature as harmoniously self-generating and amicable to human life would have been inconceivable just as his idea of nature churned into motion by constant sacrifice would have been unspeakable to the Sinic mind. The Mesoamerican would have found Chinese art devoid of energy. To the Chinese, Mesoamerican art would have appeared insanely agitated.

If none of the options used by artists in the rest of the world were available to the Amerindic artist, what was left? *Reification*. The term, 'reification,' means, in psychological or philosophical parlance, treating a subjective or abstract idea as a concrete reality. In art I use it to refer to the process of *rendering an abstract concept in such a vivid and convincing visual manner that it becomes a living presence*. As Westheim puts it, '[The Mesoamerican] interpretation of reality gave rise to a style of art based, of necessity, on symbolic representation. The realism of ancient Mexican art is a realism founded on mythology.' (81, 27) Or, Pasztory, '. . . Aztec art is not realistic in our sense of the term. What they valued as real was not a visual illusion, but a sense of vitality in the work of art.' (80, 92) Interestingly, both authors use the term 'realism,' yet both make it clear that Amerindic realism is not what Westerners call 'realism,' that is, 'visual illusion' or making the work of art appear like its subject.

The latter would indeed have been impossible because the subject of Amerindic art was the complex web of cosmological concepts which governed the Amerindic mind. The task of the artist was to make portions of that abstract web visible, tangible, and overwhelmingly real. To see how this was accomplished, turn to Plate 13. This is the famous 15th century Aztec statue of Coatlicue, sometimes called the Mother Goddess or Goddess of Birth and

Death.   Westheim calls the Great Coatlicue (there are lesser ones) 'the masterpiece of Aztec sculpture,' adding,

> Although this concept has the outlines of a human, its form and details show that it is a representation of a supernatural being not subject to human laws - a being incarnating two contrasting ideas, birth and death. As goddess of the earth, Coatlicue is the mother, the birth giver, from whom all life comes, while at the same time being, as she is called in the *Histoire du Mexique* (Thévet manuscript) the 'great monster,' to whom all living things must return in order to be reborn in another form. In the place of her head she has two serpents' heads. . . The skull which she wears as a pectoral ornament has none of the morbid and horrifying associations of that *memento mori* of Western civilization: it, too, is a symbol of resurrection. Her serpent's heads with their fangs and her clawlike feet show that she has a devilish and destructive nature.   The human hands and hearts comprising her necklace   are   references   to   sacrificial   death   and   the transfiguration effected by it.   *Many very realistic details drawn from life are thus used to increase the intensity of the religious nature of this carving.* (81, 61)

The last sentence (in italics) is what reification is about. Note that Westheim refers to the great sculpture as a 'concept,' a word one would scarcely use in referring, for example, to Michelangelo's 'David.' But a concept is exactly what the Great Coatlicue is, more specifically a synthesis of abstract concepts. Nevertheless the artist has given her an integral vitality that makes her seem incredibly real. Imagine standing directly in front of this massive eight and a half foot image. Ask yourself what it might be like to be part of a society in which this monstrous creature represented the fundamental nature of life -- your life as you were taught to understand it!

The genius of the Mesoamerican artist was to bring to life the abstract concepts of his nightmarish cosmology, combining realistic elements into fantasy constructions that seemed compellingly real:

> Most Aztec art consists of individual units each having specific symbolic meaning. . . A symbol is here defined as a frequently recurring simple motif or figure that may appear alone, but is often part of a more complex design or emblem.

Such symbols in Aztec art include the human heart, sacrificial knife, feather, flame, skull or skull-and-crossbones, shell, flower, star, planet Venus, sun, moon, spear, stone, maguey thorn, liquid (water), smoke and corn. The stylization of these symbols remains constant in the various arts. . . They are so standardized that they almost function as glyphs in picture-writing. . Each symbol was highly charged with meaning and could have multiple associations. (80, 80)

In addition to symbols, Pasztory also refers to nine ubiquitous 'emblems' found in Aztec art, an emblem being defined as 'a complex image consisting of several symbolic units that generally occur together.' (80, 81) The nine emblems (see Plate 14 for illustrations of four of them) include 'the solar disk, the earth monster, the grass ball of sacrifice, the sky band, the jaguar-eagle pair, the feathered serpent, the fire serpent, the water-fire stream, and the smoking mirror.' (ibid.) Of these emblems, the last six all represent paired or fused opposites (the sky band is generally paired with an earth band). The third emblem, the grass ball of sacrifice, represents the sacrifice required to creatively fuse order and non-order. Of the first two, the solar disk and the earth monster, Pasztory says,

These two emblems are the most important in Aztec art, and in their placement they express a conceptual opposition. The sun disk is the rational order of calendar time, as indicated by the glyph for the light of day; the earth monster is the chaos of darkness, unmeasured time, and unformed matter. (80, 82)

In other words, the two most important emblems in Aztec art refer to the basic opposition of order and non-order, cosmos and chaos. It should be noted, however, that while these two opposing symbols may be juxtaposed in art, they are never shown to be fused in creation. The Solar Disk represents the world as created, the world of the Fifth Sun, not an ordering principle. The Earth Monster, on the other hand, represents *pure* non-order, the ultimate destruction of all creation.

When the Amerindic artist wanted to portray the creative fusion of order and non-order - his most typical theme - he chose other symbols of those opposites as we saw in the Great Coatlicue. This is also exemplified in the motifs of the temple of Quetzalcoatl at Teotihuacán (Plate 15). Across the facade of the great truncated pyramid we see two alternating visages. First, there is that of the Feathered Serpent, Quetzalcoatl, stern and fanged. The same serpent heads also project at intervals from the curb of the steep stairway. We have already noted that Quetzalcoatl is the supreme symbol of *order* in Toltec mythology, the mythological intitiator of the Fifth Sun's movement and the legendary bringer of civilization to Mesoamerica. Alternating with Quetzalcoatl's image on the temple is that of Tlaloc, the 'rain god,' identified by the two goggle-like circles. Tlaloc was an abstract deity representing water or matter, that is, *non-order* . Of this unlikely pair, Laurette Séjourné says,

> These two heads are different symbolic expressions of one and the same basic concept of the Nahuatl [Toltec-Aztec] religion: the vital impulse arising from the unification of opposing elements. (52, 87)

Séjourné cites several cases of Toltec art which show the Tlaloc water (non-order) image combined with fire (order) symbols and makes an excellent case that these composite images represent the fusion of opposites. This is confirmed in one case by the appearance of the glyph for *Movement*, i.e., the creative overcoming of inertia. *But we do not see any such fusion or movement indicators on the Tlaloc of the Quetzalcoatl temple*. There we find the unredeemed, unfused, unmotivated Tlaloc. I suggest that is precisely because the purpose of the rites performed atop the temple was *to bring together the creative fusion of the Quetzalcoatl and Tlaloc principles, of order and non-order*. It would not be necessary for the artist to assume the fusion in his sculpture. It might even have been sacrilegious to do so. By presenting the two contrasting figures unfused he was announcing to the world what the purpose of the temple was: to accommodate.

the sacrificial rites by which the creative fusion of order and non-order was accomplished and the continuation of the world and life assured - *for yet a little while.*

In summary, we can say that, despite what may seem to us its horrendous presuppositions and its frequently monstrous images, Amerindic art was worthy of the greatest respect. Far from being primitive or inferior it dealt with a highly complex intellectual content by a technique of *reification* which was a unique achievement in the history of world art. And if we had any doubt after surveying the art of the other three civilizations, Amerindic art should convince us that there is no such thing as a universal aesthetic by which all civilized art can be understood and judged. *Each civilization requires its own aesthetic.*

SIX

Law: The Rules Society Lives by

The Origin of Law

Righteousness and sin, good and evil, right and wrong. These dichotomies of attitude and behavior are defined by reference to *law* - the laws of the gods, the laws of mankind, the laws of conscience. Law is a creation of the civilized mind. The precivilized mind has no need for it. Along with its repertoire of techniques for coping with the environment, a primitive society also has a repertoire of techniques for interpersonal behavior which are called its *folkways*. The degree to which members of the society are expected to conform to the folkways varies. It should not be assumed that primitive groups are completely homogeneous. They usually have some degree of tolerance for eccentricity. But at the core of the folkways there always exists an irreducible minimum of customs - called *mores* by anthropologists - which are expected to be observed by all members without exception. There are negative mores which make some kinds of conduct prohibited or taboo and positive mores which make other kinds obligatory. The primitive mind makes no distinction between the realms of the sacred, the legal, and the ethical. No primitive could have a conflict between the demands of religion and society, between those of society and his conscience, or between those of religion and his conscience. It was civilization which gave rise to such dilemmas.

Moreover, unlike civilized laws, the mores of a primitive society are self-validating. Their source is simply the past. They come with the territory, so to speak, and form the matrix of the primitive's identity as a member of a particular society. No one needs to interpret them or devise a reasoned foundation for them. The primitive, in fact, has no frame of reference on the basis of which he can evaluate or question his mores even if it occurred to him to do so. While many primitive societies allow children considerable freedom of activity, when the child, through rites of initiation, becomes an adult, his or her unquestioning adherence to the mores is taken for granted. All adult members of the society, the living and the dead, have always adhered to them and all future members will.

When civilization came into being, it had as its first rules of conduct nothing more than the mores of the pre-civilized peoples over which it extended its sway, just as it had only their technologies. Thus we find that the earliest laws recorded in any civilization are little more than collections of extant customs and practices. But the larger and more complex the civilization became the more likely was it to find itself confronted with the mores of many different subordinate societies which were often in conflict. As time went by decisions made by rulers or their magistrates tended to become precedents which might later be codified into a *corpus juris*, a body of law. When civilized societies reached the level of empire the rulers not only had to deal with divergent mores but also the native laws of civilized societies they had conquered or with whose citizens they had commerce. In Rome those laws were called *jus civile*. The primary *jus civile* was the law of Rome as it applied to its citizens although Roman jurists grudgingly recognized that the native law of other civilized societies was of the same genus. Roman *jus civile* itself was, in fact, a combination of law and primitive Roman folkways, a rather tedious and ritualistic affair. Recognizing the impracticality and undesirability (from the point of view of Roman snobbery) of using their own civil law to adjudicate cases involving foreigners and loath to make decisions based on the foreigners' own laws (for the same reason), the Romans early recognized a rather vague and imprecise kind of law called *jus gentium*, the law of aliens, which was supposed to be based on what was common in the differing laws of nations.

The development of the concept of *jus gentium* under Roman and Christian jurists and philosophers will be examined in the next section. Here I simply want to point out that the search for laws which could satisfy the needs of a heterogeneous population was a major problem for the ruling elite of all civilizations. Solving it successfully was essential to creating and preserving the unity necessary for the power elite to maintain control over the majority. Since civilization was *in essence* a usurpative form of social organization, civilized rulers had always to be on guard against and devise ways to avoid rebellion. Aristotle counsels that the tyrant, in order to preserve his tyranny as long as possible,

> . . . ought to show himself to his subjects in the light, not of a tyrant, but of a steward and a king. He should not appropriate what is theirs, but should be their guardian; he should be moderate, not extravagant in his way of life; he should win the notables by companionship, and the multitude by flattery. For then his rule will of necessity be nobler and happier, because he will rule over better men whose spirits are not crushed, over men to whom he himself is not an object of hatred, and of whom he is not afraid. (82, 1261)

Smart kings did not need a philosopher's advice. The Babylonian king, Hammurabi, having conquered all of lower Mesopotamia, proceeded to unite it under a general code of law. In that code he proclaimed,

> I am the guardian governor. . . In my bosom I carried the people of the land of Sumer and Akkad; . . . in my wisdom I restrained them, that the strong might not oppress the weak, and that they should give justice to the orphan and the widow. . . Let any oppressed man, who has a cause, come before my image as king of righteousness! Let him read the inscription on my monument! Let him give heed to my weighty words! And may my monument enlighten him as to his cause, and may he understand his case! May he set his heart at ease, (exclaiming:) 'Hammurabi indeed is a ruler who is like a real father to his people . . . he has established prosperity for his people for all time, and given a pure government to the land.' (83, I, 221)

The Code of Hammurabi was one of history's first great public relations gimmicks, although I hasten to add that the king's words, unlike those of many modern public relations specialists, were not merely rhetoric. Hammurabi did indeed promulgate a remarkably enlightened code of laws but he also made sure their effect was not to diminish his own power which, in fact, he increased considerably during his reign. Law was always a powerful instrument in the hands of the civilized ruler and its reform was often a critical factor in staving off rebellion and maintaining social unity.

The reverence and enthusiasm for law in any civilized society was directly proportional to two factors:

1. What the society understood as its source and foundation.
2. What its purpose was, i.e. toward what goal it tended.

The importance of these two factors cannot be overestimated. They determine how law is perceived and received by the people who are expected to obey it. As a child will accept a command from a parent far more readily than he will from a peer, so is the adult's acceptance of either a legal prohibition or an obligation directly proportional to his *reverence for its source*. The more closely law is connected to what a society sees as the ultimate ground of its being the more significant law is to that society. On the other hand, just as a child will accept a command which he sees will result in a reward (like, 'Go get the cookie jar'), so will an adult's readiness to obey a law be directly proportional to his *enthusiasm for its purpose*. The more closely law is linked to a society's ultimate goal, the more significant it will be. We often think of law as primarily a negative or coercive force but the fact is that it is most powerful when a people has both a reverence and an enthusiasm for it, when, in short, it is capable of producing in those who uphold it a sense of *righteousness* . Even the most humble and dispossessed of a society can derive dignity from pride in their adherence to the law. 'Righteousness,' said Aeschylus, 'is a shining in the smoke of mean houses.' We have in our own Western history the example of a people who have endured for more than three thousand years despite adversity, defeat, dispersion and persecution. And what gave that people, the Jews, their continuing identity and dignity? It was not their race or political system or even their language. The Jews are one people because they are the people of the Law, God's law as He gave it to Moses. They are a perfect example of the importance of righteousness which comes from reverence for the source and enthusiasm for the goal of law.

As we examine the nature of law in the following sections, there are three different kinds of law which it is worthwhile to note and define in advance:

Divine law is law which comes from 'God' by way of revelation and is necessary for man's 'salvation', whatever those terms happen to mean wherever one happens to be. It can be restricted to ceremonial rites and observances or include just about every aspect of human behavior, religious, moral, civil and criminal.

Natural law is law which governs the cosmic process. It may include both physical laws and moral laws, the former viewed as compulsory for the insensate part of nature and the latter as an obligation on beings possessed of free will.

Human law comprises those specific laws which are created and promulgated by rulers or legislators. It can include both what we call civil and criminal law.

These three kinds of law are not necessarily found in all civilizations. Drawing a distinction between them here is intended to provide a reference point for comparing law and legal systems wherever they are found.

While philosophical and theological considerations played an important part in the development of law, law was of great concern to the civilized mind long before formal philosophy made its appearance. One of the most interesting things about civilized societies is the way in which they would at one time interweave law, philosophy and theology only at a later time try to unravel them. Since law was, like philosophy and theology, a work of the mind, the deeper civilized man probed the basic questions about law, the more he found his search shaped by the fundamental matrix of all his thought - his mindset.

The Western Law above all laws

The earliest laws, as we might expect, came from Occidental civilization. While it is one of the most famous law codes, the Code of Hammurabi, which dates from the eighteenth century B. C., is not the oldest. Sumerian laws from the twenty-second century have been discovered and Egypt had a well-developed legal system centuries before that. It is not surprising that law, being concerned with order in society, should have been a primary and persistent concern of peoples guided by the Occidental mindset. Law was perceived by them as reflecting the ordered nature of ultimate reality. In Egypt the gods were its foundation and its source was the divine Pharaoh who was also the supreme judge, assisted in that role chiefly by the priesthood. Likewise in Rome, so noted for the development of secular law, the religious base was never lost, even under the Republic. Jolowicz observes,

> It is true that Roman law took on a secular character at a comparatively early stage in its history, but with the Romans, as with all peoples [except the Chinese, as we shall see], law and religion were not originally differentiated, and there were many spheres, even after the XII Tables [fifth century B. C.], and in later times, where the *ius sacrum*, the religious law strictly so-called, touched the ordinary civil law. The pontiffs [advisory priests] were the guardians of religious

> tradition, and, as such, would naturally be the authorities to
> be consulted in purely legal matters as well. . . By their
> different kinds of advice, the pontiffs were able to influence
> the development of law very considerably. They might even,
> under the cover of 'interpretation', create an entirely new
> institution. (84, 86)

The importance of the 'divine connection' to Roman law was,
however, actually much greater than Jolowicz' comments suggest.
The religious foundation of the Roman state had indeed become
obscured as the Republic disintegrated and the empire came to be
ruled by the arbitrary will of dictators like Sulla and Julius Caesar.
After Caesar's death in 44 B.C. Rome went through a turbulent
period during which power was shared by a triumvirate including
Mark Antony and Caesar's nephew, Octavian. It was the accession
of Octavian to absolute power after defeating Mark Antony at Actium
in 31 B.C. which gave Rome a new lease on life and the restoration of
the divine connection played no small part in the process.

If Caesar was a military genius, Octavian was a genius in the
political sphere. Although somewhat aloof and severe in his personal
living habits, he had a charismatic influence over his fellow Romans
and an extraordinary grasp of the needs of Rome. He seems to have
been perfectly aware that if Rome were to be a great empire it must
have an absolute ruler possessing divine authority. And divine
authority could no better be assured than if the emperor himself
were divine. In his lifetime Octavian never allowed himself to be
officially deified, but he was declared a god three days after his
death and that honor accrued to succeeding emperors until the
Christianization of the empire. What was perhaps most remarkable
about Octavian was the way in which he shrewdly gave Rome a
divine emperor while publicly appearing to do just the opposite.
Every accretion to his power seemed to come about at the insistence
of others. He required that eighty silver statues which had been
erected in Rome in his honor be melted down and 'the proceeds used
to provide golden ornaments for Apollo in the temple which he had

erected to him on the Palatine.' (85, 39) At the same time he allowed himself to be called (at the 'request' of the senate of Rome) *augustus*, an epithet succeeding Roman emperors retained. 'Augustus,' Jolowicz explains, 'was a rare word and had a strong religious flavour about it, its meaning being almost equivalent to our 'holy.' (84, 334) Again, Octavian, or Caesar Augustus, as he would now be called, had, after he had restored peace to the empire, 'transferred the state from his power to the management of the Senate and the People of Rome.' (84, 333). It was a magnanimous gesture which only served to heighten his prestige, but it came from a man who could afford it because he already held the posts of proconsul of the empire, tribune for life, and *pontifex maximus* (highest priest), which, combined with other minor posts, were sufficient to give him the power of an absolute dictator. The result was that Augustus had, by the time of his death, accumulated all the powers of a divine emperor whose word was the law of Rome while assiduously preserving the forms of the Republic.

Thus, in Rome as in all other Occidental societies the ultimate source of law was perceived to be divine. And, as in all Occidental societies, the ultimate definition of 'divine' was 'creator of the cosmic order'. The fundamental question which arises when law is perceived as having a divine source is: *To what extent does human law reflect the divine will?* From the time of the Greeks, the Western mind was too aware of the possibilities of corruption in human devices to accept any law as having final divine authority. The result was that legal theorists searched for a *principle* on the basis of which law, and all of government, for that matter, could be evaluated. The result of that search was the introduction in Rome of the concept of levels of law, a higher law and a lower law subordinated to it.

We have already observed earlier in this chapter the distinction made in Rome between *jus civile*, local civil law, and *jus gentium*, the law of aliens or nations. In the beginning the Romans looked down their noses at the *jus gentium*, considering it a mongrel which was

decidedly inferior to their own civil law. The centuries following the
death of Augustus saw a radical change in that attitude. In the
Corpus Juris, the sixth century compilation of law ordered by the
Christian emperor Justinian, we are told,

> All nations, who are ruled by laws and customs, are governed
> partly by their own particular laws, and partly by those laws
> which are common to all mankind. The law which a people
> enacts is called the Civil Law of that people, but *that which
> natural reason appoints for all mankind* is called the Law of
> Nations, because all nations use it. (86, 37, *emphasis mine*)

By the time of Justinian the law of nations has clearly been
elevated to a superior position. It is described as the law which
natural reason appoints for all mankind and, moreover, it has
become the standard for judging civil law. The notion of civil law has
correspondingly changed. It appears now to mean simply those laws
which are in force in various communities and which may differ in
specifics from place to place but ought not to conflict with the law of
nations. It is, in short, what I have called *human law*. The old
cumbersome Roman *jus civile* with its elaborate ritual has, in fact,
virtually disappeared, and it is that *jus civile* to which Jolowicz refers
when he says,

> [Justinian's law] is a universal system in which the
> distinction between *ius civile* and *ius gentium* has become of
> purely historical and theoretical interest. For the practical
> meaning of the distinction there is no room in a society
> where, in effect, every free man is a citizen. In fact, the
> peculiar institutions of the *ius civile* have ceased to exist.
> (84, 518)

It is all very well, you might observe at this point, to make a nice
distinction between civil law and the law of nations, but how do you
learn what the law of nations is? Civil laws and decisions based on
them are found in law books but where do you find a book of the law
of nations? That is a quite legitimate question and the answer to it

is the key to the whole structure of Occidental law as it developed first in the Roman Empire and later in medieval Christendom.

The answer came from philosophy. The Romans were not much as philosophers, so when they needed to think deeply about something they borrowed ideas from the Greeks. For more than five centuries, from the death of Aristotle to the advent of Neoplatonism in the third century A.D., Greek philosophy was dominated by the Stoics, whom I mentioned briefly in Chapter IV. I did not go into details about the Stoics in that chapter because their abiding influence was in the area of ethics and law rather than metaphysics. Stoics did not believe in incorporeal realities, whether souls, ideas or essences. Reasoning that a corporeal effect could not be produced by an incorporeal cause, the Stoics bluntly declared that all reality was corporeal. In the beginning was an ethereal, primordial matter called *pneuma*, i.e. gas or air. Permeating pneuma and inseparable from it was an internal logic, reason or ruling principle called *logos*. The Stoics identified the original ethereal pneuma and its logos with God, a conception similar to (though not identical with) that found in the opening chapter of the Gospel of John where 'Word' is used to translate the Greek 'logos':

> In the beginning was the Word [*logos*], and the Word was with God, and the Word was God. He was in the beginning with God; all things were made through him, and without him was not anything made that was made. In him was life, and the life was the light of men. The light shines in the darkness, and the darkness has not overcome it. (87, New Testament, 103)

The Stoics would not have found much to disagree with in that passage. However, while in both the Christian and Stoic views the Logos refers to the ordering principle in the creation of the world, the Christian view was that the world was created by God from nothing (*ex nihilo*) while the Stoics held that the world was an *emanation* from God, a series of condensations of the primordial pneuma. God, therefore, contributed not only the structure of the world but its substance as well. Each level of condensation was subject to an inherent logos or principle. The grosser condensations were subject to the laws of physics. Those laws comprised one part of what came to be known as *jus naturale* or natural law. But rational beings were also subject to natural law. Human souls were considered to be intense, refined emanations from the world soul, their ruling principle being *reason*. The Stoics believed that the universe was, of its innermost nature, not only physically but morally lawful. While they accepted human freedom and therefore human folly they believed it was man's highest obligation to recognize and obey the moral natural law through the exercise of reason.

It will now be clear what Justinian's Corpus Juris meant by calling the law of nations 'that which natural reason appoints for all mankind.' *Roman jurists had come to equate the Law of nations with the natural law of the Stoics.* "The Jus Naturale, or Law of Nature,' wrote Sir Henry Sumner Maine, 'is simply the Jus Gentium or Law of Nations seen in the light of a peculiar [i.e., Stoic] theory.' (86, 43) He went on to observe that,

> . . . on the whole, the progress of the Romans in legal improvement was astonishingly rapid as soon as stimulus was applied to it by the theory of Natural Law. The ideas of simplification and generalization had always been associated with the conception of Nature; simplicity, symmetry, and intelligibility came therefore to be regarded as the characteristics of a good legal system, and the taste for involved language, multiplied ceremonials, and useless difficulties disappeared altogether. The strong will and unusual opportunities of Justinian were needed to bring the Roman law to its existing shape, but the ground plan of the system had been sketched long before the imperial reforms were effected. (86, 47)

After the death of the great Stoic emperor, Marcus Aurelius, in 180, Stoicism as an independent philosophy virtually disappeared. By the time of Justinian, the empire was Christian and natural law was no longer the product of a Stoic world soul. It was the law of the universe created by the God of Genesis.

The answer to the previous question we raised about where you find the law of nations or the natural law is that it is not written anywhere but is *accessible to reason.* Reason, operating with regard to principles of justice and equity, is conceived to be 'in tune with' the natural law and capable of judging and correcting injustices and inequities in human law. *But reasonableness, justice and equity are not legal matters. They are moral values which cannot themselves be legislated.* And that is the key to the structure of Western law. It embraced not only what we think of as law *per se,* but, deriving from the Stoic-Christian conception of natural law, a moral imperative toward a just and equitable society. Reginald Dias writes,

> Unless we think of a striving toward justice as a part of the concept of law itself, we cannot distinguish between a state where 'the rule of law' prevails and a tyranny in which what are miscalled rules of law are mere objects of selfish manipulation by those who control the government. 'The rule of law' requires that the source of law itself, the state, respect a lawfulness that is not of its own creation. What a given rule of law means within a particular system depends not merely on its wording but the mode of its interpretation and application. This, in turn, cannot be controlled by legal rules but only by the moral integrity with which the legal rules are administered. (88, 151)

The 'lawfulness that is not of its own creation' was found by Roman and early Christian society in the moral natural law of God's universe. Since the natural law was, in effect, a moral imperative overseeing the administration and judgment of human law, no human laws were sacrosanct or immune to change or repeal. That had a salutary effect on the subsequent history of Western law. It did not lead to radical transformations of society because the administration of the law remained in the hands of the elite which made changing and repealing laws slow and cumbersome processes. Nevertheless, some degree of amelioration in society through the law was always a possibility.

I have already remarked that after the Christianization of the Roman Empire, the natural law of the Stoics became the natural law of the Judaeo-Christian Creator. Theologians such as St. Augustine had dealt with the problem of synthesizing the old concept of natural law with Christian theological ideas but it was not thoroughly resolved until St. Thomas Aquinas undertook the task in his thirteenth century *Summa Theologica.* Aquinas recognized natural law but since it was accessible to human reason he did not want man to suppose that his reason could penetrate and expose the mind of God. So he made natural law subordinate to a still higher level of law which he called *eternal law.* Eternal law is the law by which God actually governs the universe. It is called eternal because it is not subject to time. What eternal law is in itself cannot be known by man. Aquinas says, '. . . no one can know the eternal law as it is in itself, except God and the blessed who see God in His essence. But every rational creature knows it according to some reflection, greater or less. For *every knowledge of truth is a kind of reflection and participation of the eternal law, which is the unchangeable truth. . .'* (89, V. 2, 764, emphasis in all Aquinas quotations is mine.) In Aquinas' Christian view, natural law became '. . . the light of natural reason, whereby we discern what is good and what is evil, which is the function of the natural law, is nothing else than an imprint on us of the divine light. It is therefore evident that *the natural law is nothing else than the rational creature's participation of the eternal law.'* (89, 750) In other words, natural law is the innate structure of rationality in man, comparable to the Stoics' logos, a structure which is put there by the eternal law. As to whether human law is derived from the eternal law, Aquinas states that '. . . all laws, *in so far as they partake of right reason,* are derived from the eternal law.' (89, 766) We therefore have a *hierarchy* of three levels of law, from the eternal through the natural down to the human, and the key to their coordination from the human point of view was the use of *reason.* It is very important to note that law is both accessible and at the same time hidden. Eternal law cannot be known directly but we do get a 'reflection' of it. We can discern natural law by 'the light of natural reason' but reason can go astray, so we are told it has to be 'right reason.' All law, insofar as it is really law, reflects the eternal order of the universe but we have to work at understanding rationally what natural law requires and what human laws ought to require. Most people need a considerable amount of help in understanding such matters and it was an important function of the Church to give them direction. Medieval law was not merely a matter of arbitrary enactments of the state. According to Troeltsch,

> . . . Catholic social doctrine conceives Natural Law as existing before the State, which binds it to a positive legal working out of the organic and patriarchal theories of Christian Natural Law. In so doing it is free to take into account variation in circumstances and in suitability, but it is still bound to consider that which it creates as the working out of the principles of Natural Law, and continually to improve them according to its insight into Natural Law. Here also that means that all that is essential is already in existence, has already been 'given', that the course of Nature and of Providence of itself guides humanity into right knowledge, that the State, like all positive expressions of law, must order its life according to these principles, and that only from this standpoint do its laws attain their binding character. (90, 305)

To complete his grand synthesis of medieval law, Aquinas had to include the additional dimension of Judaeo-Christian *divine law.* The divine law was the law revealed in the Old and New Testaments. The *old law* was the Jewish law, which Aquinas says is 'like a pedagogue of children,' (89, 958), while the *new law* of Christ is 'the law of perfection, since it is the law of charity.' (ibid.) Man needs the divine law, according to Aquinas, because he 'is ordained to an end of eternal happiness which exceeds [his] natural ability,' and 'therefore it was necessary that, in addition to the natural and the human law, man should be directed to his end by a law given by God.' (89, 753)

We might say that if natural law defines good and evil, and human law defines right and wrong, then divine law defines righteousness and sin. Man can obey the laws of his society and do moral good of his own ability. But can man overcome *sin* of his own accord? The great theologian has no doubt about the answer to that question.

> Man by himself can in no way rise from sin without the help of grace. For since sin is transient as to the act and abiding in its guilt . . . to rise from sin is not the same as to cease from the act of sin; but to rise from sin means that man has restored to him what he lost by sinning. Now man incurs a triple loss by sinning . . . , viz., stain, corruption of natural good, and debt of punishment. He incurs a stain, inasmuch as he forfeits the adornment of grace through the deformity of sin. Natural good is corrupted, inasmuch as man's nature is *disordered* because man's will is not subject to God's; and when this *order is overthrown*, the consequence is that the whole nature of sinful man remains *disordered*. Lastly, there is the debt of punishment, inasmuch as by sinning man deserves eternal damnation.

> Now it is manifest that none of these three can be restored except by God. For since the adornment of grace comes from the illumination of the divine light, this adornment cannot be brought back, except God give His light anew. Hence a habitual gift is necessary; and this is the light of grace. Likewise, *the order of nature can be restored*, i.e., man's will can be subject to God, only when God draws man's will to Himself . . . So, too, the guilt of eternal punishment can be remitted by God alone, against Whom the offense was committed and Who is man's Judge. And thus, in order than man rise from sin there is required the help of grace, both as regards a habitual gift and as regards the internal motion of God. (89, 990)

Therefore, no matter how obedient man may be to the other kinds of law, he cannot of his own power fulfill the divine law or achieve salvation. He needs the help of grace and *grace means the Church and its sacraments*. When all is said and done the power of the state and its laws mean nothing without the divine sanction available only through the Church.

In concluding this section we only need to observe how the whole course of Western law is permeated with the notion of *order*. It can, of course, be said that all law deals with order - social order. In a practical sense that is true but as I said earlier the fundamental questions about the law are: *What is its foundation?* and, *What is its goal?* As we have seen, in the Thomist synthesis the *foundation* of all natural and human law is the eternal law, which according to Aquinas is 'nothing else than the exemplar of divine wisdom, as directing all actions and movements.' (89, 763) In other words, the foundation of law is God as supreme orderer of the universe. The *goal* of natural and human law is the common good, i.e., general happiness and beatitude. 'Consequently,' says Aquinas, 'law must needs concern itself mainly with *the order that is in beatitude.*' (89, 744) The goal of divine law, on the other hand, is salvation from sin. Note, however, in the previous quotation about the need for grace, how Aquinas described sin: 'Natural good is corrupted, inasmuch as man's nature is *disordered* because man's will is not subject to God's; and when this *order is overthrown*, the consequence is that the whole nature of sinful man remains *disordered.*' And note also how he characterizes the effect of grace: '*the order of nature can be restored*, i.e., man's will can be subject to God, only when God draws man's will to Himself. . . ' Clearly, the ultimate goal of all law, including the divine law which man can only obey through grace - is the restoration of the natural order which has been overthrown by sin. Aquinas certainly produced a system of law the foundation of which - God - the Christian world revered and the goal of which - salvation - inspired enthusiasm.

The genius of Western legal thought lies in its hierarchical system of law, each higher level representing a more perfect and uncorrupted order. The Western mind did not allow human laws to be confused or equated with God's laws, whether eternal, natural or divine. All human laws, insofar as they were valid, were held to 'reflect' God's law but they were no more than a reflection. It was therefore always possible that any human law might be judged invalid if it was not the product of 'right reason.' That the body of law is subject to change because it is only an imperfect reflection of a transcendent law which is not subject to change is a unique conception of the Occidental mind. As we shall see, none of the other mindsets did or could have produced it.

The Changeless Hindu Law

Although law originated in the West, Indic, or more specifically, Hindu law is the world's most longlived system still in current use. Despite the incursions of Islamic and British law, Hindu law still prevails in much of India. At the core of Hindu law is the conception of *dharma*, which means law or moral order. Indic life is totally and uncompromisingly organized around dharma and the many duties which arise from it. In fact, I know of no society, past or present, which has been so completely, meticulously and inflexibly ordered by law as Indic society. But if that is the case, you might well wonder, is that not a direct contradiction of the Theory of Mindsets? How can such a comprehensively ordered society be the result of a mindset which eschews order and insists on the supremacy of non-order? In this section I hope to show that the character of Indic law not only fails to contradict the Theory of Mindsets but that its rigidity and changelessness is best explained by the Theory of Mindsets.

In the West it was taken for granted that every social order and every legal system is corrupted by some degree of non-order (chaos). That, as we observed in the preceding section, is why the Western mind, obsessed with order, could never be satisfied with any particular set of laws but always looked beyond what was to what *ought to be*, a tendency which resulted in the conception of higher laws which transcended and guided human laws. The complete Western legal system consisted not merely of the aggregate of human laws, designated L1 to L6 in the following diagram, but also included the transcendent (eternal/natural) law (large L).

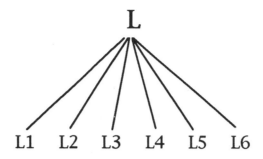

The transcendent law is the ordering principle of the system, a principle which, for the West, might be described as the furtherance of justice or equity. The system remains intact as long as it is consistent with the transcendent law. This allows specific laws to be repealed (L1 in the diagram below), amended (L3a) or added (L7) without invalidating the legal system as long as the changes result in greater justice or equity. The system maintains its order although its elements may change.

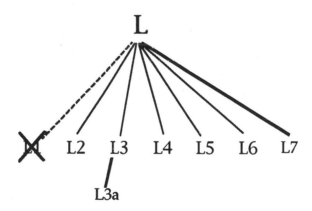

In the Hindu system, on the other hand, the only transcendent reality is the ultimate non-order, Brahman. Every level of order is relative and none has any claim to higher validity than any other. In the sphere of law there is no transcendent law to which human laws have reference. The legal system consists simply of the *aggregate of existing laws*. The figure on the following page illustrates such a system.

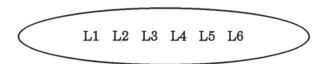

The order in this kind of system consists simply in the nature of the elements, i.e., the content of the specific laws. Suppose, now, that you wish to change, amend or repeal any of the laws. You would get something like this:

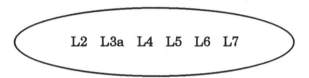

Do we now have a *changed* system of laws? No, we have a *different* system, some of the elements of which are the same as those in a previous system. You cannot speak of the same system persisting through change unless you have an overseeing principle to maintain the integrity of the system. Since the Indic mind did not accept such a principle, how, then, did Hindu law maintain its integrity? *By not changing!*

Hindu jurists maintained that their law had come down from time immemorial, had not changed and could not be changed. There were no such things in the Hindu system as Aquinas' natural law or eternal law. All law was divine law, essentially a part of the structure of the universe as it had been generated in the beginning. The *source* of law was the primordial non-order or Self-existent Brahman. And the *goal* of law? Moksha - release from the cycle of reincarnation and reunion with Brahman. Lest you think these conceptions of the source and goal can hardly be found in any legal system and that they are merely my interpretations to support the Theory of Mindsets, let us review one of the great documents of Hindu law, the *Manu-smriti* or Laws of Manu.

The Laws of Manu is a *Smriti* or metrical composition which was based on a prior *Dharma-sutra* or compilation of legal aphorisms. The Dharma-sutras were composed between 600 and 200 B.C. and the Laws of Manu are generally dated between 200 B.C. and 200 A.D. That is what the Sanskrit scholars will tell us. The orthodox Hindu, however, who is a great deal like our Christian fundamentalists when it comes to scriptures, will tell you that the content of the *Manu-smriti* comes from precisely where the *smriti* claims it does, from the Creator. In the examination of the Laws of Manu which follows I will rely on the 1886 translation by Georg Bühler which was republished by Dover Books in 1969 (91). I will, however, take one liberty with Bühler's translation. There are three Sanskrit words which are similar and likely to confuse a Westerner. The first is that for the ultimate One or the Self-existent who has many Sanskrit names. The second is that for the Creator, who is the firstborn, so to speak, of the One and who also has many names. Finally, there is the word for a member of the Hindu priestly caste which is confusing because it is anglicized differently by different translators. For simplicity I will replace the words Bühler uses with one of the following (in brackets):

Brahman - the primordial Self-existent
Brahma - the creator
Brahmin - Hindu priest

This usage accords with that of the Vedanta Society which has for many years been the most important conveyor of the Hindu tradition in the West and the one with which most English-speaking people are likely to be familiar.

In order to dispel any notion that the Laws of Manu is comparable to Western canon law or the Roman *jus sacrum* rather than a complete corpus juris applicable to civil and criminal cases as well, its contents are listened in full below. Obviously what we have in the laws of Manu is an extensive *corpus juris* covering most of the

areas included in any modern code of laws including those delights of
the legal profession, contracts and torts, but much more besides.

CONTENTS OF THE LAWS OF MANU

*Brahmin who has completed his studentship (91, vii-ix)

The code begins with a brief account of the creation of the world,
which is the author's way of establishing the divine source of the law
beyond dispute:

1. The great sages approached Manu, who was seated with a collected mind, and, having duly worshipped him, spoke as follows:

2. 'Deign, divine one, to declare to us precisely and in due order the sacred laws of each of the (four chief) castes . . .

3. 'For thou, O Lord, alone knowest the purport, (i.e.) the rites and the knowledge of the soul, (taught) in this whole ordinance of the Self-existent [Brahman], which is unknowable and unfathomable.'

4. He, whose power is measureless, being thus asked by the high-minded great sages, duly honoured them, and answered, 'Listen!'

5. This (universe) existed in the shape of Darkness unperceived, destitute of distinctive marks, unattainable by reasoning, unknowable, wholly immersed, as it were, in deep sleep.

6. Then the divine Self-existent [Brahman, himself] indiscernible, (but) making (all) this, the great elements and the rest, discernible, appeared with irresistible (creative) power, dispelling the darkness.

7. He who can be perceived by the internal organ (alone), who is subtle, indiscernible, and eternal, who contains all created beings and is inconceivable, shone forth of his own (will).

8. He, desiring to produce beings of many kinds from his own body, first with a thought created the waters, and placed his seed in them.

9. That (seed) became a golden egg, in brilliancy equal to the sun; in that (egg) he himself was born as [Brahma], the progenitor of the whole world. . . .

11. From that (first) cause, which is indiscernible, eternal, and both real and unreal, was produced that male. . ., who is famed in this world (under the appellation) of [Brahma]. (91, 1-6)

We are already familiar with this kind of creation story from Chapter 3. There are innumerable versions of it in Hindu scriptures. After this introduction Manu goes on to describe how Brahma made the universe, what kind of creatures, great and small, he populated it with and how 'in the beginning he assigned their several names, actions, and conditions to all (created beings).' (110, 12) Finally, he tells us, '. . . *he [Brahma] having composed these Institutes (of the sacred law), himself taught them, according to the rule, to me alone in the beginning . . .*' (91, 19, *emphasis in all quotations mine*) There is a good deal of inconsistency in Hindu lore about who Manu was. Sometimes he is portrayed as the first man, sometimes as a god, even as Brahma himself. But Manu's nature need not concern us, merely the fact that he was traditionally revered as India's first lawgiver and that he received the laws directly from the creator.

The important point to understand quite clearly is that the Laws of Manu are not abstract principles which can generate or judge human law. They are specific laws covering all the subjects which, in the West, would be spread between divine law, canon law and civil and criminal human law. But to the Indic mind they are all divine law, attributed directly to and revealed by the creator. Therefore, while they are subject to interpretation they are never subject to change. 'In this (work),' Manu declares, '*the sacred law has been fully stated* as well as the good and bad qualities of (human) actions and the *immemorial rule of conduct* , (to be followed) by all the four castes . . . ' (91, 27, *emphasis mine*) This does not mean that Manu claims his 'institutes' are the totality of Indic law. He naturally assumes and enjoins strict adherence to the enormous body of obligations and practices contained in the scriptures, the Vedas, which are also held to be divinely composed. About the absolute authority of the scriptures and the laws he is uncompromising:

> But by Sruti (revelation) is meant the Veda, and by Smriti (tradition) the Institutes of the sacred law [i.e., of Manu]: those two must not be called into question, since from those two the sacred law shone forth. (91, 31)

Considering all law the direct creation of Brahma makes it an intrinsic part of the ongoing cosmic process, a shining forth of eternal Brahman. How then could man dare consider changing or questioning it? Of course, Manu understood well that in that vast body of literature called the Vedas there were conflicting injunctions. His position regarding those conflicts is enough to flummox the Western mind:

... when two sacred texts (Sruti) are conflicting, both are held to be law; for both are pronounced by the wise (to be) valid law. (Ibid.)

I don't know exactly how a Brahmin judge would decide a case with two conflicting laws at hand. Since they would be equally valid, I assume he would simply have to decide which one to use. There would certainly be no Supreme Court to which an appeal could be made. Hindu law forms an all-pervading structure for the individual's life. From birth to death, from waking to sleeping, the law prescribes virtually every proper activity. Zimmer emphasizes this in his usual dramatic way:

The divine moral order (*dharma*) by which the social structure is knit together and sustained is the same as that which gives continuity to the lives [reincarnations] of the individual; and just as the present is to be understood as a natural consequence of the past, so in accordance with the manner in which the present role is played will the caste of the future [life] be determined. . . . The correct manner of dealing with every life problem that arises, therefore, is indicated by the laws (*dharma*) of the caste . . . to which one belongs, and of the particular stage-of-life . . . that is proper to one's age. One is not free to choose; one belongs to a species - a family, guild and craft, a group, a denomination. And since this circumstance not only determines to the last detail the regulations for one's public and private conduct, but also represents (according to this all inclusive and pervasive, unyielding pattern of integration) the real ideal of one's present natural character, one's concern as a judging and acting entity must be only to meet every life problem in a manner befitting the role one plays. Whereupon the two aspects of the temporal event - the subjective and the objective - will be joined exactly, and the individual eliminated as a third, intrusive factor. He will then bring into manifestation not the temporal accident of his own personality, but the vast, impersonal, cosmic law, and so will be, not a faulty, but a perfect glass: anonymous and self-effacing. (25, 52f.)

If Indic law was immutable so was the position of the individual vis-à-vis the law. That position was defined by the *caste* into which a person was born. The castes, too, came with creation which meant that gross inequalities were part of the system from the beginning:

> . . But in order to protect this universe He, the most resplendent one [Brahma], assigned separate (duties and) occupations to those who sprang from his mouth [Brahmins], arms [Kshatriya], thighs [Vaisya], and feet [Sûdra].
> . . To [Brahmins] he assigned teaching and studying (the Veda), sacrificing for their own benefit and for others, giving and accepting (of alms).
> . . The Kshatriya [ruler and warrior caste] he commanded to protect the people, to bestow gifts, to offer sacrifices, to study (the Veda), and to abstain from attaching himself to sensual pleasures;
> . . The Vaisya [commercial caste] to tend cattle, to bestow gifts, to offer sacrifices, to study (the Veda), to trade, to lend money, and to cultivate land.
> . . One occupation only the lord prescribed to the Sûdra, to serve meekly even these (other) three castes. (91, 24)

The symbolism of mouth, arms, thighs and feet is obvious. They indicate levels of purity and worth:

> . . Man is stated to be purer above the navel (than below);hence the Self-existent [Brahman] has declared the purest (part) of him (to be) his mouth.
> . . . As the Brahmin sprang form [Brahma's] mouth, as he was the first-born, and as he possesses the Veda, he is by right the lord of this whole creation. (ibid.)

Manu never misses a chance to declare that the priestly caste is preeminent even over the ruling caste:

> . . A [Brahmin], coming into existence, is born as the highest on earth, the lord of all created beings, *for the protection of the treasury of the law.*
> . . Whatever exists in the world is the property of the [Brahmin]; on account of the excellence of his origin the [Brahmin] is entitled to it all. (91, 26)

A person was born into one of the castes and with that caste went a well-defined status and equally well-defined obligations and proscriptions. One never went upward in the caste system in the present life, although there were countless ways, through his own dereliction of duty, in which a person might sink to a lower caste or even find himself with no caste at all. The position into which one was born depended on his karma in past lives and his position in the next life would depend on his current adherence to dharma. There was no question about anyone making a judgment as to your past karma. The cosmic system took care of that. You automatically were born into the caste position you deserved. But if your present status depended on your past merit or lack of it, you were also a passive victim of what Manu states to be the real reason for the caste system: 'the protection of the universe.' What he means by that, in simplest terms, is that society needed priests, warriors, merchants and servants and the caste system assured there would always be a supply.

It was not unknown in the West to have different legal standards apply to different classes but in the West there was from very early times a nagging perception that what God or the gods enjoined was a movement toward equality of all men before the law and a kind of basic equality of human status if not of station. That perception arose because Western man, believing that order was the essence of the divine plan for the world, approached that plan with his ordering faculty, *reason*, finally developing his conception of natural law based on equity and justice. In the Western world, God's will was to change the world, which meant essentially restoring it to its pristine order.

To the Indic mind, on the other hand, the world is what it is with an elaborate structure called sacred law which points ineluctably beyond the world. There is, therefore, no plan for the world, no primeval order to restore. God's will, in effect, is to reabsorb the fragmented sparks of himself which he generated in the act of creation. The faculty by which one knows that will and follows it is not reason but *spiritual intuition* resulting from meditation. The end result toward which all scripture and law tend is union with

Brahman. This is the reason we find, toward the end of the Laws of Manu, a chapter called *Supreme Bliss* , which speaks of the final goal of Brahma's revelation of the sacred law to Manu, knowledge of the Atman (Brahman as the universal Self).

> . . All that which is most efficacious for securing supreme bliss has been thus declared to you; a [Brahmin] who does not fall off from that obtains the most excellent state.
> . . Thus did that worshipful deity disclose to me, through a desire of benefiting mankind, this whole most excellent secret of the sacred law.
> . . Let (every [Brahmin]), concentrating his mind, fully recognise in the Self all things, both the real and the unreal, for he who recognises the universe in the Self, does not give his heart to unrighteousness.
> . . The Self alone is the multitude of the gods, the universe rests on the Self; for the Self produces the connexion of these embodied (spirits) with actions.
>   * * *
> . . Let [every Brahmin] know the supreme Male (Purusha [or Brahma], to be) the sovereign ruler of [all the gods], smaller even than small, bright like gold, and perceptible by the intellect (only when) in (a state of) sleep(-like abstraction).
> . . Some call him Agni (fire), others Manu, the Lord of creatures, others Indra, others the vital air, and again others eternal Brahman.
> . . He pervades all created beings in the five forms, and constantly makes them, by means of birth, growth, and decay, revolve like the wheels (of a chariot).
> . . He who thus recognises the Self through the Self in all created beings, becomes equal(-minded) towards all, and enters the highest state, Brahman.
> . . A twice-born man [Brahmin, Kshatriya, or Vaisya] who recites these Institutes [of Manu], will be always virtuous in conduct, and will reach whatever condition he desires.(91, 511f.)

To summarize, Indic law comes directly from eternal Brahman as the very order of the universe he generates from himself. It remains, therefore, unquestionable and unchangeable, and leads the soul back to union with eternal Brahman, the Self-existent beyond all order. Its source and its goal are one.

The Chinese Puzzle: Virtue or Coercion?

> It is a curious paradox that the Chinese, who have
> emphasized written records as have few other peoples, have
> placed much less stress on codes of law, and on their
> interpretation, than has been customary in the West.
>   Herrlee G. Creel *The Origins of Statecraft in China*

I find it puzzling that the Martin A. Ryerson Distinguished
Service Professor Emeritus of Chinese History at the University of
Chicago really thought that the Chinese failure to 'stress' codes of
law was a curious paradox because it is only paradoxical to the
extent that one fails to understand the Sinic mind, of which Professor
Creel could hardly be accused. In Dun J. Li's compilation (51) of 198
excerpts from Chinese writings on a large variety of subjects, only
nine deal explicitly with law and those are virtually all concerned
with enforcement and punishment. The Chinese did enact laws, of
course, the earliest known code dating from the sixth century B.C.
And a Western Chou document, the *Tso-chuan*, referred to law codes
in the Hsia, Shang, and Chou dynasties which would, if taken at face
value (which no one does with the earliest Chinese dates), date
Chinese law well back into the second millennium B.C. Whether or
not its ascription of law codes to the Hsia and Shang is more than
fictional, it is instructive to note that the *Tso-chuan* states that they
were set up at times *'when the government had fallen into disorder
under each of the three dynasties.'* (92, 162, *emphasis mine*) This
indicates a persistent Chinese attitude that there was another even
more important factor in maintaining sound government than the
promulgation of law codes and that the latter came to the fore only
when the former failed. That attitude is at the core of Creel's so-
called paradox and is predictable by Mindset Theory.

Law, wherever found, is inherently Yang, i.e., the result of an
active, ordering, 'male' principle. We found this to be equally true in
Occidental and Indic Civilizations. In the latter, while creation itself
originated as an essentially feminine giving birth by the One, it was

carried out by the firstborn male (Brahma or Purusha) who also composed and promulgated the law. But to the Sinic mind, the cosmic (and the social) process resulted from the creative interaction between Yang and Yin, order and non-order. That interaction was the Way of Nature and the healthy society followed the Way of Nature. To the Chinese mind, the purely Yang process of law could not produce a healthy society. It is not, therefore, paradoxical that the Chinese should have 'placed much less stress on codes of law, and on their interpretation, than has been customary in the West.' The operative word is *stress*, a matter of emphasis. The simple fact is that because of their mindset the Chinese were always wary of *stressing* law as the sole means of managing society and throughout Chinese history many thinkers, among them Confucius, were downright opposed to it. Kracke is right on the mark when he observes,

> As we view the Chinese political tradition in its centuries of innovation and achievement, and its further centuries of remarkable survival and adaptation to new conditions, we look for a key to its successes. Certainly no single factor holds the answer. But one aspect seems very significant - *the co-existence and equilibrium of competing political concepts that began in the Han* [202 B.C. - 221 A.D.]. The early speculators about ways of operation and control - the 'Legalists' - initiated a train of development that led to pioneering in methods of organization and personnel administration. It led also to expansion of state activity and control that tended to reach all spheres of life, within the bounds imposed by material technology. But Confucian ideology checked and mitigated this trend of thought and action, subordinating it to values beyond those of power and efficiency, and in its way acted to liberate the individual. (28, 315, *emphasis mine.*)

In Chinese civilization, as in the other three, the divine connection of the ruler was essential. The cornerstone of the Chinese empire was the concept of the Mandate of Heaven which originated during the Chou dynasty, from which time, says Creel,

> China was a state - and, since it ideally embraced 'all under heaven,' the only state - created by, and maintained under the direct supervision of, the highest deity, Heaven. Its ruler was the Son of Heaven. His office bestowed the highest glory possible to man. His officials shone in the reflection of his glory, and under weak Kings the loyalty of feudal lords was often guaranteed by the fact that it was more splendid to be second to the son of Heaven than first among rulers exercising only mundane power. (92, 94)

Continued possession of the Mandate of Heaven, however, was not guaranteed to any Chinese king. There were many reasons why he might lose the Mandate and, therefore, the throne. Impiety, principally failure to attend to the many elaborate rituals which were incumbent upon him, was a principal reason. But a king might also lose the Mandate for being too pious, i.e., attending excessively to ritual and neglecting his primary responsibility which was governing well.

> A major reason of the loss of the Mandate of Heaven was failure to attend earnestly to government. The last Kings of both Hsia and Shang 'treated the tasks of government with contempt.' The earlier Shang Kings and their ministers, on the contrary, were zealous in their administration. King Wen created a well-governed domain in the west, giving it order and harmony, and we are told by both King Wu and the Duke of Chou that it is this that attracted the attention of Heaven and led to his receiving the Mandate. (92, 96)

Incidentally, we should always bear in mind that the Chinese conception of an 'ordered' society is different from that of the West and India. In the thinking of both the latter, an ordered society is one in which the members conform strictly to the rules but to the Chinese it is one that functions smoothly like a healthy organism regardless of the rules. There is far more flexibility and fluidity in the Chinese conception. The test of a well-governed domain was, in theory, the satisfaction of the king's subjects, the 'little people,' or at least the little people who counted. Slaves, as in any civilization, did not count. And, in fact, strong public opposition to a king could result in his being deposed and even having his dynasty replaced by another. The king, or emperor, was, above all, expected to be (publicly perceived as) an example of virtue for his ministers and subjects to emulate.

> When government officials love righteousness, the common people will follow the principle of *jen* [a Confucian virtue of good will toward all], and their customs will be good. If on the other hand these officials pursue material profit, the common people will become wicked, and their good customs will deteriorate. The emperor and his ministers set examples for the common people to follow, as if they were sitting in the center of a square, with people all around who watch them constantly. . . *To cultivate actively one's own virtue and yet be fearful of one's inability to influence the common people towards the good should be the basic attitude of all government officials.* [From a discourse by the minister, Tung Chung-shu to the emperor Han Wu-ti] (51, 15, *emphasis mine*)

We are now in a position to put some content in Kracke's phrase, 'the co-existence and equilibrium of competing political concepts that began in the Han.' On the one hand there were the 'Legalists' or 'Administrators' or 'Bureaucrats' (no Chinese character can ever be translated simply). Étienne Balazs characterizes the legalist position succinctly:

> According to the legalist school of thought a universal, uniform and absolute law *(fa)*, unvarying and binding on everybody, was essential for the maintenance of the social order, and only a legal system of rewards and punishments could guarantee the authority of the ruler. The dream of the legalists was realized when the Ch'in dynasty succeeded (221 B.C.) in unifying the Chinese empire under a strong and absolutist state power based on harsh administrative and penal measures, which they considered to be the most efficient deterrent to crime. (93, 635)

Chinese law was extremely harsh. The typical law code *began* with a list of penalties including death, mutilation and bastinado (beating the feet with a cudgel). It then proceeded to the crimes. When the judge found an offender guilty he picked the punishment he thought would best fit the crime.

Opposing the legalist approach were the Confucianists. Confucius accepted the need for law as an instrument of state power but he saw it strictly as negative and punitive, not a force for creating and maintaining the ideal harmonious state. For that purpose men were needed who were *gentlemen* in the profoundest sense, cultivated in and setting an example of *jen* or good will. The Confucian gentlemen was a model of propriety *(li)* and courtesy, concerned with the manners and rituals of society and pious toward the ancestors. It was only through the influence of such men that a society, however structured by law, could become humane and benevolent.

In typical fashion, the Chinese produced a system which balanced the two opposite points of view:

> . . . the Confucianists, who had accepted law . . . as an instrument of state power, maintained that the prescriptions of the moral code were sufficient for the discipline of the upper class, and succeeded during the middle ages in mitigating the rigour of the laws, bringing them into harmony with the *li*. The combination of these two disparate elements resulted in a legal system characterized by principles that were unchanging and rigid (a draconian penal code, collective responsibility of the social group, inequality before the law in favour of the privileged nobility and officials), but which were applied by a flexible and supple procedure that took into account the special circumstances of every case. (ibid.)

This compromise system was clearly a balance between Yang or order ('draconian penal code') and Yin or non-order ('flexible and supple procedure'). It produced an attitude toward law which was unlike that of any other civilization. In the first place they had no *reverence* for the law because they recognized that all law was what I have called *human law* and its *source* was state power pure and simple. Nowhere in Chinese literature do we find any conception of *divine law* or anything equivalent to the Western idea of *natural moral law*. Derk Bodde observes:

> A striking feature of the early written law of several major civilizations of antiquity has been its close association with religion. . . . The contrast of the Chinese attitude to the belief in the divine origin of the law is indeed striking, for in China no one at any time has ever hinted that any kind of written law - even the best written law - could have had a divine origin. (Quoted in 92, 166)

Nor did the Chinese have any *enthusiasm for the goal of law* because its goal was nothing more than to deter crime and to punish those who committed it. The law was merely one tool, and not the noblest, for managing society, a task which was ultimately the responsibility of the emperor. What the Chinese did have reverence for was the emperor who had the Mandate of Heaven to create and maintain a harmonious society and what they had enthusiasm for was precisely that kind of society. Nothing expresses their view more eloquently than the words of Tung Chung-shu in an address to the emperor:

> I have heard that Heaven is the creator of all things in the universe, and it embraces everything with love and without partiality. It makes the universe harmonious by creating such things as wind and rain together with the sun and the moon. It makes the universe complete through the interactions between the *yin* and the *yang* and between the hot and the cold. Following the ways of Heaven to govern men, a sage king is likewise selfless and impartial in his love. He induces the best from men by being virtuous himself; he leads them to a moral life by teaching them righteousness and propriety *(li)* which he himself possesses. As spring is the season heaven chooses to give birth to all things on earth, a king follows the principle of *jen* to love all of his subjects. As summer is designed by Heaven for things to grow, he likewise cultivates the growth of his own virtue. Frost is the weapon with which Heaven kills; execution is the means whereby a king punishes. To harmonize man's affairs with those of Heaven is the basic principle of all times. (51, 10)

The Chinese simply never viewed law as a way of harmonizing man's affairs.

The Tyranny of Time in Mesoamerica

As we noted in a previous chapter it is doubtful that the Amerindians reached the level of abstract thought (although they certainly dealt with high mythopeic abstractions in their art as we saw in Chapter 5). For the same reason we do not find philosophy we likewise find no reflections on the nature of law in Mesoamerica. Neither do we find modern scholars writing tomes about Amerindic law. There is no Jolowicz or Creel to whom we can look to help us understand the source or the goal of Aztec or Mayan law or whether it was predominantly divine or natural or human law. Studies of Aztec life repeatedly refer to certain peculiarities of the law, such as the severe penalties for drunkenness and the fact that, contrary to Chinese practice, penalties were more severe the higher in rank and responsibility was the offender. A fairly detailed account has also come down to us of the structure of the justice system, the kinds of courts, duties of judges, avenues of appeal, and so forth. But no one that I have come across has dealt with Amerindic law as a system and explained on what it was founded and whence it derived its authority. Consequently, as with other areas of their life, we have to do our own theorizing and create our own model of the Amerindians' legal system, hoping it will approximate what they themselves might have constructed had their civilization survived a few more centuries.

It might be expected that in such religion-ridden states as those of Mesoamerica, divine law would dominate and that all *crime* would be equivalent to *sin*. It is true that when an Aztec feared that he approached the end of his life he could go to a priest and confess any crimes he had committed which had remained undetected and unpunished by the courts. Once he had made his confession, which could only take place once in a lifetime, and had undergone the penance set by the priest, the penitent was not only absolved of guilt but could no longer be punished by the law. Depending on the seriousness of the crimes confessed, the penance could be very severe as Soustelle tells us:

> When [the penitent] had finished, the priest set him a
> penance that would vary in severity: short or lengthy fasts,
> scarification of the tongue - it might be pierced through and
> have as many as eight hundred thorns or straws pushed
> through the wound - sacrifices to Tlazolteotl [goddess of
> lechery and unlawful love who also had the power of
> absolution], and various austerities. Once the penance was
> done the man could 'no longer be punished upon this earth'.
> The priest was bound to the most absolute secrecy, 'for that
> which he had heard was not for him, but had been said,
> secretly, for the deity.' (94, 200)

Tempting as it is, however, to think of Amerindic law as divine,
i.e., revealed law, there are compelling reasons against that point of
view. Although the gods could forgive transgressions which came
within their particular venues, we are nowhere told that the gods
created or revealed the laws which were transgressed. Even the
revered Quetzalcoatl, to whom the Toltecs and Aztecs attributed
nearly everything, is never credited with composing or revealing laws.

If law did not come from the gods, was it then merely *human
law?* There were certainly published laws such as the statutes of
Nezaualcoyotl but it seems to me that such statutes were more like
regulations such as, to give a modern parallel, those the Internal
Revenue Service promulgates to express and enforce the revenue laws
Congress passes. Why, for example, were the Aztecs so severe on
drunkenness? I can't take seriously suggestions by some writers
that it was simply because Indians can't handle 'fire water.' When
an Aztec's active life was over, i.e., after retirement, he was free to
drink as much *pulque* as he wished. Why, again, did the Aztecs
treat crimes by persons of higher rank much more harshly than those
of lesser rank? 'It may be observed, in passing,' says Soustelle,

> . . . that the gravity of the sentence always increased in
> proportion with the rank of the culprit: the punishment for a
> plebeian who was drunk in public was a severe admonition
> and the shame of having his head shaven; for a noble, it was
> death. It was also death for a noble who had robbed his

father, whereas a *maceualli* [plebeian] guilty of the same crime got off with penal slavery. *Duty, responsibility and danger increased with power and wealth.* (94, 143, *emphasis mine*)

This observation is so important for understanding the rules by which Amerindians lived that it should not merely be noted 'in passing.' Notice how contrary this view of the application of the law to different classes is to that of Confucius who held that while the plebeians might need the strictures of law the nobles could be trusted to depend on their honor and virtue alone. The difference between the two outlooks is that for the Chinese man depended on the universe but *for the Amerindians the universe depended on man.* And it depended more on the person in high position whose whole *raison d'être* was the religious and civil duties he *must* perform to keep the cosmic process functioning. There was no mercy for the person of high responsibility who neglected his duties because of drunkenness or offended the gods by serious crimes. The harsh laws which regulated all Amerindic societies were not, therefore, simply human laws but were, in effect, regulations to ensure that another, higher kind of law was not violated. That higher law was not legislated by man and it was not revealed by the gods but the *instrument* by which it could be understood was given to man by none other than Quetzalcoatl himself. *That instrument was the calendar!*

I went into some detail about the Amerindians' calendar in Chapter 4 to give an idea of the complex extremes to which they carried it. The importance of their calendar and the cosmic order it represented was far greater to the Amerindians than we find in any other civilization. To them the calendric order was not something which acted from the remote heavens but the very fabric of the universe and of life. Jacques Soustelle best conveys the all-pervasive character of the calendric order in the following passage from his *Daily Life of the Aztecs:*

The divinatory year of 260 days split up naturally into 20
groups of 13, each of which began with the figure 1 with a
different sign [day name] appropriated to it: 1 *cipactli*
[crocodile], 1 *ocelotl* [ocelot], 1 *mazatl* [deer], etc., and so on
until the last, 1 *tochtli* [rabbit]. Each of these groups was
considered on the whole fortunate, unfortunate or indifferent,
according to the sense of its first day; but besides this each of
the days might be good, bad or neutral according to its
distinguishing number and sign. The days which had the
numbers 7, 10, 11, 12 and 13 were held to be generally
favourable, and those with the figure 9 unfavourable. But
the influence of the figures had to be combined with that of
the signs, and the divinatory [ritual] calendar was in fact
made up of a table of 260 special cases.

Furthermore, each group of thirteen was assigned to one or to
two gods: the sun and the moon for the group 1 *miquiztli*
[death], Patecatl, god of drink and drunkenness, for the group
1 *quiauitl* [rain]; the planet Venus and the god of the dead for
the group 1 *coatl* [snake], etc. Finally, nine deities, 'the lords
of the night', made up a series parallel with that of the signs
and running in an uninterrupted sequence beside them: their
particular influence had certainly to be taken into account in
the soothsayer's appreciation of any given day. (94, 110f.)

Soustelle goes on to indicate that the complexity of the calendric
order was further compounded by 'the influence peculiar to the year
itself, and likewise that which the cardinal points of space might
have upon the signs.' (ibid.) It should not be supposed that the
calendric order was, as Soustelle's use of the term 'divinatory' in the
quotation on the preceding page suggests, merely a matter for
priestly soothsaying. On the contrary, the calendric order impinged
on every aspect of Amerindic experience and was a constant
imperative on the daily life of every Amerindian, especially those
belonging to the upper classes.

The degree to which the members of ruling class were taken up
by their duties is surprising; but one is positively astonished
when one tries to count up the time that they had to devote to
worship and to ceremonies. Of course everybody in Mexico
took part in the innumerable holidays, or rather holy days,
and in the complicated rites which took place on them; but
here again it was the dignitaries who bore the brunt.

Their presence was very often called for in the sacrifices,
dances, singing, processions and parades not only in the
town, but more than once right round the lake [of Mexico
where Tenochtitlán was situated].   The solar year was
divided into eighteen months of twenty days (plus the five
intercalary days of evil omen, during which all activity was
reduced to a minimum) and a fresh set of rites and
ceremonies belonged to each of these months.   Some at least
of these called for a very great effort from a very large number
of people, an immense amount of organisation and a very
considerable expense. (94, 144)

It seems clear that *the calendric order was, in fact, the dominant
law which ruled Amerindic life*.   But what species of law was it, if not
divine and not human.   I submit that had the Amerindians at some
future time thought about it abstractly, they would have come up
with a conception very similar to Western *natural law*.   It was a
cosmic law which ordered everything from the gods to nature to
man's moral and religious life.   Was it, like Western natural law,
accessible to reason?   To a degree it was.   The priests, over a long
period of time, had to determine what rituals and duties were *right
and proper* to each of the myriad occasions determined by the
calendric order.   What was right and proper was not set forth in a
divine revelation as it was in India.   Judgment was required.   It also
seems clear that in the Amerindic civil courts decisions were not, for
the most part, based on hard and fast rules but were generally
arrived at by lengthy (and reportedly longwinded) debate about the
right and proper way to settle matters.

   If we acknowledge that Amerindic law was a kind of natural law,
we have to acknowledge as well that it differed in character
considerably from Western natural law.   The *jus naturale*, whether
Roman or Christian was viewed as tending toward a more
reasonable, just and equitable society.   Its concern was, as Aquinas
stated, the common good.   The order it embodied was an expression
of God's eternal law which governed and upheld his creation.   But
Amerindic natural law was, in the deepest sense, independent of the
gods and not a guarantor but a test of creation.   Failure to observe

its demands could lead not merely to individual damnation or social disaster but to cosmic destruction. It was not a solution to the precarious balance between order and non-order, creation and destruction which we have seen typified Amerindic society. On the contrary, it focussed that precariousness on the most minute details of everyday life and instead of hope tended to load a terrible burden of anxiety and pessimism on the Amerindic soul, a burden of which Soustelle speaks poignantly.

> The moral climate of ancient Mexico was soaked in pessimism. The poems of the great king Nezualcoyotl are haunted by the idea of death and annihilation; and even when other poets celebrate the beauties of tropical nature one feels that the obsession is there and that 'it takes them by the throat even amidst the flowers. Religion, and the art that expresses religion through sculpture, and even the manuscripts whose glyph enclose the wisdom of this ancient people, everything crushes man with the harshness of a fate that is beyond his control. (94, 115)

Any reverence for the *source* of Mesoamerican law was thus born out of fear and any enthusiasm for its *goal* was the child of desperation.

SEVEN

Physical Discipline: Mind and Body

The Trainable Human Body

This book is about the civilized *mind* but in this chapter and the next we are going to be considering what many people think is virtually antithetical to mind - the human body. What I intend to show in these chapters is that the way in which members of each civilization understood and treated the body was profoundly influenced by their mindset. In this chapter we will see that influence manifested in the manner in which the body was disciplined and trained. The next will deal with how it affected the intimate contact between male and female.

The human body is an extraordinary system consisting of a two-hundred piece jointed framework, an equal number of binders and activators which connect and move the structural members, miles of tubing through which fluids and solids are pumped or squeezed and even more miles of delicate transmission lines over which electrical signals are constantly passing. It has organs that pump, others that filter, some that manufacture complex chemicals, some that receive and transmit external information and one that specializes in thought. The body is, in fact, the intermediary between the mind and the external world. Information about the external world comes to us in the form of such things as photons and sound waves. We do not experience photons or sound waves. They reach our sense organs where they are converted into neural messages which our brain organizes into pattens and our minds translate into experienced light and sound.

Conversely, our imaginings, our desires and our decisions get transformed into body activators which enable us to move in and manipulate our customary three-dimensional world. We exercise a considerable amount of command over some of these activators. Most of the usual regulatory functions of the body, however, operate pretty much independently of our consciousness, which is very fortunate for us. Who would want to have his consciousness taken up with the task of keeping his digestive system working? The autonomic regulation of our body's normal maintenance systems leaves us free to use our minds to direct those parts of the body for which the mind has a great deal of special use, such as the feet, hands and eyes.

There are four kinds of discipline and training to which the body can be subjected. First, we can train it to perform automatically and unconsciously functions which we usually have to think about. For example, I could sit here at my computer keyboard and consciously pick out each letter. Some people do. It is called the 'hunt and peck' system. But I long ago trained my fingers so that they can fly over the keyboard and record my thoughts almost as fast as I think them (sometimes faster). I can do the same thing with a ten-digit keypad but not with a piano keyboard because I never trained myself to play the piano.

The second form of training is related to the first but it also applies to some bodily functions which are already largely automatic as nature gives them to us. This type of training consists in increasing the power, skill, speed, gracefulness or sensitivity of those functions. We certainly use it in learning to type faster and more accurately as well as in *mastering* the piano or other musical instrument. But we can also use it in such activities as walking or running. The latter are such complex activities that if we had to think them through as we did them we would never get anywhere. Still, we can train ourselves to alter their character so that we can run a four minute mile, manipulate a soccer ball back and forth across a field with marvelous speed and accuracy using only our feet, or twist, turn and glide our way through a ballet. All of these activities, incidentally, require training in *sensitivity*. One must never think that only certain people such as artists are sensitive. *Sensitivity is the ability to finely discriminate between perceived elements.* A person's sensitivity is greatest in the field in which he specializes. A painter will be sensitive to the finest nuances of color, shape and texture. But a boxer is also sensitive, only to different experiential elements. He has to be sensitive to his opponent's style, the effect the fight is having on his stamina, how he is likely to react at any given moment to a certain kind of attack or retreat, how strong and accurate his punches seem to be and, in addition to all that, the boxer has to be aware of all the same things in himself. No one who ever heard Muhammad Ali in his prime give one of his famous post mortems after a fight could doubt the incredible sensitivity of the champion *in his own area of specialization*. You don't have to play a violin or paint with oils to be sensitive. Sensitivity appropriate to any specialization can be trained just as speed or accuracy can.

The first two forms of training, you will notice, have to do with the body's relationship to the external world. The last two arise from the body's unique status in the phenomenal world. It is the only phenomenon which we not only experience externally as one among all other objects, including other people's bodies, but internally as well. We feel only our own hunger, our own sexual urges, our own headaches, our own indigestion - no one else's. And, of course, we experience only our own pleasures and pains, joys and sorrows, daydreams and nightmares - thankfully no one else's.

All of these internal feelings and sensations arise normally in the course of life. But what if there are some we don't like and would rather be rid of or perhaps some we do like and wish to enhance? What can we do about it? We can use a third type of training, the aim of which is not to enhance our physical effect on the external world but to alter our internal perceptions or *to change our inner consciousness.*   Human history is replete with techniques for altering consciousness - drugs, Corybantic rites, revivalism, hypnosis, and psychotherapy, to name only a few.

Finally, there is a fourth method of training the body which is more esoteric than the others. It is also concerned with our internal experience but instead of attempting to change our perceptions of and attitudes toward our bodily processes it aims to change those processes themselves. Here I am not referring to the voluntary processes but the ones that are normally under the control of our autonomic nervous system. It is apparent in the West today, from our knowledge of such processes as hypnosis and biofeedback, that we are capable of considerably more influence over the autonomic nervous system than we customarily acknowledge. There are also numerous cases which show that the mind can affect the body in startling ways - cases, for example, of virtually superhuman strength summoned up in a critical situation.

The fact is we simply do not know to what extent the mind can change the body by taking control of its normally unconscious functions. The yogic tradition of India has always claimed that the extent is enormous, even extending to such phenomena as levitation although such extraordinary powers of mind over body have never been convincingly demonstrated to the West. Indic Civilization was the only one in which the assumption of direct control over the autonomic nervous system was attempted to any significant degree. But all the civilizations developed techniques of disciplining the body and those techniques involved one or more of the four types of training outlined above. How they used them depended entirely on the views they held of the body's relationship to the mind and 'soul' and its place in the scheme of things. The range of those views, as we shall see, was determined by the civilized mindsets.

Regimens of the West: Athletes and Ascetics

When all the voluntary and involuntary functions of the body proceed smoothly in consonance with a healthy, active mind we have the situation described by the poet Juvenal as *mens sana in corpore sano* - a sound mind in a sound body. But a cardinal feature of the human condition is that neither the mind nor the body is guaranteed continued soundness. Insanity is not directly pertinent to this chapter but pathologies of the body are, primarily because they are inescapable reminders of its mortality. We have only one 'interior' experience of death, one we can hardly learn from, but from the illness and death of others we learn that malfunctions of the body always carry the risk that it will simply shut down permanently. Even if the body is relatively healthy, the gradual deterioration and weakening called 'aging' points inexorably toward death.

Strong, healthy bodies send fewer premonitory signals of death, so one way in which we can deny death is to concentrate on physical development. This accounts in part for the fact that no period in time can compare with this last part of the twentieth century in the West for the sheer magnitude of its emphasis on developing and maintaining a sound body. The shelves of American book stores are studded with books on health, diet and exercise. A spate of exercise video tapes have flooded the market, ranging from the funny to the formidable.

These workout programs are methods of *physical training*. People who follow them do so because they want to be healthy, feel vital and, in no small measure, avoid the premonitions of and postpone the time of death. This is a rational purpose based on modern medical theories about how the body functions but underlying it is a belief that body and mind, 'exterior' and 'interior,' are inseparable and coterminous and that mind, to the extent that such a reality is acknowledged, is a product or 'epiphenomenon' of the body, particularly the brain.

Strange as it may seem to us, this belief is completely contrary to the body/mind understanding of Occidental Civilization, which is our heritage. From the earliest times the Egyptians held that the body was infused with a vital spirit called the *ka*. The *ka*, whose physical locus was the heart, was the soul or essence of the person and the repository of his deeds during life. At death it left the body and was judged by Osiris. If the judgment was favorable the *ka* was granted immortality, but not merely a 'spiritual' immortality. To the Egyptians life meant living in a body. They preserved the corpse by mummification so that the *ka* could return to it and live forever. Although the Jews are generally credited with originating the idea of *the resurrection of the body*, it was really the Egyptians who first conceived of such a miracle, one they expected to happen in the secrecy of the tomb.

Egypt was thus the first civilization to explicitly formulate that unique relationship between body and soul from which subsequent Western Civilization was to derive much of its intensity. In this Western view the soul was not a product or epiphenomenon of the body. On the contrary, the body was considered inherently inert, what I have called a *non-order phenomenon*, until it was given vitality by the soul. This view is reflected alike in Hebrew and Greek thought. In Genesis 2:7 we read, '. . . the Lord God formed man of dust from the ground and breathed into his nostrils the breath of life; and man became a living being.' (87, 2) Plato's *Timaeus* expresses a similar point of view about body and soul:

> Now of the divine, he himself [God] was the creator, but the creation of the mortal he committed to his offspring. And they, imitating him, received from him the immortal principle of the soul; and around this they proceeded to fashion a mortal body, and made it to be the vehicle of the soul. . . (73 , 52)

Three basic assumptions underlay the Western understanding of body and soul:

1. The soul is independent of and superior to the body;
2. The soul is intrinsically individual and specific to a particular body, that is, it is neither a 'universal' soul nor one subject to reincarnation in other bodies;
3. Since the soul does not depend on the body for life, but vice-versa, the death of the body does not cause the death of the soul.

Behind these assumptions was the ultimate assumption of Occidental Civilization that order was the essence of life and the only way that lifeless non-order (in this case, the body) could be vitalized was through the transformative power of order (the *ka* or soul). That is why the civilized West never adopted the belief that the mind is a product of the body, although philosophers did propose it from time to time.

But if the body was the 'vehicle of the soul' why was it subject to passion and perversion, disease and death? Why did it not share the immortality and perfection of the soul? This puzzle plagued Western man. Whenever he thought of physical discipline it was always with the aim of conforming the disorderly body to the order of the soul. Of the methods he devised for accomplishing this, two were most important and enduring: the Greek method, *The Way of the Athlete*, and the Christian method, *The Way of the Ascetic*. Different as these methods may seem, we will see that at the deepest level they were outgrowths of the Occidental mindset and therefore unique to Western Civilization.

The Way of the Athlete. Recall that in the passage previously quoted from Plato's *Timaeus* , God did not create the human body. He left that to his 'offspring' who made the body to be 'the vehicle of the soul.' But that was not the end of the matter. The 'assistant' gods, the passage continues,

. . . constructed within the body a soul of another nature which was mortal, subject to terrible and irresistible affect-

ions - first of all, pleasure, the greatest incitement to evil;
then pain, which deters from good; also rashness and fear,
two foolish counselors, anger hard to be appeased, and hope
easily led astray - these they mingled with irrational sense
and all-daring love according to necessary laws, and so
framed man. (ibid.)

This story, which is more poetry than philosophy, nevertheless
reflects the typical Greek view that the human body is a composite
creation of 'higher' and 'lower' components. It was not corrupted by
the influence of a cosmic fiend, as in Zoroastrianism, nor by human
sin, as in Judaism. The corruption occurred in the process of
creation, the body receiving or retaining a share of original chaos in
the process. How large a share and to what extent the mind could
bring it under the dominion of order was a problem which repeatedly
recurred in Greek thought. There was a strain in later Hellenistic
thought which took a very pessimistic outlook on the susceptibility of
the body to discipline. This strain culminated in the body-denying
school of neo-Platonism which had some impact on early Christian
theology. But in fairness to the Greeks we have to admit that neo-
Platonism was heavily skewed by Indic, Iranian, Egyptian and other
influences from the periphery of the Hellenistic world. The great
Athenian philosophers and their cultured contemporaries were far
too down-to-earth to accept a life-denying mysticism. What they did
understand and accept very well was Greece's unique and enduring
contribution to physical discipline - *athletics*.

The focus of athletics was the games, of which the Olympic
Games were foremost. Athletic competitions are mentioned about as
far back in Greek history as we can go. They were always
celebratory and generally associated with religious festivals. In the
Iliad, Homer tells of games which followed the death of Patroclus at
Troy. The Olympic Games, held in honor of Zeus, were held to have
begun in 776 B.C. and they continued every four years until they
were abolished by the Christian emperor, Theodosius I, in 393 A.D.,
a period of well over a thousand years. So important were the
Olympics that the Greeks kept track of dates by reference to them.

Each four year interval was called an Olympiad and a year was designated by the Olympiad in which it occurred, for example, the third year of the seventieth Olympiad.

Athletic discipline combined strong muscular exertion with continual attention to the *form* of the activity. Neither muscular exertion, while it was considered the healthiest form of exercise, nor muscular development were considered ends in themselves. The Greeks would have been apalled by the excesses of much modern 'aerobics' as well as the often grotesque results of so-called 'body building.' To them any activity or quality which admitted of a wide range of gradations also had a *péras* or exactly right degree which was healthy and appropriate. Aristotle called it the 'right mean.' Athletics were, therefore, to be performed not only strenuously but with graceful and beautiful form. The body which resulted from that activity was not one with a mass of knots and bulges heaped on one another like Ptolemaic epicycles but one in which clearly defined, well-developed musculature formed one component of a graceful, vital whole. It was this beautiful, athletic body which the Greek sculptors drew upon for their incomparable male figures. (See Plate 4)

Greek physical discipline was not confined to those who intended to compete in the games but was practiced by all healthy, vigorous men. Athletes such as the famous wrestler, Milo, specialized in specific events *(athelas)* but the basic training for all was the same - *calisthenics.* This term, from *kallos*, beauty, and *sthenos*, strength, accurately describes the Greek view of the goal of physical discipline - *strength combined with beauty* . It was a more profound concept than 'a sound mind in a sound body.' It denoted a body trained to suit the ideal conceived by the mind, for it was the mind that determined the 'right mean.'

But it was not merely a matter of bringing the *body* under the rule of the mind. Every Olympic competitor had to swear a solemn oath to compete cleanly and fairly. This meant that no matter how well his body was trained, his mind must also put aside those passions which can so easily corrupt athletic competition, the very things, in fact, we heard mentioned earlier in the *Timaeus:* rashness and fear, anger hard to be appeased, hope easily led astray. How many athletes (especially, it seems, tennis and ice hockey players) have been tarnished by rashness and anger and how many have been tempted to cheat by hope (of winning)? In the Greek ideal you could not train the body properly without also training the soul in virtue!

Athletics virtually disappeared from Western history for fifteen hundred years. They were only revived in the nineteenth century due to the ardent enthusiasm of the French baron, Pierre de Coubertin. The first modern Olympic Games were held in 1896, fittingly in Greece. Winter games were added in 1924. The modern Olympics, as we might expect, dispensed with both the religious and moral assumptions of the Greeks. The only vestiges of virtue associated with them were the requirement of amateurism (now no longer applicable) and the code of fair play. Nevertheless, as far as the kind of training and the nature of the events are concerned, the modern Olympics are a fair reflection of the originals and we can learn a great deal about the Greek ideal of physical discipline by examining them in more detail.

The key observation we need to make about Olympic events is that all of them, without exception, have one common characteristic: *the aggressive, controlled propulsion of objects through space.* The propelled objects are of two kinds, human and non-human, as the following table of typical events illustrates:

Events propelling human objects	Events propelling non-human objects
Running	Shot-put
Jumping	Discus
Swimming	Javelin
Diving	Hammer
Boxing	Weight lifting
Wrestling	Fencing
Gymnastics	Archery
Skiing	Shooting
Ice Skating	Most team sports

Certain sports are a combination of the two, with the human participants going along for the ride on a non-human object, e.g., cycling, rowing, canoeing, yachting, bobsledding, luge, and equestrian events. With only two exceptions, equestrian events and shooting, the propulsive power is supplied by human strength. Speaking of these events as aggressive means both that all involve extraordinary muscular or other force and that many of them subject the human body to unusually hazardous conditions. Think of hurdles and pole vault, side horse and flying ring events, 90-meter ski jumps, slalom runs, platform and springboard dives, to name only a few of the events which are inherently violent and could easily result in injury or even death were they not performed with the master athlete's nearly perfect control. Injuries are rare in major athletic competitions but they do happen and the road to those competitions is strewn with strains, sprains, fractures and even paralyses and fatalities.

It is the aggressive, near violent character of Olympic events which makes them typically Western. Once a body, human or non-human, is thrust out of a quiet state and hurled through space it becomes a paradigm of non-order, that is, of chaos and chance. The challenge for the athlete is to transform its chaotic course into a controlled series of movements with an ordered objective or form. He can only achieve that control through a specific kind of physical discipline involving the development of those special skills which are required by the nature of the event for which he is training. While all athletes benefit from general calisthenics, training for athletic events can become highly specialized. Quite different kinds of training are involved for hammer-throwing, cycling, diving and vaulting, for example. Much of the training, in fact, consists simply of 'practice,' repeating the activities of the event over and over again while gradually modifying and improving their execution. But, in addition, the ancillary calisthenics for each event have to be designed around its specific requirements.

Obviously, athletic training does not involve all the systems of the body. It is primarily concerned with the muscles, their strength and accuracy of control, and with their coordination with the senses, particularly that of sight. Greek-inspired physical discipline does not seek to alter the bodily functions which normally depend on the autonomic nervous system nor to affect the nature of the information signals transmitted from sensory receptors to the mind through the central nervous system. The stream of Western physical discipline which flows from Greece is strictly a matter of transforming non-order (the untrained body and the chaos of the raw athletic event) into order (a finely tuned body and a superbly executed event).

The Way of the Ascetic. In the fifth century A.D., a Syrian monk stood on a fifty-foot high pillar for *twenty years*. His name was Simeon and he was called Stylites from the Greek word, *stilos*, meaning 'pillar.' Simeon Stylites ate very little food, spent most of his time in prayer and, we are told, never once sat down in all those twenty years. The only time he was known to be off his feet was during the several times a day he knelt in obeisance to God. People were very impressed by Simeon. He preached to crowds from his pillar twice a day and succeeded in making large numbers of converts to Christianity.

If a modern political regime were to put a man on a pillar, expose him continually to heat, cold, wind and rain, never allow him to sit, and feed him next to nothing for twenty years, its action would be considered the most heinous kind of torture and Amnesty International would be relentless in condemning it. But no one forced Simeon Stylites to undergo those inhuman conditions. *He imposed them on himself.* In so doing he became the first of a series of so-called 'pillar saints' who appeared in eastern Christendom off and on until the twelfth century. The pillar saints practiced an extreme form of a kind of physical discipline called *asceticism*. Asceticism involved not only denial of comforts but of basic human needs such as food, sex and social contact. In addition, it often entailed self-inflicted discomfort, pain and even injury or mutilation.

The typical image of the ascetic is one of a gaunt, emaciated person clothed in rags, his eyes burning with fanatic intensity. How strongly that image contrasts with that of the Greek athlete, his body strong, graceful and beautiful. How schizophrenic, we might think, must the Occidental mind have been to have produced two such opposite physical ideals as the Olympic athlete and the Christian ascetic! What could they possibly have in common? Let us see.

To begin with, athleticism and asceticism had a *word* in common. The words, 'ascetic' and 'asceticism', are derived from the Greek word, *askein* , meaning 'to train' or 'to exercise.' It was the very same word used to denote the training undergone by Greek athletes. The Greeks, in fact, used it for all kinds of training - in virtue, in wisdom, in art as well as in athletics. So when the Church Fathers used the term to describe the kind of self-denial and 'mortification of the flesh' later carried to almost superhuman extremes by the pillar saints they were indicating that it was not simply a matter of perverse self-torture but a way of training and disciplining the body toward a specific goal. As with athletics, asceticism was a method of ordering the chaotic tendencies of the body, but the goal was not the visible order of strength and beauty. Asceticism aspired to a different kind of order, one that arose from the Christian answer to what caused the body's chaotic tendencies.

In the Judaeo-Christian tradition, unlike the Greek, the corruption of human nature was not caused by the way man was created. On the contrary, the first man, Adam, was created perfect to be lord of a perfectly ordered world. That he did not continue to enjoy that perfection was due to his own sin. He arrogated to himself the divine prerogative of judging good and evil and that brought chaos into the order of Eden. It is significant that the first evidence of man's corruption of Eden, concerned the body:

> Then the eyes of [Adam and Eve] were opened, and they
> knew that they were naked; and they sewed fig leaves
> together and made themselves aprons. And they heard the
> sound of the Lord God walking in the garden in the cool of

the day, and the man and his wife hid themselves from the presence of the Lord God among the trees of the garden. But the Lord God called to the man, and said to him, 'Where are you?' And he said, 'I heard the sound of thee in the garden, and I was afraid, because I was naked; and I hid myself.' He said, 'Who told you that you were naked? Have you eaten of the tree of which I commanded you not to eat?' (87, 3)

Obviously, the knowledge that they had no clothes on was not the dreadful sin that caused the first couple's fall from paradise. It was the *judgment* they made that nakedness was evil and ought to be covered which brought about that cosmic disaster.   God had pronounced all he had created, including the body, good, *very* good, but man, contradicting God, had pronounced the naked body evil. That was the paradigm of man's willful but futile arrogation of divine power to himself, his Original Sin. It was that sin, passed on from Adam to all the generations of man, which was the source of the corruption of human nature according to Jews, Christians and Moslems.

For Jews and Moslems, the redemption of human nature was accomplished by submitting to the laws of God as revealed by Moses and Mohammed, respectively. Those laws involved certain dietary, moral and social restrictions for all the faithful which, while they affected the body, did not require it to be subjected to any stringent discipline. Except for two peripheral Jewish sects (the Essenes and the Therapeutae) and one mystical spinoff of Islam (Sufism), asceticism was alien to both religions.

Christianity, on the other hand, held that human redemption was impossible by human effort and achievable only by divine grace. Although he went off to the desert to commune with God, as did all Jewish prophets, Jesus' own lifestyle cannot be called ascetic. His first recorded miracle was changing water to wine at a wedding feast in Cana. It was judged to be an exceptionally good wine and there is no reason to doubt that Jesus himself enjoyed a cup of it. He did not deny himself food but seemed clearly not to have concerned himself about where his next meal was coming from. Although he told his disciples to take no thought for the morrow he was concerned when people who came to hear him became hungry and made sure they had enough fish and bread to eat. He probably had a sound, healthy body because he walked a lot. The only recorded instance of his riding was when he entered Jerusalem on a donkey shortly before his death and that was for symbolic purposes.

The early Christians imitated Jesus' lifestyle. Like him they expected the imminent end of the world as they knew it and the establishment of the Kingdom of Heaven on earth. So they lived in anticipation, their communities characterized by their devotion to Jesus the Christ and loving care for each other. But though they waited and waited, the end and the new beginning did not arrive. In the meantime, many of them died, so the ones who were left had to begin rethinking what they were waiting for. They did not give up the idea of the Second Coming but it began to appear less imminent. The convert Paul solved the problem of those who had died by reviving the Jewish doctrine of the resurrection of the body. Don't worry if you die before Christ comes, was the message; when he does all the faithful will be raised in new, incorruptible bodies which will live forever in God's kingdom.

In the meantime, however, there were those Christians, particularly around the edges of the Roman empire, who were beginning to suspect that the relatively wholesome naturalness of the Christian communities was falling short of what a Christian life required. Something more severe, more disciplined was needed *as a demonstration of faith*. At first, there is no doubt that that kind of thinking was influenced by the dualistic views of gnosticism and Neo-Platonism and it was generally condemned by the mainstream of the Church. But by the third century, perhaps because the Church had undergone so many persecutions and setbacks and was beginning to wonder what was the right course, it was ready to accept the growing number of devotees called anchorites who had appeared in Asia Minor and Egypt. Anchorites were recluses who devoted themselves to prayer and typically subjected their bodies to the severe hardships of inadequate clothing, hunger and exposure and even to torments such as shirts made of coarse bristles, chains and flagellation.

The fundamental purpose of these ascetic practices was not salvation. That was already guaranteed to the faithful by God through the sacrifice of Christ. The purpose of asceticism was to *demonstrate faith*. After all, the only absolute requirement laid upon a Christian was faith in Christ. To Paul the great demonstration of faith was love but to the ascetics that was not enough. They were more acutely aware even than Paul that the natural tendencies of human nature, especially the desires of the body, were constant sources of competition with their faith. The ascetics adopted Kierkegaard's dictum that 'Purity of heart is to will one thing' many centuries before the great Danish philosopher was born. They believed that every tendency of human nature had to be subjugated to one intense movement of the will toward God. *Life was to be ordered around one total act of faith.*

Once the Church had accepted the authenticity of Christian asceticism it soon realized that its discipline produced an enormous spiritual energy which could be of great benefit to the Church as a whole. What was needed was to organize and institutionalize that energy. The first step was to organize ascetics into communities. Such communities arose spontaneously in Egypt in the third century. At first they were hardly more than loose collections of hermits called cenobites, who chose to live near each other because of certain common practices. The second and crucial step in harnessing the power of asceticism was taken by St. Pachomius who founded the first Christian *monastery* in 318. Pachomius introduced the idea of a religious 'order,' the lives of whose adherents were totally governed by a *rule* which regulated every activity of the day, hour by hour, down to the finest details. The founder of *European* monasticism was St. Benedict. The famous Benedictine Rule became the prototype for those of all the great monastic orders which were to be founded throughout the centuries. The rule was an ordering power which governed abbot and monk alike. It curbed the eccentric zeal exemplified by the pillar saints and, while the monastic orders recognized that some were called to mortify the flesh more than others, they generally discouraged excesses which tended to debilitate the individual and hinder him from carrying out the work of the order.

You do not have to be Roman Catholic to appreciate that the monastic practitioners of ascetic discipline - Benedictines, Dominicans, Franciscans, Carmelites and members of many lesser known orders - were a principle force in preserving the heritage of Western Civilization during the 'dark ages' following the collapse of the Roman Empire. The Benedictines alone were largely responsible for preserving and transmitting much of classical literature. Without their work we might know next to nothing about the ancient Olympic Games and have little but ancient ruins to tell us of 'the glory that was Greece and the grandeur that was Rome.'

Asceticism was an expression of the Occidental mindset every bit as much as Greek athletics. As the Greek trained his body, his emotions and his mind to participate in an ideal order, so the ascetic trained all three to demonstrate his faith in the order that God would eventually bring to a sinful world. Until this century, asceticism had a far more profound influence on the West than athletics. This may seem a strange thing to say because nothing could be more alien to the modern Western mind than asceticism. But we are discussing the era when Western Civilization held sway. It no longer does.

The Inward Path of the Indian Yogi

In 1936 a graduate student at Columbia University named Theos Bernard wrote his doctoral dissertation on the unlikely subject of *Hatha Yoga*. In it he described in great detail a regimen of physical exercises which sounded not only bizarre but physically impossible to his faculty examiners. To dispel their incredulity Bernard added to his dissertation a series of photographs of himself actually performing those exercises. I am certain that the exercises still seemed bizarre to some of the Columbia professors but the photographs at least proved they were physically possible.

More than half a century later, Hatha Yoga, the basic Indic form of physical discipline, is very well known in the West, where it is usually simply called 'yoga.' You will find it taught in classes at the 'Y', in numerous books by both Indian and Western authors, and even on television and videotape. These presentations of Hatha Yoga almost invariably have two characteristics in common. In the first place, the teachers tell us that the discipline is based on principles of health and well-being which do not require that you be Indian or that you commit yourself to Indic religion or philosophy. For example,

> The idea has sometimes been expressed that the union with the higher Self, which is the final objective of Yoga, cannot be achieved by westerners using eastern methods. Such views are greatly exaggerated and usually based on ignorance of the real facts. They are mostly the product of a time when Yoga was practically unknown in western countries except by a few specialists of Hindu culture who were interested in Yoga mainly from a philological and philosophical viewpoint. (95 , 13)

The truth is, however, that although 'union with the higher Self' may well be attainable by Westerners through yoga, the very concept of union with the higher Self is specifically Indic. To the extent that it is to be found in other civilizations it is certainly, as the author says, 'more or less buried.' Parallels to it in Western Civilization are to be found only on the periphery of the great religions, represented in Islam, for example, by Sufi mysticism and in Christianity by the unorthodox teachings of mystics like Eckhart, Suso and Tauler who were regarded with considerable suspicion by the fourteenth century

Church. It is true that just as you may practice calisthenics without aspiring to be an athlete, so you can practice at least some elements of yoga without aspiring to 'union with the higher Self.' But what you are doing is merely lingering on the threshold of a great system of thought and practice which is in origin and aim thoroughly Indic.

This fact accounts for the second common characteristic of modern yoga instruction, namely that what is taught is a simplified, diluted compromise between traditional Hatha Yoga and soft calisthenics. As one American practitioner says,

> I have *adapted* , *modified and 'streamlined'* Yoga so that it will be of *the very highest possible value to you today.* In so doing, I have taken full cognizance of modern advances in nutrition, vitamin-therapy, health foods, and the new systems of diet and exercise, as well as the most recent medical knowledge and research into methods of revitalizing the human body and halting the 'aging process.' (96, 10)

No lack of *chutzpah* there. The same writer tells us that 'only a few minutes' easy, practical application [of Hatha Yoga] can restore your lost youth . . . put new zest into your undertakings . . . and enable you to enjoy to the full a sense of health, energy and creative living which will make all the difference to your future happiness.' (Ibid.) With these goals in mind and only a few minutes' easy, practical application involved it is understandable why the writer had to adapt, modify and streamline the ancient discipline. The Indian yogi would spend hours, not minutes, at the discipline and while, after long practice, he might perform all the exercises with ease, it would never suit to call them easy. The reason for this is that the yogi was not training his body for 'future happiness' but to make it *the perfect vehicle for the spiritual training of the mind*.

Indian spiritual teachers have often warned against the practice of Hatha Yoga as a discipline independent of spiritual goals for several reasons. First, a preoccupation with the body obviously detracts from commitment to the development of the spiritual life.

Second, the kind of discipline yoga involves is one which effects changes in the functioning of the entire nervous system, a risky procedure. Finally, yogis have always held that their methods can produce, at some stage, formidable psychic or paranormal powers which are potentially destructive. Nevertheless, despite this cautionary attitude toward Hatha Yoga *per se*, most of its practices are well accepted as part of Raja Yoga - the royal yoga or *yoga of meditation* .

Raja Yoga is a complete psychophysical discipline consisting of three components:

1.*Pranayama* - breath control;
2.*Asanas* - body postures
3.*Dhyana* - meditation

Before we examine these three components let us backtrack to what we observed earlier about the Indic view of the world. Recall that the Indic mind conceived of this world as a vast illusion proliferated from the primal non-order (*Atman-Brahman,* the Infinite) of which one can say no more than, 'It is not this; It is not that.' That infinite, unfathomable Mystery is all that is real. All the phenomena of the universe, including our individual selves, only *seem* to be real but in truth are merely so many masks hiding the face of the Infinite. I delude myself that the 'I', my inmost self, my deepest consciousness, is nothing more than the bundle of needs, deeds, thoughts and aspirations with which I have always associated myself. Because of that delusion I crave the continuance of that 'self-bundle' (*jiva* in Sanskrit) and bind myself to reap the consequences of its past deeds and accept the future burden arising from its present deeds. I can therefore perceive myself to be the result of many past incarnations of the fascinating and vexing self-bundle and anticipate that it will carry me on to many more. That is *karma*.

But if I could break the spell of that delusion and realize that I am not really the self-bundle after all, what then would this 'I' turn out to be? To Indic psychology the answer is unequivocal: *my inmost 'I' is none other than that primal non-order which is the inmost reality of all things.* 'That thou art,' the Upanishads declare, meaning you are that infinite mystery. You are Infinite Being, Infinite Consciousness, Infinite Bliss. When that realization comes you know that you are not and never have been the restricted, suffocating self-bundle. You are, therefore, no longer bound by past karma and you will create no more. You will be free from reincarnation and abide beyond time in your true, infinite Self. That is what is meant by *moksha* (liberation) or *nirvana.*

With this understanding of life, the human dilemma is obvious: *How to get from self-delusion to Self-knowledge.* Indic religion is unique among the religions of the world in having developed an empirical system of psychophysical discipline for solving what it perceives as the human dilemma. That is the purpose of Raja Yoga. You will now readily understand why discussing the details of that discipline without explaining its religious assumptions would have been futile. For a similar reason it will be better to discuss the third of the three components of Raja Yoga, meditation, before the other two. The physical postures and breath control techniques are really methods of making the body a more suitable vehicle for meditation.

The purpose of meditation and its ancillary disciplines is *to control the thought-waves in the mind.* Thought-waves are those contents of our many states of consciousness which are constantly being generated by the 'self-bundle.' They are present when we are awake, when we are dreaming or sleeping dreamlessly, and when we are in one of those intermediate or paranormal states of which we Westerners are rarely aware and for which we scarcely have names. Thought-waves can be fleeting and desultory, vague and erratic, or they can be highly organized and goal-directed as when we are engaged in a serious intellectual effort. But no matter what the nature of the thought-waves which fill our minds, whether trivial or profound, *all* are obstacles to Self-realization. Even the deepest scientific or philosophical thoughts or the most intense artistic activity imply dualisms between thinker and thought, subject and object, doer and deed, dualisms which contradict the universal unity of all things.

How, then, do we overcome the obstacles and reach the Self? Fortunately, not all thought-waves are equally diverting or deluding. According to yogic psychology, as there are three elemental tendencies or qualities in nature, called *gunas* in Sanskrit, so also there are in the mind, which is part of nature. The first guna is *tamas* or inertia. It characterizes everything lifeless, immobile, or slothful. Next is *rajas* or activity. It is present in whatever is energetic, moving, aggressive, even violent. Finally, there is *sattwa* or tranquility. Sattwa corresponds to the ideal, the simple, the pure, what a Platonist might call the Good, the True and the Beautiful. The caricature of Indic spiritual practice as 'passive' is entirely false unless we think the only kind of activity is scurrying about and changing our environment or exercising our muscles. To the yogi, tamas (inertia) is the tendency of the mind most inimical to Self-realization. It is the dead weight, the mental laziness and rigidity which militates against changing the way we think.

Sattwa, on the other hand, is conducive to that inner peace of mind and purity of heart which lead toward final Self-realization. Rajas can be either an aid or a hindrance to spiritual progress. Let us take a sculptor as an analogy. He has, on the one hand, an inert block of stone (tamas) and, on the other, the idea of a beautiful figure (sattwa) he wishes to create from that stone. If he uses his strength and energy (rajas) with skill and care he can transform the lifeless rock into a the beautiful image he envisioned. But if he pounds away crudely and carelessly he will not only fail in his goal but destroy whatever potential his material originally had.

Exactly so, if we leave our mind's energy unbridled and undirected it is capable of being frenetic, wayward and destructive.

But there is another way we can use that energy (rajas) and that is to achieve *concentration*. Meditation is a process of concentrating the mind on what is pure and holy instead of leaving it to the mercy of the trite or futile. One specific method involves repetition of a combination of 'holy names,' names of God, which remain the same for one's entire life. These names are given in secret to the yogi by his spiritual master or *guru* and the act of repeating them is called 'making *japam*'. Meditation is not, however, a merely mechanical process. As he makes japam, the yogi also attempts to concentrate on the reality behind the words. It is a long process requiring intense dedication and extraordinary effort, but eventually japam becomes a virtually continuous activity. The mental diversions which were such a large part of the contents of his mind are displaced by the power of the mantram. His mind becomes clearer, more purified. Even when it lapses into an unconcentrated state its thoughts are dominated by sattwa rather than tamas or rajas. Eventually, of course, if not in this life then in another, the mind breaks through and transcends even the tranquil purity of sattwa, for while sattwa, as one of the gunas, is part of nature, the final goal is the Self which is beyond gunas, beyond time and nature, beyond even the gods themselves.

Yogic psychology teaches that spiritual progress is experienced concomitantly with the awakening of an energy reserve present in the body but normally unknown and unavailable to most of us. According to the physiology of raja yoga, a huge reserve of spiritual energy is situated at the base of the spine. This reserve of energy is known as the *kundalini*, 'that which is coiled up'; hence, it is sometimes referred to as the 'serpent power.' When the kundalini is aroused, it is said to travel up the spine through six centers of consciousness, until it reaches the seventh in the center of the brain. As it reaches the higher centers, it produces various degrees of enlightenment. (97, 163)

These 'centers of consciousness' are known in yogic psychophysiology as *chakras* (wheels) and are traditionally symbolized by lotus flowers. The higher the chakra in the body, the more petals in the lotus symbol. The ultimate goal of Self-realization is symbolized by the opening of the thousand-petalled lotus at the top of the brain. The location of chakras bears a remarkable resemblance to modern divisions of the central nervous system as shown in the following table.

Chakra Name	Body Site	Nervous System
Muladara	Anus	Coccygeal plexus
Svadishtana	Perineum	Sacral plexus
Manipura	Stomach	Lumbar plexus
Anahata	Heart	Dorsal plexus
Vishuda	Throat	Cervical plexus
Ajna	Forehead	*Pineal gland**
Sahasrara	Top of head	Top of frontal lobe

*The pineal gland is not a neural plexus. It is a tiny organ in the brain which has traditionally been called 'the organ of enlightenment.'

Yogic psychophysiology was not arrived at by dissecting cadavers. The location of the chakras was determined by yogis' actual experiences of the *kundalini* radiating through the successive neural centers. With this view in mind it is easy to see why the asanas (postures) are important. They serve three purposes:

1.To provide a comfortable, erect position which the body can maintain without fatigue during long hours of meditation. This is the purpose of the asana best known in the West, *padmasana,* the lotus seat. With the right foot resting on the left thigh and the left foot drawn across the right calf and resting on the right thigh, the spine is locked in an erect position from which it is virtually impossible to slump.

2. To make the body healthy, supple and smooth-functioning. This is accomplished by postures which stretch, contract, expand, compress or affect in some other way nearly every bone, muscle, organ and gland in the body. Special attention is given to the spinal cord because it is the conduit of the kundalini and to the stomach and digestive tract. For meditation the body has to be well if simply nourished and the digestive organs have to work smoothly. Few things create such distracting thought-waves as an upset stomach.

3. To enhance the general energy and vitality of the nervous system by increasing the blood supply to the spinal nerve centers and the brain.

The asanas are practiced slowly and gracefully, never with vigorous muscular exertion as in Western calisthenics. Consequently, the yogi does not develop prominent, well-defined muscles as does the athlete. Yet, while his body remains relatively smooth, every muscle is limber, supple and untiring.

While the asanas are important they are less so in Raja Yoga than *pranayama*, breath control. In yogic philosophy, *prana* (breath) involves more than the inhalation of air. Prana is the primal energy of the universe, the creative power which flows from the Infinite. As we take air into our bodies we also take in prana.

> According to yoga, how we breathe has a crucial effect on how much vital energy we absorb and how it is directed and used in the body. The object of pranayama is to rouse the kundalini and thereby control the prana, the vital energy. Prana, as has been said, manifests itself primarily in the function of breathing. Therefore, control of the prana may be obtained by the practice of breathing exercises. (97, 167)

Some breath control practices are quite simple and a good method both of relaxing and increasing vitality. They have to do with such things as how much and what parts of the lungs you fill when you breathe and controlling the length of time you take to inhale, to hold the breath, and to exhale. But there are also some very complex and dangerous practices involving long stoppages of breath which experienced yogis are the first to warn novices about. They caution that for someone who is mentally and spiritually undisciplined, rousing the enormous power of the kundalini, which is what pranayama does, can cause serious mental disturbances.

There are, in fact, dangers all along the path of the yogi because he, unlike either the athlete or the ascetic, practices a system of discipline which directly affects the brain, the central nervous system and all the vital systems of the body, not merely the musculature or sense coordination. The Indic outlook on life has often been called life-denying and it is - if by 'life' we mean that of the individual self which was of such supreme value in Occidental Civilization. But, paradoxically, in order to advance from the complicated, mostly unconscious order of the self to the purified, conscious order of the spirit and thence to the final non-order of the universal Self, the Indic yogi developed the most physiologically intimate and psychologically complete view of the self the world has ever known.

The Chinese Masters: T'ai Chi and the Martial Arts

October, 1975. 5:30 A.M. The city of Canton emerges from sleep in the gray light of morning. Hardly any automobiles are to be seen on the streets but, as streetcorner loudspeakers broadcast stirring music, hundreds of Cantonese are already streaming along the broad boulevards on their way to work. Looking down at the scene from the balcony of our hotel room, my wife and I find it remarkable that many of those we are watching are actually *jogging* to work. On the island where we live, people are reluctant even to walk to their jobs.

But directly below our balcony, in the narrow garden between the hotel and the wall which separates it from the thoroughfare, something even more remarkable is happening. Several young Chinese bureaucrats, in their customary blue cotton 'pajama' suits, are going through the motions of what seems like a slow, graceful ballet. Although the participants remain in one place, their bodies are in constant, gentle motion, arms, legs, torso, head executing a series of patterned, circular movements none of which appear to be repeated. The whole process lasts perhaps ten minutes and ends without a noticeable climax, after which the men leave the garden to assume their daily duties.

Although I had seen it many times in photographs, that morning in Canton was my first encounter with *T'ai Chi Ch'uan* 'in the flesh.' T'ai Chi Ch'uan is part of the ancient physiological heritage of China which, along with acupuncture, acupressure and herbal medicine, the communist regime has encouraged rather than suppressed, evidence of the latter's sense of continuity with the past. No one knows for sure how long the Chinese have been practicing physical discipline of the T'ai Chi type. Like Hatha Yoga, it was developed as a method of training the body in connection with meditation although in origin it probably consisted of imitating certain natural movements of animals and birds.

> There are several examples of [imitating animals and birds] in the T'ai Chi Ch'uan form, which includes movements such as Bring Tiger to the Mountain, Snake Creeps Down, Step Back and Repulse Monkey, White Crane Spreads Wings, and Golden Cock on One Leg. (64, 16)

Whatever the roots of T'ai Chi Ch'uan in the often obscure and mythicized history of China, it is clear that from the time of the great Sages down to the twentieth century, the Chinese were engaged in a continuous process of developing forms both of meditation and physical training based on world views stemming from their unique mindset. During the Eastern Han Dynasty Wei Po-yang wrote a treatise in which he set forth a form of meditation based on the *I Ching,* China's ancient and revered oracle text. Animal movement systems were pursued concomitantly.

> In the third century A.D. an exercise called the Movement of the Five Animals was invented by Hua T'o, a surgeon. He

contributed additional movements of animals such as the bear, tiger, monkey, deer and bird to the development of T'ai Chi Ch'uan. A series of eighteen forms of health exercise [were] invented by the alchemist Ko Hung (active A. D. 325). . (64, 18)

A stimulus to the progress of Chinese physical training was provided around 530 A.D. when a Buddhist monk from India, named Bodhidharma (in Chinese, *Ta Mo*), established a school of Ch'an Buddhism (*Zen* in Japanese) at a monastery called Shao Lin. It is said that Bodhidharma was concerned about the health of the monks who seemed to be wasting away in the process of meditation and invented a system of exercise to keep them in good health. The system was called Shao Lin Ch'uan, or Shao Lin Fist, indicating that it was not only a method of exercise but also one of (defensive) combat, the first of the famous *martial arts*. (Shao Lin Ch'uan become popularly known in the West through the television series, *Kung Fu*.) It seems doubtful to me that Shao Lin-Ch'uan was created by Bodhidharma in quite the *de novo* fashion tradition maintains. It seems more likely that a T'ai Chi-type discipline was already established in the Chinese population on which the Indian monk drew for recruits and what he may have done is to reorganize that discipline into a form suited to his Ch'an principles as well as convert it into an unarmed combat form suitable for peace-loving monks.

T'ai Chi itself is attributed to a Taoist monk, Chang San-feng, to whom is ascribed an uncertain date between the twelfth and fourteenth centuries A.D. In creating T'ai Chi, Chang 'reworked the original forms of Shao-Lin with a new emphasis on breathing and inner control.' (72, 59) Da Liu says of Chang's achievement,

The great Taoist master Chang San-feng, who was knowledgeable about all the ancient forms of wisdom, including the *I ching*, Confucianism, Buddhism, and Taoism, created, after a long period of meditation, the system of exercise known as T'ai Chi Ch'uan. His aim was similar to that of Ta Mo: to develop a form of discipline complementary to the practice of meditation, which would also promote health. The resulting exercise method . . . is different from Shao Lin and has quite distinct results. The movements of Shao Lin are generally strenuous and sometimes very quick. Regular practice of these forms results in the strengthening of the limbs and an increase in the size of the muscles. In T'ai Chi Ch'uan, on the other hand, the movements are done slowly, gently, and evenly from beginning to end, each posture unfolding with the same continuous rhythm. The result is an improvement in circulation and respiration and a strengthening of the internal organs, but no increase in muscles. Because of this contrast, T'ai Chi Ch'uan is sometimes called the Inner School and Shao Lin the Outer School. In spite of these differences, *both schools are, at their highest levels, forms of spiritual discipline, and both were originally developed to aid in the practice of meditation.* (64, 20, *emphasis mine*)

It is certain that throughout the centuries there were parallel and mutually interacting developments between Buddhist-based and Taoist-based martial art forms which tended to produce a distinctively Sinic kind of physical training with a number of different branches. It is also certain that although there is an interplay between Indic and Sinic ideas in Chinese meditation, the psychophysiological system and philosophical foundation of T'ai Chi Ch'uan are thoroughly Chinese. As a basic discipline, T'ai Chi Ch'uan and its cousins are as fundamental to all Chinese and Japanese martial arts as calisthenics is to Western athletics.

The first clue we have as to the deep involvement of T'ai Chi Ch'uan in the Chinese mindset is its name. 'T'ai Chi' means 'the Supreme Ultimate' or 'the Great Primal Beginning,' a strangely highflown name, we might think, for a slow, gentle exercise form. What it implies, however, is that the performance of T'ai Chi is a recreation of the fundamental creative processes of the universe which, as we saw in Chapter 4, the Chinese were fond of setting forth in diagrams called T'ai Chi T'u (Diagram of the Supreme Ultimate). Let us take another look at the T'ai Chi T'u of Chou Tun-i on page 133. Whatever its earliest forms might have been, under the guidance of Taoist thought T'ai Chi Ch'uan was formalized so that each phase of the exercises was symbolized by a part of the diagram:

> The uppermost circle symbolizes emptiness - *wu chi* . In the beginning the T'ai Chi Ch'uan player stands quietly with his mind empty. The movements of T'ai Chi Ch'uan correspond to the alternating black and white stripes of the second circle of the diagram. Downward and retreating movements represent the yin, while upward and forward movements represent the yang. The five elements in the five small circles below correspond to the five foot movements performed by the T'ai Chi Ch'uan player, while the eight trigrams of the *I ching* represent the eight movements of the player's hands. The straight and diagonal connecting lines between the five small circles are an indication of the continuous alternation of the player's steps. Finally, the bottom circle corresponds to the end of the T'ai Chi Ch'uan - a return to stillness. (64, 27)

It is no accident that the T'ai Chi T'u diagrams are full of circles because, according to Chinese thought, the processes of creation are essentially a matter of harmonious circulation, of the alternation of outward and inward movements, of projection and withdrawal. T'ai Chi Ch'uan reproduces these processes in the body by promoting the circulation of vital energy called *ch'i* (Japanese: *ti*). Ch'i is said to circulate through eight psychic channels, twelve psychic centers and twelve 'meridians.' The two principle psychic channels are:

1. The *Tu Mo*, or Channel of Control [which] runs along the spinal column, from the coccyx up through the neck to the skull, and over the crown of the head to the roof of the mouth.

2. The *Jen Mo*, or Channel of Function [which] goes through the center and front of the body. Its lower extremity is at the genital organs, and it extends up to the base of the mouth. When the tongue rests against the palate, it forms a bridge between the *Tu Mo* and the *Jen Mo*. (71, 40)

The Tu Mo is remarkably similar to and may well have been influenced by the yogic conception of the spinal channel of spiritual energy called the *sushumna*, and the idea of ch'i, or psychic energy, is much like *prana*, which we discussed in the preceding section. Also in agreement with yogic psychophysiology are the eight psychic centers located along the Tu Mo. With one exception, the psychic centers correspond to the *chakras* listed on page 256, the exception being an additional center (*yu-chen*) located at the back of the head. To these eight centers, Chinese psychophysiology adds four said to be located on the Jen Mo: in the chest, above the navel, in the navel and about three inches below the navel. You may wonder what these last four add, since they seem to correspond to some of the body sites of the chakras rather than additional nerve centers. It seems to me they are based on two peculiarities of Chinese thinking.

The first peculiarity is the Chinese passion for numerology which is a way of bringing microcosmic phenomena into harmony with macrocosmic. Thus, adding four psychic centers to the original eight produces twelve. The psychic centers, says Dai Liu,

> . . . are represented by twelve hexagrams of the *I ching,* which also represent the twelve months of the year as well as the twelve times of the day. Thus the circulation of the *ch'i* through the twelve psychic centers reflects the cyclic pattern of the cosmic processes which bring about the alternation of light and darkness as well as the changing of the seasons. Harmonizing the flow of energy within the body with the cosmic processes is essential to achieving unity with Tao, the ultimate goal of meditation. (64, 40)

The second peculiarity of Chinese thought which explains the extra four psychic centers is evidenced by the fact that three of them are located around the navel. The embryo 'breathes' through the navel and while, according to Chinese physiology, lung breathing is usual for the adult, prenatal breathing is never entirely abandoned and is utilized in meditation and T'ai Chi Ch'uan. In fact,

. . . meditation and T'ai Chi Ch'uan may be said to bring
about a union of prenatal and postnatal breathing. That
is, during inhalation, as the meditator is drawing the
postnatal breath into the lungs and down to the navel, the
prenatal breath rises up from the lower abdomen to the
navel, where it joins together with the postnatal breath.
During exhalation, as the postnatal breath rises up out of
the lungs, the prenatal breath sinks down again to the
lower abdominal region. (64, 50)

Although there are a number of similarities between Indic and
Sinic psychophysiology, the difference between the movement of
prana in yoga and its counterpart, ch'i, in T'ai Chi Ch'uan is
instructive. In yoga it is the *rising* of prana or the kundalini from the
base of the spine through successively higher centers to the chakra at
the top of the head which is the aim of the discipline, the highest
chakra being the opening to Self-realization. While this ultimate
state of enlightenment is known to Zen Buddhism and even to Taoist
meditation, the latter calling it the attainment of the Great
Quiescence, the basic intent of T'ai Chi Ch'uan is not simply the
rising of ch'i to the highest center (*ni-wan*) but its *circulation* through
the psychic routes and centers of the body. Thus,

The 'chi' is tapped at the sacrum and then proceeds up the
spine. When you watch a T'ai Chi master move you can see
the force rippling up the spine from the bottom to the top.
This energy is stored in a spot just below the navel, called
the 'tan-tien.'. . . In T'ai Chi the energy travels from the
sacrum to the ends of the fingers, circles back to the body,
and moves down to the 'tan-tien.' In Taoist meditation this
'chi' is circulated internally. (98 , 172)

It is this elemental circulation, the interplay of yang and yin, we
see embodied in the performance of T'ai Chi Ch'uan:

The play of oppositions . . . is symbolized kinetically in the
exercise. Every movement is circular and out of each motion
comes its opposite. You sink down before you stretch up; pull
back before reaching out; shift left in order to swing right.(98,
29)

We have now sufficiently well established that the archetypal Chinese form of physical discipline, T'ai Chi Ch'uan, is deeply rooted in the Sinic mindset. The fruits of this discipline are an extraordinary inner composure, an acute sensitivity to the external environment, an ability to move the body swiftly but always in balance, and a method of focussing intense energy at will, all qualities which are characteristic of the oriental *martial arts*. When we see practitioners of the martial arts in action, particularly as the practices are debased in so many movies to appeal to a juvenile audience, it might be difficult to accept that they have the profound basis I have claimed. But as Joe Hyams, an American writer who has had the opportunity to study with several masters of the martial arts, including the legendary Bruce Lee, says, '. . . for the true master, karate, kung-fu, aikido, wing-chun, and all the other martial arts are essentially avenues through which they can achieve spiritual serenity, mental tranquility, and the deepest self-confidence.' (73, 1)

Preparation for Death in Mesoamerica

The Mesoamericans played an outrageous ball game called among the Mayans *pok-a-tok* and among the Aztecs *tlatchtli*. It was one of the first things banned by the Spanish because they believed it involved witchcraft and satanic rites. But the ball courts on which it was played are still to be found among the ruins of all the great Amerindic cities of Central America and Mexico. The largest, at Chichen Itzá in Yucatan, is 545 feet long (almost twice as long as a modern football field) and 225 feet wide. Thirty-five feet up on the center of each massive side wall is a large stone ring set in a vertical position. So resolute were the Spaniards about abolishing the game that very little record remains of how it was played but we do know it involved putting a large (perhaps six inches in diameter) hard rubber ball through the ring. Exactly how that was done is obscure. Fr. Sahagún tells us the ball could not be touched by the hands but had to be butted with the elbows or buttocks. That seems an unlikely feat with a thirty-five-foot high ring and not an easy one even in other courts where the ring was just over eight feet high. In some statuettes, what appear to me to be ball players are holding a kind of bat but the texts make no reference to bats.

We do know that players, who were always from the elite classes, wore heavy padding, especially on their hands, arms, buttocks and heads, that they were divided into two sides, each possessing one side of the center line and that the game was extremely violent.

> The players threw themselves to the ground to get at the ball, and they received the full impact of it on their bodies when it was in flight; so, like modern Rugby or baseball players, they were padded and provided with knee-caps and leather aprons, and even with chin-pieces and half-masks covering their cheeks. They also wore leather gloves to protect their hands from the continual scraping on the ground. But in spite of all these precautions accidents were not uncommon: some players, hit in the stomach or the belly, fell never to rise again; and after the game most of them had *to have incisions made in their buttocks to let out the extravasated blood.* (94, 159, *emphasis mine*)

It seems doubtful to me that such injuries could result merely from contact with other players or falling on the ground. But if the 'bats' were clubs, the injuries are much more understandable. The ball game was probably a ritual war, the kind of conflict so ingrained in Amerindic life, where the two sides fought symbolically the heavenly battle for the survival of the world. The stakes were the highest:

> In Tajin, dating from, say, A.D. 800, as well as in Chichén Itzá, several centuries later, the game was strictly sacrificial, and involved decapitation. . . The principal court of El Tajin is sixty metres long, formed by two facing vertical walls, covered with splendid bas-reliefs. In one of these a player is sacrificed by the others, who brandish the ritual knife over his head. In a stela from a nearby site of the same period, seven serpents sprout from the neck of a decapitated ball player (as also occurs in a Chichén Itzá relief). (100, 124)

In later times it seems that losing the ball game did not necessarily entail being sacrificed but sacrifice was replaced by the making of enormous wagers. Losing could cause ruin and enslavement, the latter of which could, of course, lead to being sacrificed. Common sense would tell us that people whose lives are routine and secure seek out extravagant excitements while those for whom life is precarious long for safety. The Mesoamericans believed in a world the very existence of which was totally precarious, in which the gods themselves depended on human action for their sustenance (a habit of mind which the Spaniards found it hard to banish). Yet they continued to indulge in the most dangerous kind of gambling with their lives in defiance of common sense. How do we explain such an irony?

We have already seen how the Amerindians valued death in war as the highest fulfillment of life. Now we see the same attitude operating in relation to a *game*. In the previous sections of this chapter I have shown how each civilization created basic physical (and psychological) disciplines which agreed with their world views and aimed at the highest life goals those world views envisioned. In this section, although the specific material we have in relation to Amerindic disciplines is much more limited than that for the other Civilizations, I intend to show that the Amerindians also practiced a unique discipline, one that was essentially *a preparation for death*. Perhaps we will then understand their penchant for 'courting disaster'.

We cannot reiterate too often that their practice of human sacrifice does not mean that the Amerindians were 'bloodthirsty savages' or even that they were cruel. There is no evidence that they took any sadistic delight in killing and much evidence to the contrary. In fact, the more one learns about the personal attitudes of the Aztecs, who practiced human sacrifice on an unimaginable scale, the more one is impressed by the amount of tenderness and compassion they displayed in personal relationships. It is difficult to find in the literature of any civilized people expressions more humane and gentle than we find in Aztec poetry. The practice of human sacrifice was dictated by the Amerindians' world view which, in turn, was shaped by their impossibly futile mindset.   Jacques Soustelle confirms this eloquently:

> Human sacrifice among the Mexicans was inspired neither by cruelty nor by hatred. It was their response, and the only response that they could conceive, to the instability of a continually threatened world. Blood was necessary to save this world and the men in it: the victim was no longer an enemy who was to be killed but a messenger, arrayed in a dignity that was almost divine, who was sent to the gods. All the relevant descriptions, such as those that Sahagún took down from his Aztec informants, for example, convey the impression not of a dislike between the sacrificer and the victim nor of anything resembling a lust for blood, but of a strange fellow-feeling or rather - and this is vouched for by the texts - of a kind of mystical kinship. (74 , 99)

The mistake we generally make is in thinking that the one to be sacrificed was always *the other guy!*   Although, as with any system, there were ways in which power and wealth could manipulate the odds against dying in one's favor, no one, however high in the ranks of the elite, was exempt from the possibility of giving his life for the preservation of the world at some time. Sacrificial death was man's highest honor and his final sacrament. In his mind he had not only to accept it as such but desire it.

> When a man took a prisoner he said, 'Here is my well-beloved son-in-law And the captive said, 'Here is my revered father.' The warrior who made a prisoner and who watched him die before the altar knew that sooner or later he would follow him into the hereafter by the same kind of death. 'You are welcome: you know what the fortune of war is - today for you, tomorrow for me,' said the emperor to a captured chief. As for the prisoner himself, he was perfectly aware of his fate and he had been prepared from his childhood to accept it: he agreed, stoically. More than that, he would refuse a clemency that crossed his destiny or the divine will, even if it were offered him. (ibid.)

Preparation from childhood to accept death! That was the essence of Amerindic discipline. Within four days of birth the Aztec child underwent a long and complicated baptismal rite at the end of which 'the midwife begged the gods that the boy might become a courageous warrior, 'so that he may go into your palace of delights where the brave who die in battle rest and rejoice.'(74, 166) Baby girls went through a similar rite and, although their role in life was not to be warriors, they, too, were trained to accept death and, in a remarkable practice virtually unparalleled in any other civilized society, Aztec women who died in childbirth were accorded the same honors as a warrior who died in battle.

There were two kinds of schools for young Aztec males, the temple school or *calmecac*, which adjoined a temple and was run by priests and a kind of general school called a *telpochcalli* or 'house of the young men.' Those who went to the *calmecac* were destined either for the priesthood or for high office rather than for war but it was common for young priests to go off to war in order to take a prisoner, a feat which enhanced his status in the society. 'There was no night of uninterrupted sleep for the scholars of the *calmecac*,' Soustelle writes,

> They had to get up in the darkness to go into the mountains, each by himself, to offer incense to the gods and draw blood from their ears and legs with agave-thorns. They were obliged to undergo frequent and rigorous fasts. They had to work hard on the temple's land, and they were severely punished for the least fault. . The whole emphasis of this education was upon sacrifice and abnegation. (94, 170)

Strictly speaking, sacrifice and abnegation were characteristic of the *discipline* in the *calmecac*, whereas the education comprised all the knowledge which belonged to Aztec society, 'reading and writing in the pictographic characters, divination, chronology, poetry and rhetoric' (94, 172), to which I am sure we can add architecture, art, iconography and no small amount of anatomy. It takes knowledge of the human body to flay it properly or neatly remove its still beating heart, which were among the duties of the Aztec priest.

The purpose of the *telpochcalli* was training for warriors and its discipline was much more lax than that of the *calmecac*.

> There was little room in their education for the religious exercises, the fasts and the penances which had so much importance in that of the pupils of the *calmecac*. Everything was done to prepare them for war; from their earliest age they associated only with experienced warriors, whose exploits they admired and dreamed of rivalling. So long as they were bachelors they lived a communal existence, enlivened by dancing and songs, and by the company of the young women, the *auianime,* who were officially allowed them, as courtesans. (94, 171)

Soustelle sees a conflict between the two kinds of discipline, remarking on the fact that 'The god of the *calmecac* was Quetzalcoatl, the priests' own god, the god of self-sacrifice and penance, of books, the calendar and the arts, the symbol of abnegation and of culture,' whereas, 'The young men's god was Tezcatlipoca, who was also called Telpochtli, 'the young man', and Yaotl, 'the warrior', Quetzalcoatl's old enemy who had expelled him from the earthly paradise of Tula long ago by his enchantments.' (ibid.) If there is a conflict it is one with little practical significance. The warriors were expected to take prisoners in battle for sacrifice or else to be killed themselves and the priests were the ones who sacrificed prisoners on the temple altars, obviously finding their devotion to Quetzalcoatl no obstacle to that duty. Soustelle himself resolves the problem when he says,

> In a general manner, Mexican education in both its forms hoped to produce strength of mind and of body, and a character devoted to the public good *[to the preservation of the world, we might add!]*. The stoicism with which the Aztecs were able to meet the most terrible ordeals proves that this education attained its end. (94, 173)

The discipline of Amerindic societies did not, however, end with the school period. It was a lifetime matter. Very high ethical standards were demanded, especially of the elite. 'Overweening pride' was not tolerated, a humble manner and a great deal of self-control being the ideal. Transgressions against the standards of society were revealed to a priest in confession and quite severe and painful *penance* was usually exacted from the sinner. Once the penance was done, however, the slate was wiped clean as far as the gods were concerned.

Among the Amerindians, self-torture was a sacred way of purification and sacrifice. This was dramatically demonstrated in the 1986 exhibition called 'The Blood of Kings: A New Interpretation of Maya Art' presented by the Kimbell Art Museum of Fort Worth, Texas. Commenting on this exhibition, E. F. Porter, Jr. says,

> Kings and queens engaged in ritual self-mutilation, pulling thorn-studded cords through holes in their tongues and puncturing their genitals with stingray spines which themselves acquired a sacred meaning. (101)

'Blood was the mortar of ancient Maya life,' write archaeologists Linda Schele and Mary Ellen Miller, the co-authors of a fascinating book-length essay in the show's 335-page catalogue. 'Through his gift of blood the king brought gods to life and drew the power of the supernatural into the daily lives of the Maya.' (101, 8) I mentioned in Chapter 2 that although the Theory of Mindsets, which I developed before 1976, required that the Mayas were brothers under the skin to Aztecs, the prevailing view of the Mayas as a gentle, peaceable people did not support my theory. I am naturally gratified to see that the most recent scholarship is correcting the earlier opinions and demonstrating a common outlook on life for all of Amerindic Civilization.

In Aztec Tenochtitlán one of the buildings attached to the temples was

> . . . the *quauhxicalco* , 'the place where there is the
> *quauhxicalli*' or bowl for the sacrificed heart of the victims;
> and here the emperor and the priests fasted and did penance
> by thrusting agave-thorns into their legs and offering the
> blood to the gods. (94 , 22)

What we need to note here is that fasting, bloodletting and other
forms of self-torture were not simply penitential, i.e., to atone for
sins. They were part of a continuing *sacramental discipline* of which
giving one's life as a sacrifice was the ultimate deed. Amerindic
discipline was not a demonstration of faith, as was Christian
asceticism, nor was it, like yoga, a training of the body to assist the
mind to Self-realization. Perhaps we can best compare and contrast
it with T'ai Chi Ch'uan, which was developed to harmonize life with
the fundamental creative forces of nature. Amerindic discipline was
a complete inversion of T'ai Chi Ch'uan, a ritual self-torture
symbolizing and preparing for sacrificial death, through which alone
the fundamental creative forces of nature could be sustained .

Why, then, we ask again, did the Amerindians play their
notorious ball game with its life and death stakes? Why did they
engage in the dangerous, sometimes fatal *volador,* the feat of
swinging in larger and larger circles at faster and faster speeds from
ropes attached to the tops of high poles? Why were Aztecs of all
classes such inveterate gamblers, playing dice to the point of ruin?
Soustelle remarks on the 'curious fact that the Aztecs, although they
were so puritanical about drinking and although their sex-life was so
restrained, never seem to have tried to curb gambling.' (94, 160)
But I do not find their reckless excesses curious. For the
Amerindians life was inherently precarious. There can be no safe
haven in a doomed world. In such a case to gamble, to court disaster
is not reckless. *It is the essence of life and a preparation for death.*

EIGHT

Sex: Mind and Two (or more) Bodies

What has Mind to do with Sex?

'Now you have gone too far,' someone will object. 'I followed you through mythology, philosophy, art, and law, all of which are admittedly activities involving the mind and therefore amenable to the influence of what you call a 'mindset.' I also grudgingly entertained your arguments about physical discipline even though I might have been jogging or watching a football game. Now, however, you propose to inflict your methods on a subject which is about as far from the mind as one can get - *sex*. Sex is a simple thing, a biological urge we share with a large part of the animal kingdom. No one has to teach anyone, primitive or civilized, how to perform a sex act. Instinct teaches us all we need to know. In fact, it is the one sure and certain proof of our animality, *the antithesis of mind*. Why do you have to burden it with mindsets?'

A formidable objection - and very Western. The notion that sex is the antithesis of mind is the mark of a true Occidental as we shall see later in this chapter. That sex is, in part, a biological urge that we share with animals is undeniable. But how simple a matter is it in human beings? Variations in sexual behavior are extensive among all the primates and after years of studies conducted by anthropologists on primitive societies we have to conclude that the range of variations among primitives is so great that only two customs related to sex can be said to be virtually universal: marriage (in some form) and incest taboos. However based in instinct sex may be, instinct does not teach humans all they need to know about it and certainly not all they want to know.

Human sex, far from being simple, is one of the most complex areas of experience. Desmond Morris calls human sex 'super-sex', by which he means not what Cosmopolitan Magazine might mean using the word in a sentence beginning 'How to have . . . ,' but simply to name the complex activity sex becomes when it reaches the level of man, the 'super-ape.' Morris lists 'ten functional categories' of human sex:

1. Procreation Sex - 'the most basic function of sexual behavior.'
2. Pair-formation Sex - 'nowhere outside the pairing phase do sexual activities regularly reach such a high intensity.'
3. Pair-maintenance Sex
4. Physiological Sex - 'Without [periodic sexual] consummation, a physiological tension builds up and eventually the body demands relief.'
5. Exploratory Sex - '[man's inventiveness and curiosity leads] to a wide range of variations on the sexual theme.'
6. Self-rewarding Sex - 'sex for sex's sake.'
7. Occupational Sex - 'sex operating as occupational therapy, or . . . as an anti-boredom device.'
8. Tranquilizing Sex - 'anti-turmoil.'
9. Commercial Sex - prostitution and sexual display for material gain.
10. Status Sex - sex used to convey dominance, including but not confined to sadism and rape. (102, Ch. Three)

This is a very comprehensive list. But while it covers most aspects of modern sexual practice, it leaves out three historically important 'functional categories', namely,

11. Political sex - sex used as a tactic in political or business strategy, exemplified at one extreme by seduction for espionage purposes and at the other by noble marriages arranged to cement alliances.

12. Self-transcending sex - notably certain Hindu and Buddhist practices in which the sexual act itself is used as a kind of yoga to awaken the latent spiritual force in the mind-body.
13. Ritual sex - a symbolic heterosexual activity performed in civilization, usually by members of the ruling or priestly classes, as a means of reaffirming or reinforcing the relationship between society and its divinities.

About this extended list of thirteen 'functional categories' it should be noted that only the first and last are inherently heterosexual. All the rest can equally apply to homosexuals. It can also be noted that not one of the categories is exempt from the influence of mind. Today, even the first category, procreative sex, is the subject of highly-charged doctrinal disputes in religious circles. The controversies which have gone so far as to cause Roman Catholic archbishops to be stripped of much of their authority - contraception, homosexuality, and, to some degree, abortion - are centered precisely on the question of whether sex can have fully acceptable human functions *to the exclusion of procreation*. The Roman church historically accepted the first and grudgingly tolerated the second, third and eleventh functions, given certain constraints, but it never accepted any sexual function as legitimate which excluded the *possibility* of procreation.

Religious doctrines which define the legitimate functions of sex are not merely matters of concern to theologians. They have profoundly influenced the attitudes of millions upon millions of human beings towards sex and thereby the character of their participation in it. But the doctrines are products of a particular kind of civilized mind, not of animal instinct, and consequently they reflect the structure of that mind, its mindset. The mind may be said to influence the nature of sexual relations in three ways:

(1)It can *define* sexual activity, its place in the scheme of life and its legitimate or desired functions, having so many possible functions to choose from. Every religion considers such definition among its responsibilities.

(2)It can *regulate* sexual activity through voluntary or involuntary restraint or stimulation. Secular institutions have often made regulation of sex a matter of policy, encouraging the birth of 'Aryan' children by rewards as the Nazis did, for example, or discouraging it by a combination of rewards and sanctions as do many modern countries, China in the forefront, in order to control their population growth.

(3)It can *structure* sexual activity so that it more efficiently or more satisfyingly fulfills its functions. By applying thought and discipline any of the thirteen functions can be enhanced. The flood of books and television programs about sex on the market today proclaims that fact *ad nauseum*.

A mindset's influence is most directly evident at the definitional level but regulation and structuring flow directly from the way in which sex is defined, so the mindset is reflected in the whole process, as we shall see.

Sex in the Western World: Little or Nothing

The most noteworthy thing about the explicitly sexual literature of Western Civilization (i.e., the West before 1500 A.D. by definition but extending well into the twentieth century) is that it does not exist. The male and female genitalia are rarely mentioned in Western writing and when they are, as in the work of Rabelais, it is with a heavy admixture of satire and comic vulgarity. References to sexual relations are equally rare and always oblique, humorous or satirical when we find them, for example, in the work of Aristophanes, Ovid, Boccaccio or Chaucer. Examples of sexual union between gods and mortals are not lacking in Near Eastern or Greek mythology but the results are often disastrous, especially for the mortal participant. The calamities of 'passionate love' are the grist of a great deal of Greek tragedy such as Euripides' *Medea* and Greeks and Romans alike tended to regard passionate love as a kind of madness or frenzy.

When we come to the Middle Ages, we find three famous stories of passionate love, all wound about with tragedy. First, Dante's never consummated passion for the beautiful Beatrice, whose death in 1290 drove the poet to the point of madness. Secondly, the tale of the ill-fated adulterers, Paolo and Francesca, whom Dante, with magnificent irony, consigned to drift side by side through hell, eternally but, of course, *incorporeally*. And finally, one of the greatest of all love stories, that of Abelard and Heloise. The handsome Abelard was a rising star in the medieval academic world, a brilliant young teacher and theologian. Heloise was a lovely young woman whose uncle, her guardian, had taken pains to see was far better educated than was customary for the time. Abelard became her tutor, both of them living in the uncle's house. An affair began which eventually resulted in Heloise's pregnancy. Outraged, the uncle sent his kinsmen to punish Abelard, which they did by beating and then castrating him, an act which was vehemently condemned by his peers and for which some of the perpetrators were punished in a manner that fit the deed. Heloise continued to live with her uncle, but on learning that he was becoming increasingly abusive toward her, Abelard arranged for her to find shelter in a convent, where she eventually took the veil.

Despite his mutilation, Abelard continued to advance in his career, and, over the years, he and Heloise carried on a correspondence in which a once strong physical attraction became transmuted into an enduring and equally strong intellectual and spiritual relationship - a genuinely 'Platonic' relationship. Still, neither ever forgot the depth of their physical passion and, in one of

the most touchingly eloquent professions of love ever penned, Heloise,
by that time head of her convent, wrote Abelard,

> I call God to witness, if *Augustus,* ruling the whole world,
> were to deem me worthy of the honour of marriage, and to
> confirm the whole world to me, to be ruled by me for ever,
> dearer to me and of greater dignity would it seem to be called
> thy strumpet than his empress. (143, 171)

Then, as if forty-five hundred years of Occidental Civilization had
not produced enough confusion about sex, eleventh century Provence
produced what must be ranked among the world's most bizarre erotic
phenomena - the Troubadors and their code of Courtly Love. We will
return to Courtly Love later in this section because it had a profound
influence not only on subsequent Western literature but on the
attitude of Western society toward women and the nature of love
itself. But first let us consider the reasons why the West has always
been shy about sex and has never dealt with it in a straightforward
manner.

We should never make the mistake that the attitudes we call
'Puritan' or 'Victorian' began with the periods that bore those names.
Like all Western attitudes and points of view they go back much
further than that, directly to two sources - the Greek and the Judaeo-
Christian-Islamic traditions.

The Greeks were a lusty people but their sexuality was marked
by a peculiarity: homosexuality. Greek males - and some females -
practiced homosexuality openly and with social acceptance. Most
Greek men were probably heterosexual and many were bisexual.
They married and fathered children and, as Aristophanes' *Lysistrata*
demonstrates, they did not undervalue their wives' sexual favors.
Women, in addition to their value as sex objects and their roles in
childbearing, childrearing and homemaking, were acknowledged to
have the capacity for strong love relationships with husbands or
lovers. There are many examples of love-bonds between men and
women in Greek literature. But, in the Athens of the age when the

great Greek philosophers and dramatists wrote, men did not always look to women for intense erotic relationships. They often looked to other men. As we saw in the previous chapter, Greek males practiced calisthenics and athletics from an early age, striving to develop strong, beautiful bodies. Those who achieved the greatest physical beauty were not only admired but desired. Pederasty - sodomy between men and boys - was practiced and the adults were most likely to find their beautiful boys in the *palaestra* - the wrestling school or 'gym.' The intimate physical contact of wrestling was a way of sexually stimulating another man or boy. Pederasty, however, was not held in high esteem by cultivated Greeks, whose most prized erotic relationships were between 'consenting adults.'

I have mentioned this peculiarity of the Greeks not because it is a revelation but because it is common knowledge and I would like to dispel any impression that the Greeks' thoughts about the nature of sex and its place in human life were distorted by their acceptance of homosexuality. They were perfectly clear that whatever they said about sex and love applied equally well to both heterosexual and homosexual relations. And if we remember that in eleven of the thirteen categories of sex mentioned in the opening section gender is irrelevant, it is easy to see why this is so.

The most lucid Greek account of the nature of sex and love is given in Plato's *Symposium*. Of the *Symposium*, the great Plato scholar and translator, Benjamin Jowett has this to say:

> Of all the works of Plato the Symposium is the most perfect in form, and may be truly thought to contain more than any commentator has ever dreamed of; or, as Goethe said of one of his own writings, more than the author himself knew. (58, 275)

The *Symposium* takes place at an afternoon banquet on a holiday in Athens. Several cultivated Athenian men are there, including Socrates, the comic playwright, Aristophanes, and the poet, Agathon. One of the guests suggests that instead of drinking or listening to the flute-girl's 'noise', each guest in turn deliver a discourse, the subject of which is *Eros*. Eros is the Greek god of love or desire, counterpart to the Roman *Cupid*. Spelled with a small 'e', *eros* is a noun which is usually translated as 'love'. More accurately, however, it specifically refers to concupiscence - sexual desire. So the discourses at the banquet are to be in honor of the god, Eros, and about the phenomenon, eros. The guests deliver their speeches, each in its turn witty and entertaining, but the speech around which the whole work centers is that of Socrates.

Socrates, instead of giving his own views directly, attributes all his ideas to a priestess named Diotima, whom he credits with having taught him everything he knows about love many years earlier. Throughout the discourse, however, it is clear that, whatever their source, the views he expresses are his own. Most people, Socrates says, think Eros is a great and good god but he is not. Nor is he foul or evil. In fact, he is not a god at all, but a spirit or intermediary between men and the gods. His father was Plenty and his mother Poverty. He

> . . . partakes of the nature of both, and is full and starved by turns. Like his mother he is poor and squalid, lying on mats at doors; like his father he is full of arts and resources and is in a mean between ignorance and knowledge. (58, 280)

Eros, according to Socrates, is an *unfulfilled* desire of something, a wanting rather than a having. If it had that something the desire would no longer exist. On the other hand, the creature which does not have the desire would have to be inanimate because all animals have a sex drive. That is why sexual desire is *in a mean* between ignorance (inanimate lack of desire) and knowledge (fulfillment). Socrates next relates a series of questions by which Diotima helped him arrive at an understanding of what that 'something' really is which love desires. The following is a paraphrase of those questions and Socrates' answers.

Question. What does love desire?
  Answer. Beauty.
Q.What does it desire *of* beauty?
  A.To possess it.
Q.What does possession of the beautiful give?
  A.Happiness.
Q.Does momentary possession alone give happiness?
  A.No, everlasting possession.
Q.But what do we already know is the one thing alone that brings happiness?
  A.Possession of *the Good* .
Q.Then what does love *truly* desire?
  A.Everlasting possession of *the Good*.
Q.What does 'everlasting possession' imply?
  A.Immortality.
Q.And what is the fundamental principle of immortality in a mortal creature?
  A.Conception and generation.
Q.Which is propitious to conception - beauty or deformity?
  A.Beauty.
Q.Beauty is therefore not loved for itself alone but for something still more basic, which is . . .?
  A.*The love of generation and birth in beauty*.

'Because,' Diotima had explained, 'to the mortal birth is a sort of eternity and immortality . . . and as has already been admitted, all men will necessarily desire immortality together with the good, if love is of the everlasting possession of the good.' (58, 337) I have capitalized the word 'Good' above because it refers to the Platonic 'form of the good', the absolute Good which is reflected in all the experiences of good we have.

So far Socrates has argued that love gets its great motivating power from the desire for procreation or, at the human level, for 'birth in beauty.' But this is only preliminary to the thoughts he now brings forth. He recounts that the wise Diotima told him,

Men whose bodies only are creative, betake themselves to women and beget children - this is the character of their love; their offspring, as they hope, will preserve their memory and give them the blessedness and immortality which they desire in the future. But creative souls - for there are men who are more creative in their souls than in their bodies - conceive that which is proper for the soul to conceive or retain. And what are these conceptions? - wisdom and virtue in general. And such creators are all poets and other artists who may be said to have inventions. But the greatest and fairest sort of wisdom by far is that which is concerned with the ordering of states and families, and which is called temperance and justice. (58, 339)

Marvelous as these 'children of the mind' are - and Socrates gives as examples the works of Homer and Hesiod and the laws of Lycurgus and Solon - they will later be referred back to as mere 'images and idols'. For Diotima is now ready to introduce Socrates, and he us, to a new level of understanding about love. 'These are the lesser mysteries of love,' she tells him, 'into which even you, Socrates may enter; to the greater and more hidden ones which are the crown of these, and to which, if you pursue them in a right spirit, they will lead, I know not whether you will be able to attain.' (58, 340) She then explains that the lover of beauty has to begin in youth and pursue his quest in ascending stages:

1. The love of one form (person) only out of which 'fair thoughts' should be created.
2. The perception that the beauty of one form is related to that of others.
3. The realization that what one sees in every fair form is *the same beauty*.
4. Relinquishment of the 'violent love' of one to become 'a lover of all beautiful forms.'
5. Learning that 'the beauty of the mind is more honorable than the beauty of the outward forms.'
6. Seeing the beauty of the mind in institutions and laws and sciences.
7. Having 'at last the vision . . . revealed [to the lover] of a single science, which is the science of beauty everywhere.'

Now we are nearly to the end of the ascent but there is one more step:

> For he who has been instructed thus far in the things of love, and who has learned to see the beautiful in due order and succession, when he comes toward the end will suddenly perceive a nature of wondrous beauty. . . beauty only, absolute, separate, simple, and everlasting, which without diminution and without increase, or any change, is imparted to the ever-growing and perishing beauties of all other things. (58, 341f.)

Finally, in a passage worth quoting in its entirety, Diotima concludes,

> This, my dear Socrates, . . . is that life above all others which man should live, in the contemplation of beauty absolute; a beauty which if you once beheld, you would see not to be after the measure of gold, and garments, and fair boys and youths, which when you now behold you are in fond amazement, and you and many a one are content to live seeing only and conversing with them without meat or drink, if that were possible - you want to be with them and to look at them. But what if man had eyes to see the true beauty - the divine beauty, I mean, pure and clear and unalloyed, not clogged with the pollutions of mortality, and all the colors and vanities of human life - thither looking, and holding converse with the true beauty divine and simple, and bring into being and educating true creations of virtue and not idols only? Do you not see that in that communion only, beholding beauty with the eye of the mind, he will be enabled to bring forth, not images of beauty, but realities; for he has hold not of an image but of a reality, and bringing forth and educating true virtue to become the friend of God and be immortal, if mortal man may. Would that be an ignoble life? (58, 342f.)

The Platonic view is thus exactly the opposite of Freud's. Freud interpreted life's higher aspirations as sublimations of the sex drive. Socrates sees the true aim of eros as life's highest aspiration, contemplation of Beauty or the Good and its ultimate product the virtuous life. Because animals and common people do not have the intellectual and moral prowess to seek the highest, they expend eros in the lowest way, as physical sex which produces physical offspring. Some men, at a higher level, turn their eros to producing offspring of the mind, literature and laws, which, great though they may be, are nevertheless still 'images' and 'idols.'

At this point we should remind ourselves again that the Greek thinkers were, above all, *rationalists* and, in the case of Socrates and Plato, *idealists* for whom the highest abstractions were the highest reality, the phenomenal world being shadowy by comparison. The Greeks invented high level abstraction in the Western World. Before they entered Occidental history, profound thoughts were expressed in mythopeia or poetry. At a more mundane level, while the Egyptians were great masters of practical geometry, it was the Greeks, Pythagoras and Euclid, who created the abstract geometry that modern schools still teach. What Socrates describes as the 'greater and more hidden' mysteries, the eight stages I previously listed (seven plus the final 'vision') essentially involves a process of rational *abstraction*. He counsels the mind to think of beauty in more and more comprehensive terms, moving from the love of one beautiful person to the love of all to the love of the mind and its intellectual expressions and finally to the love of pure beauty 'divine and simple.' This last step is not an end in itself. It enables the one who achieves it to bring into being and educate 'true creations of virtue and not idols only', i.e. virtuous human beings rather than literature or laws. Obviously Plato considered Socrates such an educator but it would not do to have Socrates credit that high achievement to himself. That is why Socrates' views are put in the words of Diotima the Priestess to whom Plato, with tongue in cheek, attributes skepticism as to Socrates' ability to comprehend the higher mysteries.

By abstraction the Greeks attempted to bring order into the non-order of the phenomenal world. What Socrates did with the concept of eros was a model for future Occidental thinking, involving a *hierarchy of truth and value*. The further up the hierarchy one ascended the closer one came to ultimate truth and ultimate value.

But, by the same token, whatever was at the bottom of the hierarchy remained relatively non-ordered and unorderable. That is exactly where Greek thought left sex, that crudest form of eros which is most *'clogged with the pollutions of mortality, and all the colors and vanities of human life.'* Order could be brought to *eros* but only by leaving physical *sex* far behind. It is small wonder, then, that the Greek mind did not deign to explore the intricacies of sex or treat it as a subject for systematic research or thought. And it was from Plato's *Symposium* that we inherited the idea of Platonic Love.

Until the thirteenth century revival of Plato's most brilliant successor, Aristotle, Christian theology relied almost exclusively on Platonism for its philosophical foundation. Perhaps I should say 'Neo-Platonism' because in the third century A.D. the great Alexandrian thinker, Plotinus, produced a remarkable synthesis of Platonism, gnosticism and other lines of thought which came to be called Neo-Platonism. Whatever other ideas converged in Neo-Platonism, however, its structure, particularly its hierarchical organization, was thoroughly Platonic. It was Neo-Platonism which impacted on the Jewish theologian, Philo, on Muslim theologians, and on the two most influential theological writers of the early medieval Church, St. Augustine and the Pseudo-Dionysius. The most important element Neo-Platonism added to Plato was mysticism. Plotinus probably got it from gnosticism, a near-Eastern religious movement which thought of the soul as imprisoned in evil matter. Salvation to the gnostic meant freeing the soul from the body and returning it to the perfect immaterial realm from which it came.

We will have occasion to mention gnosticism again later in this section but suffice it to say here that although gnosticism - and the gnostic elements of Neo-Platonism - were great temptations for the Church Fathers, already strongly influenced by asceticism, in the end they rejected its view of the human body and sexuality for two reasons. First, God had created the human body in His own image and pronounced it *good*. Therefore it could not be considered either unreal or evil in itself as the gnostics would have it. Second, Christ had been *incarnated*, born in human flesh. While the gnostics maintained the incarnation was an illusion, the Church insisted it was real and that Christ was perfect *in the flesh*.

What then was to be the attitude of the Church toward sex? To begin with, the faithful had the examples of Jesus, Paul and the Christian ascetics. Jesus had a profound respect for the strongly monogamous Jewish family of his time. He insisted on fidelity and confinement of sex to marriage. 'On the other hand,' says Ernst Troeltsch, 'Jesus reminds His hearers that sex will not exist at all in the Kingdom of Heaven; that situations may arise in which it may be necessary to renounce the joys [and responsibilities] of family life in response to some imperious spiritual demand, and that the missionary vocation may require men to 'have made themselves eunuchs for the Kingdom of Heaven's sake." (90, 61) Paul also had a deep reverence for the family but he had himself become one of the 'eunuchs for the Kingdom of Heaven's sake' and he advised others to do the same. Nevertheless he counseled that it was better to marry than to 'burn' with sexual desire.

The examples of Jesus and Paul are of men who have renounced sex in favor of a higher purpose in life. But, although from a different perspective, that is exactly what Socrates advocated in the Symposium. The Church Fathers discerned the similarities between Christian asceticism and the Platonic life of virtue and saw how they could adapt the thought structure of the latter to the faith process of the former. For love of the Good they could substitute the Christian ideal of perfection - the love of God and man. But when it came to the bottom of the hierarchy they could accept neither Greek sensuality nor the gnostic idea of the evil of the flesh. God had not made man to be a libertine nor had he told him the body was evil. He had simply equipped man and woman to 'be fruitful and multiply.' Presumably, had Adam and Eve not sinned they would have remained naked in Paradise and consorted together like teenagers in the freshness of first love. And Eve would have conceived children painlessly by the natural childbirth method. But the Fall changed everything, including sex and its results. East of Eden, their bodies now covered with garments, the first couple were never to know that innocence. To Eve God said,

> I will greatly multiply your pain in childbearing; in pain you shall bring forth children, yet your desire shall be for your husband, and he shall rule over you.[Gen. 3:16] (87, 3)

It was therefore a woman's duty and desire to have sex with her husband even though pregnancy would bring the terrible pain of childbirth. That was punishment for being Adam's temptress, a stigma from which Western women would never quite be exonerated. Moslems have been particularly severe in reminding women that they are temptresses. But both Jews and Moslems accepted sex as God-given and necessary for procreation as long as it was kept within the bounds prescribed by their laws and rules of decorum. Except in rare and unorthodox cases, Jews and Moslems never believed in a 'higher,' more virtuous life which excluded sex.

Christians, on the other hand, did believe in such a 'higher' life. At the bottom of the value hierarchy the Church adopted the basic Jewish view of sex for procreation, rejecting both the Platonic and gnostic views. The vast majority of Christians were subject to the sexual ethics of marriage, monogamy and fidelity. But at the upper end of the hierarchy of value monasticism was recognized as the highest expression of Christian life and chastity was obligatory for the monk. This notion of a higher and lower life-style, did, however, present a major problem with which Christian theologians struggled over the centuries and which was not finally to be resolved until the great synthesis of Platonism, Aristotelianism and Christianity constructed by Thomas Aquinas in the thirteenth century. The problem was the danger of having two entirely different ethics, one lower and one higher, within the structure of one faith which promised salvation to all. The solution, which went far beyond considerations of sex, was an organic conception of life in which each segment of the Christian Body had its own responsibilities and gifts to give to the whole.

> Thus the duty of those who live 'in the world' towards the whole is that of preserving and procreating the race - a task in which ascetics cannot share, while they for their part have the duty of showing forth the ideal in an intensified form, and of rendering service for others through intercession, penitence, and the acquisition of merit. (90, 242)

The whole system of organic relationships between higher and lower ways to perfection was not a system of nature, of course, but was held together and sustained by Divine Grace through the sacraments of the Church. But Divine Grace, it must be admitted, did nothing to make sex or erotic love more acceptable than it had been to Socrates. The Church finally wound up approving only one of the categories of sex - sex for procreation. Even pair-bonding and pair-maintenance were not completely relegated to sex. The former was primarily a social matter, the latter a sacramental one. And that is where Greek and Christian views left sex in Occidental Civilization.

But everyone knows, you will be justified in objecting, that the Western world produced a notion of love which is unique - *Romantic Love*. And you are absolutely right. Romantic love - in the sense of a passion for enduring union with a single person - is found explicitly in no other civilization. Its importance to the literature, poetry, drama, music and the nature of male-female relationships themselves from the late Middle Ages to the present cannot be overestimated. When we talk about being in love, about courtship, about loving and cherishing our spouses, these notions are not products of instinct or chance. They stem from a tradition of ideas which can be gathered under the heading of romantic love. As we have seen, however, nothing either in our classical or Judaeo-Christian-Islamic traditions prepares the way for such a strange notion as romantic love. It is an outrageous idea which bursts all constraints and flaunts all the fears with which Western Civilization confronted passion before the second millennium A.D.

Where did this outrageous idea come from? Elizabeth Salter tells us,

> Nearly everyone agrees that the origin of romantic love can be found in the phenomenon of *courtly love* which appeared rather suddenly at the end of the eleventh century. It was first expressed in the poetry of the troubadours who sang their lays in the feudal courts of southern France (Provence). It was not merely a poetic conceit but portrayed a real and radically new kind of relationship between men and women. The character of the love celebrated by early troubadour poets is dramatic in the extreme. The lover is always in a position of servitude; he must obey his lady's wishes, however capricious or unjust they may be. But it is his privilege, not his misfortune, to exist subject to her, for love, whether rewarded or not, is regarded as the source of all true virtue and nobility. *Such virtuous erotic love is not possible within marriage because marriage is a sacramental relationship defined by a Church which does not accept eroticism.* Thus the courtly lover habitually addresses the wife of another, and secrecy is therefore one of the important conditions of any favour granted to him. The ritual which surrounded the whole situation was observed reverently and devotedly; as later developments make even clearer, *the courtly lover often thought of himself in a semireligious context, serving the all-powerful god of love and worshipping his lady-saint.* (103, 664, *emphasis mine*)

In contrast to Christian marriage in which the husband was the ruler, in courtly love the lady rules over her servile lover. Courtly love was clearly incompatible with marriage; it was essentially adulterous but typically it was neither consummated nor, in all likelihood, expected to be. The courtly lover was in love with love, that ever unfulfilled spirit, in direct opposition to all the fundamental values of Western Civilization. What, then, could be the source of such a maverick phenomenon? That question puzzled scholars well into the twentieth century. In 1936, C.S. Lewis acknowledged,

It is, at any rate, certain that the efforts of scholars have so far failed to find an origin for the content of Provencal love poetry. Celtic, Byzantine, and even Arabic influence have been suspected; but it has not been made clear that these, if granted, could account for the results we see. (104, 219)

It was not until 1940 that Denis de Rougemont published a book called *L'Amour et l'Occident* which was translated into English as *Love in the Western World* . In it he argued persuasively that the fundamental ideals of courtly love, which turned the Christian ideal of marriage upside down, were derived from Catharism, a heresy derived from *gnosticism*. Provence, the original venue of the troubadours, was also that of the Cathars. These Cathars (meaning 'the Pure') decried

. . . the [Catholic] sacrament of marriage joining two bodies even where there is no love between them, a sacrament which the Cathars never stopped attacking as *iurata fornicatio* [legal fornication]. (105, 134)

But that did not mean the Cathars praised erotic love. On the contrary, like all gnostics, they believed the soul was imprisoned in the mortal body and that its destiny was to fly 'upward' from that prison to the immortal realm in which it originated. The Cathars believed that it was primarily sexual passion which bound souls to mortality and what released them was another kind of passion, that for 'a feminine principle, held to have pre-existed material creation.' This feminine principle was analogous to 'the Sophia-Pistis of Gnosticism' and was, to the Cathars, 'Maria, symbol of the pure saving Light, intact (immaterial) Mother of Jesus.' De Rougemont stops short of saying that courtly love *is* veiled Catharist mysticism but he states without reservation that 'it was *at least inspired* ' by it. (82, 101) His conclusion is that romantic love 'is nothing else than *a lawless invasion and flowing back* into our lives of a spiritual heresy the key to which we have lost.' (82, 137)

In other words, romantic love is not a product of the Western civilized mind at all but of an anti-Western way of thought which perpetuated itself for centuries on the fringes of Western Civilization. Gnosticism in all its manifestations - Manicheism, Docetism, Catharism - was a recurring threat to the supremacy of rational order in Western Civilization. For that reason it was always ferreted out, rejected and persecuted by the Church. The troubadours were not advocates of romantic love as we know it. But the emotions and rhetoric they created were transformed in the thirteenth and fourteenth centuries into the language of courtship, the 'pedestalization' of women, and the idealization of marriage *as the embodiment of love*.

Romantic love could only flower once Western Civilization began its radical transition to the modern era. It is one of the delicious ironies of history that a perennial anti-sexual heresy should have been the source of the most distinctive model of male/female relations in the modern Western world. We can only agree with C. S. Lewis that is difficult to imagine

> . . . in all its bareness the mental world that existed before [romantic love] - to wipe out of our minds, for a moment, nearly all that makes food for both modern sentimentality and modern cynicism. We must conceive a world emptied of that ideal of 'happiness' - a happiness grounded on successful romantic love . . . (104, 216)

But make no mistake about it, romantic love was, in its origin and as it unfolded in the modern world, non-sexual. It was the presupposition of all the love stories which came out of Hollywood from the thirties to the sixties and which never went beyond a chaste kiss. Yet Lewis was right: a world emptied of romantic love would be quite a different world. But if he could look at the United States today, he might see just such a world in the making.

Sex in the Indic World: Everything and Then Some

In the movie, 'Passage to India,' which was based on E. M.
Forster's novel, there is a scene in which a young, well-bred, virginal
Englishwoman is riding a bicycle along unfrequented paths to see the
Indian countryside. Full of curiosity she turns down a narrow,
deserted side path hemmed in by tall grass. After a short distance
she is startled to see the stone face of an Indian god overlooking the
path from a low bank, its body and pedestal hidden by brush.
Beyond the idol is a grove of trees. There the woman sees something
even more startling - the walls of a ruined temple decorated with bas
reliefs of larger than life-sized men and women, their bodies
beautifully entwined in passionate embrace. The expressions on the
faces of these couple, captured by the sculptor at the peak of sexual
intercourse, are filled with an ecstasy that far transcends the merely
sensual. These *mithuna* - loving couples - are completely sexual, yet
at the same time completely religious. They are a recurrent theme in
Indic art and unique to Indic Civilization. Their like is to be found
nowhere else in the world.

And nowhere else in the world was sex accepted, explored and
given such prominence as in what some people have called 'life-
denying' India. Even in China, where sex was the fundamental
symbol of the cosmic process, sexuality was never treated with the
reverence, awe and total fascination that it was in India. We have
seen that in the Western world only one category of sex was finally
and fully accepted. In the Indic world, all of them were accepted,
although some were appropriate to certain situations and
philosophies of life, others to different ones. How one reconciles this
fact with the austere discipline of yoga and the Indic desire for
moksha (release) or *nirvana* takes a bit of explaining.

Recall the story in Chapter 3 which told how the primordial
'man,' Prajapati, *generated* the gods, the demons and the entire
world from himself. It probably occurred to you that this generative

process was like giving birth, a feminine activity rather than the masculine kind of construction ascribed to the God of Genesis. The Indic mind did, in fact, think of creation as birth and the creative principle as feminine. The nineteenth-century Hindu saint, Sri Ramakrishna, said,

> The Primordial Power is ever at play. She is creating, preserving, and destroying in play, as it were. This Power is called Kali [Goddess of birth and death]. Kali is verily Brahman, and Brahman is verily Kali. It is one and the same Reality. When we think of It as inactive, that is to say, not engaged in the acts of creation, preservation, and destruction, then we call It Brahman. But when It engages in these activities, then we call It Kali or Sakti. The Reality is one and the same; the difference is in name and form. (25, 564)

From very early times in India woman was seen as the embodiment of the divine creativity. Another Prajapati story from the Brhadaranyaka Upanishad tells us that

> Prajapati (the Lord of Creation) thought to himself: 'Let me provide a firm foundation.' So he created woman. When he had created her, he honored her below. Therefore one should honor women below. He stretched out for himself that stone which projects [lingam or penis]. With that he impregnated her. Her lap is a sacrificial altar; her hairs, the sacrificial grass; her skin, the soma-press. The two lips of the yoni [vagina] are the fire in the middle. Verily, indeed, as great as is the world of the person who performs [a certain important sacrifice], just as great is the world of him who practices sexual intercourse knowing this. (106, 12)

Seen in this light sexual intercourse becomes a religious rite and woman becomes the holy flame into which the gods themselves cast the seeds of creation. 'Woman is fire,' says another passage in the same scripture,

> . . . her haunch the fuel; the hairs on her body the smoke; the yoni , the flame; intercourse, the coals; the fits of enjoyment, the sparks. The gods offer seed in this fire. From this offering man springs forth. (106, 11)

Contrast this enraptured affirmation of woman with the woeful condemnation of the temptress, Eve, in Genesis. True, the Indic view of woman was not that of a 'full person' in the modern sense nor an object of romantic love. But the religious symbolism in which she was garbed was positive, not negative, as in the West. By the same token sexuality was seen in India as the microcosmic expression of macrocosmic creativity. It would make no sense to the Indic mind to say that sex was acceptable *merely* for procreation when procreation was the essence of the world process. Sex made the world go round.

In the Indic view there was no hierarchy of truth and value, no higher order to which man could aspire in order to achieve immortality. All orders, whether of gods, demons, humans or ideas, were equally relative before the absolute non-order out of which they had arisen. From this point of view all order was transitory and illusory and eventually to be transcended through release from the illusion. But until the soul was ready to begin that ascent to the Source, its purpose was to live that life it had been given to the fullest. No one had to feel guilty because he was young and vigorous and wanted to make the most of sex.

So it was that one of the *trivarga* - India's three worldly philosophies of life - was the *kamashastra*, the science of *kama* or pleasure, particularly sexual pleasure. Kama, according to Zimmer,

> . . . denotes the whole range of possible experience within the
> sphere of love, sex, sensual gratification, and delight. Kama
> is wish, desire, carnal gratification, lust, love, and affection.'
> (25, 145)

In other words, *kama* means about the same as the Greek *eros*. There were many treatises written about kama but the one best-known is the *Kama Sutra*. It was written in an aphoristic style *(sutra)* by Vatsyayana probably in the third or fourth century A.D. and purports to be an abstract compiled from much longer works by the author's predecessors. There is nothing salacious or pornographic about the Kama Sutra. It never really needed to be sold 'under the counter' in the West because it is not meant to titillate or to arouse sexual desires.   It is, in fact, a rather dull book, a sort of comprehensive *technical manual* which gives detailed prescriptions for everything having to do with sex including its social context, the eligible types of partners and the ones to be avoided, the physical setting in which it takes place, the entertainment skills which accompany it, the kinds of embraces, the positions for intercourse, and so on. The book is divided into seven parts (106, 57ff.):

Part One: Society and Social Concepts
Part Two: On Sexual Union
Part Three: About the Acquisition of a Wife
Part Four: About a Wife
Part Five: About the Wives of Other Men
Part Six: About Courtesans
Part Seven: On the Means of Attracting Others to Yourself

For an idea of the book's detail, following are the chapters in Part Two:

I   Kinds of union according to dimensions [of the sexual organs], force of desire, and time; and on the different kinds of love
II   On the embrace
III   On kissing
IV   On pressing or marking with the nails
V   On biting, and the ways of love to be employed with regard to women of different countries
VI   On the various ways of lying down, and the different kinds of congress
VII   On the various ways of striking, and on the sounds appropriate to them
VIII About females acting the part of males
IX   On holding the lingam in the mouth
X   How to begin and how to end the congress.   Different kinds of congress, and love quarrels.(83, 59f.)

Despite all this detail, Vatsyayana does not pretend to have exhausted the subject and strongly recommends exploratory sex (Morris' fifth category):

An ingenious person should multiply the kinds of congress after the fashion of the different kinds of beasts and of birds. For these different kinds of congress, performed according to the usage of each country, and the liking of each individual, generate love, friendship, and respect in the hearts of women. (106, 115)

What I have called 'political sex' was explicitly recognized by Vatsyayana. He says that, apart from marital sex, having sex with women of the lower castes, with women excommunicated from their own castes, with public women and with women who have left their husbands for another man is all right *as long as it is merely for pleasure*. But it is wrong to have sex with another man's wife merely for pleasure. There have to be special reasons, of which he gives a long list. Most of the special reasons are political as the following examples illustrate.

> This woman has gained the heart of her great and powerful husband, and exercises a mastery over him, who is a friend of my enemy; if, therefore, she becomes united with me she will cause her husband to abandon my enemy.
> By being united with this woman, I shall kill her husband, and so obtain his vast riches which I covet.
> The union of this woman with me is not attended with any danger, and will bring me wealth, of which, on account of my poverty and inability to support myself, I am very much in need. I shall, therefore, obtain her vast riches in this way without any difficulty. (106, 82)

Vatsyayana is not concerned with whether treachery, murder or avarice are morally right or wrong, merely whether it is within the rules of society to use sex with another man's wife to further such purposes and he judges that it is. This is unabashed political sex. Along with political sex the Kama Sutra approves all ten of Morris' categories, including, of course, the first:

> When Kama is practiced by men of the four classes, according to the rules of the Holy Writ . . ., with virgins of their own caste, it then becomes a means of acquiring lawful progeny and good fame . . . (106, 81)

Morality (dharma) does not affect sexual practices as far as what you do, only who you do it with and why. Sex is a sphere unto itself, not subject to suspicion and moral condemnation as it was in the West. Vatsyayana himself expresses this attitude of compartmentalization of life's aims very well:

> Man, the period of whose life is one hundred years, should practice Dharma [moral and religious duty], Artha [acquisition of wealth and power], and Kama at different times and in such a manner that they may harmonize, and not clash in any way. He should acquire learning in his childhood; in his youth and middle age he should attend to Artha and Kama; and in his old age he should perform Dharma, and thus seek to gain Moksha, that is, release from further transmigration. (106, 63)

The last two categories of sex, self-transcending sex and ritual sex also found a rich expression in India but not as part of kamashastra. The most profound Indic approach to sex was found in the Tantra school of thought and practice which emerged both in Hinduism and Buddhism. It was Tantrism which was being expressed through the *mithuna* reliefs I referred to at the beginning of this section. The god whose serene face startled the cyclist was *Shiva* .

In India God is worshipped in a vast number of forms but Indians recognize that those many forms are manifestations of the One. Their scriptures make that abundantly clear. Nevertheless some forms have a special fascination and are widely revered. Among these is Vishnu, especially in his avatar (incarnation) as Krishna. Another is Kali, the black goddess, divine mother and goddess of death. And then there is Shiva, god of storm and destruction, yet also the embodiment of divine creative energy, of cosmic sexuality. The *Nataraj*, Shiva as Lord of the Dance, a slender, four-armed figure dancing ecstatically in a circle of fire, is probably the Hindu symbol most widely-known to the rest of the world. It is said that with Shiva's every footfall a world is created or destroyed. There is little shocking to the Western mind about the graceful Nataraj, despite his four arms. What has shocked many Westerners is the other symbol through which Shiva is worshipped over much of India - the Shiva *lingam* or penis, a vertical stone carved in a very realistic likeness of the male organ. It is the lingam which was referred to as 'the stone that projects' in the Prajapati story above. It is perhaps necessary to abandon some of our Western ascetic mentality in order to appreciate that the lingam does not represent simple penis-worship. It is the symbol of Shiva, the divine male partner in cosmic *procreation*. Shiva is *shakti*, 'energy, force power, potency.' (25, 77) In Tantrism shakti is feminized as the spouse of Shiva, the supreme goddess.

> Typical of the Tantric system is the concept of *sakti* : the female as the projected 'energy' (*sakti*) of the male . . . Male and female, God and Goddess, are the polar manifestations (passive and active, respectively) of a single transcendent principle and, as such, in essence one, though in appearance two. The male is identified with eternity, the female with time, and their embrace with the mystery of creation. (25, 62)

Tantrism, then, celebrates the cosmic process instead of attempting to attain release from it as does yoga. The goal of life is still to experience the Oneness of all things but *within* the world of multiplicity, not *beyond* it. Make no mistake that this is an affirmation of order. To be sure, the world is ordered, but the order is purely relative. There is no meaning or purpose to it. You will not get anywhere by trying to fathom its true essence. It is the divine *play (lila)* or dance. But to know it is the *divine* play, that it is one with the Absolute, is quite different from thinking it is a cruel joke. Experiencing that is the aim of Tantric practice.

Instead of withdrawing from the world and practicing yoga, the Tantric student, the *sadhaka*, was 'taught not to think that we are one with the Divine in Liberation only, but here and now, in every act we do. For in truth all such is Sakti. It is Siva who as Sakti is acting in and through the Sadhaka . . . . When this is realized in every natural function, then, each exercise thereof ceases to be a mere animal act and becomes a religious rite.' (25, 577) You will recall that in the previous chapter we came across the three gunas, tamas (inertia), rajas (activity) and sattwa (tranquility). We saw that the yogi uses rajas to overcome tamas but gradually cultivates sattwa as the path to Self-realization. The sadhaka, on the other hand, cultivates and disciplines rajas. He has to be a very special kind of person. He is called a hero *(vira)* because he has the strength to treat those things as sacramental which are forbidden to the yogi, particularly the 'five forbidden things': wine, meat, fish, parched grain, and sexual intercourse. (25, 572) Genuine, not symbolic, sexual intercourse was an integral part of Tantric practice, a *sacrament*. This has brought visions of licentiousness and orgies to many a Western mind. But, as Zimmer explains,

> The Tantric ritual of wine, meat, fish, parched grain, and sexual intercourse is accomplished not as a lawbreaking revel, but under the cautious supervision of a guru, in a controlled state of 'nondualist'. . . realization, and as the culminating festival of a long sequence of spiritual disciplines, through many lives. (25, 574)

The ritual aspect of Tantric sex involved long advance preparation of the mind in which the male was identified with Shiva and the female with Shakti. The psychophysiology underlying the rite was same as we found in yoga, that of the *chakras* or nervous centers through which the *kundalini* (spiritual energy) rises. Whereas in normal sexual intercourse only the lower three centers are involved, Tantric sex involved a kind of *coitus interruptus* which avoided orgasm and stimulated the flow of the kundalini to the higher centers. 'The spiritual emotion of the adept is *prema*: ecstatic, egoless, beatific bliss in the realization of transcendent identity.' (25, 574)

Thus we find that what *kamashastra* left out, self-transcending sex and ritual sex, *Tantrism* provided, leaving no category of sex missing from the Indic repertoire. It makes one wonder if the Westerner who first called the Indic mind 'life-denying' even knew that there *were* thirteen categories of sex.

Sex in the Sinic World: Battle of the Sexes

The Tantrists wrote about sex as a sublime cosmic ritual; Vatsyayana wrote about it like an anthropologist. But the Chinese wrote about sex like no one else ever has. Contrast the following passages about sex involving more than one partner. The first is from the Kama Sutra:

> When a man enjoys two women at the same time, both of who love him equally, it is called the 'united congress.'
> When a man enjoys many women altogether, it is called the 'congress of a herd of cows.' (106, 115)

Not exactly titillating, is it? Consider, however, the second passage which describes one of The Nine Glorious Postures as described by a Wise Maiden to China's legendary Yellow Emperor:

> *The Gobbling Fishes*
> Lady Precious Yin and Mistress White Jade lie on top of each other, their legs entwined so that their Jade Gates press together. They then move in a rubbing and jerking fashion against each other like fishes gobbling flies or water-plants from the surface. As they become more excited, the 'mouths' widen, and choosing his position carefully, Great Lord Yang thrusts between them with his Jade Root. They then move in unison until all three share the Ultimate simultaneously. (14, 133)

If the enjoyment of the activity were not enough, the Wise Maiden adds,

The triple flow of Vital Essence will strengthen bones and sinews as well as the breathing. It will also assist the Great Lord Yang to avoid the Five Overstrainings and the Seven Sex-injuries. (ibid.)

This is not merely to say that sex is salutary but that it is an expression of the same overall attitude which brings good into every aspect of life - the harmonization of opposites. Good politics, good art, good health, good sex - all arise from the harmonious resolution of conflict and each has a beneficial effect on the others.

In the ancient *Su-nü-ching*, conversations between Huang Ti (The Yellow Emperor) and the Wise Maiden, the following dialogue emphasizes the need for 'harmonious spirit':

Yellow Emperor : Now there is this problem of the Jade Thrusting Root failing to rise and stiffen. When this happens my face reddens and I am soaked in sweat. I breath hard, my desire is strong, I press furiously at the Gate - yet there is no sign of life. How can I avoid this mortifying situation?

The Wise Maiden : This is a problem that afflicts many men. Unless one is physically exhausted it is because one has retired to the bedchamber in the wrong mood. With a harmonious spirit the Jade Stem will always stiffen, with a mood that is dark or bitter, it is like a thorn piercing one's own flesh. (14, 143)

The Chinese did not organize their world as the West did, in hierarchies of value with sex at the very bottom of the ladder. Neither did they believe the world was an illusion or the meaningless play of the divine. Consequently they did not accept the compartmentalization of life exemplified in the Indic trivarga with different life functions rigidly separated, each following its own rules. To the Sinic mind every sphere of life followed the same rule and that rule was the rule of harmony and balance, the Way of Nature.

The basic paradigm for the Way of Nature in China was sex, its most expressive symbol the Yin-Yang. The Most Noble Tung wrote in the T'ang Dynasty,

It is my belief that all things under Heaven are wondrous, but that Man is the most wondrous of all. This distinction is because of the unique nature of his sexual urge and its part in the harmony of Yin and Yang, and therefore of Heaven and Earth. If a man follows the Natural Laws, and understands them, he will nourish indefinitely his Vital Essence, prolong his life, and know gratification to the end of his days. If a man defies the Natural Laws, and abuses the Truths, his Essence will dry up before the end of his days and his life will be brief and sad. (14, 19)

Yang and Yin are opposites. Although, as we saw earlier, each bears the seed of the other in it, signifying their ultimate unity as aspects of Tao, they are inherently in conflict. Yang is order, maleness, light, power. Yin is mystery, femininity, shadow, passivity. They are drawn into battle, 'drawn' because each is incomplete without the other, 'battle' because they are so different that they are a challenge to each other.

The terminology and the precision with which sex positions are explained owe much to their association with the idea of intercourse being a battle for ascendancy. Out of the Yin-Yang contest would come the wonderful peace of the final Harmony - though usually in a manner that favoured the male ego and his pleasure. Both the Taoist and the Buddhist influences in his life, drawing much of their message and their wisdom from nature and the other species of life, accepted the belief of conflict within harmony. Whether the sexes were equal, or one was superior to the other, the Chinese acknowledged certain realities very early in their history, namely that there was an eternal War of the Sexes. (14, 135)

The Chinese produced civilization's most massive volume of sexual literature - treatises, illustrated instruction manuals, poetry and novels, much of the last forthrightly pornographic with a heavy infusion of Rabelaisian humor. Only the postcivilized Western world has rivalled the Chinese in that area, in quantity although rarely in quality. What gives much of Chinese sexual literature its zest is its descriptions of the sexual encounter as a battle. For example, Li Yü, the author of the seventeenth-century novel, *Jou-pu-t'uan* (The Night-time Scholar), asks,

> Are there really any differences, apart from the numbers involved, of battles between armies and those fought in bed? In each instance the first requirement is for the commander to survey the terrain and to assess his opponent. In sexual encounters the man's first curiosity is about the hills and valleys of the woman, and hers about the size and fire-power of his armaments. Which of them is to advance and which to retreat? As in war, to know oneself is as important as knowing the enemy. (14, 136)

Li Yü's hero, the Night-time Scholar, is a young man afflicted with a tiny penis. He has the good fortune to meet a Master of Medicine who successfully grafts a huge canine penis onto his. 'For the battle that lay ahead,' Li Yü tells us,

> . . . the Scholar now possessed a piece of equipment not only of remarkable dimensions but as yet of untried power. How would he manage it? Could he control it? Would it turn savage with the spirit of its former canine owner? (ibid.)

The rest of the novel describes the sexual encounters the Scholar has with his remarkable 'piece of equipment.' They are truly Rabelaisian and it takes a total absence of humor (or an Occidental mind) to consider them salacious.

We had to explain the Occidental attitude toward sex just because it seemed so contrary to human feeling and the joy of life. But the Chinese attitude toward sex needs minimal interpretation because, to the Sinic mind, it was the quintessence of life, in full accord with its views about everything else. If the Chinese made little of the last two of our categories of sex (self-transcending and ritual), they certainly made the most of the first eleven.

Sex in Mesoamerica: Tender Comrades

The Franciscan friars who so faithfully and compassionately recorded what the Amerindians told them about their lives before the great defeat did not include details of Mesoamerican sexual relations. After all, it was not a subject for inquiry in their own repressed civilization, so they could hardly be expected to send notes on Aztec or Mayan sex back to Madrid or Rome. As we had to do with other areas of Amerindic life, in the absence of explicit information about sex we will have to venture into deduction and interpolation.

In contrast to Sinic Civilization, the basic paradigm of Amerindic Civilization was not sex but sacrifice. What we always need to keep in mind when we are dealing with the Mesoamericans is the purpose of the sacrificial *leitmotif* which dominated their lives. Sacrifice was essential to the preservation and continuation of the gods and the cosmic process. Even after the Spaniards had 'Christianized' the Aztecs they found this attitude hard to change. Under Spanish rule,

> . . . Christian worship was acknowledged without a distinction among the degrees of worship, and *Indians continued to act as if the object of worship relied upon the worshiper for its sustenance and upkeep.* Indians confessed but the Aztec preference for confession in time of crisis [as a penitential or sacrificial act] competed with the Christian requirement that confession be performed at least once a year. (107, 101, *emphasis mine*)

As with everything else in Amerindic life we might expect that sexual relations would be constrained by the conception of life as preparation for sacrificial death. Sahagún tells us that Aztec girls

> . . . were told that three precepts above all others should guide their lives: they should serve the gods, they should be chaste, and they should love, serve and look up to their husbands. (94, 174)

'Although they were heathens,' the friar added, 'the Mexicans were not without good customs.' (ibid.) Sahagún's approval in itself tells us that the Aztec attitude toward sex had a good deal in common with its austere treatment in Western Civilization. Prostitution was accepted but held in low repute. The *auianime* or courtesan-companions of the young trainees of the *telpochcalli* were a different matter. Their role was religiously prescribed and approved for the benefit of the young warriors-to-be.

> The profession of the *auianime*, whom the Spanish chroniclers tend to treat as whores although at the same time they state that 'they gave their bodies for nothing', was not only recognised, but valued; they had their own place reserved for them, beside the young warriors whose companions they were, in the ceremonies of religion. (94, 184)

Marriage was taken very seriously and in it sex was probably confined primarily to its first three functions, procreation, pair-formation and pair-maintenance, somewhat broader in scope than in the Occident. The seriousness of marriage is shown by the severe penalty imposed for adultery: death. It was the same for husband and wife, high-and low-born alike, provided that proof was rigorously established by independent witnesses. In my opinion the first three functions of sex were probably invested with more significance in Amerindic Civilization than in any of the other three. Children were important in the other Civilizations, in the West for continuation of the species (and swelling the ranks of the faithful) and in India and China because of the ritual duties children, especially sons, were expected to perform on behalf of their parents. But in Mesoamerica, every child of both sexes was a new life enrolled in the process of world-preservation, a potential sacrifice. For this reason children were treated with extraordinary tenderness and respect. The ceremonies surrounding the birth, naming and dedication of a newborn child were lengthy, elaborate and beautiful. 'Times beyond number the baby was compared to a necklace, to a jewel of precious

stones, to a rare feather.' (94, 164) After the ritual washing of a
newborn girl,

> . . . the midwife and the relatives, in a touching ceremony,
> spoke to the cradle in which the little girl would lie, calling it
> Yoalticitl, 'the healer by night', and saying, 'You who are her
> mother, take her, old goddess. Do her no harm; watch over
> her kindly.' (94, 167)

It is hard to believe that this tenderness did not carry over into
the relationship of husband and wife. Certainly, the amount of
respect afforded women in Aztec society was not exceeded, if indeed
equalled, by any other civilization. This was nowhere more evident
than in the honor paid to a woman who died in childbirth:

> It was clearly understood that a woman who died in
> childbirth was upon the same footing as a warrior who died
> in battle or as a sacrifice. . . It was said that the woman
> (dead in childbed) did not go to the underworld but into the
> palace of the sun, and that the sun took her with him
> because of her courage. . . The destiny of the 'valiant woman'
> in the hereafter was therefore exactly equivalent, the
> counterpart, of that of the warriors who died in battle or
> upon the sacrificial stone. (94, 190f.)

In a world so beset by life's precariousness it is not surprising
that the tender and the poignant should be so evident. 'Flowers and
death, like twin obsessions, adorn all Mexican lyric poetry with their
brilliance and their shadow,' says Jacques Soustelle. (94, 240)

> Let us be happy.
> Does one take flowers along to the land of the dead?
> They are only lent to us.
> The truth is that we go;
> We leave flowers and singing and the earth.
> The truth is that we go . . .
> If it is only here on the earth
> That there are flowers and singing,
> Let them be our wealth,
> Let them be our adornment,
>   Let us be happy with them. (94, 242)

What can we conclude about the attitude toward sex in Mesoamerica? When dealing with other areas of life, we have sometimes found it instructive to contrast the Amerindic way with its opposite, the Chinese way. We found that the Chinese approach to sex was modelled on war, a creative battle between the sexes. I suspect that the sexual metaphor in Mesoamerica was also a martial one. But it would not have been a battle *between* the sexes. All the evidence we can marshall about the Amerindic approach to sex, meager as it is, would suggest that the Amerindic man and woman approached sex as *fellow warriors,* as tender comrades in a cosmic war that might at any time call upon either of them to forfeit their lives.

NINE

The Twentieth Century

Two Ways of Thinking about History

> The belief that man is in fact approaching a historic climax in our own age is well-nigh universal. The evidence is sufficiently clear and overwhelming; what is lacking is any common understanding or generally accepted inter-pretation of its significance.
>
> Roderick Seidenberg
> *Post-Historic Man*

It seems to me that these two sentences of Roderick Seidenberg are quite accurate. But while it is true that we lack a 'common understanding or generally accepted interpretation' of the significance of this time of ours, we can distinguish two broadly different interpretations of its significance. The first springs from what we might call the 'Technogenic View' of human history shared by such writers as V. Gordon Childe, Kenneth Boulding and Alvin Toffler. Kenneth Boulding, for example, calls the current period 'The Great Transition' while Alvin Toffler refers to it as 'The Third Wave.' Such writers, thinking basically in economic and technological terms, tend to ignore the psychic factors which controlled the development of civilization. Therefore Boulding and Toffler cite as their 'First Transition' or 'First Wave' the Neolithic agricultural revolution which began around 8000 B. C. and produced the economic and technological base for civilization. The 'Second Wave,' in their view, appears as the Industrial Revolution of the Modern Era. I have already pointed out in Chapter 1 why this approach is inadequate. It ignores the mental leap which resulted in the radical restructuring of human society with a consequent discontinuity between history and prehistory. Roderick Seidenberg, while he seems at first glance to be more sensitive to the psychic factor, really belongs in the camp of Boulding and Toffler. In his book, *Posthistoric Man* , he sees history as a period of struggle in which intelligence gradually but painfully overpowers and controls instinct:

> This relationship [between man and his environment] has actually passed through three phases: in the first stage [man] was himself part of the natural panorama, dependent wholly upon his instinctual, unconscious adaptations; in the second stage he diverged from the biologic series into conscious awareness of his environment, guided now by his intelligence to ever greater mastery over his surroundings; in the third stage, which he has reached only today, science has enabled him to adjust himself to the basic laws of nature rather than to nature in her immediate and visible presence. (108, 41)

In other words, in the second stage man deals with nature as farmer and engineer. In the third stage he becomes a scientist and deals with it by conforming to 'the unvarying laws behind the changing face of nature' and adjusting his way of life to 'the unchanging verities of these laws.' (108, 71) Seidenberg theorizes that the decisive step in man's establishing 'his conscious independence from the biologic scheme of things' was 'probably the addition of agriculture to his meager repertoire.' (108, 41) Therefore, what he is really talking about in the relationship between intelligence and instinct is less a matter of psychic evolution than the increased use of one part of the psyche (intelligence) over another (instinct) to deal with nature. Consequently, like Boulding and Toffler, he also views history as beginning with the Neolithic revolution rather than with the mental revolution of the fourth millennium B.C. He provides the diagram on the following page (108, 55).

Up to a certain point in human development, instinct dominates intelligence but its dominance progressively diminishes until the we see the two lines cross. At this crossing point, which is 'tentatively assumed to lie within the historic era' by Seidenberg, 'the weight of influence of instinct and intelligence upon the affairs of man would reach an unstable equilibrium' and, furthermore, that point constitutes 'a *vital moment or era of transition* dividing man's development into two phases - an earlier phase under the dominance of the instincts, and a later phase under that of intelligence.' (108, 55, *emphasis mine*) In Seidenberg's view, that vital moment or era of transition is *right now*. He thus agrees with Boulding and Toffler on the crucial nature of our time, which, in fact, he calls 'The Crucial Epoch.'

PREHISTORIC   HISTORIC   POSTHISTORIC

   INSTINCT   INTELLIGENCE

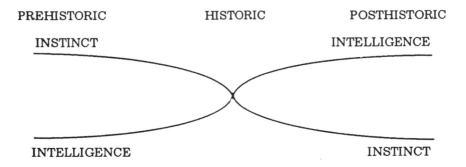

   INTELLIGENCE   INSTINCT

We shall have occasion later to consider what Seidenberg thinks are the implications of the right half of his diagram, that is, what will be the nature of 'Posthistoric Man,' but first let us consider the alternative 'Psychogenic View' of history as exemplified in the writing of Gerald Heard. All of Heard's thought had one underlying theme which he expressed as follows in *The Ascent of Humanity* .

> . . . all the material evidence of civilization being recognized as symptoms of an immaterial evolution, *it becomes apparent that the one underlying continuous process in human history is the evolution of consciousness* . . . The evolution of consciousness itself is not simple. It does not proceed in a straight line but in a spiral. Man has passed from the diffusion of the co-conscious to the intensity of individuality, but individuality is evidently not final. The inner urge of his psyche's evolution will not let him stay there. Individually he is a 'transitional creature.' He has to attempt a larger stability, a new union. . . Looking at the accumulation and ruin of civilizations, the simple belief in material progress gives

way before a conviction that history can only be interpreted as a series of collapses. . . When we realize that
the only true evolution, the only possible progress, is the
evolution of consciousness, then we can understand
history as a whole and see the periodic rise and fall of
civilization as that of a yeasty crust of material rising
under the urge of an invisible energy and falling back as
that energy, having raised the stubborn mass to rupture,
escapes - only to gather again under the crust and again
to raise it. (109, 230, *emphasis mine*)

Heard saw human psychic evolution as continuous through the
Neolithic agricultural period, still preserving 'co-consciousness'. But
he interpreted the following 'Heroic Age' as a fracture of
consciousness, a breaking of the social concensus and the emergence
of the individual. It was this individuation which produced what I
referred to as the proto-kings and -priests. For Heard, the fracture of
consciousness which preceded civilization and made it possible was a
Fall as he attempted to show in *Is God in History?*, an evolutionary
interpretation of the Christian doctrine of the Fall. But he also
pointed to the presence of redemptive processes in history and made
it clear that he believed the spiral of history to be turning upwards
from the struggle and conflict of individualism to a new level of
wholeness which he called 'superconsciousness.' 'Perhaps,' he
suggested, 'we may look upon our Fall as an inoculation with despair
to rouse resistance-reactions in our nature, which otherwise would
have sunk into that fatal complacency of stabilization, which is
painless death. Certainly Redemption is not to return us to
effortless comfort but to spur us to Sanctification, a new Wholeness.'
(109, 227)

These two views of history, the Technogenic View of Boulding,
Toffler, Childe, Seidenberg, et al., and the Psychogenic View, produce
quite different understandings of when the crucial turning points of
history occurred. The Technogenic View schematizes the past
something like this, the dates given being the critical turning points
in human development:

Pre-Neolithic	Agricultural Era	Industrial Era	Postindustrial Era
	8,000 B.C.	1650 A.D.	1955 A.D.
	(1st Wave)	(2nd Wave)	(3rd Wave)

Toffler explains this scheme as follows:

> For the purposes of this book [*The Third Wave*] we shall
> consider the First Wave era to have begun sometime around
> 8000 B.C. and to have dominated the earth unchallenged
> until sometime around A.D. 1650-1750. From this moment
> on, the First Wave lost momentum as the Second Wave
> picked up steam. Industrial civilization, the product of this
> Second Wave, then dominated the planet in its turn until it,
> too, crested. This latest historical turning point arrived in
> the United States during the decade beginning about 1955 -
> the decade that saw white-collar and service workers
> outnumber blue-collar workers for the first time. (110, 14)

In other words, from 8000 B.C. to 1650 A.D. nothing happened
that was nearly as important as the invention of agriculture at the
beginning of that epoch. The advent of civilization in the Fertile
Crescent in 3500 B.C. is completely ignored. But are we then to
suppose that civilization was a natural outgrowth of an agricultural
economy? There were before and after the beginning of civilization
many agricultural societies which never made the leap to civilization.
The great Zulu empire of the nineteenth century had an agricultural
base but it was non-literate and non-civilized. So, as we have
previously seen, were the Incan and Minoan societies. It is perfectly
conceivable that the world could still be populated today by
internally cohesive, non-literate, agricultural societies, some of them
quite elaborate and widespread but still founded on social
concensus. But it isn't. It is structured the way it is today because
in the fourth millennium B.C. some men made a gigantic
psychological leap to a new level of social organization called
'civilization.'

The Psychogenic View of the past produces a time scale like this:

Pre-civilization	Civilization West	India	China	America	Modern Era	Trans-ition	Post-civilization
| Agriculture |	|	|	|	|	|	|	|
8000 BC	3500 BC	2500 BC	1500 BC	500 BC	1500 AD	1900 AD	2000 AD

This view locates the crucial changes of history at the times when *the mind* changed radically, not when technology changed. We can agree that the 'Neolithic Revolution' was an important transition but it was important because it represented a radical change in the human mind which, in turn, produced a new focus on a settled society and a technology suitable to such a society. But the second and even more important transition was the advent of civilization. The 'Industrial Revolution' was built on the crumbling edifice of Western Civilization as a *socioeconomic system* but it could not have been built without the *Western mindset* and its intellectual heritage. Thus, although Toffler locates a crucial change in the latter half of the seventeenth century, the Psychogenic View locates it around 1500 A.D., at the beginning of the Reformation. In fact, we cannot even speak of a truly 'industrial' society in the West until the early nineteenth century and that powerful system would have been unthinkable without the religious, intellectual and political revolutions which preceded it.

The Psychogenic View interprets the twentieth century as the final phase of the modern era in which the basic structure of civilization has been progressively dismantled and, at the same time, as the transition toward *post-civilization*. When I say that the Modern Era in the West (since 1500) has seen the progressive dismantling of the structure of civilization I am referring to several developments, each of which can best be evaluated in terms of the General Theory of Civilization which I will repeat here to make the point clearer:

Civilization is a type of social organization in which a relatively small power elite, in pursuit of its own goals, exercises authority over and preempts the production of a large, powerless majority through the monopolization of written language, the sanctification of myth, the centralization of key institutions and the utilization of regimented armed force.

Decivilizing the Modern World

In the Modern Era each of these key characteristics has been dramatically altered if not eliminated in the Western democracies:

1. The trend toward *democratization* has seriously limited the power of elites over society.

2. The trend toward *economic liberalism* has helped to assure a fairer distribution of the rewards of production, leaving more in the hands of the producers. Although *socialism* corrected some of the most egregious conditions of exploitation by the elite, in the Soviet Union it did not displace the essential structure of civilization but simply replaced its feudal elite with a new political elite. The relatively sudden demise of the once formidable Soviet empire signalled not merely the collapse of a communist socioeconomic structure but of the anachronistic structure of civilization itself. In China the willingness of the elite to tolerate a considerable degree of economic freedom while suppressing political freedom is, in fact, a balancing act typical of Chinese civilization but the handwriting is on the wall (often literally in China). The tragedy of Tienanmen Square was only the opening scene in the Chinese quest for political freedom.

3. Wherever political and economic power has been wrested from the hands of power elites, the control of written information has been surrendered to the whole society. Mass literacy, extensive libraries, other public resource institutions, and now inexpensive personal computers along with newly acquired legal rights to all but the most sensitive kinds of information have made monopolization of knowledge virtually impossible in the modern Western world, barring a repetition of some grotesque atavism of the Nazi type. Gorbachev's

policy of *glasnost* (openness) was a remarkable step toward demonopolization of knowledge in the Soviet Union and that policy has been maintained against powerful opposition by President Yeltsin.

4.The disestablishment of religion and widespread skepticism about religious ideas have made it unrealistic for anyone to try to use mythology as a method of social control or mobilization except in the case of relatively small cults. Only in a few countries, such as Iran, is religion still a powerful instrument of social control. The revival of religion in the Soviet Union has, in fact, been an expression of newfound freedom. Fundamentalism in the United States does have a great deal of social and even political influence but its leaders, when they are not corrupt, are too individualistic and the movement as a whole lacks the unity necessary for widespread political discipline. It may, however, still unify itself further and remains a substantial foe of liberalization in American society as the 'Right to Life' movement witnesses.

5.While there are still strong central governments in most modern countries, they are responsible in the Western democracies to an electorate, and state and local governments function with considerable autonomy. In the typical civilized society local officials such as state governors and city officials were responsible to and usually appointed by the central government. For that to be the case today is an anachronism. Furthermore, there is a growing sentiment in society, notably American society, that something needs to be done to prevent elected 'representatives' from entrenching themselves in power as a political elite.

6.Finally, the populations of the Western democracies no longer live under the threat of military force. Local problems tend to be dealt with by local police or, in dire emergencies, by military forces under regional control. There are, of course, still countries, China and Iraq, for example, which still make unabashed use of military power for internal repression.

We can conclude, therefore, that the socioeconomic structure of human society in the Western democracies, has changed to a major extent in every important respect from what we defined as civilized. People no longer have to be subjugated to a mighty few. They no longer have to give up most of what they produce for the use of that few. They are no longer kept ignorant and denied access to means of learning. They are no longer told they have their place, however humble, in the divine scheme and that they had better accept their lot. They are no longer kept out of the decision-making process. And they no longer have to live in fear of the sound of jackboots and hammering on their doors in the dead of night.

This does not mean, of course, that the twentieth century has seen the end of civilization. Within the lifetime of many of us we have seen Adolf Hitler attempt to create his thousand-year empire - *The Third Reich*. What has been generally overlooked, precisely because we had no clear definition of civilization, is that what Hitler was attempting was nothing less than *the restoration of the basic structure of civilization*. Could there be any better characterization of the Third Reich than the General Definition of Civilization? Monopolization of knowledge had, in earlier times, been accomplished by the simple means of restricting literacy to the elite. At the time of Hitler's rise to power, however, Germany was a highly literate country. So the Nazis had to devise different ways of monopolizing knowledge. They burned books, rigidly censored the press, and created a propaganda machine unequalled in previous history. Nor did they fail to realize the importance of 'the sanctification of myth,' as their revival of the Teutonic sagas and the complementary myths of the superiority of the Aryan race and the conspiracy of the Jews demonstrates. As for centralization of key institutions, never since Roman times had power been so centralized through hierarchical institutions and so completely concentrated in the hands of one tyrant. Even the Romans allowed considerably more autonomy to their provinces and satrapies than did the Third Reich. Finally, with regard to the use of regimented armed force, the names 'Gestapo' and 'SS' have become synonymous with terror and repression. We tend to view Nazism against the background of the growth of humanistic values since 1500 but if we compare their 'crimes against humanity' with those of many of the great civilized societies of the past we will have to admit that those crimes had abundant precedents. The Third Reich was quintessential civilization in its structure but with none of the redemptive qualities that managed to emerge from time to time in earlier civilized societies.

The Third Reich was, however, not unique in attempting a reactionary restoration of civilization in the twentieth century. The Shiite theocracy in Iran is a current instance and until recently the 'Republic' of South Africa was a grotesque example of a nation trying schizophrenically to extend the benefits of modern liberal developments to one segment of its population while subjecting the majority to the kind of repression and dispossession which characterized civilization. Throughout the world we find one country after another partly civilized and partly modernized, its people yearning for progress, its leaders afraid to relinquish the structures of power which guided civilization for five thousand years. We may expect that for a long time to come there will be pockets of civilization in the world, stubbornly resisting the dismantling process, let alone the psychological shift to a postcivilized mind. After all, there are still neolithic and even paleolithic societies in the world today after all these millennia of civilization.

These pockets of resistance and reaction aside, however, we have to look now at the twentieth century in terms of what is happening in that part of the world where the *decivilizing* process has gone the furthest - in the Western democracies in general and the United States in particular. In the rest of this chapter we will be considering the twentieth century mostly as the end phase of the modern era during which we are becoming increasingly decivilized. In the next and final chapter we will try to anticipate what the *post-*

civilizing process will produce. You will recall that I said in the opening paragraph of this book that civilization is both a socioeconomic system and a cognitive structure. What has been breaking down since the beginning of the modern era is the socioeconomic side of civilization. What we are now confronting is the breakdown of the cognitive structure, *of the Occidental Mindset itself*.

The Western Mind Triumphant

To many people today the current period in the West seems little more than a time of 'psychological turbulence' as described by Toffler in *The Third Wave:*

> Throughout the affluent nations the litany is all too familiar: rising rates of juvenile suicide, dizzyingly high levels of alcoholism, widespread psychological depression, vandalism, and crime. In the United States, emergency rooms are crowded with 'potheads,' 'speed freaks' and 'Quaalude kids,' 'coke sniffers' and 'heroin junkies,' not to mention people having 'nervous breakdowns.'

> Social work and mental health industries are booming everywhere. In Washington a President's Commission on Mental Health announces that fully one fourth of all citizens in the United States suffer some form of severe emotional stress. And a National Institute of Mental Health psychologist, charging that almost no family is free of some form of mental disorder, declares that 'psychological turbulence . . . is rampant in an American society that is confused, divided and concerned about its future.' (110, 365)

In the time since Toffler wrote those words, the conditions he described have gotten far worse. But this kind of 'psychological turbulence' is not unique in human history. It seems to precede any great psychosocial change. For example, it happened at the end of the Middle Ages, just before the mental revolution which brought on the modern era. I believe it was Aldous Huxley who described the Europe of the late Middle Ages as 'one vast insane asylum.' Huizinga confirms that description somewhat less dramatically:

At the close of the Middle Ages, a sombre melancholy weighs on people's souls. Whether we read a chronicle, a poem, a sermon, a legal document even, the same impression of immense sadness is produced by them all. It would sometimes seem as if this period had been particularly unhappy, as if it had left behind only the memory of violence, of covetousness and mortal hatred, as if it had known no other enjoyment but that of intemperance, of pride and of cruelty. (111, 31)

And psychologist Rollo May concurs:

The last two centuries of the Middle Ages were pervaded by feelings of depression, melancholy, skepticism and much anxiety. . . Almost all of Michelangelo's human beings, powerful and triumphant as they appear at first glance, present on closer inspection the *dilated eyes which are a telltale sign of anxiety*. One would expect an expression of intense apprehension on the faces of the figures in his painting 'The Damned Frightened by Their Fall,' but the remarkable point is that the same frightened expression in less intense form is present in other figures in the Sistine Chapel as well. (112, 157f.)

However, although there are parallels between the late Middle Ages and our own time, which W. H. Auden called 'The Age of Anxiety', the two periods are quite different in significant ways. The Italian Renaissance was the final flowering of Western Civilization but it was the spectacle of exquisite blooms rooted in decay and corruption. Nothing illustrates the collapse of Western Civilization as a system better than the history of the papacy in the fourteenth and fifteenth centuries. In 1302 Boniface VIII had issued the papal bull, 'Unam sanctam,' which proclaimed in the strongest terms ever the supremacy of papal authority. Yet, a year later Boniface died a prisoner in the Vatican, deposed by Philip IV of France. In 1309 the French pope, Clement V, moved the papal seat from Rome to Avignon, thus beginning the 'Babylonian captivity' of the Church which lasted nearly seventy years only to be followed by the forty years of the 'Great Schism' during which there were two popes, one in

Rome, the other in Avignon. The decline in the authority of the papacy during the fourteenth and fifteenth centuries reached a nadir in 1492 with the election of the libertine Roderigo Borgia as Pope Alexander VI. Considering the deplorable condition into which the Church had sunk it is not remarkable that those last two centuries of the Middle Ages are almost devoid of creative achievements. There were a few great names scattered through the period, particularly in literature and art: Dante at the very beginning, da Vinci near the end, Chaucer, Boccaccio, Petrarch, Fra Angelico, van Eyck, Giotto, Donatello. But compare that scattering over two centuries with the men who were born just in the last four decades of the fifteenth century and whose creative efforts would come to the fore in the early sixteenth century:

Pico de Mirandola	Nicholas of Cusa	Erasmus
Holbein the Elder	Machiavelli	Albrecht Dürer
Michelangelo	Thomas More	Titian
Martin Luther	Raphael	Ulrich Zwingli
Andrea del Sarto	Thomas Cranmer	Ignatius Loyola

This period also saw the birth of Rabelais, for whom the intellectual sterility of Scholasticism was to be a prime target for satire. Unlike our time, therefore, we have to view the late Middle Ages as an intellectual wasteland dotted with a few oases of creativity waiting for the flood of psychic energy which was to burst forth in the Renaissance and the Reformation. As John Addington Symonds wrote:

> By the term Renaissance, or new birth, is indicated a natural movement, not to be explained by this or that characteristic, but to be accepted as an effort of humanity for which at length the time had come. The history of the Renaissance is . . . the history of the attainment of self-conscious freedom by the human spirit manifested in the European races . . . The arts and the inventions, the knowledge and the books which suddenly became vital at the Renaissance, had long been

neglected on the shores of the Dead Sea which we call the Middle Ages. It was not their discovery which caused the Renaissance. But it was the intellectual energy, the spontaneous outburst of intelligence, which enabled mankind at that moment to make use of them. The force then generated still continues, vital and expansive, in the spirit of the modern world. (113, 123)

The current Western world, on the other hand, does not get its psychological turbulence from the failure of the mind, the decay of moral authority or the atrophy of institutions as did the late Middle Ages. The reason for the mental havoc of our time is that the 'vital and expansive' force of mind which began nearly five hundred years ago has not abated but, on the contrary, has accelerated to such a fever pitch that it has burst through the containing walls provided by the Occidental Mindset. During the Modern Era, while the socioeconomic structure of Western society was being radically altered, the Occidental Mindset remained virtually intact. As the old forms of order were being displaced, the mind was anxiously searching for viable new ones. The authority of the one Church was superseded by the authority of the Bible. The absolute power of royalty was supplanted by democratic power expressed through institutions founded on abstract but nonetheless absolute principles such as the 'inalienable rights' of man. Philosophers such as Descartes, Kant and Hegel sought to replace the grand synthesis of medieval Scholasticism with systems of equal certainty. Science strove, to repeat Roderick Seidenberg's words, to discover 'the unvarying laws behind the changing face of nature.' Clearly the West had not given up its passion for order. The significance of the Industrial Revolution was that it focussed that passion on the development of *technology*, creating new means of production which were not under the control of the old landed elite but under that of the modern entrepreneur and capitalist. The American Civil War struck the final blow against the old elite by ending that hallmark of civilization, slavery.

On the threshold of the twentieth century the Western passion for order climaxed in a creative crescendo unparalleled in human history. Between 1895 and 1905, the Western mind literally began to reconstruct our whole way of thinking about the world, ourselves included. Consider some of the names which made major contributions to human thought during that brief period:

Wilhelm Roentgen	Guglielmo Marconi	Louis Pasteur
A. H. Becquerel	The Curies	Max Planck
Ernest Rutherford	Albert Einstein	Henri Bergson
Henri Matisse	Paul Cezanne	Jacob Epstein
Havelock Ellis	Sigmund Freud	Pablo Picasso
Bertrand Russell	John Dewey	William James

These and many more were not merely adding to our perception and understanding of the world but taking that world apart and putting it back together in ways no one had ever dreamed of before, just as Picasso took people and events apart and put them together as his unique vision dictated. Every stale preconception we had inherited from thousands of years of civilization was being questioned and dissected and radically new ways of ordering experience were being created amid the fragments. *We were still operating within the confines of the Occidental Mindset but with outrageously powerful new analytical methods.* Equipped with new techniques of investigation, new systems of logic and mathematics, new ways of perceiving and depicting 'reality,' new methods of understanding and changing behavior, and a new confidence that our rational science and technology could vanquish all mystery and cure all ills, we seemed to be on the threshold of a great era of progress.

Then came the Great Depression followed by the Second World War. As that war ended we found ourselves confronted with two horrors, the Holocaust perpetrated by the Nazis and the other holocaust perpetrated by the world's greatest democracy on Hiroshima and Nagasaki. The most frightening thing about those two horrendous deeds was their incredible rationality. The Nazi atrocities were not perpetrated by people running amok and engaging in spontaneous death orgies. They were planned and executed with the utmost attention to organization and efficiency. Nor was the atomic bomb the result of some mad scientist's nightmarish dream. It came about through the concerted effort of our most brilliant scientists and administrators, again with consummate organization and efficiency.

It was in the 1950s that we began to become self-conscious about the Occidental Mindset with its passion for order, rationality, analysis, and, most recently, technology. The 1950's were a grim period in American history. The Iron Curtain had descended and two superpowers, each in its own way a product of the Western mindset, glowered across the world at each other from forests of super weapons. Mao Tse-Tung had just established his rule over China, thus enabling Communism to glower at us from the other direction. The French defeat in Indochina and the concerns about Communism in that area led to the 'Domino theory,' which eventually spawned the Vietnam War. In the United States itself the 'Cold War' between Russia and the Western democracies was reflected in the ideological inquisitions of Joseph McCarthy and the House Un-American Activities Committee. Pogo's pronouncement that 'We has met the enemy and he is *us!*' reflected a real concern among many scientists, educators, and politicians that the worst enemy just might be *us* or at least something *in the way we think*. Scientists like Robert Oppenheimer and Arthur Holly Compton, who had participated in the development of the atomic bomb, were deeply worried that our rational-technical achievements, the crowning accomplishment of the Occidental Mindset, had unleashed a force on the world that we might not have the moral resources to control. Their concern was not so much that we might use our technology irrationally but that our thralldom to analytic rationality itself had left us blind to any broader context of value or purpose. So at universities all over the nation, a new emphasis was placed on the 'humanities,' in hope that a thorough exposure to Plato and Aristotle would help save the world from nuclear destruction.

But while a resurgence of humanism and even an interest in religions took place in undergraduate schools, social scientists were bringing the rational-technical mind under close scrutiny and trying to understand where it was leading us. In a book to which I referred earlier, *Posthistoric Man*, Roderick Seidenberg viewed the last phase in man's history, the triumph of rationality, as allowing him to conform his behavior to 'the unvarying laws behind the changing face of nature' and adjust his way of life to 'the unchanging verities of these laws.' (108, 71)   In other words, the postcivilized or posthistoric mind would be the rational, organizational mind *par excellence,* divorced from the instinctive, prerational mental processes of the past and bent on mechanizing human relations and thwarting deviations. Seidenberg predicted that,

> In place of the immanent values that arose in the incipient stages of their development, out of the primal instincts, man will come to depend, under this new dispensation, upon increasingly rational and wholly extrinsic solutions of his problems. In short, a new manner of approach in the very perception and appraisement of phenomena, social no less than natural, is fashioning the world. . . The extent to which the formulations of intelligence may come to supplant the directive guidance of the instincts is virtually unlimited, from our point of view; and however different life may come to be in the far future from what it is today, the integration of society will be effected, we may be sure, on the basis of conscious procedures and organized efforts. (108, 178)

Thus Seidenberg was envisioning a time when prerational instinct would be displaced by an architectonic rationality. He predicted a human world transformed into a changeless, thoughtless, insect-like social structure:

> The organization of society will unquestionably proceed until its final crystallization shall have been achieved ecumenically, because of the relationship of this trend with the inherent dominance of the principle of intelligence. But the process, once dominant, implies in turn a steady decrease and retardation of social change - the gradual slowing down of the momentum of history until, indeed, we shall be confronted by the inverse of our historic ascent in ever more delayed sequences of stability and permanence in the conditions of life. And thus, in a period devoid of change, we may truly say that man will enter upon a *posthistoric age* in which, perhaps, he will remain encased in an endless routine and sequence of events, not unlike that of the ants, the bees, and the termites. (108, 179)

There were obvious echoes in this view of Orwell's *1984* and Huxley's *Brave New World*. Huxley was well aware of current developments and theories which tended to confirm his predictions of 1931. He had not yet written *Brave New World Revisited* but it was already growing in his mind. It was he who first recommended for English translation one of the most powerful arguments for the view that the postcivilized mind was to be one of triumphant rationality and mechanistic social control, French sociologist Jacques Ellul's *La Technique*. Ellul's 1954 book, published by Alfred A. Knopf, Inc. under the English title, *The Technological Society*, was an extremely difficult book to translate and edit. Knopf himself called it one of the most difficult editorial tasks Alfred A. Knopf, Inc. had ever undertaken. But it was well worth the effort. The most distinctive thing about *The Technological Society* was not its scholarship or method of argument, both of which received some criticism, but the passion and power of Ellul's conviction that *technique,* the instrument of analytic rationality, was completely absorbing the modern mind and becoming not only its means but its end, its *raison d'être.* 'Without exception in the course of history,' he contended, '*technique belonged to a civilization* and was merely a single element among a host of nontechnical activities. Today *technique has taken over the whole of civilization.*' (114, 128, *emphasis mine*) 'Certainly,' he goes on to say, 'technique is no longer the simple machine substitute for human labor.   It has come to be the 'intervention into the very substance not only of the inorganic but also of the organic.' (Ibid.) And of the psychological, we might add.

Ellul defined 'technique' as

> . . . the translation into action of man's concern to master things by reason, to account for what is subconscious, make quantitative what is qualitative, make clear and precise the outlines of nature, take hold of chaos and put order into it. (114, 43)

In other words, *what Ellul calls technique is the climactic product of the Occidental Mindset*. In every chapter of this book we have seen that the Occidental Mindset is the one obsessed with transforming chaos into order, regardless of who does it - God or man. But while in Western Civilization the ultimate determinant of order was God or a principle transcending human order, *the dominance of technique means that the human power of ordering is conceived as an end in itself, the pure art of the possible, unconstrained by nontechnical values*. That was how the Occidental Mindset led us to Ausschwitz and Hiroshima.

We can summarize Ellul's argument by saying that whereas in the past technique, i.e., the most efficient, direct and rational method, was used to help solve problems which were defined and presented in a larger life context, today life is being reduced to the level of those problems we can technically define and solve. Life is therefore in danger of losing all its dimensions except those with which technique can deal. The results of this conclusion can be bizarre indeed, according to Ellul:

> None of our wise men ever pose the question of the end of all their marvels. The 'wherefore' is resolutely passed by. The response which would occur to our contemporaries is: for the sake of happiness. Unfortunately, there is no longer any question of that. One of our best-known specialists in diseases of the nervous system writes: 'We will be able to modify man's emotions, desires and thoughts, as we have

already done in a rudimentary way with tranquillizers.' It will be possible, says our specialist to produce a conviction or an impression of happiness without any real basis for it. Our man of the golden age, therefore, will be capable of 'happiness' amid the worst privations. Why, then, promise us extraordinary comforts, hygiene, knowledge, and nourishment if, by simply manipulating our nervous systems, we can be happy without them? The last meager motive we could possibly ascribe to the technical adventure vanishes into thin air through the very existence of technique itself. (114, 436)

Predictably, *The Technological Society* ends with a pessimistic sigh:

But what good is it to pose questions of motives? of Why? All that must be the work of some miserable intellectual who balks at technical progress. The attitude of the scientists, at any rate, is clear. Technique exists because it is technique. The golden age will be because it will be. Any other answer is superfluous. (ibid.)

Ellul thus agreed broadly with Seidenberg, with Huxley in his more pessimistic moments, and with many others of the fifties and early sixties. If you accepted their conclusions, you were merely accepting that the order-dominated Occidental mind would continue into the indefinite future, that the Western Mindset would be the structure of the postcivilized mind even though the socioeconomic characteristics of civilization would have been displaced.

Not surprisingly, both Seidenberg and Ellul considered, as did Huxley and Heard, whether there was any escape from the encroachment of rational control on modern life. In particular they wondered whether the creative and ecstatic possibilities of human life were not feasible escape routes or counterforces. The answer was negative. Seidenberg concluded that the effect of the superrational, organized, mentally mechanized posthistoric society would be precisely to suppress those 'psychic mutations' or mystical eruptions which alone could save society from ankylosis. 'It is clear,' he said,

> . . . that the very source and fountainhead of spiritual enlightenment, in the emergence of privileged souls, is certain to be closed by the drastic suppression of all deviations from the dominant norm. Moreover, in this sovereignty of the masses we may likewise perceive a gradual displacement of an inner by an outer approach to the values of life; and even the more intangible and inscrutable aspects of existence are certain to be approached from the point of view of scientific intelligence rather than religious feeling - not because they are necessarily antithetical in nature but because they represent an inversion of values in harmony with the dominant trends of man's development. . . Religion offers us truth sheathed in mystery; science offers us mystery enveloped by truth. (108, 225f.)

In Seidenberg's view, religious creativity, indeed any creativity, will have the mystery and hence the life squeezed from it *by* society before it has a chance to exert a redeeming influence *on* society. But Ellul was of a different view, a far more perceptive one, in my opinion. Whereas Seidenberg thought rational-technical society could *suppress* creative expressions, Jacques Ellul's best insights illustrated how it could much more effectively *contain* and *diffuse* them. Recognizing that the creative life had previously been thought to be diametrically opposed to the mechanical control of life, Ellul pointed out that, on the contrary, technique encourages the revolutionary spirit to new levels of innovation and expression *but*, at the same time, diffuses and contains that spirit so that it never has a truly revolutionary impact on society. 'Human impulses,' he says,

> . . . are confined within well-defined limits, and become the objects of propaganda, profit-seeking, contractual obligations, and the like. The vast extent of the technical apparatus makes the 'payoff' inevitably the primary consideration, in money in the capitalist world, in power and authority in the Communist world. Technique as a means, however, encourages and enables the individual to express his ecstatic reactions in a way never before possible. He can express criticism of his culture, and even loathing. He is permitted to propose the maddest solutions. The great law here is that all things are necessary to make a society and that even revolt is necessary to make a technical society. . . The expression of criticism is permitted because its repression

would be even more catastrophic. But it is permitted only on condition that it entail no serious consequences, or better put, so that no serious consequences to the power of the state can result. The technical apparatus, in fact, assures this by confining the most violent explosions of human ecstasy within itself and by satisfying without danger and at small cost to itself certain spiritual needs of the citizen reader. (114, 424)

Ellul gives a number of examples of how the technical society contains and diffuses revolutionary energy, two of which are particularly important to mention, not least because he wrote in the fifties. The first refers to the novelist, Henry Miller. 'Henry Miller's erotic petard,' says Ellul,

. . . launched onto society like a plastic bomb, finds a reader whose sexual life is thwarted, who is upset by the conditions of his work, his lodgings, his political life. This has created in him a thirst for revolt. And he finds his thirst powerfully and well expressed by Miller. The pornographic element unfetters his imagination and plunges him into an erotic delirium that can satisfy his contracted needs. But Miller's book, far from pushing a man to revolt, vicariously satisfies the potential revolutionary, just as the sexual act itself stills sexual desire, or jazz soothes the Negroes' bitter longing for freedom. (114, 425)

The last part of this quotation brings out the second important example - *jazz* - of which Ellul says, 'We have noted that jazz has become universal. The reason is now clear: it is the music of men who are satisfied with the illusion of freedom provoked by its sounds, while the chains of iron wind round them ever tighter.' (ibid.) Ellul thus recognizes the existence of a 'thirst for revolt' which is incited by the technical society but then insidiously diffused and contained in two ways: (1)by paying off those who voice that thirst, either economically or politically; (2)by quenching the thirst with illusion and vicarious satisfaction.

We have seen a host of revolutions since 1500. They all started with the ideas of intellectuals which were later translated into policies and programs of action. Each revolution - the religious, the

philosophical, the political, the economic, the artistic - contributed to
the next in turn and each freed Western man a little more from the
institutional structures of Western Civilization. But none of them
allowed him to escape the Western Mindset. The Dionysian urge,
which Nietzsche championed, remained captive to the Apollonian
sense of restraint. We could explore our freedom as far as we wished
as long as we did not cross two forbidden thresholds, the first
leading to *mystical ecstasy* and the second to *sexual abandon*. The
pessimistic conclusion of Ellul and Seidenberg was not only that we
could not escape our mindset at the present time but that the
increased efficiency of social control made possible by twentieth-
century techniques would further entrench that mindset and render
it inescapable at any time in the future.

Revolt

But scarcely a decade after Ellul and Seidenberg reached their
gloomy conclusions, a series of unthinkable revolts took place in
America which were to shake Western man loose from the bonds of
his five thousand year-old mindset. Some commentators call the
extraordinary phenomena of the sixties 'revolutions' but that is a
misnomer. Revolutions have a resolution. Sexual liberation and the
introduction of psychedelic drugs were *revolts* against the iron grip of
the Western Mindset but they have not yet resulted in the emergence
of a new mind or a new level of social concensus. Nevertheless,
unresolved as they are, they are still with us and neither the big
payoff nor the attempt to turn them into vicarious channels has yet
succeeded in bringing them under rational-technical control *although*
the means for and the pressure to do so are far more powerful than
they were in the fifties and sixties. No jazz musician ever dreamed
of being paid what a rock star is today.

The contemporary revolt, which began in the sixties and is
continuing, should not be understood as a political revolt although it

has a significant political dimension. It is essentially a revolt of the mind.   Its major significance was that it crossed the forbidden thresholds of sexual abandon and mystical ecstasy into areas with which the Western Mindset had never been able to cope. Oddly enough, the revolt was sparked by a most unlikely hero. He came out of Mississippi and spoke with a country drawl. He looked like one of the million teenagers who thronged the drive-ins in the late fifties.   In the movies he starred in, not one profane word ever crossed his lips and he never appeared nude or simulated sexual intercourse. Yet his musical performances were blantantly erotic. On stage he became a combination of satyr and the boy next door, managing to satisfy the remnants of romanticism and puritanism in his young audiences while delivering a message of unabashed sexuality through his music. They reverently called him 'The King.' They still do. Like a Pied Piper, Elvis Presley disarmingly led his followers toward the sexual revolt, all to the beat of a new music of freedom - *Rock and roll.*

Ellul had correctly observed that sex and jazz had been diffused and contained by technique. But rock music was revolutionary in a way that jazz had never been. To much of the older generation it seemed little more than a primitive din but its beat heralded the mind-explosion of the sixties. It was the music of the drug culture and sexual liberation. Its sounds were of freedom and passion and breaking out, often violent and angry sounds. 'Rock and roll is only rock & roll if it's not safe,' said Mick Jagger in an interview, '. . . Violence and energy - ... *that's* what rock & roll's all about.' (115a, 34) Of course, subsequent musicians such as the Beatles added other dimensions to rock, dimensions of intelligence, emotion, value, and protest but it has never lost its energy or its powerful sexual base. *La Technique* has commercialized, prostituted, and corrupted Rock but has failed to suppress its message, which remains the theme music of the ongoing contemporary revolt. The sexual freedom at the core of the revolt is a *fait accompli,* not a Millerian fantasy.

People who think of psychohistorical change in grandiose terms, a vast upheaval based on supernova-like explosions of technology or great creative syntheses of ideas, will doubtless find it crass to suggest that a principle driving force of the contemporary revolt, the most significant in human history, is to be found in something as base as sex. But why should that surprise us? For reasons I outlined in Chapter 8, the Occidental Mindset was *never* able to cope with sex in a direct, accepting and meaningful way. Sex has been the single most painful thorn in the side of Western man, simply because he never found a way to make it comply with his obsessive need for order. Far removed as it may at first seem from any significant psychic revolt of our time, sexual liberation is, in fact, at the heart of that revolution. We saw in Chapter 8 how civilized mindsets shape even our understanding of sexuality. Is it not obvious, then, that as the Western Mindset explodes and a new mind emerges, that the old, ascetic crust which squeezed the life out of our sexuality must be vaporized in that explosion?

An important aspect of sexual liberation was the gay liberation movement. When homosexuals spoke about gay liberation they were often voicing articulate arguments for the broader sexual revolt. Until the nineteen seventies, homosexuality was generally regarded as a sexual 'inversion' or 'perversion,' as unnatural or a psychological illness, although there was no concensus on what kind of illness it was. Freud originally assumed pathological causes for homosexuality but finally had to admit that at least some instances of it were 'congenital.' Much of the public still thought of homosexuals in terms of Keenan Wynn's famous phrase in *Dr. Strangelove* as 'deviated preverts.' Yet one of the astounding conclusions of the Kinsey Report was that fifty percent of American males would have had at least one homosexual experience by middle age and that fully ten percent of American males were either exclusively or predominantly homosexual. *And that was in 1948!* Even if correcting the much-criticized sampling errors of the Kinsey Report reduced that percentage by half or more, it would still be an astounding conclusion, especially for a time twenty years before 'gay liberation.' While many people today still think of homosexuality as abnormal or pathological, the American Psychiatric Association considers it an 'alternate life-style.' It is undeniable that some degree of homosexual behavior has been found in many primitive societies and in every civilized society. But the significant thing about the homosexuality issue for the whole society is the emphasis it places on sexuality *per se*. For the first time in the history of any civilization we have a massive movement, 'gay rights,' based solely on sex, not *gender* but *sex*. Dennis Altman wrote,

> Western societies rely on very considerable hypocrisy about sexual behavior, preferring epidemics of venereal disease and crippling back-yard abortions to any honest acceptance of the realities of sexual life. Nowhere is this more obvious than in the case of homosexuality, and both gays and straights have been caught up in a gigantic game of pretending that in fact it does not exist. In the new mood of the counter-culture, it is not surprising that such pretense is rejected; to be told not to come out publicly because of social consequences becomes merely a reason to be more blatant. When gay liberationists proclaim 'We are going to be who we are,' they are echoing the mood of the broader counter-culture. The very directness of the counter-culture's language, its rejection of euphemisms, which distinguishes both the gay and the straight radicals from more traditional groups, is in part rejection of hypocrisy, although there is also a desire to assault the old consciousness by shock tactics and to find phrases that cannot easily be co-opted by the mass media. (116, 182)

While I think Altman is correct as far as he goes, it seems to me that the sexual liberation movement, 'gay and straight,' is challenging something far deeper in the Western psyche than hypocrisy and is, therefore, itself involved in a far more profound transition than it realizes. Altman was aware of the relationship between sexual liberation and the broader psychic revolution of our time when he wrote,

> Gay liberation is part of a much wider movement that is challenging the basic cultural norms of our advanced

industrial, capitalist and bureaucratic society and bringing about changes in individual consciousness and new identities and life styles. It is a movement that is political, not in the traditional way that we have used that word, but *because it challenges the very definitions and demarcations that society has created.* (116, 234, *emphasis mine*)

The sexual revolt in general not only challenged those 'definitions' and 'demarcations' but virtually *demolished* them. The extraordinary western notion of romantic love was chief among its inevitable casualties. As romantic love had been portrayed by Hollywood, guy and girl always maintained a chaste relationship and when the guy finally got the girl it always meant marriage. In plots which involved sexual relations outside marriage, the ending was nearly always tragic. Sex, as distinguished from passionate kissing, was never explicit on the screen. At the end of the sixties, however, censorship was abandoned in favor of the rating system. The 'R' rating allowed nudity, simulated intercourse and unrestricted use of what had formerly been considered obscene language. After the sixties virtually everything sexual could be seen on the movie screens of Main Street and later, of course, on cable television. The only thing relegated to the 'X' rating was real intercourse and close-up photographing of the genitals.

The plots also underwent a radical transformation. The guy and the girl frequently went to bed early in the story and only much later began wondering about whether they wanted to be joined in something other than sex. The primary question was no longer whether to marry but, first, whether to remain 'involved,' second, whether to have a 'relationship,' third, whether to 'live together,' and, occasionally and finally, whether to marry. Women, no longer on the pedestal to which romantic love had consigned them, were freed from the requirement to be chaste until marriage and thus achieved a considerable boost in independence. In less than one decade, all the constraints which western civilization had placed on the relations between men and women had simply evaporated for a significant portion of the American population.

The mind of the future, the postcivilized mind is not going to be a science fiction brain floating in a solution and connected to a computer by wires. It will be a mind in a body with its sexuality intact. The sexual revolt will continue and expand, despite the powerful reactionary force of the ascetic tradition. To date its principal function has been to help overthrow the Western Mindset. As time passes, however, its purpose will change from revolt to revolution as postcivilized man learns *to harmonize the new mind and its sexuality in ways which were not possible as long as the Western Mindset reigned.*

Sexual abandon, then, was the first threshold crossed in stepping out of the Occidental Mindset. Mystical ecstasy was the second. That was the meaning of psychedelic drugs. Taking LSD, George Harrison of the Beatles said, 'was like opening the door, really, and before, you didn't even know there was a door there. It just opened up this whole other consciousness, even if it was down to, like Aldous Huxley said, the wonderful folds in his gray flannel trousers. From that smaller concept to the fact that every blade of grass and every grain of sand is just throbbing and pulsating.' (115b, 47) What was happening was an expansion of the mind not only beyond the confines of the Western ascetic tradition but of the Western Mindset itself. 'We are going to have to face the fact,' said Timothy Leary in 1966,

> . . . that psychedelic drugs do take us fast and far beyond our normal conceptual framework. But the term 'going out of your mind' shouldn't really be that disturbing. We recall that most of the great religions have taken this goal, *ex-stasis,* the going beyond the rational, as their central program. The fact that we now possess the chemical means for guaranteeing this process should be a cause for rejoicing - for those who take their religion or their neurology seriously. (117, 25)

Leary's notion that 'most of the great religions have taken this goal, *ex-stasis*, the going beyond the rational as their central program,' is, of course, mistaken, as this book has consistently demonstrated. It was, in fact, antithetical to the 'program' of Western religion, which is what makes the impact of mind-expanding drugs on the West revolutionary. While drugs may be a dangerous way of 'going beyond the rational' rather than a guarantee, the fact has to be recognized that psychedelic drugs played a major role in the process of exploding the Western mindset with its excessive rationality and asceticism. It was again the ubiquitous Aldous Huxley who experimented with LSD and pronounced it productive of genuine mystical experiences as he had done earlier with mescalin. Huston Smith, in an article entitled *Do Drugs Have Religious Import?*, argued that some psychedelic experiences seemed identical to religious experiences which occurred without the use of drugs:

> If there is one point about which every student of the [psychedelic] drugs agrees, it is that there is no such thing as the drug experience per se - no experience which the drugs, as it were, merely secrete. Every experience is a mix of three ingredients: drug, set (the psychological makeup of the individual) and setting (the social and physical environment in which it is taken). *But given the right set and setting, the drugs can induce religious experiences indistinguishable from ones that occur spontaneously* . (117, 158, *emphasis mine*)

In the revolt of the sixties and seventies, the royal road to 'cosmic consciousness' was through drugs. They were *mind-expanding*. Once again, however, *La Technique* stepped in through the cooperation of science and drug cartels and turned the use of drugs into a vast *'mind-blowing'* enterprise. Government cooperated by outlawing the genuinely mind-expanding drugs, even the relatively innocuous *cannabis*. Again, however, the spirit of the revolt was not lost. We discovered that mind-expanding experiences are achievable in many ways, including the many forms of meditation advocated by our modern gurus. Many thousands of Americans, who had little familiarity with yoga, began practicing 'transcendental meditation.' There also seemed to be an increasing frequency of their *spontaneous* occurrence, especially among highly rational people such as scientists. Compare, for example, George Harrison's experience with LSD and the spontaneous experience related by Fritzjof Capra in *The Tao of Physics:*

> Five years ago, I had a beautiful experience which set me on a road that has led to the writing of this book. I was sitting by the ocean one late summer afternoon, watching the waves rolling in and feeling the rhythm of my breathing, when I suddenly became aware of my whole environment as being engaged in a gigantic cosmic dance. Being a physicist, I knew that the sand, rocks, water, and air around me were made of vibrating molecules and atoms, and that these consisted of particles which interacted with one another by creating and destroying other particles. I knew also that the earth's atmosphere was continually bombarded by showers of 'cosmic rays,' particles of high energy undergoing multiple collisions as they penetrated the air. All this was familiar to me from my research in high-energy physics, but until that moment I had only experienced it through graphs, diagrams, and mathematical theories. As I sat on that beach my former experiences came to life; I 'saw' cascades of energy coming down from outer space, in which particles were created and destroyed in rhythmic pulses; I 'saw' the atoms of the elements and those of my body participating in this cosmic dance of energy; I felt its rhythm and I 'heard' its sound, and at that moment I *knew* that this was the Dance of Shiva, the Lord of Dancers worshipped by the Hindus. (118, xix)

Both sexual freedom and expanded 'transrational' consciousness appear to have become permanent factors in the postcivilized world. Thus sex and drugs were the spearhead of a broad revolt against the Occidental Mindset which is still not only continuing but expanding. This revolt is not against the mind as such but against the mindset. It is anti-rational (as the Western mind understood reason), anti-organizational, anti-technical, anti-ideological, anti-everything that tends to confine life and restrict reality to the orderable. Mick Jagger summarized the feeling underlying it very well:

It's the freedom of choosing your own personal experience and
these questions of freedom - whether you wanted to take
LSD or *not* to go to Vietnam - were sort of major legal and
philosophical points at the time. It still seems absurd to me
now that anybody can actually be put in jail for smoking
marijuana or even selling it. It's absurd. Certainly this
became one of the major arguments of the time: 'This is my
body, and you can't legislate what I do with it.' (115a, 32)

Here Jagger has put his finger on the leitmotif of the contemporary
revolt: *radical freedom* - freedom *from* and freedom *to*. That is the
essence of the revolt and it has penetrated virtually every crevice of
contemporary life. Let us review its impact on those areas of
experience we covered in Chapters 3 through 8.

Religion. In the 1960's a group of young American theologians
stirred up a minor tempest over what was referred to as 'the death of
God.' The tempest even made the cover of one of the national news
magazines. Dr. Thomas Ogletree lists several 'interesting
similarities and points of contact' between the 'death of God'
theologians:

(1)the assertion of the unreality of God for our age, including
the understandings of God which have been a part of
traditional Christian theology; (2)the insistence upon coming
to grips with contemporary culture as a necessary feature of
responsible theological work; (3)varying degrees and forms of
alienation from the church as it is now constituted; and
(4)recognition of the centrality of the person of Christ in
theological reflection. (119, 26)

Here we find clear expressions of the contemporary revolt within
the context of serious Christian thought. In Ogletree's first point we
see anti-rationalism, for 'traditional Christian theology' was a highly
rational body of doctrine and dogma. The second point is a direct
reference to the contemporary revolt because that was the principal
and most troubling feature of 'contemporary culture.' The third point
reflects the anti-organizational trend of the revolt. People who are
demanding radical freedom are not the least bit interested in being

directed and confined by 'sacred' institutions. It is not surprising
that the theologians centered their attention on the *person* of Christ
because there is no clearer model of *radical freedom* in history than
Jesus. To be sure, he was also a model of radical responsibility but
the Gospels make it clear that that responsibility was freely chosen.
The power of Christ was displayed in human relations and social
interactions. And, for the 'death of God' theologians, God became
meaningful, if at all, only in terms of those interactions. Ogletree
mentions a German theologian, Herbert Braun, who, in 1961,

> . . . published a programmatic essay which in effect is a
> proposal for a theology without God. Braun makes use of the
> word God throughout his essay, but he is careful to translate
> it wholly into human relationships and experiences. He
> speaks of the special character of Christian existence as
> involving a peculiar sort of interaction between the sense of
> 'being taken care of' and of 'being obligated.' This experience,
> he contends, is something which comes to us not from the
> universe in general but from and through other human
> beings. Consequently, the word 'God' can, according to
> Braun, be interpreted to mean the 'whence' of my being taken
> care of and being obligated as it has come to me through my
> fellowman. Or even more succinctly, *God is a kind of relation
> with one's fellowman*. (119, 25, *emphasis mine*)

With this kind of thinking the divine hierarchy of order which had
characterized traditional Christian theology was perceived as
irrelevant and *immanentalism* became the watchword of the day.
The Ecumenical Institute in Chicago sent teams all over the world
teaching that we no longer live in a 'two-story universe.' It espoused
an 'operational theology' in which God was defined as life's limits,
Christ as the possibilities which arise within those limits, and the
Holy Spirit as the life-style which springs from recognition of the other
two. Operational theology involved a somewhat wider perspective
than that of Braun's, the Trinity essentially being defined as the
fundamental structure of human experience.

Immanentalist theology had a liberating effect on many
Christians (although to others it was about as obscene as sex and

drugs). It delighted in theologians and philosophers who tend to rattle the brain and shake the mind loose from the transcendentalist accretions of centuries, thinkers like Søren Kierkegaard, Rudolf Bultmann and Dietrich Bonhoeffer. It was a message of mental and spiritual freedom and ranks high among the important thrusts of the contemporary revolt.

Philosophy and Science. Modern physical science may be justly regarded as the highest flowering of the Western Mindset, one that is least likely to produce seeds of revolt against it. Yet it has done precisely that. Scholasticism, the school of thought based on the theological-philosophical synthesis of Thomas Aquinas was a system which included everything and explained nothing. The new breed of thinkers in the modern era could not put it behind them fast enough. In place of its dogma and deductive logic they wanted a method of finding truth by experiment and inductive logic. David Hume expressed their feeling perfectly in the mid-eighteenth century when he wrote in his *An Essay Concerning Human Understanding*,

> It seems to me, that the only objects of abstract science or of demonstration are quantity and number, and that all attempts to extend this more perfect species of knowledge beyond these bounds are mere sophistry and illusion. . . When we run over libraries, persuaded of these principles, what havoc must we make? If we take in hand any volume; of divinity or school metaphysics [i.e., Thomism or Scholasticism], for instance; let us ask, *Does it contain any abstract reasoning concerning quantity or number?* No. *Does it contain any experimental reasoning concerning matter of fact and existence?* No. Commit it then to the flames: for it can contain nothing but sophistry and illusion. (120, 689)

At the time Hume wrote, however, he was expressing more a dream of a new method of inquiry than an actuality. While many of the modern philosophers were mathematicians - Leibnitz was one of the inventors of calculus - and most were well acquainted with developments in experimental science, none of them were experimenters of any significance. Perhaps it is not surprising, therefore, that for the most part they ignored the two ideas which scientists themselves combined to form the first scientific cosmology. The first idea was that of *natural law*, an idea which, as we have already seen, made its way into medieval philosophy from Stoicism. But natural law, though given a great deal of moral and legal content in Scholastic thought, nevertheless remained little more than an abstraction as applied to the physical world. In the modern era, however, the formulation of physical laws, such as the Law of Gravity and the Laws of Motion and Thermodynamics became a principal goal of science. The second seminal component of scientific philosophy was *atomism* which stemmed from Democritus and had been lying on the shelf collecting dust since Lucretius had written his philosophical poem, *De Rerum Naturae,* in the first century B.C. While several philosophers and scientists, among them Bacon, Déscartes and Newton, had entertained the notion that natural processes were the result of the combinations and interactions of minute, indestructible particles, atomic theory did not receive a clear formulation until the notion of chemical *elements* had been well established and several dozen elements identified. In 1808 John Dalton published *A New System of Chemical Philosophy* which set forth the following principles.

1. Matter consists of indivisible atoms.
2. All the atoms of a given element are identical in weight and in every other property.
3. Different elements have different kinds of atoms. In particular, the atoms of different elements are different in weight.
4. Atoms are indestructible, and chemical reactions are merely a rearrangement of atoms.
5. The formation of a compound from its elements takes place through the formation of 'compound atoms' containing a definite (and small) number of atoms of each element. (121, 704)

The combination of natural law and atomism was a philosophy which would have delighted Hume. *'Does it contain any abstract reasoning concerning quantity or number?*' he would have asked and the answer would have been a resounding 'Yes.' It was exactly the mathematical nature of the new natural laws which made them so precise and powerful. *Does it contain any experimental reasoning concerning matter of fact and existence?* Again, Yes. The theories of scientists such as Bernouilli, Dalton, Gay-Lussac, and Avogadro gained ready acceptance just because they could be tested and confirmed by experiment.

Atomic theory was the crowning philosophical achievement of the Western mindset. Set within a fixed matrix of Newtonian space and time, following mathematically precise laws, indestructible atoms combined to produce molecules which in turn combined to produce more complex compounds right up to the incredibly complex organism we call a human being. True, the theory never came up with an explanation of how those little particles which possessed only extension, motion and mass produced the visible, audible, tasteable, smellable, tangible world we experience but it hoped to *associate* the phenomenal world with processes and structures in the noumenal atomic world. That was good enough for the practical purposes of science and, moreover, it ensconced *absolute order* in the form of strict *cause and effect* relations as the fundamental substructure of experience, the great dream of the Greek philosophers.

The story of science in the twentieth century has been a series of explosions which have torn that objectively ordered atomic world apart. Einstein's Special Theory of Relativity (1905) and even more his General Theory (1916) broached a world the characteristics of which could no longer be ascertained in isolation from a frame of reference derived from specific operations applied to it. The scientist ceased to be a passive observer of an ordered world independent of himself and became an active participant in discovering relations of events, the nature of which relations depended, in large part, on how the process of determining them was decided. In studying the macrophysical world, it was still possible to preserve the relative distinction between observer and observed. But in the atomic world it was no longer possible. In 1938, Werner Heisenberg was awarded the Nobel Prize for his 'uncertainty principle', a mathematical proof that both the position and velocity of an electron could never be specified at the same instant. Heisenberg stated some of the philosophical implications of the uncertainty principle in a series of lectures delivered at the University of Chicago in 1929.

> Particularly characteristic of [discussions about the uncertainty principle] is the interaction between observer and object; in classical physical theories it has always been assumed either that this interaction is negligibly small, or else that its effect can be eliminated from the result by calculations based on 'control' experiments. This assumption is not permissible in atomic physics; the interaction between observer and object causes uncontrollable and large changes in the system being observed, because of the discontinuous changes characteristic of atomic processes. The immediate consequence of this circumstance is that in general every experiment performed to determine some numerical quantity renders the knowledge of others illusory, since the uncontrollable perturbation of the observed system alters the values of previously determined quantities. (122, 555)

The uncertainty or indeterminacy principle is not due to imprecise or imperfect methods of measurement. It is an irremediable indeterminacy rooted, as Heisenberg says, *'in the discontinuous changes characteristic of atomic processes.'* The discontinuous changes to which he refers are the changes in subatomic fields which can appear either as waves or as packets of energy called 'quanta.' The apparent contradiction between the fact that radiation can appear in both guises gave rise to quantum theory which, in turn, led to the Heisenberg principle. This apparent contradiction was resolved, Capra tells us,

> . . . in a completely unexpected way which called in question the very foundation of the mechanistic world-view - the concept of the reality of matter. At the subatomic level, matter does not exist with certainty at definite places, but rather shows 'tendencies to exist,' and atomic events do not

occur with certainty at definite times and in definite ways, but rather show 'tendencies to occur.' In the formalism of quantum theory, these tendencies are expressed as probabilities and are associated with mathematical quantities which take the form of waves. This is why particles can be waves at the same time. They are not 'real' three-dimensional waves like sound or water waves. They are 'probability waves,' abstract mathematical quantities with all the characteristic properties of waves which are related to the probabilities of finding the particles at particular points in space and at particular times. All the laws of atomic physics are expressed in terms of these probabilities. We can never predict an atomic event with certainty; we can say only how likely it is to happen.

Quantum theory has thus demolished the classical concepts of solid objects and of strictly deterministic laws of nature. At the subatomic level, the solid material objects of classical physics dissolve into wavelike patterns of probabilities, and these patterns, ultimately, do not represent probabilities of things, but rather probabilities of interconnections. A careful analysis of the process of observation in atomic physics has shown that the sub-atomic particles have no meaning as isolated entities, but can only be understood as interconnections between the preparation of an experiment and the subsequent measurement. (118, 56)

The solid objects and strictly deterministic laws of nature' which Capra states that quantum theory has demolished were the very foundations of atomism. He goes even further than that, noting that some of the most advanced theorizing about the nature of subatomic particles 'implies, ultimately, that the structures and phenomena we observe in nature are nothing but creations of our measuring and categorizing mind.' (118, 266) 'That this is so is one of the fundamental tenets of Eastern philosophy,' he further notes (ibid.), and goes on to conclude that Indic and/or Sinic philosophy coordinate much better with current subatomic physics than anything in Western philosophy. So we see that atomism, which was the last bastion of the Western Mindset in philosophy, has crumbled in the very process of being explored to the fullest. This does not mean that irrationality has superseded reason and that science is stultified. It simply means that order is not the independent and transcendent characteristic of reality which the Western mind has always believed it to be.

Law. Religion and law, as expressions of order, are the most carefully guarded embodiments of the Western mindset because the consequences of entertaining new ideas and new perspectives in those areas impact so directly and gravely on life, far more than in other areas of experience. This is clearly demonstrated in the reaction of both Christian and Islamic fundamentalism to modern ideas, which arises not because fundamentalists are merely stupid or stubborn, but because in their thought-world the surrender of certain beliefs involves eternal salvation or damnation, a consideration not to be taken lightly (as long as it is taken seriously). In perhaps not quite so ultimate but nevertheless quite significant way, ambiguity, inconsistency, unpredictability, or innovation in law can severely threaten established social values or the legitimization of newly emerging ones. But as the contemporary liberation movement gathered force, American courts were called on again and again to judge to what degree the radical freedom those movements demanded would be sanctioned by government. Remarkably, in one key decision after another, on issues such as abortion, homosexual rights, and free speech as it involved obscenity and pornography, the courts upheld the principle of radical freedom demanded by the liberation movements. At the beginning of the sixties, for example, explicit sexuality and 'dirty words' were confined to 'blue movies' which were illegal and available only through an underground market. By the end of the same decade, virtually every restriction on what could be said or done on the screens of Main Street had been removed.

That such a radical movement of the law could take place so smoothly was made possible by a peculiar concept which underlies the American Constitution and which is unique in the history of jurisprudence. To appreciate its uniqueness we have to look back to the early modern era. The legal theorists of the sixteenth and seventeenth centuries found little of value in the Scholastic conception of law. Aquinas had integrated all levels of law into one hierarchical system and had given the Church a central role in guiding man's reason as it endeavored to understand law. That, of course, was unacceptable to humanists and Protestants alike. Consequently, a new basis for law had to be found and the early modern philosophers therefore felt themselves compelled not only to develop new theories of nature but of the law and government as well.

Prominent among the new legal theorists was John Locke who did most of his work in the seventeenth century, dying in 1704. Locke was a devout Anglican who believed that God had created the world, that Jesus was the Messiah and that a Christian was called to live a Christ-like life. However, he did not base his governmental theories on dogma but on two theoretical premises. The first was a theory of natural law stemming from the Creator. Other legal theorists such as Grotius had revived the idea of natural law as the basis of jurisprudence but their theories tended to view it as a matter of obligation, of what people *ought to do.* Locke's brilliant contribution to the theory of natural law was to construe it, not in terms of obligations or moral duties, but, as the Declaration of Independence says, as an *endowment* of 'certain inalienable rights' on man by the Creator. For Locke these God-ordained rights were summed up in the words, 'freedom' and 'equality.' In his *Concerning Civil Government,* he says,

> To understand political power aright, and derive it from its
> original, we must consider what state all men are naturally
> in, and that is a state of perfect freedom to order their
> actions and dispose of their possessions and persons as they
> think fit, within the bounds of the law of nature, without
> asking leave, or depending upon the will of any other man.

> A state also of equality, wherein all the power and
> jurisdiction is reciprocal, no one having more than another;
> there being nothing more evident than that creatures of the
> same species and rank, promiscuously born to all the same
> advantages of nature, and the use of the same faculties,
> should also be equal one amongst another without
> subordination or subjection. . . (120, 404)

The radically innovative nature of this doctrine cannot be overstated. No man, no government, no document, it proclaims, *gives us freedom or equality. Freedom and equality come to us as basic endowments of our humanity.* The second premise of Locke's theory of government was that a community, or commonwealth, is based on a *social contract,* the purpose of which is to preserve and enhance the freedom and equality of all its members. Anyone participating in such a commonwealth *delegates* (not surrenders) one aspect of his inherent freedom, namely, the right 'to judge of and punish the breaches of that law [of nature] in others as he is persuaded the offense deserves, even with death itself, in crimes where the heinousness of the fact in his opinion requires it.' (120, 437) Breaching the law of nature means nothing more complex than depriving someone else of his inalienable right to 'life, liberty, and estate.' As citizens of a commonwealth we delegate our right to personal retribution, which inheres in our freedom, to the community which then, in Locke's phrase, 'comes to be umpire.' In contrast to other thinkers, such as Hobbes, Locke contends we can never lose our inalienable rights. Not only can no one else take them away from us, we cannot lawfully (according to 'natural law') surrender them by taking our own lives or selling ourselves into slavery. Furthermore, if the leadership of the commonwealth tries to become tyrannical and deprive its citizens of their rights, 'the people are at liberty to provide for themselves by erecting a new legislative, differing from the other, by the change of persons, or form, or both, as they shall find it most for their safety and good.' (120, 493). Nor do they have to wait for tyranny to reach full growth: '. . . men can never be secure from tyranny if there be no means to escape it till they are perfectly under it. And therefore it is that they have not only a right to get out of it, but to prevent it.' (ibid.)

Virtually all previous systems of law had been founded on obligations of the people toward higher authority, human or divine. *The radical nature of American law is that is founded on the inherent freedom of the people and their only fundamental obligation is to maintain that freedom.* It is because of that fact that the contemporary revolt was able to achieve legal recognition so quickly. It is difficult for some people, even eminent jurists, to understand that the United States Constitution *confers no rights.* Our so-called 'Bill of Rights' is, in reality, a bill of restrictions on Congress. It prevents Congress from making laws which would restrict certain important rights *with which we are endowed by birth.* Those rights were ones which the founding fathers recognized would be the first ones infringed upon in the attempt to establish a tyranny. They were a way of implementing our right to prevent a tyranny, as Locke said, rather than merely to get out of one. It was a sad spectacle to see a jurist of Robert Bork's standing fumbling before the Senate Judiciary Committee over the importance of the ninth and tenth Amendments to the Constitution because those are precisely the ones which make it clear that rights are an endowment of birth and that the first eight amendments by no means enumerate them all.

The concept of inalienable rights was in itself a revolt against the Western Mindset. But because a principle of radical freedom was enunciated in the seventeenth century and found its way into the United States Constitution does not mean that it was either fully appreciated or implemented. The Dred Scott decision was proof of that. Throughout our history legal and moral doctrines founded on other principles derived from our civilized past have influenced legislation. The Volstead Act is one invidious example but there are also many of a more subtle character. The fact that so many cases arising out of the liberation movements had to be carried as far as the Supreme Court is testimony to the prior existence of a large body of anti-liberation laws. Without exception those laws are based on belief in a moral and legal order transcending human freedom and choice, a belief which is the product of the Western Mindset. Overturning them can unquestionably be viewed as carrying on the revolt against that mindset which was started by our founding fathers.

Art. There is a common perception that artists, by their very nature, are prone to revolt against social norms. Like most common perceptions that one is false. As we saw in Chapter 5, artists were principal articulators of the world views of their civilizations. In that chapter I made the point that Occidental art, from its earliest development in Egypt to the beginning of the Modern Era had been preoccupied with *the eternal* and that the eternal referred to a perfect, unchanging order above the flux of temporal phenomena. In Greek art that order manifested itself as the timeless ideal and in Christian art as God's divine plan. The subject matter of art in the Christian era was centered around God's plan as revealed in Christ and as carried out in the events of the Bible and the acts of the saints. The *significant experience* which it is the purpose of art to produce derived primarily from its *subject matter* and secondarily from the way in which it was presented, the painter's object being to enhance the force of the subject in as masterly a way as he could achieve. The work of Michelangelo, particularly the murals in the Sistine Chapel, was a watershed between the art of Western Civilization and that of the modern era. In joining the power of Greek idealism to that of Christian faith, the great Florentine achieved a virtual fusion of subject and form. Although those murals are a powerful statement of faith, the non-Christian can be gripped by them to a degree that it is unlikely to be by any previous Christian art. But from that point on, throughout the modern era, the significant experience to be derived from painting was no longer predominantly the effect of Christian subject matter.

Religion, of course, continued to provide themes for painting, but most artists treated religious motifs exactly the same as they treated pagan themes, secular events, portraits, and landscapes. Until the late nineteenth century there is a remarkable consistency in what Western painters of all periods and schools attempted to achieve. Their purpose was to create what Maurice Grosser characterized as a *'planned picture with a subject,'* no matter what the subject, and that picture almost always consisted of intelligible three-dimensional figures in three-dimensional space. The human figure, depicted realistically though often with some degree of distortion, and the impressiveness of landscape were the twin preoccupations of painting in the modern era. At one extreme, space might shrink to the size of a room (although not infrequently the room would have a window opening on a countryside vista). At the other extreme, the sheer power and beauty of nature might dwarf or altogether exclude human figures. But it is safe to say that virtually all Western painters of the period can be located somewhere on the continuum between those two extremes.

The kind of painting produced in the modern era has not entirely disappeared. It remained until a few decades ago the 'official' or 'academic' style in France. Grosser observed,

> The Academic tradition . . . was principally concerned with the planned picture. All the academic devices of underpainting, color theory, composition, anatomy, drawing from nude models and painting from these drawings, historical research in costume, literary research in the classics, and so on, which are still taught at the Academie des Beaux Arts in Paris, had as their sole end the production of a planned picture with a subject. Even today in Paris, a student competing for the *Prix de Rome* in painting, is shut up *'en loge,'* in a studio with a bed, food, paints, canvas, access to books and models, and a subject *(Caesar on the Rubicon, Achilles in His Tent, The Death of Cleopatra)* and is expected to paint without help and in a given time a picture by which his merits as a painter can be judged. (123, 84)

Yet when Grosser wrote that passage (1955), 'Academic' painting had already been an anachronism for eighty years, having fallen victim to a movement called *Impressionism* which made its appearance in 1874. Impressionism was revolutionary and shocking to the art-viewing public and critics. Its theme was not solid subjects in space but *light and color* :

> The small brush strokes already used for reproducing reflections in water were now applied to trees, houses, sky, hills - all the elements of the landscape. The colours became systematically lighter and the shadows themselves were coloured. The transitional greys and browns used by Corot gave way to the pure colours of the spectrum, harmonized or contrasted according to the law of complementary colours. Coherence of vision brought in its wake unity of technique, the exaltation and vibration of light as the dominant principal, and consequently *the abandonment of contour, of modelling, of chiaroscuro, and of over-precise details, the over-all composition retaining the vigour of a sketch, with the incomplete, unfinished look that so shocked contemporaries.* (124, 127, *emphasis mine*)

Considering how radical its innovations were, it is not surprising that Impressionism was at first scorned by critics and academics alike. Nevertheless it captured the minds of the most talented painters of the day and, with the felicitous exception of Manet (who had other ways of shocking his contemporaries), those who continued to paint with the traditional orientation were eventually relegated to obscurity Impressionism's 'abandonment of contour, of modelling, of chiaroscuro, and of over-precise details' meant, of course, abandonment of the whole approach to art in the modern era. That was what made it the greatest revolution in painting since the Quattrocentro, not so much what it started, though its own productions were often remarkable, but what it put an end to. *From the time of the Impressionists, no artist, whether Expressionist, Cubist, Realist, Surrealist, or Abstractionist, felt bound to create a three-dimensional scene with an intelligible subject.*

The Renaissance artist who epitomized pre-impressionist art and who was revered as its unapproachable master was not Michelangelo but Leonardo da Vinci, whose Mona Lisa was widely regarded as the greatest painting in the Western world. Nothing could have better symbolized the radical break the new painting was making with the past than Marcel Duchamp's 1919 work, 'L.H.O.O.Q.' - a reproduction of the Mona Lisa *with a moustache*. Duchamp himself had been a participant in the Armory Show held in New York in 1913. Among the other artists represented were Matisse, Picasso, Braque, Léger, Derain, Vlaminck, Kandinsky and Brancusi. Duchamp's own most famous contribution was 'Nude Descending a Staircase,' which one critic described as 'an explosion in a shingle factory.' Although the Armory show was viewed with horror and greeted with derision by many critics, it was nevertheless a watershed on the other side of which Western painting was permanently freed from the 'subject-in-a-setting' matrix.

Thus liberated, painting since the advent of Impressionism has been involved in a constant flux in which one 'school' or 'method' emerges and remains popular for a time, only to be displaced by another. Nevertheless, art remained true to the Western Mindset well through the first half of this century in one very important respect. Perhaps the single strongest conviction that artists had about their work was its *seriousness*. They (Dadaists and Fauves excepted) had a calling, a responsibility to a higher level of vision and understanding. Whether they chose an objective, non-objective or symbolic style they saw themselves as presenting a superior view of reality, as rendering orderly the chaos of the world, the senses or life experience. Then, suddenly, they began to play. They dribbled and smeared and threw their paint, with results that became increasingly whimsical and downright disorderly. The aesthetic categories used to analyze the art of Western Civilization and of the modern era became increasingly irrelevant to the new variety of painting. How can you think in terms of space, balance, movement, color harmony, or composition when the whole canvas is painted a uniform red? Or when you are confronted with a Campbell's Soup can?

That was the abrasive, arrogant symbol of the final revolt - Andy Warhol's soup can. Whatever Warhol himself or those who took him seriously thought, his soup can told us two things. First, artists have neither the responsibility nor perhaps the ability to interpret or make sense of this world. Second, as a corollary, they have the radical freedom to present whatever 'turns them on' and to do it in whatever style they choose. As Jean Dubuffet said, art can be 'anything: as long as it doesn't bore.' Warhol chose American 'icons' such as the soup can, Marilyn Monroe and the Playboy Bunny, which, while they do not bore, produce little more than a sense of nostalgia. If, as claimed in Chapter 5, art aims to produce a *significant* experience, on a significance scale from 1 to 10, nostalgia rates perhaps a 2 (possibly a 3 in the case of Norman Rockwell). In a sense, this was a revolt against art itself as an endeavor to communicate a significant experience. Art ceased to be an attempt to communicate because the artist had nothing significant to communicate. One fad, called 'minimalist art,' was faithful to its name. The heart of the matter became the doing, the artistic event and whatever the viewer got out of it was his or her affair. On August 14, 1987 the Cable News Network aired a story about a 'Conceptual Art' event in San Francisco. Titled 'Art from Hell,' the event consisted of a series of moving mechanical monstrosities which lumbered, jerked, roared, crashed and made a frightening din. I found them ingenious and fascinating. Yet when an interviewer asked one observer, 'What does it mean?', the observer answered, 'Nothing!' I dismissed that response on the basis of the well-known dictum that stupidity is in the eye of the beholder. But when one of the creators of 'Art from Hell,' was asked, 'What's it about?', he replied, *'What it's about is your personal reaction to it.'* When the artist leaves the meaning of his work to the observer and the observer says it means nothing, art, for better or worse, has clearly been freed from the last vestiges of the Western Mindset - or any mindset, for that matter.

Physical Discipline .

> . . . To die, to sleep;
> To sleep: perchance to dream: ay, there's the rub;
> For in that sleep of death what dreams may come,
> When we have shuffled off this mortal coil,
> Must give us pause. . .
> Hamlet, Act III, Scene I (125, 752)

Civilized Westerners, of whatever age, never doubted that man had a *soul*. What they wondered about, like Hamlet, was what happened to the soul after death. Shakespeare, like Dante before him and Milton after, lived in a three-story universe. Born into the middle world of God's creation, what man did in his limited life in that world determined whether, at death, his soul would fly up to Heaven to dwell with the angels in the sight of God or would be cast down to endure Lucifer's endless torments in Hell. As the modern transition progressed in Europe and then America, skepticism about man's immortal soul gradually grew (along with skepticism about God and the Devil and Heaven and Hell). Still, it is fair to say that until the dawning of the twentieth century the belief that man had a soul that was in some sense independent of, superior to, and not terminated by the death of the body was held by a majority in the modern West.

But the contemporary revolt, ignoring transcendent values and notions of order and rejecting religious and moral constraints, has likewise discarded that belief. In fact, the exact opposite view, that the soul or mind, if they exist at all, are products of the body and neither pre-exist nor survive has become commonplace. *When you're dead, you're dead!* This view is not new. It characterized earlier movements of a liberal intelligentsia and a cynical proletariat away from religion. But its general acceptance by a whole generation in revolt *is* new.

A corollary of our forsaking belief in the soul and its survival of death is a new emphasis on the body and its health. The new generation, free of the athletic-ascetic dichotomy inherited from Western Civilization, is able for the first time to accept and affirm the body for just what it is, our vital, sensual focus of being in the world. We no longer have to sit out the physical side of life if we aren't the stuff Olympic competitors are made of or, on the other hand, keep our body's troublesome appetites under control for fear of losing our soul. It is now considered important to exercise our bodies, feed them with discretion, and keep them healthy simply that they might be better vehicles in which to live for as long as we can. Not surprisingly, the physical revolt has been strongly embraced by women, who had always experienced the suppression of the body more than men. Books and tapes like Jane Fonda's remain some of the most popular aids to physical fitness for either sex. The affirmation of the body is also reflected in the widespread use of natural childbirth methods and the ubiquity of nudity in magazines and movies. There is a second and more somber reason for the new interest in training the body but we will treat of that later.

Sex. Since sexual liberation is one of the booster rockets of the contemporary revolt, I have already remarked extensively on it. One additional observation deserves making. That is that was the dominant functional purpose of sex in the civilized West, sex for procreation, is clearly on the decline. Scarcely fifty percent of foetuses in the United States are now carried to term. Homosexuality, which precludes procreational sex, has long been on the rise, at least in visibility. Coupled with those social facts is a peculiar biological one: fertility also seems to be declining. Whether the latter is due to a genetic change is uncertain but social and biological factors do seem to be conspiring to inhibit procreation in the contemporary West.

There are, of course, many other aspects to the revolt against the Occidental Mindset but one in particular bears mentioning because it played such an important role in putting to rest the notion that rationalism or *la Technique* might still dominate the modern mind

and turn society into the likeness of a termite colony. Jacques Ellul
had written,

> For a long time it was believed that technique would yield a
> harmonious society, a society in equilibrium, happy and
> without special problems [Seidenberg's view]. This society
> would resign itself to an easy life of production and
> consumption based on an untroubled commercial ideology.
> This model of bourgeois tranquility seemed to correspond
> exactly to the preoccupations of technology. The *summum
> bonum* was comfort, and the ideal type was capitalist
> Switzerland or socialist Sweden. The sudden plunge of the
> technically most advanced societies into war and mutual
> destruction was a rude awakening for the *bourgeoisie*. An
> aberration? Scarcely. It had been forgotten that technique
> means not comfort but power. The bourgeois countries had
> developed their technical systems at a comfortable pace, until
> these systems had fully exploited their possibilities of orderly
> growth. Then technology, with its accelerated tempo, took
> over. The smaller nations were unable to keep up. And the
> great technical countries had willy-nilly to abandon their
> languid pace and accommodate themselves to the real tempo
> of the technical society. The result was that disproportion
> between the leisurely bourgeois mentality and the explosive
> tempo of technique to which we give the name *war*. A by-
> product of this ecstasy was a certain mystique. *The
> American myth was born, presenting exactly the same religious
> traits as the Nazi or Communist myth. But it is different, as
> we have noted, in that it still is in a spontaneous phase; it is
> not yet organized, utilized, and developed technically.* (114,
> 421f., *emphasis mine*)

Writing not long after World War II, Ellul clearly believed that
the American 'myth' *would be* 'organized, utilized, and developed
technically,' i.e., put to the service of *la Technique* . What was that
myth? There were two aspects to it. The first was the so-called
American Dream, the idea that comfort and prosperity would flow
over our great land as the bounty of what John Kenneth Galbraith
called 'the new industrial state.' We are already well aware of the
flaws in that part of the myth. Our homeless, our medically
unprotected, our crime, our embattled middle class, and our appetite
for drugs offer eloquent testimony to the limitations of the new

industrial state. The other part I call 'the *myth of the Dragonslayer.*' Considering the massive power of the propaganda machine the United States had developed during World War II and the Cold War mentality which followed, in which many saw America as St. George confronting the great dragon of Communism as it had confronted the dragon of Nazism, the myth might well have taken hold as a permanent structure of our political life. The 'McCarthy era' certainly tried to institutionalize it. But our faith in the myth of the Dragonslayer was rudely shaken by the Korean War. When Douglas MacArthur, the personification of that myth, was abruptly dismissed by President Truman, the Dragonslayer image of America was severely impaired. And when our leadership tried to resurrect it and involved us in a futile war in Vietnam, the myth was anathematized by the most massive groundswell of popular outrage in the history of this country, if not in world history. The Vietnam war protest doomed not only the war itself but the myth of the Dragonslayer. Any president who leads America to war today has to face the phantom of Vietnam. To avoid it he has to make sure his forces arc certain of victory and that they get in and get out *quickly* with as few casualties as possible, such as Reagan did in Granada and Bush in Panama. Fear of the phantom of Vietnam may even result in a conflict being aborted too soon, as may have been the case in Kuwait.

But more than ending a war and destroying a myth, the Vietnam protesters demonstrated the bankruptcy of the notion that rational-technical control of society, even with the benefit of overwhelming propaganda resources and internal police power, could cap the new wellhead of human values. *Whatever the postcivilized mind was to be, it would not be the insect mind predicted by Seidenberg and Ellul.*

Reaction and Escapism

In terms of our earlier analogy of the mindset as a cognitive lodestone, the contemporary revolt is based on ignoring, abandoning or rejecting the single direction of the Occidental Mindset. That opens up the possibility of kinds of behavior and experience which were traditionally off limits to the Occidental Mindset but within the familiar ambit of other mindsets. But we should not make the mistake that those involved in the revolt are adopting one of the other mindsets. On the contrary, what is happening is that their minds have become *unset*, free of *any* mindset. Freedom from any mindset implies that the whole circumference of possible experience is open. The mind can go in any direction.

That, of course, can be a terrifying prospect, both for many of those who have participated in the contemporary revolt and for those who have avoided the revolt itself but cannot ignore its results. The reason it can be terrifying is that we always assumed that the cultural product of our mindset (we were unaware of the mindset itself) reflected the nature of reality. We believed that the way we thought about the world and the kinds of behavior and experience we understood to be appropriate to it bespoke the way the world *really is*. The assault on mindsets *per se*, which is the essence of the contemporary revolt, is consequently seen as an assault on what is real to us and is therefore fraught with danger. No wonder some people felt justified in echoing Nietzsche's phrase, 'God is dead.' No words could better encapsulate the fear provoked in a great many minds by the contemporary revolt.

There are three ways we can respond to such a fear. The first is the way of *reaction*, fighting to turn back the clock and restore what has been lost. The second is to flee, to try to *escape* from the full awareness of what is happening and from responsibility for doing anything about it. We will examine these two responses briefly in this section and leave the third way, *resolution*, for the next.

Reaction. There are many forces of reaction in contemporary American society, many of them deriving simply from the urgent need of an entrenched elite to hang on to their power and wealth. Then there are the ideological reactionaries. particularly Christian fundamentalists and Roman Catholic hierarchs. Far from accepting the notion that God is dead, these Christian reactionaries have been exerting enormous effort to demonstrate that he is as alive and well as he was in the nineteenth century and that, like the leopard, he has not changed his spots. A distinction has to be made between fundamentalists and Roman Catholics in this respect. Roman Catholics tend to be reactionary mostly in the area of sex, whereas fundamentalists are reactionary about everything. For example, the Roman church has long since reconciled itself to treating the Genesis story and other parts of the Old and New Testaments, such as Revelation, as symbolic or allegorical. It has accepted the Theory of Evolution with the proviso that the human animal, unlike the others, receives a soul at conception. Not so the fundamentalists who insist on the literal truth of the Bible in every respect. For this reason, the Theory of Evolution is anathema to fundamentalists. Fundamentalists have tried again and again, fortunately with diminishing success, to get their so-called 'scientific creationism' admitted to the public education curriculum either in place of or alongside the genuinely scientific, if admittedly incomplete, theory.

What makes fundamentalists reactionary rather than simply conservative or quaint is their attempts to turn back the clock through the use of political power. The battle between the contemporary mind and fundamentalism is by no means over. The lengths to which it has gone to try to replace evolutionary theory with its bogus 'scientific creationism' merely illustrates the vigor and ingenuity in its reactionary arsenal. In my opinion, fundamentalism would like nothing better than to restore theocracy in some form with all the social controls that implies, as Islamic fundamentalism has already done in Iran. The simple fact is that it has been pushing on every front for the re-establishment of religion, censorship and banning of books, and the substitution of dogma for science in America. The power it can bring to bear is no better illustrated than in the area in which fundamentalists and Roman Catholics, particularly the Catholic hierarchy, are in profound agreement - sex. Both groups of Christian reactionaries are bent on contesting the hallmark issues of the contemporary sexual revolt: abortion and homosexual rights. Major decisions on each of these issues have already been made by the Supreme Court but each issue is extremely complex with many ramifications which have not yet been tested. This is why there was such an intense debate over the appointment of Judge Robert Bork to the Supreme Court. It was not a simple issue of conservative versus liberal. The eventual acceptance of a conservative was a foregone conclusion. But a judge who did not acknowledge a general right to privacy as a basic element of liberty had all the potential of making decisions which could undermine the freedom so prized by the contemporary mind if not the essential meaning of the constitution itself.

Throughout the Western world fundamentalism, Christian and Islamic, is a formidable obstacle to the postcivilizing trend. It is essentially an effort to preserve the Western mindset and stop the dismantling of civilized forms of social organization. *As mythology was the earliest expression of the civilized mindset it is the last refuge of that mind under threat.* So far the reactionary efforts of American fundamentalism have been rebuffed by the laws of a society which is advancing toward postcivilization. If that rebuff continues, those who wish to remain hardcore fundamentalists may eventually have to fall back on escapism and insulate themselves, like the Amish, from the society around them. But they are indomitable in their fight to turn back the clock and I am certain they still have a great deal of energy to pour into that effort before they are ready to quarantine themselves.

Escapism is a modern word which denotes almost the opposite of *escape*. The latter means a movement from bondage *to* freedom, while the former means one *from* freedom to bondage or illusion. In an early work on the phenomenon of escapism, Eric Fromm (127) called attention to the ambiguities involved in freedom, particularly the tension between its great possibilities and the anxiety generated by its lack of clear direction and our feeling of inability to cope with it. The latter eventuated in the need to 'escape from freedom,' the phrase with which Fromm entitled his book. The 'mechanisms of escape' he described were *authoritarianism, destructiveness, and automaton conformity*. However, the freedom which Fromm was examining in 1941 was the limited kind of freedom produced by liberal democracy, hedged as it was by tradition, archaic laws and the dominance of the Occidental Mindset. The freedom created by the contemporary revolt is far more radical and the level of anxiety it has generated is an order of magnitude above that of the first half of this century. It is that level of anxiety which powers the vehemence of the fundamentalist reaction but it has also led to more intense and imaginative 'mechanisms of escape.' The most prominent among these mechanisms today are *drugs, religion, television, sports, and physical fitness*.

With an estimate of between twenty and thirty million users of cocaine alone, one scarcely needs to argue that *drugs* are a primary aid to escapism in the United States. The psychedelic effect, which was the principal positive aspect of the early drug movement, has given way to the habitual 'high' and the addictive 'fix' which clearly seem to be unrelated to the expansion of consciousness. Rather than lifting the mind to new levels of awareness, the current drugs simply allow the user to go temporarily - sometimes permanently - out of that mind which has to face the daily anxieties of a new world into a dream mind which becomes more and more independent of and less and less integrated with the whole person. Instead of experiencing new realities we embrace illusions.

The escapist side of contemporary *religion* is particularly exemplified in TV evangelism. It truly boggles the mind to witness the enormous crowds which throng to hear preachers like Oral Roberts, Jimmy Swaggart, and Jim Bakker (before, that is, the last two fell into Elmer Gantryism). These men are, for the most part, not doctrinaire reactionaries like Pat Robertson or Jerry Falwell. They are entertainers to a vast, sympathetic audience which wants nothing more than to escape the enormous possibilities and problems posed by the contemporary revolt and drown the mind in a sea of emotionalism and sentimentality. The hours their followers spend in the arena stands or watching them on television are hours spent in an illusory world with no roots in the realities of our time or perhaps any time, very much on a par with the lost hours of the drug user.

Television is the most prevalent vehicle of escapism for those who avoid drugs and have little use for gospel salesmen. Like the 'holodecks' on the U. S. S. Enterprise, television creates layer upon layer of illusory worlds you can live in twenty-four hours a day. Without ever leaving your house you can be in a galaxy a million lightyears away, in a legendary world of sorcerer kings and musclebound heroes, in bed with your favorite sex idol, killing 'VC' in the jungles of Vietnam, or attending a rock concert. Modern television is a creation of *la Technique* more vast and powerful today than Ellul ever imagined in the 1950s but it works on the mind in exactly the way he foresaw, by containing and diffusing the revolutionary spirit. It is the medium of wishful thinking. Through it we can get our sex, kill the rapists and murderers who infest our streets, fight the Vietnam War over again (winning the second time around), and even bring the evil Galactic Empire to its knees. We don't have to *do* anything. It's all done for us and if we don't like the way it is done on one channel we have forty others to choose from (assuming we have cable TV). It might be thought that television helps the contemporary revolt by expressing many of its values. That is true to a limited extent. But what is more to the point, as

Ellul pointed out, once you start enjoying the revolt vicariously you are no longer participating in it. Yet if the contemporary revolt is to become a revolution worthy of the name it cannot allow itself to be contained or trivialized, even though the television and motion picture industries may make billions of dollars trying to do just that.

Sports are a peculiarly Western phenomenon. Although they have spread to other parts of the world, they remain a unique product of the Occidental Mindset. Unlike athletics, sports are *abstract*, like chess or checkers. Many, if not all, athletic events have some roots in real activities. It was not too long ago that civilized people actually did throw javelins and shoot arrows in war and there have always been good practical reasons for skiing, horseback riding, swimming, running, jumping, and so forth. But it is hard to imagine any useful life skill which relates to bashing a hard leather ball four hundred feet over a fence or dropping an inflated one through an overhead hoop. Sports are essentially irrelevant to any useful activity, but within the limits of their own definitions and rules they are examples of meticulously ordered and regulated activities. The only thing left to chance is who wins. Consequently it is no mystery that the emphasis on sports has accelerated to the degree it has in a contemporary world in which everything else seems to be so uncertain. The worlds of sports are self-contained realms of vicarious enjoyment which have no connection with reality but all the trappings of the ordered world we have left behind us. They are the Occidental Mindset distilled and bottled for consumption on Sunday afternoon.

It may seem surprising that I mention *physical fitness* as a mechanism of escape when I highlighted the new affirmation of the body as an important aspect of the contemporary revolt. But recall that I also said there was a second and more somber reason for our current interest in physical discipline. That is that our liberated generation, no longer believing in a soul or an afterlife, *has to face death more nakedly than people at any other time in Western history.*

Are we prepared to face it squarely and lucidly? Psychiatrist Ernest
Becker thinks not.

> The knowledge of death is reflective and conceptual, and
> animals are spared it. They live and they disappear with
> the same thoughtlessness: a few minutes of fear, a few
> seconds of anguish, and it is over. But to live a whole
> lifetime with the fate of death haunting one's dreams and
> even the most sun-filled days - that's something else. . . It is
> only if you let the full weight of this paradox sink down on
> your mind and feelings that you can realize what an
> impossible situation it is for an animal to be in. I believe
> that those who speculate that a full apprehension of man's
> condition would drive him insane are right, quite literally
> right. (128, 27)

I am not convinced that the spectre of death is quite as
maddening as Becker claims it is, partly because there is a good deal
of ambiguity about what 'man's condition' really is. At times we do
become aware of dimensions to life which transcend the 'animal.'
But except for those who have gone the route of spiritual exploration,
one by-product of the contemporary revolt is a heightened awareness
of death and a sparse sense of self which can be summed up in the
words Djuna Barnes wrote in *Nightwood:* '*We are but skin about a
wind with muscles clenched against mortality.*'

What do we do about it? We tan the *skin*, massage it, tighten it
with surgery, and diet the 'cellulite' out from underneath it. We save
the *wind* by giving up smoking and practicing aerobics. We restore
the strength and resilience of the *muscles* by calisthenics, yoga and
t'ai chi ch'uan. But even with all that strenuous effort *we often
remain terribly afraid.* Afraid of the microscopic virus, afraid of the
trace of toxic chemical, afraid of the invisible radiation which can
bring all our strident attempts to preserve youth and deny death to
nought, afraid of cancer, afraid of AIDS. Because we believe in
nothing before birth, beyond life or after death, we go to
extraordinary lengths to subdue the premonitions of death. In her
excellent book, *Women Coming of Age,* Jane Fonda tells us,

> The passing of my father placed all of this [thoughts about middle age] into a far deeper context. While living, our parents are the barriers between us and mortality. When they pass on, we step up to the head of the line. Being with my father during the months of his decline, shattered any childhood illusion of living on forever. I realized then, sitting at this bedside those many days, that it was not so much the idea of death itself which frightened me as it was being faced with the 'what ifs' and the 'if onlys' when there's no time left, arriving at the end of the third act and discovering too late it hasn't been a rehearsal. (129, 14)

To prevent us from dying too disappointed Fonda proposes we get ourselves in shape to get as much out of life as we can while we can. And, although she doesn't say it, the implication is clear that the more we are concentrating on how well our body feels and looks, the less we will be dwelling on death. It is unquestionably true that the idea of an atomic soul which can survive death and live eternally in some sort of heaven has been an unsalvageable casualty of the contemporary revolt. Until and unless we find something to replace it, physical fitness with its emphasis on remaining young, vigorous and sexy, will undoubtedly continue to provide an escape from thinking about the inevitability of death.

Resolution

When we look at the contemporary revolt without the venom of the reactionary or the illusions of the escapist it is clear that it presents us with enormous problems which we have not even begun to resolve. If no resolution is reached then the only options we will have are to retreat to the past, surrender to illusion, or fall into psychological anarchy, all of which are happening to many people today. Resolution essentially involves creating an intelligible and practicable orientation toward the great variety of new experience which is resulting from our radical freedom. Attempts to provide such an orientation are at the root of the so-called New Age movement. Apart from the charlatanism, quackery and plain nonsense which pervades this hotchpotch of widely divergent ideas and practices, its inability to persuasively address the needs of the contemporary revolt arise from a failure to understand the underlying unity of the revolt, no matter by what route people may have joined it. This produces an eclecticism with no central creative core. 'The New Age movement,' says Christopher Lasch,

> . . . tries to combine meditation, positive thinking, faith healing, rolfing, dietary reform, environmentalism, mysticism, yoga, water cures, acupuncture, incense, astrology, Jungian psychology, biofeedback, extrasensory perception, spiritualism, vegetarianism, organic gardening, the theory of evolution, Reichian sex therapy, ancient mythologies, archaic nature cults, Sufism, Freemasonry, cabalistic lore, chiropractic, herbal medicine, hypnosis, and any number of other techniques designed to heighten awareness, including elements borrowed from the major religious traditions. But such a concoction, though it can sometimes furnish temporary relief from the symptoms of spiritual distress, cannot bring about the equivalent of a religious conversion, a real change of heart; nor can it bring about even an intellectual conversion to a new point of view capable of standing up against rigorous questioning. (130, 81f.)

Of course it cannot because it is trying to solve a radically new problem with an eclectic stew of old solutions. But contradictory as its expressions might seem, the contemporary revolt nevertheless has one common ground, the rejection of the Occidental Mindset, *our* mindset, as the exclusive key to reality. No generation has ever done that before. That is why it is a radically new kind of problem. But by understanding what its central issue is we can now address the contemporary revolt not merely as a problem of how we interpret and what we do with our freedom, but *of how we think about reality without the guidance of a mindset.* The essence of the contemporary revolt is that we have cast off our dependence on the past, to the Occidental Mindset that guided our five and a half thousand years of civilization. We can no longer look to the past for rules to put our life in order or resolve our problems. We wanted to be free and now we are. But we cannot continue to be careless about how we understand and use our freedom. Nietzsche's *Zarathustra* might well have been challenging us today when he said:

> Free, dost thou call thyself? Thy ruling thought would I hear of, and not that thou has escaped from a yoke.
> Art thou one *entitled* to escape from a yoke? Many a one hath cast away his final worth when he hath cast away his servitude.
> Free from what? What doth that matter to Zarathustra! Clearly, however, shall thine eye show unto me: free *for what?*
> Canst thou give unto thyself thy bad and thy good, and set up thy will as a law over thee? Canst thou be judge for thyself, and avenger of thy law?
> Terrible is aloneness with the judge and avenger of one's own law. Thus is a star projected into desert space, and into the icy breath of aloneness. (131, 65f)

What is our 'ruling thought' to be? Can we create our own system of values, our own good and bad and hold ourselves accountable to it? The civilizers did it long ago. They had a big advantage, the mindsets, which kept them on course. But even though we have abandoned mindsets, we now have an advantage that they did not. We have the *experience*, the mental charts which not one but *four* civilizations made before us. We cannot count on any civilization to guide us but we can certainly draw on all the civilizations to teach us. To do that we have to cast off any last vestiges of bondage to the Occidental Mindset, to *any* mindset. If we are to avoid reaction, escapism and anarchy and make sense of our freedom, there is only one course open to us, to endure the 'icy breath of aloneness' and make the next mental leap - to the *postcivilized mind*.

TEN

The Postcivilized Mind

The Itch for Infinite Freedom

> Do you think that we can learn to abandon the world after
> death, the sacredness of motherhood, the holiness of sex, the
> intoxication of national patriotism, the itch for infinite
> freedom, and the respect for industry, in favor of man-centered
> population restriction involving sex for fun and implying world
> government, managed ecology, and education for leisure? - And
> do it all before the twentieth century has run out?
>
> We don't have to, you know.
>
> It's just that if we don't, our civilization will be destroyed in
> thirty years, that's all.
>
> Isaac Asimov
Today and Tomorrow and . . .

What an ironic passage from the late dean of science fiction!
Asimov first put this challenge to us in 1973 and it stands without
comment in the 1983 edition of the book. Yet, with one exception,
the values he asked us to abandon are precisely those which the
contemporary revolt had already abandoned. The only people today
who still cling to them are reactionaries who, by definition, are
committed to hold fast to them. The irony of the passage lies in the
fact that what the contemporary mind abandoned them *in favor of*
was not the geo-humanistic values Asimov suggests but the value of
infinite freedom, or what I earlier called 'radical freedom,' freedom
unbounded, unconstrained and unregulated. Since the 'itch for
infinite freedom' is the core of the contemporary mind, the moot
question is not what the contemporary mind can abandon but *what
it will decide to take responsibility for.* What and how it decides will
determine whether the contemporary revolt will become a genuine

revolution and whether the contemporary mind will become a true *postcivilized mind*. Let us consider what resources the contemporary mind has to draw on to make that sort of decision.

The Heritage of the New Mind

I said in the last chapter that the mind which has gone through the revolts of the last several decades has become or is becoming *unset*. That means it is losing both the comforts and the limitations of dependence on mindsets inherited from the past. But why should we expect the unset mind to be anything more than the *unsettled* confusion it so often manifests itself as today? The primitive mind had a structure, the cognitive *map*. The much more complex civilized mind also had a structure, the *mindset*, which I likened to a *lodestone* pointing in a single direction. Mindsets constrained the range of experience within the civilization but the constraint had the positive function of preventing creativity from becoming dissipated. Is it not the case, then, that while the range of the contemporary free mind is unlimited, its creative energies will be dissipated? Frequently, yes. It is happening all around us. Such dissipation is an inevitable threat to the free mind. But while it is true that when your mind becomes free, i.e., *unset*, you lose the constraints of the lodestone and its prejudicial effect, it is not true that you must be left with no sense of direction. On the contrary, what you can hope to gain is an *overview* of the four directions (mindsets). As you do you will find yourself with a *compass*, calibrated to show alternate directions which, instead of being compulsory, can be freely chosen. The result is that *the whole circumference of experience and choice will be opened up to you* . You can wholeheartedly pursue rationality and order at one time and intuition and mystery at another without having to despise the one while in pursuit of the other or, alternatively, you can follow your own choice of a rational or intuitive path without denigrating the person who does the opposite. This is what allows Fritzjof Capra to say,

> I see science and mysticism as two complementary
> manifestations of the human mind; of its rational and
> intuitive faculties. The modern physicist experiences the
> world through an extreme specialization of the rational mind;
> the mystic through an extreme specialization of the intuitive
> mind. The two approaches are entirely different and involve
> far more than a certain view of the physical world. However,
> they are complementary, as we have learned to say in
> physics. Neither is comprehended in the other, nor can either
> of them be reduced to the other; but both of them are
> necessary, supplementing one another for a fuller
> understanding of the world. To paraphrase an old Chinese
> saying, mystics understand the roots of the *Tao* but not its
> branches; scientists understand its branches but not its
> roots. Mystical experience is necessary to understand the
> deepest nature of things, and science is essential for modern
> life. What we need, therefore, is not a synthesis, but a
> dynamic interplay between mystical intuition and scientific
> analysis. (133, 297)

The 'dynamic interplay' which is possible for the unset mind is, not of course, limited to the polarity of mysticism and science. It involves all the traditional polarities of experience: female and male, creativity and calculation, compassion and direction, paranormal and normal, dreaming and waking. To some this might seem to mean that the unset mind is simply a new version of the Sinic mind, affirming both order and mystery. But this is not the case because, as I pointed out in Chapter 2, the Sinic mind could never affirm either *wholeheartedly*. It had to keep them in balance and that meant placing limitations on how far you could go in either direction. That is why the Chinese, brilliant as they were, never pushed rational science to the height it reached in the West or mysticism to the height it reached in India. They always backed off before exaggerating either emphasis. The Sinic mind, like the others, was a *set* mind, which means in essence that it believed the cognitive structure which it used to deal with reality was the structure of reality itself. *But reality is not a balance between order and non-*

order, nor a precarious conflict between them, nor a cosmos defying
chaos, nor a primordial One veiled by an illusory many. It is all of
those things and none because they are the ways in which civilized
man experienced reality and his experience was filtered through his
mindset. Each civilized mind viewed reality through different-colored
glasses and each thought reality was the color of its own glasses.
The unset mind understands that reality is, in fact, multi-colored
and it shows you the color you are looking for. You can indeed 'raise
the multi-colored trapdoor of the mystery' and find that the whole
circumference of experience has been opened up to you.

Thus radically free, the postcivilized mind will have to adopt a
new structure which reflects that radical freedom. In speculating
about what kind of structure that might be, we need to realize that
while structure is essential if the mind is to think and choose, a *fixed*
structure is not. The primitive mind had a fixed structure based on
the cognitive map which was passed on from generation to
generation and admitted of very little change in cultural product.
The civilized mind had its mindset which was a fixed matrix for an
enormous variety of cultural product. But the only cognitive structure
consistent with a totally free mind is the *hypothesis*, i.e.,

A tentative theory or supposition provisionally adopted to
explain certain facts, and to guide in the investigation of
others.' (5, 1083)

When it comes down to the bottom line, what else can the
postcivilized mind be but a hypothesizing mind? The civilized mind,
of whatever civilization, was based on certainty. There was nothing
tentative or provisional about its pronouncements on life and reality.
But what do you, my freeminded friend, know for certain? You don't
believe in God, at least not with much enthusiasm. If you
acknowledge He was once alive, you're more than half convinced He's
dead. You don't believe you have a soul, so no one can tell you you
must do this or not do that to keep your soul from winding up in
Hell. You flirt with the idea of reincarnation but it strikes you as

nearly as unlikely as immortality. You don't believe in the sanctity
or lifelong commitment of marriage, so you are skeptical about
getting married at all. You no longer obey an independent moral
order and you observe that no one else, from stockbroker to terrorist,
seems to be obeying one either. You certainly don't believe in your
country right or wrong. And if you once thought that science, at
least, was one solid bastion of certainty, you now know, as one
writer observed, that 'the quantum theory of the ultimate nature of
matter seems to raise questions that simply cannot be resolved.'
(135, 74) If your contemporary, unset mind is to complete the
revolution to the postcivilized mind, there is *nothing* you can take for
granted. Whatever model of reality you choose *must* be hypothetical.
If, of course, you want to begin the adventure of the third
millennium. That is one alternative. The other is to let your mind
simply drift in the present or deposit it in some past century of
civilization, a not uncommon practice today. Whichever alternative
you choose you will not be alone but the choice must be made 'in the
icy breath of aloneness.' Never were words of Huxley's *Orion* more
appropriate than today:

> The choice is always ours. Then, let me choose
> The longest art, the hard Promethean way
> Cherishingly to tend and feed and fan
> That inward fire, whose small precarious flame,
> Kindled or quenched, creates
> The noble or ignoble men we are,
> The worlds we live in and our very fates,
> Our bright or muddy star. (136, v)

In the devising of hypotheses for postcivilized life, the record of
civilized experience will be indispensable. The civilized mind
produced marvelous charts of experience which are invaluable guides
as long as we understand that they are not charts of reality. Science
and mysticism, as Capra observed, lead to extreme experiences of
order and mystery respectively and our primary guides to those
experiences are to be found in the cultural products of Occidental and

Indic civilizations. But neither encourages behavior which leads to the sense of balance and harmony which so engrossed the Sinic mind, a sense which is most relevant to social and ecological concerns. We may never again have an architectonic world view which embraces all areas of experience, not because of any limitations of the postcivilized mind but, on the contrary, because for the free mind experience will be unlimited. With no mindset to tell us where we may not venture we will dare to venture anywhere and that will produce a range of discovery that no world view will be able to keep up with. Any postcivilized social concensus will need to incorporate a broad tolerance for diversity and the Sinic tradition will be an invaluable guide in that area. And what about the Amerindic mind, which took man's need to take responsibility for the entire universe so seriously? I believe the more we understand about the central place of humanity as the cutting edge of creation (at least on our planet) the more pertinent the Amerindic self-understanding may seem to us. In particular, we may have to formulate a new understanding of *sacrifice*, a concept which seems so alien to the modern Western mind. All the civilized traditions will have to be taken into account in constructing the hypotheses and models the postcivilized world will need.

Hints of the New Mind

In Chapter 2 we saw that each of the four civilizations was beset by a dominant concern which could be attributed directly to its mindset. Thus the Western mind was particularly gifted in dealing with nature, the physical world of space and mass, the Indic with the inner world of the self, the Sinic with society, and the Amerindic with time. All the civilizations, however, had to deal with those four basic realities in some way, however ineptly in some cases, and the postcivilized mind will have to deal with them as well. Out of today's ongoing mental revolution, we are already beginning to see hints of how the new mind will conceive self, society, nature and time.

Self. As I pointed in Chapter 2, the self was always troublesome for the Western mind. The concept of self inherited by the twentieth century was composed of two elements - body and soul. In Christian thought, man was a special kind of creature, differing from other animals in his possession of a soul which survived the death of the body. The Roman Catholic Church, unlike biblical fundamentalists, finally accepted that human beings were the result of a long process of biological evolution but insisted that they were unique in receiving souls at conception. As the twentieth century progressed, however, the existence of the soul became less and less relevant to the concept of self. The psychodynamic theories of Freud were grounded in biology. No soul could be found in the Freudian trinity of id, ego and superego and no major psychological theory made any reference to one. The dominant form of experimental psychology, behaviorism, was even more explicit in its rejection of the soul as a meaningful concept. It would not even countenance the use of the term 'mind' which had become a substitute for 'soul' in sophisticated thought. The behaviorist attitude toward the human mind is well summed up by an educational psychologist, J. Stanley Gray, who, writing in 1935, declared smugly,

> The scientist does not deny that mind exists. He merely says that until it becomes evident to the senses through some form of sensory extension, we will ignore the fact that it might exist. The physicist no longer assumes that each physical object possesses a mind, as was formerly believed, but neither does he deny it. The biologist completely ignores the fact that a mind may exist in his laboratory animals and plants, but he does not deny such a possibility. The scientific psychologist proposes to adopt the same procedure in his study of humans. Perhaps we have minds, but until it is demonstrated, we shall omit that postulate from our basic position. (139, 39)

There were many other factors, of course, which tended to shrink our concept of self: philosophical and practical materialism, the increasingly one-dimensional picture of life projected by Hollywood, and, by no means least, the liberal theologians who dreaded finding themselves intellectually isolated from other academicians when they talked about things like souls and Heaven and Hell. And so we arrived at the sixties with a concept of self even more impoverished than the body/soul composite which had come to us through five and a half millennia of Western civilization. To put it starkly, we had come to the conclusion that the self is the body and the mind is the brain, both of which are physically determined, with no freedom of choice, and both of which exist in awful isolation in a universe that is vast beyond comprehension and utterly devoid of plan or purpose.

Thus stripped down to the most meager concept of self with which human beings have ever had to live, we are beginning to develop a new, hypothetical concept for the future. To begin with, we are discovering that being a body with a brain is not the simple mechanical thing we have become accustomed to think of it as. Our physical being is embedded in a matrix of universal fields, a primary characteristic of which is not determinism but *indeterminacy*. A number of scientists and philosophers are hypothesizing that human freedom of choice derives in some way from quantum indeterminacy or a comparable indeterminacy in far-from-equilibrium conditions in brain processes. Again, the field of psycho-neuroimmunology is uncovering an incredible set of systems within the brain/body complex which has all the hallmarks of intelligent communication. *Something* is operating to make us what we are other than a set of chemical and electrical processes, a something which is intelligent and free to choose. Scientists are no longer afraid to call that something 'mind.' 'Mind,' says psychoneuroimmunologist Candace Pert, 'is in a different realm from the molecules of the brain.' But mind, in today's context, does not mean the same old half of the body/mind or body/soul composite we inherited from the past. It is a far richer concept with much deeper connections to the core processes

of the universe. In fact, we are on the threshold of grasping the idea
that a universal mind may be the source of all physical processes,
that *those processes are the thoughts of that mind.* I say 'on the
threshold' because to argue that hypothesis would take far more
time and space than this chapter has can provide. A major part of
my next book, *The Future of Mind,* will be devoted entirely to arguing
it. But we can, I believe, say with assurance that the self-concept of
the postcivilized mind is not going to be restricted to individuality or
to our biological organism. This fact is being discovered today by
many people of different backgrounds and different life situations. It
is illustrated dramatically in an incident Shirley MacLaine records in
Don't Fall Off The Mountain. After trying unsuccessfully to fall
asleep in an unheated shelter one frigid night in the Paro Valley of
Bhutan, MacLaine recalls,

> Then I remembered the orange circle.
>
> 'You have a center in your mind,' [her yoga] instructor had
> said. 'It is the source from which all your thoughts spring. It
> is your nucleus, the center of your universe. Find it.
> Concentrate. It will come. Relax with it. That is meditation.
> Allow nothing to divert your conscious or unconscious
> attention. Not fear. Not pain. Sorrow. Cold. Nothing.
> Stare into your interior. You will see it. It will look like a
> tiny sun. The sun is the center of every solar system and the
> reason for all life on all planets in all universes. So it is with
> yours.'
>
> I closed my eyes, searching for the center of my mind. If only
> I could find that tiny sun. I will concentrate on the real sun, I
> thought, the sun I know, the sun I have seen. I will find that
> in my mind, and it will be hot.
>
> The room left me. I felt my knotted muscles begin to relax.
> The freezing room and the windy granite mountains outside
> began to drift out of my conscious mind.
>
> Slowly in the center of my mind's eye, a tiny round ball
> appeared. I stared and stared at it. Then I felt I *became*
> the orange ball. Slowly, slowly the center grew. It seemed to
> generate hear and light. The heat spread down through my
> neck and arms and finally lodged in my stomach. I felt

droplets of perspiration on my midriff and forehead. The light grew brighter until finally I sat up on the cot with a start and opened my eyes, expecting to find that someone had turned on a light. Perspiring all over, I was stunned to find the room dark. I lay back. I felt as though I were glowing. Still perspiring, I fell asleep. The instructor was right; hidden beneath the surface there was something greater than my outer self. (134, 237f.)

Greater than but not *alien to*. The outer self is the exposed tip of the deeper Self. The creativity which passes from the Self to the self does not proceed from some external source but from the depths of our own being, the vastness of which we have scarcely begun to fathom. To truly, fully grasp that fact is essential to the self-concept of the postcivilized mind. We saw in Chapter 1 how the civilizers, overawed by their own creative efforts, placed the source of that creativity outside themselves, in the gods. They balanced their own extraordinary achievements with a self-concept that made themselves mere vessels of vastly greater powers. It was a conceit which shielded them from the full responsibility for their actions. Among the Greeks, failure to maintain that conceit was called *hubris*, arrogant pride. Today the New Age movement is resurrecting the same conceit under the guise of ancient sages speaking through 'channelers' or visitors from outer space who are given credit for giving us poor, uncreative humans everything more complicated than the safety pin. To that extent the New Age movement is escapist and inimical to the postcivilizing task. The truly contemporary mind is the mind with an 'itch for infinite freedom' and to look for help to spirits or extraterrestrials is to surrender that freedom. The postcivilizers will understand that their own central core of creativity is the source of their achievements but also that that core is far more prodigious than we yet realize.

Nature. The emergent awareness of a multi-dimensional self is intimately connected to the postcivilized concept of nature. I suggested before that the physical world flows from a universal intelligence, which means we can relate to it as mind to mind, not mind to mindless matter. This implies a new relationship between ourselves and nature, one of respect and kinship rather than one of alternately detached observation and ruthless exploitation. The new morality which underlies today's ecology movement and groups like Greenpeace is not derived from traditional sources but stems instead from free minds choosing to be responsible for endangered life forms and for whole environmental systems up to and including that of the entire planet. In 'the icy breath of aloneness,' some human beings have decided that whales have 'certain inalienable rights' as well as themselves and have been willing to risk their lives to defend those rights. That is indeed a new morality arising from radical freedom. Whether or not the Gaia hypothesis, that the earth is a single vast self-regulating system, is sustainable, we are beginning to perceive it as such. Our former conception of nature as mere space and mass to be manipulated into whatever kind of order we willed is being displaced by one which views it as one living organism of which we are integral parts.

Society. When we began the democratic revolution of the modern era, we had to forego the security of the divinely established social order of the past. The only things divinely established about democracy are our inalienable rights. To make a society out of nothing but rights, to establish a social order out of nothing but freedom, we had to invent the *social contract*. The social contract simply means that we agree to live together in a society and to abide by certain laws which we recognize are for the common good and individual protection.

The free mind recognizes several problems for this understanding of a democratic society. In the first place, it understands that the very idea of God-given inalienable rights is an abstract fiction that we have chosen to believe in. In the second place, it understands that these abstract rights are encrusted with social taboos, familial restraints, personal neuroses, and biological dispositions. Genuine freedom of the mind has to constantly contend with all those limitations. Finally, it acknowledges that we are free to choose to what extent we wish to uphold the social contract. From its indulgence in drugs to its unprecedented financial ripoffs of a trusting public, the unset mind has often shown the utmost contempt for the social contract. And there is an even darker side. From at least the time of the tribal stage in human evolution, there has been one virtually universal social taboo: incest. Yet in the United States today, according to some accounts, we have one in five female children and one in seven males suffering sexual abuse by some member of their own family.

This forces us to realize that there is more to a viable society than rights and a social contract. Those formed the *legal* system of American society. Equally important, however, was its *value* system which was broadly founded on the precepts of Judaeo-Christian religion. But while those values remain as part of the heritage of the free mind, they no longer carry the same divine authority and there is no penalty for ignoring them or exchanging them for others. This is a frightening prospect. It accounts for the frenzy surrounding the current call for a 'return to traditional values,' which is, in effect, a call to reinstate a conservative, Judaeo-Christian moral code as the legal and social basis of the new society. But for the free mind, God, in the traditional sense, *is* dead and, as Nietzsche so brilliantly pointed out, when God is dead, man alone is responsible for choosing his own law to live by. If we choose radical freedom we are responsible for choosing and maintaining our own values. The more radical the freedom, the more responsibility it places on us. 'Freedom *for what?*' Zarathustra asked.

Free choice of values and responsibility for implementing and maintaining them, then, will have to be the basis of postcivilized society. Postcivilized society is crystallizing around core areas of *concensus*. Some people have *decided* that all women, for example, should have the right to control their own bodies. Around that decision a broad concensus has grown and no legalism or dogma will be allowed to interfere with it for long. Others have *decided* that homosexuals should have the same rights as heterosexuals and that decision, too, has gathered concensus. Still others have *decided* that the fate of the environment cannot be left to industrial greed and political indifference and there again a new concensus is arising. The examples are endless, some issues being confined to small groups, others having nationwide support The concensual groups often overlap to a considerable degree and thus a deeper and broader value concensus emerges.

In postcivilized society, the political structure will lose its preeminent place. Since the dawn of civilization, creativity has been viewed as proceeding from the top down. It is, however, already becoming evident that the postcivilized mind no more wants the establishment of a political elite than it wants a religious elite. Political leaders will have to be far more responsive to the concensual values around them or they will be replaced by popular insistence. The national election of 1992 may well be the political watershed between the civilized past and the postcivilized future. The Republican Party adopted the ideology of the religious right and the economic policies of the rich elite, while the Democratic Party showed itself to be more sensitive to emerging concensual values. If the governance of President Clinton and Vice-President Gore remains responsive to those values, then the political processes of the United States may well be structured quite differently after the year 2000.

I said in Chapter 6 that the effectiveness of law depends on our *reverence for its source* and our *enthusiasm for its purpose*. In a postcivilized democratic society that can mean only one thing. Those laws will be enacted, followed and respected which are 'of the people, by the people, and for the people.' They will be effective because the people revere and respect themselves and because they reflect the purposes the people have chosen.

Time. What view of *time* is consistent with a postcivilized mind? Until the nineteenth century, the Western conception of time was relatively static. Time had a beginning, Creation Day, and would have an end, Judgment Day. Between the two, the great institutions of religion and government changed but little and were essentially dedicated to maintaining the *status quo*. With the increasing awareness of the age of the earth and of life in the nineteenth century as well as the increasing acceptance of evolution, our concept of time exploded into the future, which now seemed to extend endlessly ahead of us as a vast region of discovery and progress. Two world wars and the invention of superbombs gave cynics ample opportunity to deprecate our pretensions to progress but no one could seriously doubt that we continued to make astounding and accelerating progress in technology despite all its hazards. So we anticipated the expanse of time ahead of us as one of more and more wonderful technological advances, one in which we would eventually fan out into the universe in marvelous spaceships just as our fifteenth- and sixteenth-century ancestors spread across the earth in their wooden sailing ships. But the intriguing fantasies of *Star Trek* notwithstanding, that scenario seems highly improbable. Although physics may someday discover a way to travel faster than the speed of light, nothing in current physical theory encourages that possibility. (The theoretical particles called 'tachyons' would travel faster than light but never slower.) Even were a 'warp drive' possible, the technology required for even a modest 'starship' seems a far-off dream and the resources available pitifully inadequate. The prospect of even a modest 'space station' hangs uneasily in the balance today. For the foreseeable future mankind's destiny seems wedded to that of planet Earth.

Perhaps that is a good thing. Is it mankind's destiny to carry its war machines into the wider universe, to repeat the mistakes of the past on a galactic scale? I think not. *Star Wars* is not our future. I suggest that our destiny in the coming decades is *to enrich the texture of time present,* to be the *redeemers of time past and the conservators of time future.*

Enriching the texture of time present means devoting our creativity to the quality of life and more and more of our resources to the benefit of all life, including the earth itself. It also involves exploring those dimensions of time and space at the existence of which altered states of consciousness have always hinted. But as you proceed with these new ventures you will have to simultaneously dismantle the mental barriers which restrict your own possibilities and those of all the other people who inhabit your world. You will begin with yourself, watching for the remnants of unfreedom in your own mind and carefully dispelling them. Then you will have to reach out to others you can help to cope with their unfreedom, those whose minds are still *set*. You will have to actively confront sexism, racism, ethnic hatred, and materialism. You will even have to formulate a strategy for reaching the fundamentalists - there are so many of them with so much untapped creative energy - and rescuing them from their tunnel vision. You cannot restrict your caring to whales and dolphins. Your own species is threatened as well.

How can you be *a redeemer of time past?* Haven't you always heard that you can't change the past? How wrong that cliché is! The past is not something *behind you*. It exists as a living structure in the present and *only* that. As such it is always with you, producing both pernicious and salutary influences on your life. One of the most powerful ways in which the past informs the present is through *archetypes*. Archetypes do not necessarily come from far back in human history. They may be relatively recent although their power is arguably rooted in much older material. One of the best examples of a recent archetype is that of Nazism. The primary emblem of that archetype, the swastika, still evokes a deep psychic response in many people, in some one of loathing, in others one of awesome potency.

It is the latter response that makes the swastika the common symbol of neo-Nazis and white supremacists. Redeeming the past with respect to Nazism means allowing no future generation to forget the horror that was perpetrated under its cruel emblem. It means remembering with honor the young soldiers of all nations and the millions of innocents who died because of a monstrous ideology they neither understood not shared. It means remembering the dead civilians of Berlin and Dresden as well as of London. And it means never forgetting the Holocaust. Redeeming the past also involves such things as reviving in current memory the forgotten contributions of men and women who have been excluded from the history books because of cultural or racial bias, the significant but little remembered work of African Americans being a case in point.

Another archetype we have inherited in the West is our peculiar concept of the relation between male and female. In *all* civilizations the socioeconomic structure was dominated by the male elite. In *all* civilizations the male, *yang,* was identified with order, rationality, light and activity, the female, *yin,* with mystery, intuition, darkness and passivity. But only in the West did *yang* qualities become *excessively and exclusively dominant in principle* over *yin,* whereas in India, China and Mesoamerica they did not. What made the West unique in this respect was, therefore, determined neither by the socioeconomic prepotence of men or with anything inherent in either the universal male or female archetypes. The latter are, in fact, not products of civilization at all but are rooted well back in our precivilized heritage. But to the civilized mind, maleness and femaleness were a fundamental polarity which had to be structured by its mindset. Thus while the West's identification of rationality with maleness flowed from the universal male archetype, *obsession* with rationality flowed from its mindset. The reason the male archetype assumed the character it did in the West was simply that the order-obsessed Western mindset placed the stamp of its *a priori* cognitive structure on the relationship between maleness and femaleness just as it did every other order-mystery pair. With the collapse of the Western mindset the female archetype is now free to reemerge and be explored by men and women alike. This process, however, has a long way to go and the invidious tenacity of male dominance is reflected in the prevalence of rape and spousal abuse in our society as well as the everpresent 'glass ceiling' in employment.

The most important factor in redeeming the past is, of course, *understanding* it. If we make a real effort to understand the past, we will be less apt to impose ideological misfits like Marxism on it. We will also be less likely to treat seriously people who tell us civilization was brought to earth by gods from outer space. As postcivilized people we are already highly sensitive to environmental pollution. But we must be equally sensitive to mental pollution. Life is not simply, as a character in Mitchener's *Chesapeake* put it, 'carrying everything forward.' What we carry forward has first to be decontaminated, purged of the spores of deceit and distortion with which it has been so abundantly infected. It is my hope that this book will contribute to a different understanding about what our civilized past has been, wherever in the world we live.

Being *conservators of time future* implies that the future must be approached with foresight and the intent to shape it responsibly instead of treating it as the dumpsite of all our thoughtless mistakes. This implies a new breed of conservatives, not, like the old breed, clinging to the past but rather caring for the future. The four trillion dollar debt the United States government has thrown forward in time to be the burden of future generations is an obscenity to the postcivilized mind as much as is the spoliation of forests and the proliferation of poverty, homelessness, and starvation. The postcivilized mind will be known by what it considers obscene. Conserving the future is perhaps the most sensitive task of all. In one of Robert Kennedy's favorite quotes, 'The present speaks with a loud voice, the future whispers.' Let those with ears to hear, listen well.

Some writers speak almost ecstatically about the prospects of the postcivilized mind. In 1979, Dr. W. Brugh Joy wrote,

> For me, the cataclysmic prophecies that are rife in current
> literature foreshadow a revolution of the most astonishing

proportions, but instead of being a revolution in the physical plane it is a revolution in consciousness, a revolution of the mental plane. I sense the approach of a psychological earthquake the magnitude of which has not been experienced in the human awareness for millennia and may not have been experienced in the human awareness ever before. (141, 281)

And Peter Russell, in a book entitled *The Global Brain,* prophecies not merely a revolution in consciousness but an *evolutionary leap:*

Humanity could be on the threshold of an evolutionary leap, a leap that could occur in a flash of evolutionary time, a leap such as occurs only once in a billion years. The changes leading to this leap are taking place right before our eyes - or rather right behind them, within our own minds. (142, 7)

I resonate with predictions like these but I cannot join in them. While I have, indeed, used the terms 'revolution' and 'leap' with regard to the postcivilized mind, my predictions about the nature of that mind are more measured and less ecstatic simply because they are *hypotheses* based on my preceding analysis of the civilized mind and what we might expect from a mind which has lost civilized constraints. I have no theoretical or evidentiary basis for predicting anything more spectacular. Nevertheless, I believe it will be an exciting adventure, building the postcivilized world. I have no idea how long it will take or how it will look in comparison to today's world. Not much different for quite a while, I expect. The vast majority of people will probably not be much different either until new models have been created which will attract their allegiance. One thing we often overlook is that most people in the period of civilization still operated out of a primitive mentality, that is, they took what the civilizers handed them as a cognitive map and never participated in the creative possibilities of the mindset. In the era of postcivilization, *mutatis mutandis,* many people will be tempted to make sects out of concensus groups. They will want civilization with

all its certainty resurrected and the postcivilizers will have to take
their fears into account while getting on with the business of literally
building a new world of constant caring and change.

The Theology of Infinite Freedom

> It is not God who will save us - it is we who will save
> God, by battling, by creating, and by transmuting matter
> into spirit.
>
> But all our struggle may go lost. If we tire, if we grow
> faint of spirit, if we fall into panic, then the entire Universe
> becomes imperiled.
>
> Nikos Kazantzakis
> *Saviors of God* (137, 206)

I can well imagine that had the Aztecs or Mayans survived and
developed for another five hundred years, one of their number might
have penned something like these lines. In them we find the same
sense of the precariousness of the universe and the need for human
struggle to save it that we find in Amerindic thought. But there is
more in Kazantzakis' words than the Amerindic mind could have
comprehended, a sense that the universe is incomplete, that it not
only needs to be preserved but that the process of creation must be
continued, not by a superhuman being but *by and through us*. We
are the cutting edge of creation.

If you are a free mind on the brink of becoming postcivilized,
beware! You have two formidable groups of adversaries who will do
anything they can to stop you. The first are the reactionaries of
every stripe who hate the freedom of the contemporary mind and will
do anything in their power to restore the past. The second are those
who have gone through the contemporary revolt, whose minds are
free like yours but who understand that freedom only as a license for
unbridled greed, unlimited power, and utter contempt for human life,
indeed, for the earth itself. The adversaries have the power now.
You do not. But you have the advantage because you understand

them while they do not understand you. You are an evolutionary step ahead of them and you will discover new kinds of power and learn how to use it wisely. What is needed *now* is that you 'get your act together,' that you approach experience with as comprehensive as possible an understanding of what you are doing and that you involve yourself totally in acting out of that understanding. You will have to pour all the energy into your efforts that you would if God Himself were drawing you like Moses through the desert to a rendezvous on Sinai. But you will have to do it believing there is no God, no high holy place and no tablets of law except as you create them yourself.

Because, like it or not, the key to postcivilized theology, *the theology of infinite freedom,* is that whatever God did for us in the past, like a good parent He is gradually cutting us loose and leaving it to us to do more and more of what is to be done. As Teilhard so incisively put it, '. . . evolution, by becoming conscious of itself in the depths of ourselves . . becomes free to dispose of itself - it can give or refuse itself.' That puts a far more crucial choice to us than those with which Asimov challenged us, the literal choice of giving or refusing the next step in our own evolution. We can be infinitely free but with infinite freedom goes infinite responsibility. We can no longer pass the buck to a higher power.

We are that higher power.

APPENDIX A
Stages in Social Evolution

In Chapter 1, I drew a contrast between primitive or pre-civilized societies and civilization. That simple dichotomy was adequate for the argument at hand but it was not meant to imply that all precivilized societies are the same. On the contrary, they can be differentiated into several levels which are identified below, beginning with the most primitive. In presenting those levels, I want to make it clear that I consider they represent *stages in social evolution*. For a long time anthropologists, particularly those field anthropologists who studied 'primitive' societies and developed great empathy for them, were loath to characterize one society as more 'advanced' or further up the ladder of evolution than another. They believed that societies could not be compared except, for example, in terms of their 'synergy,' that is, how well they functioned by their own internal standards. Among societies of the same level, that is probably true, although any one of them, not having an anthropologist's benign perspective, would undoubtedly think it was better than all the others. I believe, however, that it is perfectly legitimate to compare different levels of society in terms of 'evolutionary advancement.' What that means, however, is not that a higher level society is *better* than a lower level one. It means that its *range of possibilities* is greater. Each advance in social evolution opens up a wider spectrum of thought and action choices to its human population. Those choices, however, may result in destructive as well as constructive programs and activities, so only what is accomplished at each level can be evaluated in terms of better or worse, not the level itself. Being a civilized Greek is not in itself 'better' than being a precivilized Cretan or a Navaho. It merely has greater potential. This will be obvious in the way I characterize the following stages in pre-civilized social evolution.

1.The *band*. While we have little direct knowledge of humans operating in simple bands, the band is almost certainly the first form of human society. As it is among the great apes, it would have been organized around a dominant male who would have kept as many females and their offspring to himself as he could manage as a foraging unit while keeping weaker males at bay. Spin-offs from the band would have produced more bands resulting in a proliferation and spreading out of the species. Within any given forage area, however, the proliferation of bands would have resulted in inter-band competition and conflict. It would also have required greater risk-taking in the pursuit of food and created greater exposure of the band to predators. Thus, the band was an extremely hazardous form of social organization and severely limited in its possibilities.

2.The *tribe* began as a binding together of several bands. While its members lost a degree of freedom, they gained security and enhanced power. Rather than having women and children with them all the time, some of the males could leave the encampment to hunt while leaving others behind to protect their families. The freedom lost was due to the inevitable introduction of taboos and mores into the tribal mind so that, *inter alia,* access to females was no longer simply the privilege of being the strongest male present.

3.The next stage was the *nation,* but the word is not used here in the sense of a modern nation-state but in the sense that we speak of the Apache, the Sioux, the Zulu or the Mongol nation. Unlike the tribe, the nation arose by division of a tribe into sub-tribes, probably because its size had become too large for its traditional area of operation. The new tribes had, however, passed the stage of creating fundamental folkways and mores. While forming new socioeconomic units, their basic tribal identity remained intact. The Oglala were still Sioux, the Chirikawa still Apaches, and the Oirat and Khalkha still Mongols. Expansion as a nation was a creative step in human social development because it allowed a tribe to split up without breaking up. Tribes are inherently inimical to other tribes, which they generally regard as less than human. Becoming members of one nation with one identity allowed what were functionally different tribes to be allies and brothers even though they were widely dispersed. The danger always existed, of course, that tribalism would reemerge within the nation and produce internecine warfare as the history of the Mongols amply demonstrates.

4. The *agricultural collective* was made possible by the Neolithic revolution which occurred (in the Occidental world) around 8000 B. C. The term 'agricultural collective' is one which I have had to invent because of the confusion in the literature about what constitutes a civilization. To most archaeologists and historians, as I pointed out in Chapter 1, the Minoan society of Crete and the Incan society of Peru are counted as civilizations. In my view they were not; they were agricultural collectives. The collectives, representing a settled population based on farming, tended to be peaceful, increasingly hierarchical as time passed, but nonetheless neither divisive. nor exploitative. That is, while there were privileged and even revered classes, no internal group was exploited or repressed by force. The collective was, for this reason, an extremely stable form of society based on concensus. Its religion was oriented around those chthonic and meteorological elements which supported its agricultural activity. The great achievement of the agricultural collective was to harmoniously combine all man's skills and inventions in a stable, enduring socioeconomic form.

The stage of the agricultural collective can be broken down into several substages. While the societies of the Minoans, the Zulus and the Mississipians, for example, were all agriculture collectives, a good case could be made that they exemplified different 'levels' within that broader category. Although it is beyond the scope of this book, a comparative study of the cognitive structures of pre-civilized societies as they changed from one evolutionary level to the next would be a fascinating project. In this book, however, I have had to be content to study civilization which appeared as the fifth but not final stage in human social evolution.

APPENDIX B
Models of History

Time: 313 A.D. Place: Milan. Present: Constantine and Licinius, two of the three self-proclaimed emperors of the Roman Empire.

Licinius. I am deeply concerned about your recent decision. This edict tolerating all religions and giving the Christians back their property is a dangerous one.

Constantine. On the contrary, my dear Licinius, it greatly strengthens our position. The old religions have done nothing for us but look at the successes my army has had since I had my soldiers paint crosses on their shields. And, in case you hadn't noticed, Christians are getting richer and more powerful by the day. Think of how much taxes they will contribute to the imperial coffers. Besides my own mother is one, you know, and she isn't at all subversive.

L. But that vision they say you had - of a cross! Was that true?

C. I have sworn to it, have I not? That makes it true. But what difference does it make? The empire needs unity. Jupiter certainly hasn't provided it, so why not Christ? *In hoc signo vince!* Those were the words of the vision and I am convinced that with that sign going before us we shall conquer. I have already disposed of the usurper, Maxentius. While I finish our business in Gaul, you will rid us of Maximinus in the East. Then we can resume running the empire the way Diocletian planned it - you as Caesar Augustus in the East and I in the West.

L. (departing) Farewell, then, Caesar. May your new god bring you speedy victory in Gaul while the old ones ensure I defeat Maximinus.

C. (alone) Yes, Licinius Caesar, defeat the last usurper for me and continue to believe in old Diocletian's faded dream of two empires and two emperors. But Rome is one and her destiny has always been one empire with one august Caesar over all the world. The time will come when I will rule unchallenged over a single empire from Britain to Syria. And when I have deposed you from the East, I will build a new city, the City of Constantine, where your dreary old Byzantium stands, a fitting capital for the undisputed master of the world.

Time: 240 A.D. Place: Pataliputra. Present: the Buddhist emperor Asoka and his son, Mahendra.

Mahendra. The warriors are speaking among themselves, father. They wonder what will become of the empire now.

Asoka. You are very young to concern yourself with such grave matters, my son. The empire is tranquil and I have set my edicts in stone at its boundaries so all may know ours is a land of peace and justice. What more can the warriors want?

M. They are asking when you will conquer the south and add it to the empire.

A. To that question I must answer, 'Never.' My grandfather conquered many territories. He even recovered our lands from the heirs of the great Alexander. My father consolidated his achievements into the Maurya empire. In my turn, I led my warriors into Kalinga but my heart was aggrieved by the terrible suffering and death that caused. I will no longer be a conqueror.

M. Are we then to remain as we are and add nothing to the greatness of the Mauryas?

A. No, we will add to the greatness of the Mauryas in another way. In my youth I practiced *kama* as a young man should. I have that to thank for you, my son. Then I practiced *artha*, carrying on the political aspirations of my fathers. Now it is time for *dharma*. I must follow the teachings of the Lord Buddha. I will assemble here a great council of Buddhist monks and charge them to set forever the true doctrine and carry it forth to all of India. The Mauryas will be remembered as conquerors of the south, even as far as Sri Lanka, but we will conquer not by arms but by the light of the Buddha.

*Time: 123 B.C. Place: Ch'ang-an. Present: the emperor Hsiao Wu-ti
and his advisor, Chang Ch'ien.*

H̲s̲i̲a̲o̲.̲ I am deeply concerned that the northern barbarians may
yet destroy us. It was they who nearly brought down Liu Pang and
now they constantly raid our territories, killing our people, pillaging
our lands, and driving off our herds.

C̲h̲a̲n̲g̲.̲ Most noble Lord, it is not fit for you to worry so. The
Mandate of Heaven has been given to the Han and against it the
barbarians cannot prevail.

H̲.̲ But is it not possible that I have lost the Mandate of Heaven?

C̲.̲ Lord, when the last lord of the Shang became dissolute a
great drought afflicted the land and the people suffered. It became
known throughout the territory of the black-haired people that the
Lord of Shang had lost his virtue and it was only then that King Wu
came forth from Chou and put an end to the Shang. The kings of
Chou ruled for many years until their virtue declined. Then the
many states warred upon each other until Shih Hang Ti, a king of
great virtue, united the realm and built the Ch'in empire. But Shih
died too soon and again the world was torn by strife until your
ancestor, Liu Pang, was granted the mandate of Heaven and
founded the Han empire.

H̲.̲ But, alas, I am not Liu Pang and my realm is beset by foes.

C̲.̲ Nevertheless, great Lord, for many years I have travelled far
in the West and I have never once heard it said that the virtue of the
Lord of Han has declined or that he has lost the Mandate of Heaven.
Everywhere it is said that the empire is merely resting, regaining its
vitality until the great Hsiao is ready to restore its grandeur.

H̲.̲ But when will that time come?

C̲.̲ It has come, Lord of Han. Now is the time for you to put forth
missions to your friends and armies against your enemies. South
and north will fall before you. The barbarians will be obliterated

from the earth and their herds will be the spoils of Han. The virtue of Chou will be reestablished in all the lands.

Time: 1519 A. D. Place: Tenochtitlán. Present: Emperor Moctezuma II and his brother, Vice-emperor Tlacaeltzin.

Tlacaeltzin. The time has come to act, my brother. The strangers are approaching but they are only a few hundred in number. If we attack them now we can crush them before they advance another foot.

Moctezuma. Perhaps you are right, Tlacaeltzin. Yet the decision falls not on your head but on mine. For long now my mind has been disturbed by the thought that this day must come. I have sought for signs and all have portended the doom of Moctezuma. I have even played the great ballgame in hope of encouragement but, alas, the gods saw me defeated. I have sent emissaries to the bearded one they call Cortés and they have returned telling of wonders - tubes of metal that roar with fire and earth and strange beasts half man and half a fierce fourfooted creature that runs like the wind over the earth.

T. But I have heard that the men only sit astride the beasts they call 'horses' and the fire tubes must rest and be ministered to before they can belch fire again. We could crush the invaders if we swept down on them in force.

M. No, my brother, that is not to be. All the signs have convinced me that this Cortés is the bearded one whose coming from over the sea was long foretold. Look how easily he mastered the Tlaxcalans and how readily they joined him to march against us. Everything foretells the end of Moctezuma.

T. If it is your will that we do not fight, what will you do?

M. I will cross the great causeway to meet the bearded one and escort him to the palace of Axayacatl from which he shall henceforth be guardian of our people. Thus will the prophecy be fulfilled.

The characters in these dialogues were real. They did have conversations in the places and approximately at the times given. Although the words I have attributed to them are fictitious, the deeds are not. Constantine did issue a monument of religious toleration called 'The Edict of Milan' in 313 A.D. Maximinus died before his armies were defeated by Licinius and Constantine later regained power over the Eastern Empire and built Constantinople, the magnificent city on the Bosporus which is now called Istanbul. Asoka did convene a great gathering of Buddhist elders in Pataliputra and devoted much of his energy for the rest of his life to the peaceful promulgation of Buddhism. His son, Mahendra, is credited with having converted Sri Lanka. At the instigation of Chang Ch'ien, the emperor Hsiao Wu-ti extended his power through both military and diplomatic means over most of China. He put a decisive end to the Hsung-nu nomadic raiders in the north, brought his breakaway southern provinces once more under imperial control, and even added Korea to the Han empire. Moctezuma did have his fatal meeting with Cortés and, in one of history's most bizarre decisions, gave the Aztec people into the Spaniard's keeping. Oppressed by Cortés' lieutenant, Pedro Alvarado, the Aztecs later revolted and Moctezuma was killed by a stone throne by one of his own subjects while trying to calm the rebellion.

I argued in Chapter Two and have attempted to demonstrate in the succeeding chapters that Civilized Mindsets were the matrices of history. They did not rigidly determine its content but acted as powerful guidelines which kept successive societies within their sway from falling victim to the chaos of unrestrained variations. They allowed broad variety but kept the four Civilizations, each with its many derivative civilized societies, from going off on uncontrolled tangents. But if a Mindset was a matrix of history, would it not also affect the fundamental dynamics of civilized societies, their rise, progress, regress and fall? Can we derive from Mindset Theory models of history which help to explain its *movement* in the way Marx and Toynbee attempted? Answers to those questions would require a far more extensive review of history itself than I could make in this book, but in the four vignettes which began this appendix I was suggesting an affirmative answer. History was made neither by individuals nor by the masses, but by the interaction of the two. Individuals utilized their imaginations and made crucial decisions but history moved only when their visions were communicated to and adopted by masses of followers, whether by inspiration or force.

The key question for history, from the point of view of Mindset Theory, is 'How do leaders think?' When they make a decision about what course they want their societies to follow, on what are they basing that decision? What are their values, their principles, their understanding of what historical movement is all about? Knowing that the Mindsets affected every other area of life, is it likely that they had no influence on historical decisions? The possibility that the Mindsets do significantly affect the pattern of historical movement occurred to Toynbee. Although he was not thinking in terms of Mindsets as such, he realized that his original 'Hellenic' model of history, based on a segment of Occidental history, did not fit all civilized societies. Parts of it fitted some periods of some civilizations but left other periods unintelligible. It was disconcerting to him to find that the Hellenic model applied to Egypt *backwards*. Whereas the Hellenic model called for unification only after a long series of exhausting wars, Egyptian civilization achieved that unification very early on, under Narmer. That is somewhat equivalent to a modern astrophysicist presenting a theory which works quite well if you assume that the Big Bang comes in the future rather than fifteen or twenty billion years ago. There were also cases where Toynbee forced his model on societies which were not at all amenable to it. He did not realize, for example, that he was performing intellectual contortions in maintaining that the Hellenic model applied to Meso-american civilization, basing his contention on the requirement that 'we now regard civilization in Middle America as being continuous and unitary, and see the Aztec Empire as its universal state in the making.' (3, 57)   That view is, of course, confuted by everyone who has studied the so-called Aztec Empire.

In order to make up for the inadequacy of the Hellenic model, Toynbee entertained another model, that of the Chinese who saw their own history as a series of periodic 'yang' expansions and consolidations and 'yin' dissolutions and dormancies.   He acknowledges the general validity of the Sinic model to Chinese history after the establishment of the Ch'in 'unitary regime' in 221 B. C. but claims that prior Chinese history followed the Hellenic model of 'revolutionary change from disunity to unity as a result of ever more devastating wars which have brought the civilization to grief before political unity is achieved.' (ibid.) He dismissed Chinese unity under the Shang and Chou dynasties, in effect, as an unwarranted extrapolation into the past of the 'later configuration which did not establish itself before 221 B. C.'   But while our knowledge of the Shang is sketchy at best and while it is true that it is not accurate to speak of a 'Chinese Empire' before the Ch'in dynasty, it is indisputable from contemporary records that there was a Chinese 'unitary state' established under the Chou dynasty which began at least as early as 1037 B. C.   It is also indisputable that the basic models of Chinese statecraft date from that period and, furthermore, that the rulers of the Chou gave some credit for their models to the Shang and even the legendary Hsia dynasties.   In my opinion, the Chinese model of their own history is more accurate than Toynbee's attempt to fit the pre-Ch'in era into his Hellenic model.

Toynbee finally wound up using a hybrid of Hellenic and Sinic models in his monumental *A Study of History*.   Unfortunately, the way he organized that work vitiated whatever explanatory power his model might have had.   Had he reviewed each civilization in turn, applying his model to its history, he might have demonstrated some efficacy of the model.   Instead he organized his work around successive phases of the model itself, allowing him to select illustrations from various civilizations which best exemplified each phase and gloss over ones which did not.

The Sinic model of history is *prima facie* evidence that Mindsets do shape the course of history within their respective Civilizations. The evidence for the sudden and cataclysmic demise of more than one Meso-american society also indicates a likely connection with the Amerindic Mindset and the Indic view of the ultimate meaninglessness of everything temporal affected the course of Indian history profoundly. I believe it is possible to construct dynamic models of history for Sinic, Indic and Amerindic Civilization based on their respective Mindsets but that would still leave us with a major gap in our understanding of history. Apart from the theories of Marx and Toynbee, both of which are fatally flawed, *there is no generally accepted model for Western history*. Perhaps what we have learned about the Occidental Mindset can assist in filling that void.

APPENDIX C
Mindsets in the Kitchen

I had originally considered including a chapter about the influence of mindsets on methods of food preparation for two reasons. First, since I contended that mindsets mold every civilized activity, I wanted to follow their influence to the most mundane levels and cooking is about as mundane as you can get. Second, my hobby is cooking in several traditional styles, particularly French, Sichuanese, Indian and Southeast Asian and I have a natural interest in understanding why those styles are so different.

Nevertheless, because I tried as much as possible to rely on the interpretations of prominent scholars in the preparation of Chapters 3 through 8 rather than devise my own, I did not want to depart from that practice in writing about food preparation. Therein lay the rub. While there are thousands of cookbooks available there are very few books about the philosophy of cooking in various traditions. Consequently, I thought there would be too little scholarly evidence available and too much *ad hoc* interpretation on my part, so I cancelled the food chapter.

After *Beyond Civilization* was finished, however, to my surprise and delight, I came across a book edited by K. C. Chang entitled *Food in Chinese Culture: Anthropological and Historical Perspectives.* Chang's book certainly encourages one to think that mindset theory is, in fact, relevant to the differences in civilized food traditions. In his introduction he tells us:

> In the Chinese culture, the whole process of preparing food from raw ingredients to morsels ready for the mouth involves a complex of interrelated variables that is highly distinctive when compared with other food traditions of major magnitude. At the basis of this complex is the division between *fan,* grains and other starch foods, and *ts'ai*

vegetable and meat dishes. To prepare a balanced meal, it must have an appropriate amount of both fan and ts'ai, and ingredients are readied along both tracks. (140, 7)

Chang calls this division of ingredients the *fan-ts'ai* principle. Is there any justification for treating this principle as an order/non-order distinction. It seems to me that there is. In the first place, one can note that *fan* and *ts'ai* stand in clear opposition to each other. While they may be 'put together' in some dishes such as Chinese ravioli or dumplings, steamed buns with fillings or wonton they are 'not mixed up, and each still retains its due proportion and own distinction. . . ' (ibid., 8) *Fan,* generally prepared quite simply, appears to be the 'anchor' of the Chinese meal. It lends stability to the menu while *ts'ai* performs a spirited dance around it, giving the meal its variety.

> For the preparation of *t'sai,* the use of multiple ingredients and the mixing of flavors are the rules, which above all means that ingredients are usually cut up and not done whole, and that they are variously combined into individual dishes of vastly differing flavors. Pork, for example, may be diced, sliced, shredded, or ground, and when combined with other meats and with various vegetable ingredients and spices produces dishes of utterly divergent shapes, flavor, colors, tastes, and aromas. (ibid.)

The balance exemplified by the *fan-ts'ai* principle is not the only kind of balance applicable to Chinese food. First, there is the *yin-yang* principle with which we are by now thoroughly familiar:

> The bodily functions, in the Chinese view, follow the basic *yin-yang* principles. Many foods are also classifiable into those that possess the *yin* quality and those of the *yang* quality. When yin and yang forces in the body are not balanced, problems result. Proper amounts of food of one kind or the other may then be administered (i.e., eaten) to counterbalance the yin and yang disequilibrium. If the body is normal, overeating of one kind of food would result in an excess of that force in the body, causing diseases. This belief is documented for the Chou period, several centuries before Christ, and it is still a dominant concept in Chinese Culture. (139, 10)

A comparable distinction and requirement for balance is also made in parts of China between 'cool' *(liang)* and 'hot' *(jê)* foods. And finally we may note one more principle mentioned by Chang: frugality. As we saw earlier in the book, the Chinese mindset deplored overindulgence of any kind and counseled moderation. 'Overindulgence in food and drink,' says Chang, 'is a sin of such proportions that dynasties could fall on its account. At the individual level, the ideal amount for every meal, as every Chinese parent would say, is only *ch'i fen pao* ('seventy percent full').' (ibid.)

It seems that, despite the fact that Chinese cuisine is one of the two most prolific and diverse in the world (the Occidental, if all its traditions are grouped together as the Chinese do, being the second), that there are certain generalizations which can be made about it and that they do suggest the influence of the Sinic mindset. One would likely find that the overall distinct character of Chinese cuisine would be even more prominently highlighted if one were to do the kind of comparative study of cooking in the other civilizations that I did for other subjects in Chapters 3 through 8.

In the West, do we find the obsession with order exerting its influence on cooking? When we talk about Western cuisine in its most developed form we are inevitably referring to French cuisine. The French inherited very little of importance from their Roman forebears except, perhaps, Rome's obsession with meat.

> The Roman taste for meat was carried to an extreme. The consumption of meat became so exaggerated that more than once restrictive measures had to be taken. Under Alexander Severus meat had risen to such a high price that it was expressly forbidden by law to kill sows which had recently littered, sucking pigs, cows and heifers. (140, 295)

Writing 1400 years after Severus, the Palatine Princess described the meat-heavy diet of Louis XIV as follows:

> I have seen the King eat, and that very often, four plates of different soups, an entire pheasant, a partridge, a large

plateful of salad, mutton cut up in its juice with garlic, two good pieces of ham, a plateful of cakes, and fruit and jams. (140, 30)

Louis had obviously not only inherited the Roman appetite for meat but their general tendency to gluttony as well. It was against this background that the great French *chefs de cuisine* made their contributions to the world's most rationally ordered system of food preparation and service. Until the end of the sixteenth century, the Italians were the acknowledged masters of cooking but from the reign of Henri IV, French chefs began charting their own course. They accepted their rôle with highminded seriousness, too much so for the snide Montaigne who reported a conversation with one of them in the following way:

> He discoursed on this science of cookery with a gravity and a magisterial air as if he was discussing with me a great point of theology. He interpreted for me the differences in appetite, that which one has on an empty stomach, that following on the second and third course, the means to arouse it and to stimulate it; the order of his sauces, first of all in general and then particularising the quality of their ingredients and their effects. And all this in rich and magnificent phrases such as one would use to discuss the government of an empire. (140, 299)

Note that in the late sixteenth century Montaigne uses the phrase 'science of cookery.' If by 'science' we understand simply a rational, ordered approach to comprehend and organize a field, then the phrase is appropriate. And that, more than anything else, is what distinguishes French cookery from other cuisines. Early books on cooking had appeared as early as the fifteenth century but *La Fleur de toute cuisine* by Pierre Pidoux, which appeared in 1543, was the first of the great French works on cookery, culminating with those of Escoffier, Nignon and Salles at the beginning of this century. The intellectual thrust of these scientists of cookery is exemplified in the work of Antonin Carême, who died in 1833 and is regarded by *Larousse Gastronomique* as the founder of "*la grande cuisine,*' classic

French cookery.' 'Carême's life,' says *Larousse,*

> . . . is a model of probity and nobility. Money meant nothing
> to him. His art alone was important. He prized nothing but
> the glory of his profession. His very conception of the culinary
> art is in tune with the grandeur of his character. It was
> always Carême's ideal to present sumptuously the culinary
> marvels with which he enriched the tables of kings. (140,
> 212)

Carême himself said, 'The fine arts are five in number, to wit:
*painting, sculpture, poetry, music, architecture - whose main branch is
confectionery.*' He was, in fact, well grounded in classical architecture
and made meticulous drawings for 'set pieces, aspics, galantines,
baskets of fruit, etc., or even simple borders.' (140, 213) His whole
life was dedicated to bringing classical order into the culinary
endeavor. He wrote extensively on the composition of menus and the
history of cooking, injecting into the latter his own contempt for what
he considered unworthy meals.   His was thus an extremely
important influence on setting standards for French cuisine,
standards on which, for example, the famous Michelin ratings for
restaurants are based. Carême was both preceded and followed by
great chefs as well as famous gastronomes, all of whom contributed
to the rationalization and order of *'la grand cuisine.'* How far these
men (they *were* almost exclusively men) went in bringing order to the
mundane field of cookery is well illustrated by the contents of
Carême's book, *La Pâtissier royal parisien:*

> The plan of this book is extremely methodical. The subjects
> with which he deals are marketing and provisions, with
> observations on their freshness, quality and season, details
> and organization of the larder, major and minor sauces,
> *consommés, hors-d'oeuvre,* frying, sweets, the cold buffet, in
> short, all the details relating to the direction of the kitchen.
> Carême added to this treatise a vocabulary where he
> establishes the spelling of many of the names of dishes which
> had been travestied by so many practitioners. (140, 214)

It is to the rationalizing efforts of the French chefs and gastronomes that we owe the structure and ambience of a fine meal right down to the exact number of knives, forks and spoons and how they are to be placed. Misplacing or misuing even one utensil introduces an unacceptable element of chaos into a French meal. This was impressed upon me one day when my wife and I were travelling from Paris to Madrid on the Sud Express. There were many courses served in the dining car and each array of utensils was positioned meticulously. At one point in the meal, my wife used *the wrong spoon!* The maître d', who was moving through the speeding car with the grace of a ballet master noticed it immediately and on his next tour replaced the misused spoon and removed the one which ought to have been used, all without comment. The Western mindset in a dining car!

One of the most impressive examples of the order the French masters have brought to cookery is to be found in their inventory of *sauces*. Every great chef, including, of course, Carême, invented many sauces. There are over two hundred of them in the French repertoire and their classification and use is one of the most ordered aspects of '*la grande cuisine.*' Some of the sauces are named after their inventors but many were named after nobles who were the employers of the chefs. It is very important to remember that French cuisine was a development of Western *civilization* even though most of its development took place in the modern decivilizing era. While Carême's career took shape after the French Revolution, it was inextricably associated with the elite. He worked at various times for the Russian Czar, the Viennese court, the British embassy in Paris and for Baron de Rothschild, none of which were significantly affected by the decivilizing trends of the modern era.

So it seems we do have a clear contrast between Western (French) and Chinese approaches to food, one which *prima facie* appears to reflect the difference in mindsets. Time has not permitted extending the inquiry to Indic or Amerindic cookery. I leave that undertaking to someone else.

BIBLIOGRAPHY

Note: All references to the Encyclopedia Britannica are to the 1969 edition unless otherwise indicated.

1 Primitive Views of the World, Stanley Diamond, ed., Columbia University Press, New York, 1960
   a.Stanley Diamond, 'Plato and the Definition of the Primitive.'
   b.A. Irving Hallowell, 'Ojibwa Ontology, Behavior, and World View.'
   c.Kurt Goldstein, 'Concerning the Concept of 'Primitivity."

2 David G. Mandelbaum, 'Civilization and Culture: Concepts of Civilization,' Encyclopedia Britannica, Vol. 5, William Benton, Chicago, 1969

3 Will and Ariel Durant, The Lessons of History, Simon and Schuster, New York, 1968

4 Arnold Toynbee, A Study of History - a new edition revised and abridged by the author and Jane Caplan, Weathervane Books, New York, 1972

5 Webster's New International Dictionary of the English Language , G. and C. Merriam and Co., Springfield, Mass., 1914

6 Herbert J. Muller, Freedom in the Ancient World, Harper and Brothers, New York, 1961

7 Peter Farb, Man's Rise to Civilization, E. P. Dutton & Co., Inc., N.Y., 1968

8 V. Gordon Childe, Man Makes Himself, Mentor Book, The New American Library of World Literature, Inc., New York, 1952

10 John S. Mbiti, African Religions and Philosophy, Anchor Books, Doubleday & Company, Inc., Garden City, New York, 1970

11 Diane Wolkstein and Samuel Noah Kramer, Inanna - Queen of Heaven and Earth, Harper and Row, New York, 1983

12 William McNeill and Jean Sedlar, Eds., Classical China, Oxford University Press, New York, 1970

13 Peter M. Warren, 'Minoan Palaces,' Scientific American, July, 1985

14 Charles Humana and Wang Wu, The Ying Yang - The Chinese Way of Love, Avon Books, New York, 1972

15   Thorstein Veblen, The Theory of the Leisure Class, The Modern Library, Random House, New York, 1934

16   Arnold Toynbee, A Study of History, Oxford University Press, 1962

17   Sherman E. Lee, A History of Far Eastern Art, Prentice-Hall, Inc., Englewood Cliffs, N.J., 1973

18   Eric Berne, M.D., Principles of Group Treatment, Grove Press, Inc., New York, 1966

19   David Grene and Richard Lattimore, Eds., The Complete Greek Tragedies, The University of Chicago Press, 1959

20   The Egyptian Book of the Dead (The Papyrus of Ani), E. A. Wallis Budge, trans., Dover Publications, Inc., New York, 1967

21   Sherwood L. Washburn, 'The Evolution of Man,'   Scientific American,Vol. 239, No. 3, Sept. 1978.

22   Otto Neubert, Tutankhamun and the Valley of the Kings, Granada Publishing Inc., New York, 1977

23   W. Y. Evans-Wentz, trans., The Tibetan Book of the Dead (Bardo Tödol), Oxford University Press, London,1976

24   Swami Prabhavananda and Christopher Isherwood, trans., Bhagavad-Gita: The Song of God, Marcel Rodd Co., Hollywood, 1949

25   Heinrich Zimmer, Philosophies of India, Pantheon Books, N.Y., 1951

26   Lin Yutang, trans., The Wisdom of Laotse, The Modern Library, New York, 1948

27   Joseph Needham, 'Science and China's Influence on the World', The Legacy of China, Raymond Dawson, ed., Oxford Univ. Press, 1971

28   E. A. Kracke, Jr., 'The Chinese and the Art of Government', Op. cit. 27 above.

29   Victor Wolfgang von Hagen, The Ancient Sun Kingdoms of the Americas, Thames and Hudson, London, 1962

30   Sol Tax, 'Indian, Latin-American,' *Encycl. Britannica,* Vol. 12

31   Howard La Fay, "Children of Time ," *National Geographic*, Vol. CXLVIII, No. 6, National Geographic Society, Washington, D.C.

32   George C. Valliant, *The Aztecs of Mexico,* Penguin Books, 1951

33   William H. Prescott, The World of the Aztecs, Tudor Publishing Company, New York 1974

35   Steven Weinberg, The First Three Minutes - A Modern View of the Origin of the Universe, Basic Books, Inc., New York, 1977

36   John B. Noss, Man's Religions, MacMillan Company, New York, 1951

37   G. Van der Leeuw, Religion in Essence and Manifestation, J. E. Turner, trans., George Allen & Unwin Ltd., London, 1938

38   Stuart Piggott, Prehistoric India, Penguin Books, Harmondsworth, Middlesex, 1950

39   Paul Tillich, Systematic Theology, Vol. I, The University of Chicago Press, Chicago, 1951

40   The Holy Bible, Authorized King James Version, Collins' Clear-Type Press, London and New York

41   Morse Peckham, Beyond the Tragic Vision, George Braziller, New York, 1962

42   Huston Smith, The Religions of Man, Harper Colophon Books, Harper and Row, New York, 1958

43   The Koran, E. H. Palmer, trans., Oxford Univ. Press, London,1949

44   Robert O. Ballou, ed., World Bible, The Viking Press, New York, 1944

45   Vedanta for the Western World, Christopher Isherwood, ed., The Marcel Rodd Company, Hollywood, 1946

46   Edwin Arnold, The Light of Asia, Roberts Brothers, Boston, 1889

47   Vergilius Ferm, Ed., An Encyclopedia of Religion, The Philosophical Library, New York, 1943

48   Helmut Wilhelm, 'Chinese Mythology,' Encyclopedia Britannica, Vol. 5,, p. 642, William Benton, Chicago, 1969

49   Hsün Tzu, in *Classical China,* William H. McNeill and Jean W. Sedlar, eds., Oxford University Press, New York, 1970

50   E. Zürcher, 'Buddhism in China', The Legacy of China , Raymond Dawson, Ed., Oxford University Press, London, 1971

51   Dun J. Li, Ed., The Essence of Chinese Civilization, D. Van Nostrand Company, Inc., Princeton, N.J., 1967

52   Laurette Séjourné, Burning Water: Thought and Religion In Ancient Mexico, Grove Press, Inc., New York, 1960

53   John Burnet, Early Greek Philosophy, Adam & Charles Black, London, 1948

54   John M. Warbeke, The Searching Mind of Greece, F. S. Crofts & Co., New York, 1947

55   Lecomte du Noüy, Human Destiny, Signet Books, New York, 1949

56   Gerald Heard, Is God Evident?, Faber and Faber Ltd., London

57   Abû Hamîd Muhammad al-Ghazâlî, Excerpt from 'That Which Delivers From Error,' The Islamic World, William H. McNeill and Marilyn Robinson Waldman, eds., Oxford University Press, 1973

58   B. Jowett, The Dialogues of Plato, Random House, New York, 1937

59   James H. Dunham, 'Platonism,' A History of Philosophical Systems, ed. by Vergilius Ferm, The Philosophical Library, New York, 1950

60   S. Radhakrishnan, Indian Philosophy, The MacMillan Company, New York, 1951

61   M. Hiriyanna, The Essentials of Indian Philosophy, George Allen & Unwin Ltd., London, 1949

62   A. C. Graham, 'The Place of Reason in the Chinese Philosophical Tradition, The Legacy of China, ed. by Raymond Dawson, Oxford Univ. Press, 1971

63   Mo Tzu. Basic Writings, trans. by Burton Watson, Columbia University Press, 1963

64   Da Liu, T'ai Chi Ch'uan and Meditation, Schocken Books, N.Y., 1986

65   Helen Gardner, Art Through the Ages, Harcourt, Brace & Co., N.Y., 1948

66   George Santayana, The Sense of Beauty, Dover Publications, Inc., New York, 1955

67   Nathan Knobler, The Visual Dialogue, Holt, Rinehart and Winston, Inc., New York, 1971

68   Percy Bysshe Shelley, John Keats and Percy Bysshe Shelley: Complete Poetical Works, The Modern Library, New York

69   Richard E. W. Adams, 'Río Azul,' National Geographic, Vol 169, No. 4, April 1986, National Geographic Society, Washington, D. C.

70   Leroy Nieman, in a radio interview with Larry King over the Mutual Broadcasting System, 1980

71   Lionel Casson et al., Ancient Egypt, Time-Life Books, Alexandria, Va., 1978

72   Irmgard Woldering, The Art of Egypt , Greystone Press, New York, 1963

73   A. E. Taylor, Plato: The Man and His Work, Meridian Books, Inc., New York, 1960

74   Pierre Francastel, 'Space and Time,' Encyclopedia of World Art, Vol. XIII, McGraw-Hill Book Co., New York, 1967

75   John Addington Symonds, The Life of Michelangelo Buonarroti, Modern Library, New York

76   Enrico Castelnuovo, 'Stained Glass,' Op. cit. 74 above.

77   Milton C. Nahm, Genius and Creativity, Harper Torchbooks, Harper & Row, New York, 1956

78   Ananda K. Coomaraswamy, 'The Theory of Art in Asia,' *Aesthetics Today,* Morris Philipson, ed., Meridian Books, The World Publishing Company, 1961

79   Michael Sullivan, 'The Heritage of Chinese Art,' Op. cit. 27 above.

80   Esther Pasztory, Aztec Art, Harry N. Abrams, Inc., New York, 1983

81   Paul Westheim et al., Prehispanic Mexican Art, Lancelot C. Sheppard et al., translators, G. P. Putnam's Sons, New York, 1972

82   Aristotle, Politics, ed. Richard Mckeon, Random House, New York, 1941

83   Will Durant, The Story of Civilization, Simon & Schuster, New York, 1954

84   H. F. Jolowicz, Historical Introduction to Roman Law, Cambridge University Press, 1965

85   Heinz Kähler, The Art of Rome and Her Empire , Greystone Press, New York, 1965

86   Sir Henry Sumner Maine, Ancient Law , Dorset Press, 1986

87   The Holy Bible, Revised Standard Version, Thomas Nelson & Sons, New York, 1952

88 Reginald Walter Michael Dias, 'Jurisprudence,' Encyclopedia Britannica, Vol. 13

89 Basic Writings of Thomas Aquinas, ed. Anton C. Pegis, Random House, New York, 1945

90 Ernst Troeltsch, The Social Teaching of the Christian Churches, trans. by Olive Wyon, George Allen & Unwin Ltd., London, 1931

91 The Laws of Manu, trans. by Georg Bühler, Dover Publications, New York, 1969

92 Herrlee G. Creel, The Origins of Statecraft in China, University of Chicago Press, 1970

93 Etienne Balazs, 'Chinese Law,' Encyclopedia Britannica, Vol. 5

94 Jacques Soustelle, Daily Life of the Aztecs, tr. Patrick O'Brian, Stanford University Press,1985

95 Alain, Yoga for Perfect Health, Pyramid Books, N. Y., 1961

96 Desmond Dunne, Yoga Made Easy, Mayflower Books, London, 1973

97 Patanjali, How to Know God: The Yoga Aphorisms of Patanjali, Swami Prabhavananda and Christopher Isherwood, tr., Harper, New York, 1953,

98 Tem Horwitz and Susan Kimmelman with H. H. Lui, Tai Chi Ch'uan: The Technique of Power, Chicago Review Press, Chicago, 1976

99 Joe Hyams, Zen in the Martial Arts, Bantam Books, New York, 1982

100 Nigel Davies, The Ancient Kingdoms of Mexico, Penguin Books,1983

101 E. F. Porter Jr., 'The Art of the Maya,' St. Louis Post Dispatch Sunday Magazine, July 20, 1986

102 Desmond Morris, The Human Zoo, Corgi Books, London, 1971

103 Elizabeth Salter, 'Courtly Love,' Enc. Britannica, Vol. 6

104 The Middle Ages, Vol. II: Readings in Medieval History, ed. Brian Tierney, Alfred A. Knopf, New York, 1970

105 Denis de Rougemont, Love in the Western World, trans. by Montgomery Belgion, Princeton University Press, 1983

106 Vatsyayana, The Kama Sutra of Vatsyayana, trans. by Sir Richard F. Burton, E. P. Dutton, N.Y., 1964

107 Charles Gibson, The Aztecs Under Spanish Rule, Stanford University Press, Stanford, California, 1964

108 Roderick Seidenberg, Posthistoric Man, Viking Press, New York, 1974

109 Gerald Heard, The Ascent of Humanity, Harcourt Brace, New York, 1929

110 Alvin Toffler, The Third Wave, Bantam Books, New York, 1980

111 J. Huizinga, The Waning of the Middle Ages, Doubleday Anchor Books, New York, 1954

112 Rollo May, The Meaning of Anxiety, The Ronald Press Company, New York, 1950

113 Quoted by Lynn Thorndyke, 'Renaissance,' Encyclopedia Britannica , V. 19

114 Jacques Ellul, The Technological Society, Vintage Books, 1964

115 Interviews in Rolling Stone, Issue 512, Nov. 5th - Dec. 10th, 1987 a.Mick Jagger b.George Harrison

116 Dennis Altman, Homosexual, Discus/Avon Books, New York, 1971

117 LSD: The Consciousness-Expanding Drug, David Solomon, ed., Berkley Medallion Books, New York, 1966

118 Fritzjof Capra, The Tao of Physics, Bantam Books, New York, 1984

119 Thomas W. Ogletree, The Death of God Controversy, Abingdon Press, New York, 1966

120 The English Philosophers from Bacon to Mill, Edwin A. Burtt, ed., The Modern Library, New York, 1939

121 Edward Wichers, 'Atom,' Encyclopedia Brittanica, Vol. II

122 Werner Heisenberg, Selection from speech at University of Chicago published under the title, 'The Higher Physics are Indeterminate: One Can't Say 'For Sure," The Autobiography of Science, Forest Ray Moulton and Justus J. Schifferes, eds., Doubleday, Garden City, N. Y., 1946

123 Maurice Grosser, The Painter's Eye, A Mentor Book, New American Library, New York, 1956

124   Dictionary of Modern Painting, General Eds. Carlton Lake and Robert Maillard, Tudor Publishing Co., New York

125   William Shakespeare, 'Hamlet,' The Complete Works of William Shakespeare, The Blakiston Company, Philadelphia, 1936

127   Erich Fromm, Escape From Freedom, Avon Books, New York, 1965

128   Ernest Becker, Denial of Death, The Free Press, New York, 1973

129   Jane Fonda with Mignon McCarthy, Women Coming of Age, Simon & Schuster, New York, 1984

130   Christopher Lasch, 'Soul of a New Age,' Omni Magazine, Oct. 1987

131   Friedrich Nietzsche, 'Thus Spake Zarathustra', The Philosophy of Friedrich Nietzsche, The Modern Library, N. Y.

132   Isaac Asimov, Today and Tomorrow and . . . , Dell Publishing Co., N.Y., 1983

134   Shirley MacLaine, Don't Fall Off The Mountain, Bantam Books, New York, 1986

135   James Trefil, 'Quantum physics' world: now you see it, now you don't,' Smithsonian Magazine, August, 1987

136   Aldous Huxley, 'Orion,' quoted in The Choice is Always Ours, Dorothy Berkley Phillips, ed., Richard R. Smith, NY, 1948

137   Nikos Kazantzakis, The Rock Garden, tr. Richard Howard, Simon and Schuster, New York, 1963

138   Heloise, Abbess of the Paraclete, letter, *The Middle Ages, Vol. I: Readings in Medieval History*, ed. Brian Tierney, Alfred A. Knopf, New York, 1970

139   J. Stanley Gray, Psychological Foundations of Education, American Book Company, New York,1935

140   K. C. Chang, editor, Food in Chinese Culture: Anthropological and Historical Perspectives, Yale University Press,1977

141   W. Brugh Joy, *Joy's Way*, J. P. Tarcher, Los Angeles, 1979*

142   P. Russell, *The Global Brain*, J. P. Tarcher, Los Angeles, 1983*

*The quotations from 141 and 142 are from Kenneth Ring, *Heading Toward Omega*, William Morrow, New York, 1985

ACKNOWLEDGMENTS

Permission for use of the plates reproduced in the chapter on Art is gratefully acknowledged.

Plate 1: Victor R. Boswell, Jr., NGP, Copyright National Geographic Society

Plate 2: The Metropolitan Museum of Art, Museum Excavations, 1928-1929 and Rogers Fund, 1930. (30.3.31)

Plate 3: The Metropolitan Museum of Art, Fletcher Fund, 1932. (32.11.1)

Plate 4: Hirmer Fotoarchiv, Munich

Plate 5: Eliot Elisofon, Life Magazine, Copyright Time Warner

Plate 6: Archaeological Survey of India

Plate 7: Reprinted by permission of the publishers from ANCIENT INDONESIAN ART by A. J. Bernet Kempers, Harvard University Press, Cambridge, MA: Copyright 1959 by N. V. Boekhandel antiquariaat en Uitgeverig C. P. J. van der Peet, Amsterdam

Plate 8: Chinese, Tripod Cauldron *(ding)*, Shang dynasty, c. 1700 - c. 1050 B.C., 11th century B.C., ht.: 24.4; diam. 18.9 cm., Lucy Maude Buckingham Collection, 1928.167. Photograph by Robert Hashimoto

Plate 9: Chinese, Bird-shaped wine container *(Niao Zun)*, bronze, Shang dynasty, c. 1700 - c. 1050 B.C., 12th-11th century B.C., ht. 15.9 cm.; l. 13.3 cm., Lucy Maude Buckingham Collection, 1936.139

Plate 10: Memorial Art Gallery of the University of Rochester; Mrs. Charles H. Babcock Fund

Plate 12: Merle Greene Robertson, Copyright 1976

Plate 13: Museo Nacional de Antropologia, Mexico City

Plate 14: Aztec emblems reproduced by courtesy of Esther Pasztory

INDEX

Abelard and Heloise: 277f.
Adam and Eve: see Genesis
African societies: sense of time, 11
Al-Ghazâli, Abû Hamid
  Muhammad: 109
Amenhotep III: 157
American myth: 356ff.
Americans, Native: 32
Anchorites: 247
Aquinas, St. Thomas: 206ff., 287,
  346
Asimov, Isaac: 368
Aristophanes: 278, 279
Aristotle: 15, 120, 124, 143, 196
Art: Ch. 5; civilized, 153ff.;
  defining, 141ff.; 'from Hell,'
  353; general definition, 145ff.;
  Impressionism, 351; meaning in,
  148; 'planned pictures' in the
  Modern Era, 350f.; 'Sugar-
  coated Pill' theory of, 144;
  traditional distinctions ignored,
  153
Artistic vision: 146
asanas: 252
Asceticism: 244ff.
Asoka: 393, 396
Athletics: 239ff.
Atman: 83, 124
Atomism: 117, 341f.
Augustine, St.: 206, 285
Aurelius, Marcus: 204
Aztecs: 59ff., 95ff.

Ballgame, Amerindic: 265
Basil, St.: 72
Beauty: 141f.
Benedict, St.: 248f.
Berenson, Bernard: 147
Bernard, Theos: 249
Berne, Eric: 33, 34, 58
Bhagavad Gita: 48
Bodhidharma (Ta Mo): 260

Boniface VIII: 319
Bork, Robert: 348
Borobodur: 171
Boulding, Kenneth: 308f.
Brahman: 83,124, 211ff.
Brahmins (Hindu priests): 47, 70
Bronzes, Chinese: 177, *Pl. 8 & 9*
Buddha: 85f.
Buddhism: 86, 93ff., 122f., 131,
  178,179
Buddhist thought: Vijñavadin
  school, 124
Caesar, Julius: 200
Caesar, Augustus: 200ff.
Calendar, Mesoamerican: 135ff.,
  231ff.
Calisthenics: 241
Capra, Fritzjof: 337, 343, 370, 372
Caste system (India): 217ff.
Catharism: 290;
Cathedrals, Gothic: 163ff.;
  Chartres, 165; Rouen, 148ff.
Chac-Mool: 103
chakras: 255
Chaitya (Buddhist hall): 170
Chan San-feng: 260
Chichen Itzá: 265
Childe, V. Gordon: 7, 308
Chou Dynasty: 177
Christianity: 78ff.
Chuang Tzu: 90
ch'i ('vital energy'): 262
Civilization: Ch. 1; attributes, 5;
  common socioeconomic system,
  26; general definition of, 4, 14;
  opposite to precivilized societ
  -ies, 6; problem of defining, 2;
  thousand year intervals, 64f.
Civilization, Amerindic: date, 27;
  Mesoamerican peoples identi-
  fied: 56ff.; purview, 56ff.
Civilization, Indic: date, 27;
  purview, 45ff.